THE YEMENI CIVIL WAR

THE YEMENI CIVIL WAR

The Arab Spring, State Formation and Internal Instability

Elham Manea

UNIVERSITY
of
EXETER
PRESS

First published in 2024 by
University of Exeter Press
Reed Hall, Streatham Drive
Exeter EX4 4QR
UK

www.exeterpress.co.uk

Copyright © 2024 Elham Manea

The right of Elham Manea to be identified as author of this work has been asserted by her in accordance with the Copyright, Designs and Patents Act 1988.

https://doi.org/10.47788/JPJL8437

This publication is licensed, unless otherwise indicated, under the terms of the Creative Commons Attribution 4.0 International (CC BY-NC-ND 4.0) licence (http://creativecommons.org/licenses/by/4.0/), which permits use, sharing, adaptation, distribution, and reproduction in any medium or format, provided you give appropriate credit to the original author(s) and source, link to the Creative Commons licence, and indicate any modifications.

Any third-party material in this book is not covered by the book's Creative Commons licence. Details of the copyright ownership and permitted use of third-party material are given in the image (or extract) captions. If you would like to reuse any third-party material, you will need to obtain permission directly from the copyright holder.

Despite careful editing, all information in this publication is provided without guarantee; any liability on the part of the author, the editor, or the publisher is excluded.

This publication was financially supported by the Swiss National Science Foundation (SNSF).

British Library Cataloguing in Publication Data
A catalogue record for this book is available
from the British Library.

ISBN 978-1-80413-057-5 Hardback
ISBN 978-1-80413-058-2 ePub
ISBN 978-1-80413-059-9 PDF

Cover photograph © Mohammed Hamoud/Getty

Typeset in Adobe Caslon Pro by S4Carlisle Publishing Services, Chennai, India

Contents

List of Maps	vii
List of Figures	viii
Introduction	1
1. The Arab Spring and its Outcomes	13
2. The Yemeni Civil War and the Youth Uprisings	33
3. Legacies of Geography, Tribes, and Religious Beliefs	49
4. The Narrative Dilemma	81
5. Legacies of Ottoman Imperialism	91
6. Legacies of Colonization	105
7. The Cunning State and the Politics of Survival	135
8. The Role of the Cunning State	155
9. Conclusion: Yemen's Transition Towards Chaos	197
Notes	213
Interviews	247
Bibliography	253
Index	263

THE YEMENI CIVIL WAR

Maps

Map 1: Ancient Yemen—Arabia Felix. (Adapted from Wikimedia Commons (Schreiber/Rowanwindwhistler; CC BY-SA 4.0 DEED))

Map 2: Upper and Lower Yemen. (Creator: Brinkley Messick)

Map 3: Governorates and districts of modern Yemen. (Public Domain—Library of Congress: https://lccn.loc.gov/2005625554)

Figures

Figure 7.1: Zaydi core elites remained a constant in the Imamate Statelets, the Mutawakkilite Kingdom, and the Northern Republic. What changed was their tribal affiliation.

Figure 7.2: Core strata groups' relations to power in Mutawakkilite Kingdom (left) and Republic (right).

Figure 7.3: Regional/tribal representation in the traditional power base of the Socialist Party/army.

Figure 7.4: The regional/tribal affiliations of the Zumra and Tougmah, the two fighting factions in the 1986 Southern civil war.

Figure 7.5: Traditional power base of President Saleh's regime.

Figure 7.6: Traditional power base of Houthi militia.

Figure 8.1: Role of the state in cementing societal ethnic divisions and overlapping group grievances.

Figure 8.2: The factions that supported President Saleh in the 1994 civil war.

Introduction

History matters. To understand what is happening today, one has to know what happened in the past. But to know history, one has to first discern and then unpack the layers of narratives, of the past as much as the present. For history is also a construct. It is based on narratives, and often they are shaped by perceptions, and moulded by anger, fear, pride, strength, weakness, pain, and grievances. Sometimes the narratives do not mirror what *actually* happened: they are articulated so as to bend historical facts to conform to the narratives. Sometimes only half of the story is told. Sometimes all of the story is distorted. And most of the time, history is used, recounted, and narrated as a means to justify political, social, and religious orders. To unite but also to divide people. To make peace and to start wars.

One recent example is the war in Ukraine. Russian president Vladimir Putin used his angry narrative on the history of Ukraine, implying it was a creation of "Bolshevik, Communist Russia" and "never really a state", to justify Russia's invasion of the country, annexing three of its regions, and in the process attempting to recreate what he grandiosely called the "historical Russia known as the U.S.S.R [Soviet Union]".[1] His intended audience was not really the international community, but rather his own people. How else could he justify launching a war and attacking the sovereignty of a neighbouring country, destroying its cities and infrastructure, and sending Russian soldiers there to die?

This may be an odd introduction to a book on the Arab Spring (henceforth Arab uprisings) and its various outcomes using the Yemeni civil war as a case study. These uprisings in different Arab countries and their divergent outcomes are very much part of the present. The Yemeni civil war, which started in

September 2014, is still going on with no end in sight. A new multi-polar world order is in the process of being shaped. And yet history, perceptions, narratives, and emotions are all tied directly to the present-day developments in the state formations of these countries and the prevalent regional rivalries in their external environments.

How?

The different outcomes of the Arab uprisings are tied to history—or more accurately to the historical DNA of the states in question and their divergent experiences of state formation. The current Yemeni civil war is one of many that have marred the history of this country. Instability has been a symptom of historical grievances repeatedly rising to the surface, reflecting a process of state formation that failed to actually produce a modern state. Moreover, the country's core elites are defined by (and at the same time exploit) ethnic markers, perpetually fighting each other across Yemeni history. These three elements—historical grievances, failed state formation, and the ethnic markers of elites—stand at the core of the Yemeni dilemma.

This understanding of the conflict has ramifications for any peace process. Sustainable peace in Yemen has to address the three elements; it will require moving beyond a pattern of simple conflict resolution, which has so far failed to address the historical roots of Yemen's recurrent crises. It also has to go beyond the assumption that those fighting are driven only by material interests. People do not always act for rational reasons. They can also react out of anger: at perceived unaddressed grievances, or humiliation, or injustice. And that anger can be easily manipulated.[2]

At a regional level, the Arab Coalition, led by Saudi Arabia, became a party to the conflict in Yemen. Acting on the official request of the deposed Yemeni president, Abdrabbuh Mansur Hadi, on 26 March 2015 it began a military campaign against the Houthi militia, a sectarian militia that follows a radicalized version of the Zaydi tradition of Islam. Saudi Arabia's actions were in fact precipitated by (a) a perception that, through its activities in Yemen, Iran posed a threat to Saudi national security; and (b) frustration with the United States for ongoing negotiations with Iran in Lausanne (started on 17 March 2015) over a much-anticipated nuclear deal.[3] The Saudi perception may have exaggerated the actual threat Iran posed at the time in Yemen, but its actions turned that perception into a self-fulfilling prophecy.

INTRODUCTION

Today, Iranian influence and support in the Houthi-controlled areas are a fact.

In the same vein, Saudi frustration with the United States was over a changing world order, where its trusted ally, the United States, was calling on Saudi Arabia and other Gulf countries, privately and then publicly, to "reform" and "share" the region with Iran.[4] That call, which may have been necessary despite its naivety, was driven by America's strategic pivot towards China and the Asia–Pacific, which required it to withdraw from the troubled Middle East and North Africa (henceforth the MENA region).[5] The Asia Pivot is a geopolitical reality today and it continues regardless of which president resides in the White House.

Left on their own, after the buck-passing of the United States, regional powers in the MENA region scrambled to fill the vacuum and balance the power among themselves. In the absence of a realist rationality mitigated by responsibility, this geopolitical shift has had dire consequences for the stability of many countries in the region.

These two factors—state formation and regional rivalry—are key to the thinking both within this book and within the larger project of which this book is the first volume. As such, they make up the core of this project's proposed framework of analysis. Its point of departure is the question: How can we explain the divergent outcomes of the 2010–2011 Arab uprisings that reverberated in the region?

Countries that experienced popular uprisings had a range of outcomes: some countries, such as Tunisia and Egypt, experienced respectively a fragile (now shattered) democratization process and a reversion to forms of authoritarianism. In these cases, the state remained intact, albeit shaken. Other countries, such as Yemen, Syria, and Libya, experienced a meltdown of the political order, along with civil war and fragmentation. The state was torn between competing factions and groups, in the process exposing its ethnic character.

The question of this book is straightforward: Why?

In this volume, I present the first part of my argument that the interaction between different types of state formation and regional rivalry can explain, respectively, the disintegration of countries such as Yemen, Syria, and Libya, and the preservation of the Bahraini system, despite its ethnic nature. Egypt and Tunisia provide further variants in their solid statehood and sense of national identity—which provide their ability to withstand the shocks their systems have been experiencing. This is not to say that these two states are immune to new uprisings or political instability. What it does mean is that the kind of violence they are likely to experience will not be of an ethnic nature of the kind we have seen in Yemen, Syria, and Libya.

Across the two volumes of this project, *The Yemeni Civil War: The Arab Spring, State Formation and Internal Instability* and *Gulf Rivalry and the Yemeni Civil War*, I will apply Joseph A. Maxwell's approach of critical realism to qualitative research. In essence, this approach captures the complexities of reality shaped by narratives and perceptions and allows me to make sense of the divergent and contradictory narratives of the different Yemeni warring factions. It combines a realist ontology with a constructivist epistemology. In other words, it recognizes that there is a real world that exists independently of our beliefs and constructions.[6] For example, historically, Yemen as we know it today was only united twice in its modern history: in the seventeenth century (1636–1732) and in the twentieth century, when the Yemen Arab Republic (North) and the People's Democratic Republic of Yemen (South) united in 1990.

At the same time, this approach accepts that our knowledge of this world is inevitably our own construction, created from a specific vantage point.[7] An example is the imagined construct of Yemen as a united political entity in an integrated geographical state, with defined territory that spans North and South and includes Asir and Najran, within today's Saudi Arabia. This historical narrative is embraced by many Yemenis, especially from North Yemen, though no historical evidence exists to support the narrative.

It is important to emphasize that I do not subscribe to the radical position of constructivism, which rejects any possibility of fathoming or capturing an objective reality.[8] I hold that there is an objective world out there that can be understood and discovered. How we make sense of it may differ according to our perspectives. Again, turning to the Yemeni examples, regardless of the historical narratives of Yemeni unity, historically the country was divided between different political entities. This is a fact that cannot be disputed by narratives. By the same token, on a regional level the Saudis' exaggerated

INTRODUCTION

perception of the Iranian threat in 2015 does not change the fact that Iran actually provided only limited material resources to the Houthi militia at the time, despite the boosting rhetoric of some Iranian hardliners.[9]

This rejection of radical constructivism is shared by Maxwell's critical realism: it discards the idea of "multiple realities", that is, "independent and incommensurable worlds that are socially constructed by different individuals or societies", but it does accept the presence of "different valid perspectives on reality".[10] I prefer to use the term "comprehended perspectives", rather than Maxwell's term "valid perspectives". To perceive something as true does not make it true, unless it is supported by facts. If the perspective is divorced from reality (from what actually took place), it cannot be valid, no matter how strongly some may hold it. In other words, some perspectives are truer than others. For example, some members of the Southern separatist movement of the communist state, the People's Democratic Republic of Yemen (1967–1990), perceived it as an embodiment of law and order, where all regions were united in harmony and peace, but that perception diverges drastically from the actual history of the state and the recurrent regional/ethnic conflicts that took place.

This distinction is crucial when addressing the historical grievances in the conflict zones of the MENA region. An accurate understanding of what actually happened in the past is key to designing suitable tools of reconciliation for the present. In other words, a clear grasp of the state's history and formation is vital to peace making and conflict resolution for one simple reason: we cannot understand today's conflicts without an accurate depiction of the history of these conflicts and the roots of their groups' grievances. Too often, peace processes tackling the current wars and crises in the region are stuck because they focus only on the present. That is, they seek to find solutions to the current crises in their present forms, ignoring their historical roots. In doing so, they confine themselves to treating the symptoms of an illness without considering its causes.[11]

Other theoretical frameworks will also inform my discussions; I describe them in their respective chapters. Suffice here to say that Roger D. Petersen's work on the role of emotions in understanding ethnic violence will inspire some deliberations in the first part of the project,[12] which deals with the internal causes of Yemeni civil war and the legacies of that history. And in the second level of the theoretical framework, which will be addressed in a separate second volume, *Gulf Rivalry and the Yemeni Civil War*, I will modify and adapt Raymond Hinnebusch's "complex realism" approach to the foreign policies and international relations of countries in the MENA region in order to address the regional and operational contexts.[13]

Significantly, this project was informed by more than 100 interviews with Yemeni stakeholders from all parties to the conflict, with regional experts and personalities who have close contacts with core elites in their respective states, and with international diplomats who have expertise in the region and Yemen. I conducted the interviews between March 2020 and the end of October 2021: first via Zoom due to Covid-19 pandemic travel restrictions; and then, once restrictions were eased, in person in Egypt, Turkey, and the Sultanate of Oman. The book is also informed by my personal contacts in Yemen, and in work, research, and fieldwork over the last thirty years. I also made use of several archives, especially the Records of Yemen 1798–1960, the virtual archives of the Yemeni National Archive, and the Arabian Gulf Digital Archives.

The field travels and use of archival materials were only possible due to the generous support of several research foundations at the University of Zurich. In this space I would like to express my gratitude and acknowledge the generous support of the Foundation for Research and Science and the Humanities at the University of Zurich and the Privatdozenten Foundation of Zurich University (PD-Stiftung). Without their support, this project—especially my field visits and the gathering of archival data—would not have been possible. Finally, I want to express my gratitude to the Swiss National Fund for their generous support in making this publication open access. In the following sections, I will explain my own positionality and the terminology used in this study.

Author's Positionality

It has not been easy to write this book. The process was painful because it made me realize how deep the roots of instability are in Yemen, my country.

I am an Arab scholar of Yemeni–Egyptian origins and Swiss nationality. This is how I define myself, a kind of mixed salad. My father comes from

INTRODUCTION

North Yemen, from the Bani Hushaysh district north of Sana'a (on his father's side) and from Sana'a (on his mother's side). Those familiar with the tribal structures of Northern Yemen would immediately tell you that Bani Hushaysh belongs to the al-Abnna lineage, the descendants of intermarriages between local Yemeni women and Persian invaders in the sixth century. In fact, I was reminded of this lineage by a prominent Houthi figure when I interviewed him in Cairo for this book. There is another reason for his mentioning it: Bani Hushaysh supported the imamate regime during the 1962–1967 Northern civil war, just as they support the Houthis now.

Not my father. He was a force of nature, fiercely independent, critical of both the imamate regime and the Republic. He was a diplomat, a freethinker, and a humanist. Coming from the Bani Hushaysh would put him in the Zaydi Qahtani Bakili boxes. He never subscribed to these identity boxes, and yet he would insist on his Qahtani (rather than Persian) ancestry. He came from a poor background. An orphan, he worked three jobs as a child while studying. He would get up in the early hours of the morning to go to the big mosque in Sana'a, the only building with electricity, to study. The oil for the lantern was too expensive for his relatives. This resilience allowed him to become one of the Famous Forty, the first Yemeni students in modern history to be sent by Imam Yehia to study and learn outside North Yemen.[14] His education made my education possible.

My mother, an Egyptian by birth and socialization, was the daughter of a Yemeni immigrant from Al Udayn, Ibb, and an Egyptian mother from Alexandria. Her father, the son of a sheikh, fled Yemen during the imamate regime to avoid becoming a hostage of Imam Yehia (it was customary to hold the sons and brothers of tribal leaders (sheikhs) hostage in the capital, Sana'a, for political leverage). He settled in Mahal al-Kubra (where I was born). The two were raised in the Sunni Shafi'i tradition. The Egyptian dialect my mother spoke became my first language.

I lived outside Yemen for most of my life, but Yemen never left me. My father made that impossible. His Yemen was an ideal that he never saw realized. A republican, he had close friends in high positions in the post-imamate regime, but he complained that the Republic was being hijacked by a handful of military tribesmen.

"Only a donkey would want to be president of Yemen," he famously told Judge Abdul Rahman Yahya al-Eryani. That was before al-Eryani became president after another coup in November 1967. He was against the imamate system, but some of his best friends were Hashemites (the class that ruled the imamate regimes in Northern Yemen). And he remained fair, seeing the imamate in its historical context and not joining the anti-Hashemite hysteria that arose after the 1962 coup.

I have come to learn that the Yemen he described never existed. It was a construct. And the more I researched, the more I did fieldwork, the more I realized how difficult it would be to bring his Yemen to life. And as I painfully cut the umbilical cord that connected me to him, I began to see Yemen from a different perspective, using different terms than he and his generation used. For example, what happened in 1962 was a military coup, not a revolution. Words are important. How else can we address the core of a problem if we do not call it by its name? He remained wise. When the youth uprisings (another term I use deliberately) started in 2011, he was one of the few who insisted that the uprisings would bring Yemen to the brink of collapse. Despite his belief in his Yemen, he knew only too well how deep the roots of instability ran. The universe was kind. He died before his prophecy was fulfilled.

Have I been shaped by all this? Yes, of course. I have always been a bridge—not only between East and West, but also between Upper and Lower Yemen, between the different Yemeni religious traditions, and between North and South.

Does this background make me biased? No.

I certainly have my point of view—a vision of a Yemen that embraces its diverse population on equal terms. A vision of a state that fulfils its obligations to its citizens—whose dignity and equal rights are protected. This is my position, a position informed by love and concern for this country and its people. But this position does not make me naïve, ignorant of the context in which Yemen operates. My three years working at Sana'a University after graduating from Kuwait University, my involvement in politics, and my recurrent fieldwork over the past thirty years have made me aware of what it means to live in a failed state. No book can prepare you for this reality. What my position does do, however, is make me painfully honest about where the roots of Yemen's instability lie.

I do not think my father would have liked to read this book. But knowing him as I do, he would have remained fair and therefore silent. This book is my tribute to his vision of the Yemen he wanted.

Terminology

There are two terms in this book that may cause a certain amount of controversy: tribe and ethnicity.

Tribe is a controversial term. It has been accused of conveying a negative, pejorative meaning and an ideologically charged image.[15] This is due to the sensitivity of postmodern and postcolonial paradigms. I respect the motivation of these paradigms. They are trying to avoid a legacy of colonial studies that looked down on other cultures. But I stand by the use of the term tribe as a social organization to explain the social fabric of certain regions of Yemen. Yemenis themselves use the Arabic equivalent (*qabilah*), and some describe themselves in tribal terms.

The tribe in Yemen, as Marieke Brandt has aptly argued, is an "emic", that is, "an indigenous representation"; part of the local population has always referred to itself as a tribe (pl. *Qabail*) and "uses the term with pride as a matter of course".[16]

I use Brandt's definition of the Yemeni tribes, as follows:

> Tribes are social groups that exhibit a blend of fundamental characteristics: first, they are typically linked to a specific territory, homeland, or tribal areas. However, they use non-territorial criteria, such as *qabyalah*, a general code of conduct, to distinguish between members and non-members. Second, genealogy also plays a crucial role within tribes, as members often share a dominant common origin, which emphasizes group cohesion over external interests and internal differences. Finally, tribes do not exist in isolation, but rather maintain dynamic relationships with both their tribal and non-tribal environments.[17]

Significantly, in my discussion of the tribal structure in Yemen, I am careful not to present it as a static social organization. Tribes are organic social organizations. They are shaped and influenced by social, political, and economic factors that lead to their structural transformations. A group of prominent Yemeni scholars share this view. In a 2009 study on the political role of tribe in Yemen, they agreed that the tribe is the basic unit of social organization in parts of Yemen. It is based on common interests, protecting its members, and regulating the use of natural resources within its territory.[18] However, they also stressed that kinship alone is not the basis of tribal society at all levels of tribal configuration:

> Many political and economic factors played a role in the formation and reorganisation of tribal confederations through the system of fraternisation. [For example], some tribes broke away from the Madhaj tribal confederation and joined the Hashid and Bakil tribal confederations. Thus, association at the level of tribal confederations is an association based on loyalty and patronage [as opposed to blood].[19]

In addition, the politics of survival and the calculated politics of patronage employed by former president Ali Abdullah Saleh changed the nature of the relationship between tribal leaders and their constituencies.[20] His system of largesse and privilege, which gave the sheikhs freedom from accountability to their constituencies, eroded tribal codes and norms and led to the alienation of tribesmen from their leaders—who often resided in the capital, Sana'a. This does not mean, however, that tribesmen stopped relying on their tribes for support where possible.[21] The dependence has only become more pronounced during the civil war.[22]

Finally, throughout this book, I have refrained from problematizing Yemeni tribes or tribal structures because research has shown that it was the way in which statelets, kingdoms, and republics instrumentalized, reconstructed, and exploited tribal identities in a divide-and-rule fashion that made the tribe politically relevant.

Another term that may be controversial is the use of the adjective "ethnic" to describe the Yemeni conflict. As Chapter One will show, I tend to distinguish between different variants of states in the MENA region. Yemen is not Egypt or Tunisia. In Egypt and Tunisia, if there is a civil war or violent conflict, it will not take on an ethnic character like in Yemen. What makes the three countries different is the context of their state formations. In Egypt, the religious identity of the Coptic Christian minority is important. But it is not used to mobilize as an ethnonationalist identity to challenge Egyptian state authority. Their national identity remains strong, despite the discrimination they have suffered because of the state's exploitation of forms of political Islam since 1952.

Ethnicity, like tribe, is a contested concept. It has been widely used in the social sciences, but it is still difficult to define. Myra A. Waterbury tells us that "ethnicity is an identity category that signifies membership in a group bounded by shared descent, history, myths, symbols, and cultural practices".[23] The widest definition of ethnicity is the one provided by Anthony D. Smith (1986): a group is an ethnic group if its members share the following traits: a common name, a believed common descent, elements of a shared culture (most often language or religion), common historical memories, and attachment to a particular territory.[24]

While classical scholarship on ethnicity and ethno-nationalism has carefully distinguished religion from ethnicity, Smith's definition provides a space to include it. Thus, religion may form the common culture that partly constitutes ethnicity, but ethnicity also requires a territorial and descent dimension.[25]

I am fully aware of the importance of avoiding essentialist fallacies and tropes: most people have multiple identities, and these are sometimes in flux, with the emergence of new identities and the disappearance of old ones, especially in times of crisis.[26] The personal story of "sushi" I tell in Chapter Four testifies to this awareness. However, when these ethnic group identities become the basis for political mobilization, competition, and conflict, they become relevant to our study.[27] This is the case in the Yemeni conflict, where group identities—ethnonationalist identities—have played an important role, not only in challenging the authority of the state, but also in denying its legitimacy and, in some cases, its right to exist in its current form.

Again, as in the case of state manipulation and exploitation of Yemen's tribal structures, the state's role in exploiting Yemeni group identities is central to the creation of these conflicts. Some of these group identities have existed throughout Yemen's history. However, their political significance in relation to their group grievances has been heightened by the role of the state.

Stuart Kaufman's analysis of ethnicity as a generator of conflict illustrates these instrumentalist and constructivist perspectives. Ethnic identities, he argues, are not a new phenomenon. They can be traced back through history. And ethnic difference does not in itself cause conflict. It becomes a means of mobilizing people for violence only under certain circumstances.

Experts disagree about these circumstances. According to the instrumentalist school, "ethnic identity is little more than a tool used by elites to compete for material goods like economic opportunity". There is no such thing as "ethnic conflict" from this perspective. Ethnicity does not cause or generate conflict. It merely provides a framework or label within which other kinds of competition take place. Another school, the "psychocultural" school, argues that ethnic conflict is very real. It alludes to conflicts—such as those over the status of holy sites in Jerusalem—to show how they often stem directly from the way people define their ethnic identity, rather than being primarily about the participants' desire for material goods. Ethnicity can therefore be—but does not necessarily have to be—a generator of conflict.[28]

1 The Arab Spring and its Outcomes

An Arab Spring?

The Term Itself

Why was this sequence of events called the Arab Spring? Analysts disagree on the point of reference used for this expression. They agree that the term in English was first used by Marc Lynch, a professor of Political Science and International Affairs, in the American journal *Foreign Policy*[1] published on 6 January 2011, two days after the death of Mohammed Bouazizi, the Tunisian fruit vendor whose self-immolation on 17 December 2010 sparked the uprisings in 2010.

In a blog with the title "Obama's Arab Spring", Lynch, who also directs the Institute for Middle East Studies at George Washington University, observed the spread of "seemingly unrelated protests and clashes through a diverse array of Arab states". He asked if they might be the "beginnings of an Obama administration equivalent of the 2005 'Arab Spring'" in Beirut.[2]

He was alluding to what was popularly described in Lebanon as the Lebanon Spring or Lebanon Independence, a wave of popular protests sparked by the assassination on 14 February 2005 of Prime Minister Rafik al-Hariri, forcing Syria, which was blamed for Hariri's murder, to withdraw its troops from Lebanon.

Mohammed ElBaradei, the Egyptian winner of the Nobel Peace Prize, also used the expression "Arab Spring" in an interview with the German magazine *Der Spiegel*, published on the day of the first Egyptian mass protests, 25 January 2011. But he used it in reference to a different uprising: that in Prague. Asked whether he agreed with the "domino effect" theory which argued that the revolution in Tunis was only the beginning, he expressed the hope that the region was experiencing the "first signs" of an "Arab Spring"—similar to the Prague Spring of political liberalization in Czechoslovakia in 1968.[3]

Some Arab commentators used the term to allude to the Damascus Spring, a short period of opening, political liberalization, and intense debate that followed the death of Syrian President Hafez al-Assad in 2000. Just like the Prague Spring, which ended with a Soviet invasion, this spring was over in less than a year, when Bashar al-Assad reverted to his father's authoritarianism. And still others argued that it was named after the European revolutions of 1848, called "springtime of the peoples" and "spring of nations".[4]

The fact that the first reference to the Arab Spring was in an American foreign policy journal, and used by an author who openly advocated for including Islamists in the MENA region's political systems—arguing "that mainstream Islamists served as a firewall against more violent extremists"[5]—made the expression open to critique, if not to outright accusation of conspiracies. Some saw in this a diminishing of its importance—a mirror of "some subtle Orientalism". Rami Khouri argued that on the streets of various Arab states people were describing these events as "Revolutions" or "Uprisings". The expression "Arab Spring", he insisted, "plays down the severity of the challenge to existing regimes and downgrades the intensity of the courage that ordinary men and women summon when they dare to take on their well-armed national security services".[6]

To be fair to Marc Lynch, he did express his regret for coining the term Arab Spring, saying it did not do justice to the nature of the changes taking place. On the one hand, they did not yet indicate a story of democratic transitions; in fact, only in Tunisia did such a transition occur, and in 2021 it came to an abrupt end, paving the way to strongman control. On the other hand, they were not revolutions.[7]

If we accept the definition of a revolution as a rapid change of an entire social and political order,[8] Lynch does have a point here despite the expected outcry and reservations. He contended that the phenomenon was a "simultaneous explosion of popular protests" across a region united by a "shared transnational media and bound by a common identity" but "playing out differently across the region". Hence, Lynch opted instead for the term "uprisings" in his 2012 book *The Arab Uprising: The Unfinished Revolutions of the New Middle East*.[9] Other critics, such as Joseph Massad, espousing a Marxist approach, saw in the term Arab Spring a "US strategy of controlling [the uprisings'] aims and goals", instituting "measures of representativity and accountability" but manipulating them to avoid meeting the demands for the "social justice agenda".[10]

The transitional periods that followed the toppling of many leaders in the region—in Tunisia, Egypt, Yemen, and Libya—did in fact focus mainly on the political transition process, while the economic demands of the protesters were relegated to a secondary position. This was a major weakness in the Tunisian democratization process and popular frustration with the lack of economic progress may in fact explain why the country reverted to authoritarianism.

Finally, some dabbled with conspiratorial arguments. For instance, Egyptian professor of modern history, Asim Dasuqi, argued in an interview that launching the term "Spring" is an indication that it falls in the interests of "American strategy". He acknowledged the existence of internal reasons for people's uprisings, but in his opinion an "external factor" played the decisive role in spreading them. He sees a "conspiracy", an attempt by the United States to change the political order in the region, to follow in the steps of former Secretary of State Condoleezza Rice's New Middle East project,[11] to divide the region into smaller parts based on ethnicities, to bring in Islamist parties, which insist on applying religious laws, and to provide the space for the Jewish religious nature of the Israeli state.[12] Such strong perceptions are still widespread in the MENA region and in certain cases have been promoted by the authoritarian regimes themselves, in an effort to discourage their citizens from any protests and organizing for change.

In any case, the term Arab Spring was quickly dropped in favour of other expressions: Arab revolutions, Arab revolts, Arab awakening, Arab protests, Arab Winter, Arab upheavals, and so on. And some Arab intellectuals prefer to go beyond the use of a single term and describe what happened by pointing to their core feature: breaking the barrier of fear.[13]

I favour the term "uprisings". It expresses what took place and is still happening in the region, without predicting its outcomes: popular protests that brought together different segments of society, frustrated by economic and political stagnation in their societies, demanding radical change, with divergent outcomes.

The Drivers

The locations where the uprisings began in 2010 testify to the main driver of these protests: economic marginalization. Sidi Bouzid—located in the hinterland about 265 kilometres southwest of the capital Tunis—is the town where the Tunisian uprisings commenced. Mohamed Bouazizi, a street fruit seller, set himself on fire on 17 December 2010, after local officials confiscated his merchandise.

No one was surprised that this suicide, repeatedly shown on Al Jazeera TV, ignited strong protests in this agricultural town. The region was marginalized during the regimes of presidents Habib Bourguiba and Zine al-Abidine ben Ali, and compared to coastal regions it had dramatically lower levels of socioeconomic development. Figures support this argument: in the final budget of the Ben Ali regime, "82 percent of state funds were dedicated to coastal areas, compared to only 18 percent for the interior".[14] Signs of unrest were becoming clear. In fact, 2008 saw the first popular demonstration by women workers in the Mining Basin in the south of Tunisia, a protest that swept the Gafsa Region. The women were protesting against unemployment, the cost of living, nepotism, and the unfair recruitment practices of the major employer in the region, the Gafsa Phosphate Company.[15]

Economic marginalization, combined with regional disparity, unemployment, systemwide nepotism, corruption, and no real chances to climb the social ladder: these were the main drivers of the uprisings in Tunisia.[16] And they mirrored the economic drivers of the uprisings in many Arab states.

In some countries, the impact of climate change (droughts, desertification, and falling levels of water) has compounded this disparity and marginalized large segments of the population in rural areas. Consider Syria. According to John Waterbury, shortly before the Syrian uprisings, 1.3 million Syrians living in the northeast were severely affected by drought, their agricultural lands devastated, 85% of their local livestock lost, and 160 villages abandoned.[17] Seeking employment in Syria's larger cities, they formed disenfranchised belts of disparate communities surrounding Hamah, Homs, and Daraa;[18] the latter was the site of the first violent confrontation between protesters.

Frustration among youth was an especially important driver of these protests. At the end of 2010, 60% of the population in the MENA region was under 25 years old, making it one of the most youthful regions in the world, with a median age of 22 years compared to a global average of 28. This youth bulge was (and remains) especially problematic because youth are unable to access employment and then form families.

In 2009, youth made up an estimated 51% of the total unemployed in the region, according to that year's UNDP Arab Human Development Report. The huge youth bulge, caused by rapid population growth, put immense pressure on the region's labour markets, as enormous numbers of new workers entered the MENA labour markets, far exceeding the rate at which employed workers retired and new jobs could be created. And the unemployment bulge made it far harder to marry and begin a family, clearly a major rite of passage for young people. In 2009, nearly 50% of men between the ages of 25 and 29 were unmarried. Marriage requires funds: couples must invest in housing, furniture, wedding ceremonies, and so on, and now many more lacked the economic means to do so.[19]

Political stagnation was another driver of the protests. Disgusted by a pluralistic system that resulted in neither accountability nor alternation of power, those who went to the streets demanded dignity, respect for basic rights, and an end to police brutality. Arab states adopted a shallow form of representative systems, which failed to include the normative pluralistic essence of a democratic system: tolerance, rule of law, protection of basic rights, accountability, and real alternation of power.[20]

But the political frustration so often articulated by middle-class political activists does not by itself explain the success of these uprisings in mobilizing the streets of many Arab capitals in the first waves of uprisings.[21]

Success in Mobilization

In fact, the types of groups and organizations that came together and coordinated the protests made a real difference in their success at mobilization. In Egypt, in the early years of the new millennium, security forces were rarely alarmed by the engagement of middle-aged, middle-class democratic activists. One such group is Kifaya (*Enough* in Arabic), a protest movement, founded in November 2004, by 300 Egyptian intellectuals from various ideological backgrounds. It was a coalition of political forces united only by a shared call for an end to President Hosni Mubarak's rule. It achieved very little, few people participated in its constant demonstrations, and it failed to penetrate grassroots Egyptian society, operating instead in circles of intellectuals and political activists.[22]

But even young political activists, unattached to this generation, were aware that they had limited influence among the masses. As one activist told a group of civil society actors in a European capital in 2007, "we live in our activist bubble. When we call for a protest, we summon tens, or if we are lucky, a hundred protesters, only to find ourselves surrounded by double our number of security and police members".[23]

This limited capacity to move the streets started to change in 2008. Then, young activists, armed with their social media tools, began to support the economic demands of the unionized workers in Mahal al-Kubra, the birthplace of Egyptian labour unions and the centre of textile production, along with members of the professional syndicates. This combination had a potent impact, especially as many Egyptians were feeling the painful results of long decades of structural readjustment and economic liberalization: perhaps necessary, but applied without alleviating social safety nets.[24] Similarly, in Tunisia, the uprisings in the hinterland only gained momentum when the powerful Tunisian Workers' Union (Union Générale Tunisienne du Travail (UGTT)) in the centre of Tunis joined, mobilized its local union cells, provided an efficient organizational structure, and played the most decisive role in sustaining the protests.[25] The factors leading to the success of mass mobilization in Egypt and Tunisia are similar, but they may not be applicable to other countries, such as Yemen, Syria, Libya, and Bahrain. I will explore this in Chapter Two.

In general, however, the shared causes of popular resentments combined with the impact of social media for mobilization may explain the domino effect of the Tunisian uprisings. The scene of Mohamed Bouazizi setting himself on fire somehow hit a sensitive nerve in the region. And the success of the Tunisians in forcing President Zine al-Abidine Ben Ali to step down and flee the country in January 2011 sparked something that the region had lost long ago: hope.

A Framework of Analysis

More than a decade after the first wave of uprisings, that hope, for a new political order catering to the wellbeing and dignity and rights of its citizens, was crushed. The uprisings, using the words of Raymond Hinnebusch, were "spectacularly the product of agency". But the structures, "the durable inheritances from the past", and the regional settings of these structures, I add, "have constrained the outcomes of agency".[26] A reversion to authoritarianism, a meltdown of the state, and civil wars: these were some of the political outcomes of this first wave of uprisings.

However, before elaborating on this dimension, a word of caution is warranted. Despite these developments that shocked and destabilized the region to its core, the revolts succeeded in creating a form of social awakening, as people began to discuss issues that were once considered socially taboo, such as religious traditions, women's rights, sexuality, and sexual orientation. Many of those breaking these taboos are paying a high price for doing so, with their freedom, safety, and jobs. But that process has started and it is creating interesting trends. Social media, including Instagram and TikTok, are buzzing with postings that push the limits of what was once unimaginable.

Representative Arab Barometer surveys in the MENA region indicate a generational divide. Youth differ from their older counterparts in several ways. One is greater frustration with the existing system: compared to older generations, they tend to be less religious (more respondents describe themselves as "non-religious"), they lack trust in religious leaders, and they are less interested in politics and more likely to be engaged in social media. On gender issues, a majority of youth across the region tend to be supportive of equal rights for women: majorities say women should have an equal right to access divorce, along with the right to be the head of government and to receive an education. Still, they remain attached to traditional roles in family and against equal inheritance.[27]

One manifestation of the generational divide has been clearly expressed in the anti-sectarian slogans used in the second wave of uprisings in the region.

In Iraq (2018 and 2019), Sudan (2018), and Lebanon (2019), in addition to the essential economic demands and reforms, protesters were calling for a civil political order based on citizenship, not sectarian identities. This divide has also asserted itself in unorthodox manners of protest, challenging strongly held stereotypes. For example, in January 2021, female protesters demanded economic parity in Gafsa, in the south of Tunisia. A group of women protesters petitioned the governor for a collective divorce because they face discrimination in applying for jobs. Women applying for jobs in that governorate are asked about their marital status—a clear denial of their constitutional rights. Those who are married see their applications summarily rejected, with the excuse that their husbands have jobs. To bring attention to their situation, they have petitioned for a collective divorce.[28]

The above notwithstanding, the political outcomes of the first wave of uprisings remain sobering. Six countries experienced massive protests: Tunisia, Egypt, Yemen, Libya, Bahrain, and Syria. In all six, the outcome was one of two unsatisfying results.[29] One was a return to some form of authoritarianism: military in Egypt, strongman grip in Tunisia, and a sectarian monarchical domination in Bahrain. The other was a civil war combined with a meltdown of the central state, as in Yemen and Libya, or loss of control over some regions, as in Syria.

To explain these outcomes, I propose a Contextual Realist approach that integrates elements of realist and constructivist theories. This serves as a prism for analysis and is divided into two interconnected levels within this project's discussion: First, an internal level focusing on the state formation of the observed country. Second, a regional level, examining the operational context within which each country is functioning, and the type of actors involved in its political affairs. This regional-level examination will be explored in *Gulf Rivalry and the Yemeni Civil War*.

Internal Context: State Formation

Countries in the Arab MENA region exhibit one of two types of state formation:

- Countries of old states and old societies. These are characterized by a long tradition of centralized state apparatus and the existence of a strong

national identity. This group includes Egypt, Tunisia, and to a lesser extent Morocco.
- Countries of new states and old societies. These are characterized by the youth of their states, the lack of a coherent national identity, and the division of society along ethnic lines (tribal, religious sectarian, linguistic, and/or regional lines). The Arabian Peninsula countries, Syria, Libya, and Iraq are examples of this group.

The difference between these two groups of states can be seen in their types of political elite and can explain to a great extent why it was possible for the Tunisian and Egyptian presidents to step down without bloodshed and why, in contrast, the removal of the Yemeni and Libyan presidents, and the attempt to do so in Syria, led to their countries' meltdown and the outbreak of civil wars.

Within these two groups of old and new states, the core elite plays a decisive role in the development of the state's policies. Volker Perthes refers to them as the politically relevant elite (PRE); he argues that they "wield political influence and power, make strategic decisions on a national level, contribute to defining political norms and values, and directly influence political discourse on strategic issues".[30] Perthes distinguishes between three concentric circles of the PRE. The first is the inner circle, a core elite, who make decisions on strategic issues. The intermediate elite exerts significant influence on decisions of lesser importance, but not strategic ones. Finally, the sub-elite are less influential elites capable of indirectly influencing strategic decisions or contributing to national agenda-setting through their position in the government and administration.[31]

In my 2012 book *The Arab State and Women's Rights: The Trap of Authoritarian Governance*, I distinguished between two forms of the core elite power base. I argued that lack of legitimacy led many states' political core elite to depend on their traditional or clientlist power base to remain in power.

Traditional Power Base of Countries of New States and Old Societies

In states shaped by ethnic features, countries of new states and old societies, such as Libya, Syria, Bahrain, and Yemen, the traditional power base is defined as the sectarian, tribal, religious, and/or regional groups from which a state's political elites come, or on which they depend, and whose support is vital if the political system as a whole is to endure and survive.[32]

Syria is a good example here. The traditional power base on which the Syrian ruling elite has depended was sectarian, religious, and tribal. Two circles have developed: the inner and outer.

The inner circle of the power base includes the immediate clan members: al-Assad's immediate tribal/sectarian clan from Qardaha in the Latakia province of western Syria. Members of the president's immediate clan fill the key ranks of the security and military apparatus.[33] The circle also includes the extended clan, a larger tribal and sectarian group; we see this in the way the Assads—both father and son—rely on members of their tribe, the Kalbyia, and other tribes of the Alawite minority including the Khayatin, the Haddadin, and the Matawira, to secure their power. This reliance, however, has rarely been based on trust, since the main challengers to their power come from within the Alawi community. And it does not prevent members of that community from feeling alienated by the actions of their strongmen.[34]

The wider circle of the Syrian traditional power base features both diversity and fluctuation. It includes those religious, sectarian, tribal, or regional groups, such as Christians, Ismailis, and Druze, that were historically marginalized or discriminated against during the Ottoman imperial period, who feel threatened within an increasingly Islamized society, or simply seek to share some of the regime's political, economic, and business privileges.[35]

Here the regime plays the role of the guarantor, the power that can keep the minority groups safe against the "tyranny of fundamentalism" or the "Sunni majority". Again, minority groups in Syria, like the Alawites, are pushed to believe that the survival of the regime and their own wellbeing are one and the same.[36]

Traditional Power Base in Countries that are Old States and Old Societies

In countries like Egypt and Tunisia that are not characterized by ethnic markers, countries that are both old states and old societies, the power base is defined in terms of cliental and patronage relations without a distinct ethnic marker.

THE ARAB SPRING AND ITS OUTCOMES

Take Egypt as an example. Egypt's internal and external policies, Gamal Abdelnasser argues, are shaped by a wide range of people from state institutions and civil society. Following Volker Perthes's PRE model, the first circle of elites consists of three groups: politicians of the ruling party, state technocrats, and military leaders. In the second circle, the most influential groups are businessmen, trade unionists, and members of parliament. The third circle includes two new emerging groups: the judges of the supreme constitutional court and influential NGO activists.[37]

President Hosni Mubarak and his son Jamal were at the centre of the two main groups in the first circle. The president appointed the first ranks of state technocrats, the military men, and the administration. In addition, he was chair of the National Democratic Party (NDP), which held over 80% of the seats in the people's assembly.[38]

Nevertheless, though Egypt's political system is highly centralized, indeed autocratic, the ruling elite have long come from various social backgrounds, with military affiliation and access to higher education providing the means for social mobility. The criteria by which they are chosen are generally their party (and now) military connections and education, along with personal and patron–client relationships. Ethnic criteria, such as tribal or clan affiliations, and sectarian and religious affiliations, do not play obvious roles in this context.

In other words, looking again at the core elite in what I have defined as these two groups of countries, we see that they differ according to their respective contexts, but one can argue that the main difference between the two is the presence or absence of a powerful core ethnicity. That is, the core elites in new states tend to be members of a closed ethnicized group (sectarian, confessional, religious, tribal, and regional), whereas the elites in the second set of old states, specifically Egypt and Tunisia, are more diversified and not shaped by ethnic considerations.

The difference explains to a great extent how the army in each set of states acted towards the uprisings. In Egypt, the army is perceived as a national army—a national institution that often acts to defend "the state".[39] More to the point, Hosni Mubarak and his family were just a family, and as influential as they may have been, it was possible to pressure them to step down without threatening the collapse of the whole system.

On the other hand, in countries such as Syria, Libya, and Yemen, the armies were and are still based on ethnic affiliations. At the time of the uprisings, these were: in Syria the Alwaite and other minorities; in Libya the Qadhadfa, al-Warfalla, and al-Magariha tribes;[40] and in Yemen the Sanhan clan and Hashid tribal confederation. As a result, each national army acted as an ethnic bodyguard of the ethnic core elite. In the demise of these ethnic core elites, it saw its own downfall.

Conversely, it saw that protecting the elites would guarantee the system's overall survival. As a result, getting rid of the incumbent core elites was destined to be bloody; hence the bitter civil wars in Yemen, Syria, and Libya so driven by their identity politics.[41]

Given the ethnic nature of these states' institutions, they play a decisive role in perpetuating ethnic divisions within society. Unequal distribution of resources is not just a matter of priorities, policy preferences, or negligence. It is tied to historical rivalry, antagonism, and even hatred. Particular regions and areas are deliberately undermined and excluded. Just as violence—like the breakout of civil wars—has its history and grievances, economic exclusion also carries a powerful logic. I will say more on this in the process of discussing the Yemeni case.

The nature of the core elites in the countries of the Arab uprisings is one part of the puzzle and is strongly tied to these countries' different paths to state formation.[42] Which brings me to my main argument in this section: to understand the divergent outcomes of the first waves of uprisings, we need to bring the state itself back into our analysis; to look at its formative moments and evolving processes, and understand its formation in relation to specific contextual factors.

Achieving this necessitates an interdisciplinary approach, entailing a departure from entrenched paradigms. The Eurocentric lens, which historically fixates on state formation within the European and North American contexts, will be abandoned. A critical concern arises as well from the postcolonial standpoint, haunted by colonial guilt, where the regional historical narrative is deemed relevant solely from the moment of colonial arrival in the region. Preceding events hold limited relevance within this framework, reflective of a selective historical engagement.

The impact of colonization on the process of state formation within the MENA region has been readily undertaken by prominent scholars, including scholars from the region.

THE ARAB SPRING AND ITS OUTCOMES

Scholars diverge on what Ghassan Salamé called the "original sin of the Arab state": to what extent were these states created by a foreign, alien, hostile will? Illiya Harik insists that Arab countries are not only old societies but also old states. Harik argued that these states all have histories dating back to the nineteenth century or earlier, and that cultural and/or economic embryos of states existed in various parts of the region, except for Iraq, Syria, and Jordan.[43]

Others, like Nazih Ayubi, suggest that while the existing Arab states were not entirely manufactured by the colonial powers, their current borders were certainly drawn by them.[44] Benjamin MacQueen qualifies this assertion. Yes, "the most direct manifestation of European control was the territorial definition of the new political entities, each of which would form the modern-day states of the MENA region". However, "this was not purely artificial, with Ottoman policies of centralized bureaucracy around major urban areas as well as deeper historical communities, helping to provide the logic for these new polities", and their borders.[45]

Few question the role of colonial powers in the formation of states in the Arab region. All agree that the periods of Ottoman rule and colonization were formative in the history of Arab states.[46]

I agree. The influence of both Ottoman and colonial imperialism has profoundly shaped state configurations in the region. But the approach proposed here goes beyond these two important influences. It introduces other factors of equal importance. I focus on the observed state and ask the questions: What characterized the state under study before the Ottoman arrival? What regions did it consist of? What political and social structures and religious beliefs prevailed? How did these structures, together with the political implications of the religious tenants and the geographical features of the observed state, shape and determine its state-forming? I also ask the question: How did ideologies (pan-Arabism and Islamism) affect the shape of post-independence states? What kind of core elites came to power after the Ottoman and colonial departures? What policies did they pursue? In other words, this approach essentially refuses to be bound solely by the influence of "external" powers. Instead, it looks inward, examining the internal dynamics and recognizing the agency and voice of the observed society and its political elites.

Hence, bringing the state back into the contextual analysis of the MENA region should be tied to the main factors that played decisive roles in shaping each state's formative moments. It is a contextualized approach. Some factors, such as religious dogmas, may not be significant in one state, but they are significant in another. This approach examines the formation paths of Arab states and recognizes their diverse and disparate historical and institutional trajectories. The result of these different processes of state formation has been the emergence of different variations of state configurations within the region.

I see five internal and external factors as the most important that have played a role in state formation in the region. They are:

a. the types of social structures and the roles they play, combined with the legacy of geography;
b. religious beliefs and their political impacts, when applicable;
c. legacies of Ottoman and colonial rule;
d. ideologies including pan-Arabism and pan-Islamism; and
e. the role of the political elites in the post-independence/Protectorate period.

The Libyan case can be used to illustrate this approach. In order to understand the current situation in Libya, we must consider how these five factors play out there.[47]

Social structures and legacies of geography. The three distinct geographical regions of Tripolitania, Cyrenaica, and Fezzan have had different historical paths and distinct political forms, along with different economic and political ties with neighbouring regions/countries: Tripolitania with today's Tunisia and Cyrenaica with Egypt. Also crucial are the historical rivalry and antagonism between Tripolitania and Cyrenaica, and the roles the tribes play in them.

Ottoman rule. The heavy-handed Ottoman policy depended on leading tribes to provide its governance. It also had different relations with the three regions. It helped defend Tripolitania against the Spanish invaders. With Egypt, it forcefully subjugated Cyrenaica and it engaged in constant military campaigns to control Fezzan. Clearly these relations had differential impacts on the institutional capacities in the three regions.

Colonial rule. The Italian colonizers played a key role in dismantling the Ottoman bureaucracy, military, and financial establishment, and imposing an entirely Italian administration. In doing this they depended, once again, on particular tribes to exert control. Most importantly, Italy and later Britain played key roles in "uniting" the three regions into one political unit.

Ideology. Pan-Arabism played a key role in efforts to unify the three regions under King Idris, despite his reluctance and hesitation given the antagonistic history between Cyrenaica and Tripolitania.

Political elites. Finally, the personalized extractive dictatorship of President Qaddafi eroded any possibility of creating a united nation. He depended on specific tribes and excluded others. He ethnicized the security institutions, and deliberately undermined and excluded Cyrenaica and its population, both economically and politically. Cyrenaica is known for its support of King Idris, whom Qaddafi deposed in a military coup.

In other words, the approach I propose involves an examination of the internal and external legacies of both the past and the present. It goes beyond classical Eurocentric approaches to state formation, which take the European nation state as their point of reference. It also goes beyond the fixation on colonial legacies prevalent within postcolonial studies, which regrettably tend to overlook crucial aspects such as the pre-Ottoman periods and Ottoman rule, treating 400 years of Ottoman imperial rule as a footnote, ignoring the role and agency of the post-independence core elites in shaping, or destroying, the future of their countries. A measured and balanced approach to the factors involved in the internal landscape of state formation and development is thus the first level of the analytical framework I propose. The second level of this analytical framework is the regional context.

Regional Context: Survival and Complex Realism

If we understand the regional relations of the MENA region as a product of two factors—politics within states and politics between states[48]—then it is only logical that the regional context of the 2011 Arab uprisings played a decisive role in shaping their outcomes. Imagine the outcome of the Bahraini uprisings without the Saudi–Emirati intervention? But think at the same time about the internal drivers of the Saudi actions—specifically its demographic structure and the location of the bulk of its oil fields. I will discuss this further in my second volume, but at this point suffice it to say that the roots of the uprising were certainly internal, but the outcome was a product of the interaction of both internal and regional structures in and between these states.

Explaining the regional actors' behaviour towards the Arab uprisings requires a coherent framework of analysis: one that is applicable to the MENA region. All too often, theories of international relations are developed to explain the behaviour of core states in the international system. But this perspective does not suffice for the MENA region. It does not capture the complexity and history of these states nor their preoccupation with their regional surroundings. In fact, compared to core international powers, such as the United States, countries of the MENA region are likely to have foreign policies more oriented towards their region. Why? The reason is straightforward. The main threats that have challenged the national security of states and the survival of regimes (the two are not always congruent) have often emanated from their own region.

Think of the ideological divide in the region in the 1950s and 1960s and how pan-Arabism led to the destabilization of the region and even to the toppling of several regimes, including the Mutawakkilite Kingdom in the North of Yemen in 1962 and the United Kingdom of Libya in 1963. Think as well of the Islamic Iranian Revolution in 1979 and its attempts to export its revolution to the Gulf, and how Baathist Iraq under President Saddam Hussein threatened the sovereignty of Kuwait and the stability of the Gulf region in general.

Certainly, survival and national security lie at the heart of MENA countries' foreign and regional policies: they are concerned with guarding their national security and survival, constantly struggling to withstand regional pressures from hegemonic or competing neighbours. In fact, some are relentlessly attempting to change the behaviour of other states following what Peter Calvert calls the "the international rules of the game".[49]

For all these reasons, we may be content to confine our approach to realism.

Realism is a school of thought that emphasizes the competitive and conflictual side of international relations. It argues that international affairs are a struggle for power among self-interested states. It has several assumptions. First, the state, a unitary actor, is the principal actor in international relations. In addition, decision-makers are rational actors pursuing national interests; and states live in a context of anarchy, in which no one is in charge internationally. This conjunction of egoism and anarchy results in the imperatives of power politics.[50]

However, by itself, a realist approach cannot explain the whole range and complexity of regional actors' foreign policy decisions. State formation, perceptions of threats, the ideological orientation of states and core elites, and the personalities of leaders are all important factors to consider as well. One cannot understand the MENA regional politics without taking these dimensions into account. Hence, I argue that a critical realist approach, which combines a realist ontology with a constructivist epistemology, is warranted here. This is Maxwell's concept, which I introduced earlier. Translated into international relations terminology, a modified form of complex realism provides a suitable theoretical framework for understanding the MENA regional actors' foreign policies in the aftermath of the 2011 Arab uprisings.

The term complex realism was first developed and introduced by Raymond Hinnebusch in the several editions of his book, *The International Politics of the Middle East*, and in his 2014 volume, co-edited with Anoushiravan Ehteshami, *The Foreign Policies of Middle East States*.[51] Complex realism is a form of realism that accepts some realist assumptions but argues that any analysis must consider other levels of state behaviour, notably both the internal (domestic) and the international systemic level, as they have major impacts on state behaviour and international politics.

Complex realism accepts that the basics of realist thinking are applicable because Middle Eastern policymakers are "quintessential realists", preoccupied with the threats so pervasive in the MENA region. It agrees with two key claims of the realists. First, insecurity generates struggles for power and foreign policy seeks to counter security threats to regime survival, state interests, sovereignty, and territorial integrity. Second, some states have ambitions for regional leadership, international acceptance, and economic development, but these can only be pursued when security is established.[52]

However, it sees the limits of a purely realist approach and considers several realist assumptions as problematic. Most significantly, it argues that "states are not necessarily cohesive actors" and that "some states are so fragmented, or their sovereignty is so compromised by dependency, that their foreign policies might reflect regime interests but less obviously national interests".[53]

It also argues that the environment in which foreign policy makers operate is more multi-layered than the picture the realists paint. Hence, in addition to the regional inter-state system, foreign policies are affected by the "trans-state identities and the global hierarchy in which regional states are also embedded".[54]

The limits of realism call on us to integrate several assumptions and concepts from other theories. For the purpose of this research project, constructivism and historical sociology are of relevance. Constructivism[55] emphasizes the impact of ideas and beliefs on world politics, and helps us understand trans-state identities, where sub- and supra-state identities compete with state identity, inspire trans-state movements, and constrain purely state-centric behaviour. Historical sociology highlights the importance of state formation and shows how the "kind of states—their level of state formation—that dominate a system shape its dynamics". Finally, we must open the black box of decision-making processes, to reveal the role of internal leadership and policy processes in any state's response to environmental pressures.[56]

A final note regarding this approach. Hinnebusch's work has a tendency to overstress the colonial and imperial forces in shaping the region, and its decision-making processes. He overlooks the fact that the states concerned and core elites have often been adept at exploiting the seams of the international system to their advantage. Therefore, the author adds two further important dimensions to which Hinnebusch has attributed little importance, in the state- formation legacy of MENA states. These are, first, the Ottoman Empire's role and policies, and second, the post-independence state's role in shaping and forming state systems in the region.

The adapted complex realism approach, I argue, is suitable to explain the role of regional players in shaping the divergent outcomes of the 2011 Arab uprisings. To underline this argument, consider the Saudi regional intervention in the Bahraini 2011 uprisings, which sealed their fate.

A simple explanation of the Saudi (together with Emirati) military intervention of 14 March 2011 via the Gulf Cooperation Council Peninsula Defence Shield[57] would look at it only as an attempt to stop the advance of democratic movements in the region, lest that movement spread outside its boundaries. That argument is certainly plausible; many scholars have used it. They may look at it from a purely realist perspective, focusing on the rivalry between

Iran and the Saudis and their balance of power in the region. This is indeed a core issue. But it cannot be understood without adding analysis at the state level, with a focus on state formation and the sectarian factor in both Saudi Arabia and Bahrain.

Saudi Arabia and Bahrain are new states that were officially created in 1932 and 1971 respectively. One cannot understand their relationship without looking at the tribal ties in their ruling dynasties: the Sunni Al Khalifa tribal dynasty that rules Bahrain immigrated in the eighteenth century from Najd, a middle region in today's Saudi Arabia, and the Saudis' traditional power base. We must also look at their demographic structures in relation to the Sunni–Shia sectarian divide: a majority of the population in Bahrain (estimated to be between 60% and 70%) are of the Shia tradition. Called Baharina, they are the original farming and fishing inhabitants of Bahrain. On the other hand, a minority of the Saudi Shia population (estimated to be between 10% and 15%) are concentrated in the Eastern Region, right opposite Bahrain, where the main Saudi oil fields are located.

Now add in the fact that the Shia populations in both states are followers of the Iranian Twelvers tradition: they enjoy close cultural and religious ties with Iran, and in both countries, they are discriminated against and treated as second-class citizens. And major Shia political actors in Bahrain enjoy good if not close political ties with Iran. Considering all this, from the perspective of Saudi Arabia the developments in Bahrain are hardly just internal. The uprisings in Bahrain were certainly expected: just consider the history of the country's uprisings, every decade in the last century.[58] But for Saudi Arabia, what takes place in Bahrain does not remain in Bahrain; it threatens to spill over to the Eastern Region and shake its own stability. It is a matter of acute national security, especially if we consider the location of the oil fields.

To summarize my points in this introductory chapter, in this project I propose a framework of analysis for the divergent outcomes of the 2011 Arab uprisings. I adopt a critical realist approach and introduce two interconnected levels of analysis.

The first is an internal level, focusing on the state formation of specific countries. At this level we bring the state back into our analysis, look at its formative moments and evolving processes, and understand its formation in relation to five specific factors: (a) types of social structures and their roles in combination with the legacy of geography; (b) religious beliefs and their impact, when applicable; (c) Ottoman and colonial legacies; (d) ideologies, pan-Arabism and pan-Islamism; and (e) the role of the political elites in the post-independence/Protectorate period.

The second level is regional. I examine the operational context within which each country is functioning, and the types of actors involved in its political affairs. I apply complex realism. It accepts some of the realist assumptions but argues that other levels of analysis, notably the internal (domestic) and the international systemic level, have major impacts on state behaviour and international politics. Hence, in addition to considering the regional inter-state system, this approach also looks at "trans-state identities and the global hierarchy in which regional states are also embedded", along with the impact of ideas and beliefs on world politics, importance of state formation in the states observed, and the role of leadership and policy processes in states' response to environmental pressures.[59]

The 2015 Yemeni civil war will serve as a case study. This volume addresses the first level of analysis. A second volume, with the title *Gulf Rivalry and the Yemeni Civil War*, will focus on the regional dimension.

If we turn our attention to the internal level of Yemeni civil war, three legacies, formed by the five factors outlined above, will be illuminated. Legacies of geography, religious beliefs, and tribes; legacies of Ottoman imperialism and British colonization; and the legacy of the cunning state and politics of survival. Chapter Two will discuss the Yemeni youth uprising in detail. Chapters Three to Eight will discuss the aforementioned three legacies. A concluding chapter will highlight the relevance of these legacies for sustainable peace in Yemen. Sustainable peace, I argue in this volume, must go beyond an end to violence. It must address the roots of Yemen's recurrent civil wars and political instability.

2 The Yemeni Civil War and the Youth Uprisings

It is difficult to write about Yemen. It was difficult before and it is even more difficult now. Yemen, I have argued elsewhere, is many Yemens, with many histories, political units, formative moments, and evolving processes. Telling its story entails untangling the many layers and factors, internal and external, that make up its history and shape its present. How do you tell this story without distorting the picture of a magnificent land, once called in Arabic مهد الحضارات (the cradle of civilization) and in German a *Märchenland* (fairyland)? How do you narrate it without degrading its people, proud people brought to the brink of starvation by this latest cycle of violence? This is a man-made humanitarian disaster caused by multiple warring actors, Yemeni and regional alike (my use of a gendered term here is deliberate). And how do you study this history without painfully shattering deep-rooted myths, held dear by many Yemenis?

It is even more difficult to write about Yemen *today*. The current civil war has brought this country to the centre stage of world politics. Powerful countries in the region are holding the strings of Yemeni affairs. Depending on the regional side to which a writer/scholar/expert leans, they would narrate a different story, sometimes laying the "blame" squarely on one or two regional actors to the exclusion of others; and sometimes the story conveniently ignores the regional role altogether.

A plethora of scholars, tied to Western, regional, and Yemeni think tanks, and some attached to elite universities, are engaged in a new form of "knowledge production".[1] They explain Yemen from different perspectives, rarely taking account of the Yemeni voices inside, and they focus on the narratives of English-speaking Yemeni elites, each tied to a party in the conflict. The type of each one's think tank, their government ties, and most importantly their donors: all these naturally shape the knowledge being produced.

That does not mean these think tanks do not produce serious scholarship. They do. But it does mean that this knowledge production is often formed by specific perspectives and interests. Yemeni interests may not always be their priority. It also means that very often the analysis produced is focused on the present. Looking back to state formations and history: that is a luxury, an exercise that cannot be allowed in during fast-paced knowledge production. It is the conflict in its current shape that becomes the focus. With this perspective, the roots of the recurrent Yemeni crises are often concealed and different narratives about the current civil war become dominant: it may be called a proxy war between regional rivals, a sectarian war with a focus on the Sunni versus Shia division, and a failed state with implications for security and terrorism.[2] All these narratives capture symptoms, but what caused those symptoms remains elusive.

Writing about this civil war is even more complicated.

Where do we start our analysis? The starting point is a choice and that choice may indeed shape policy decisions. It can lead to a totally different story, and thus a different remedy. Should we start with the Yemeni youth uprising? That is certainly a plausible point of departure and even suggested in a TV interview by Jamal Benomar, the first UN Special Envoy for Yemen.[3] The youth uprising, with its different starting dates in January or February 2011, can tell us a lot about the complexity of the Yemeni story and how the core elites with their simmering power struggle used this uprising to settle their differences.

Or should we begin with the Gulf Initiative, designed by the Gulf Cooperation Council (GCC) in May 2011 to provide Yemen a safe exit from an explosive situation? That would highlight the region's role in Yemeni affairs, and the priorities of some Gulf states, but also the way that the Initiative set the parameters and glass ceiling that inadvertently determined the outcome of the transitional period that followed.[4]

How about using the starting date of the war? Those who support the narrative of the war offered by the Houthi militia, which some analysts and journalists erroneously describe as a Shiite militia, may set the starting date of the war as 26 March 2015. This was the date when the Arab Coalition (made up of nine Arab countries and led by Saudi Arabia), acting on a "request" by former President Abdrabbuh Mansur Hadi, launched its Operation Decisive Storm. The purpose of the attack, as the Saudi Ambassador to Yemen stated on that very day, was to "defend and support the legitimate government of Yemen and prevent the radical Houthi movement from taking over the country".[5]

Others, to highlight the central role of the Houthi militia in starting the war, would counter with another date: the war started on 21 September 2014, when the Houthi militia took over Sana'a, the capital of the Yemen Republic, a move that further consolidated and expanded its control southward and along the Red Sea coast.[6]

And some would argue, as did Asher Orkaby, that a "more manageable historical origin narrative begins in September 1962, at the contentious founding of the modern Yemeni republic".[7] That year marked the end of an era: the overthrow of a Zaydi Kingdom in North Yemen and the adoption of a republican system. It is also the year that saw North Yemenis fight on different sides, supported by different regional actors (this time Egypt and Saudi Arabia), over the future nature of the Northern Yemeni system.

How about the six Sa'ada wars (2004–2009) between the Houthi militia and the Yemeni government? And the 1994 civil war that witnessed an unsuccessful attempt by some Southern leadership to separate the South from the North? These too, as Jamal Benomar, the first UN Special Envoy for Yemen, reminds us in an interview with this author, may be looked at as the historical origins of the current civil war.[8]

But if we look back at these formative moments of North Yemeni history, should not we do the same for South Yemen? This is not just a matter of courtesy. It is crucial to understand South Yemen with its divided actors, if we are to understand the complexity of this war. If we do not include it in our analysis, we get a distorted picture: a binary of a Houthi militia versus an internationally recognized government operating from Riyadh and Aden. And this war is anything but binary. It is a war between competing groups and forces within the North, within the South, and between the North and the South. And that statement covers only the internal actors in this war.

THE YEMENI CIVIL WAR

So, if we do look at South Yemen, which date should we choose? 1994, the above-mentioned date of a civil war between North and South Yemen? Or 1990, the date of the unification between the North, the Yemen Arab Republic, and the South, the People's Democratic Republic of Yemen? Or perhaps the year 1986 is more adequate? That is the date of a ferocious Southern civil war that still divides Southerners, even today. Better yet, we should trace the date back to the very creation of a unified South Yemen in 1967.

All of these points of departure are relevant, plausible, and practicable. But I tend to look back even farther, as Orkaby also suggests. For the story of Yemen has often revolved around these very same two markers of the 1962 Northern civil war and the 1967 creation of South Yemen: internal causes of disputes—rooted well back in history, and external interventions—exploiting these divisions for their own interests. The combination was not good for Yemen.

If we focus in this volume on the internal dimension, it becomes clear that the 2015 civil war was not the first. Sadly, it is one of many. Yemen experienced several civil wars before and after unification in 1990 and it has a long history of political instability—in North and South Yemen alike. That instability is not restricted to the modern history of the twentieth century and later. It goes much farther back.

The roots of these recurrent crises, I argue, have to do with the DNA of Yemeni state formation. This is the level I will address in the next six chapters, as I try to understand what went wrong with Yemeni state formation, explaining it in relation to the factors proposed by this project's framework of analysis. More specifically I look at (a) the type of social structures and their role; (b) geography, religious beliefs, and their impact, when applicable; (c) Ottoman and colonial legacies; (d) ideologies (pan-Arabism and pan-Islamism); and (e) the role of the political elites in the post-independence/Protectorate period.

Tailored to the Yemeni context, I will present three forms of legacies: those of geography, religious beliefs, and tribes; those of Ottoman hegemony and British colonization; and that of the cunning state and politics of survival.

But before we embark on this journey in the next chapters, and since the Arab uprisings are the first point of departure for this project, it is necessary to introduce the Yemeni youth uprising, looking especially at how it was hijacked and unintentionally led to the meltdown of the Yemeni state.

Trapped Between Aspirations and Structures

Remember Hinnebusch's argument? The uprisings in the MENA region were an outcome of agency and aspirations. The youth revolted against troubling features of their respective countries, only to be confronted with the structures of their states: the "durable inheritances from the past". Karl Marx, Hinnebusch reminds us, said something similar: "men [people] make their own history but not in circumstances of their own choosing".[9]

This in a nutshell is what happened with the Yemeni youth uprisings. Young Yemeni men and women dreamt of change and went to the streets in their limited numbers. Their protests gained momentum as they were joined by others, only to see their demands for change hijacked by disgruntled core elites, engaged as they were in their own power struggle. The elites recycled the uprisings into their own vehicle for grabbing power and in the process destabilized the whole political system.

This deserves an explanation. Those who sparked the youth uprisings in Yemen were members of the civil society. They were a small and diverse group of actors. Diverse in ideologies, they included socialists, Nasserists, liberals, and some with no affiliation. They wanted change in a fundamental sense: as they put it, "our objective was bigger than *leave*. Our aim was to build a civil state";[10] and "we needed a revolution, an end to corruption, nepotism; come on, thirty-three years! There was nothing new."[11]

Leave was the slogan that became a trademark of all the Arab uprisings: calling on the incumbent head of state to step down from power. At that point, Ali Abdullah Saleh had been president for thirty-three years: more than enough for the young person quoted above.

The young people's frustrations and demands for change were understandable. Corruption permeated every level of the state's institutions. In fact, in 2011, Yemen stood (with Libya) among the most corrupt regimes within the MENA region and worldwide, ranking 164th out of the 182 countries on the Corruption Index. Nepotism was deep seated, a small elite monopolized economic power with no trickle-down effect, and poverty was widespread.

More than 45% of the population was living under the poverty line, 30% of citizens did not have basic food security, and unemployment was conservatively estimated at 35%.[12]

The economic pains and corruption were aggravated by the way the regime made a farce of democracy: holding up the shell of a democratic legal organization that resulted in neither accountability nor real alternation of power. The shell was promising: political parties could work freely, the press allowed for critique and debates that "made their counterparts in the Arabian Peninsula blush with envy",[13] and the electoral system included a bicameral legislature. But this very electoral system and its results lacked credibility and elections were often subject to manipulation. The president who competed with others in the 2006 presidential election had in fact held the office since 1978. And just like other presidents in the MENA region at the time, President Saleh was grooming his own son Ahmed, head of the elite National Guard, to be his successor.

A great deal of the country's political action took place in an unofficial sphere of politics: a "sphere where decisions are made that bypass the law and the constitution, sometimes with the specific aim of rendering shallower the state's institutional reality".[14] Powerful men and their entourages were never held accountable. Their excesses included land grabbing, corruption, and human rights violations. In fact, some of them, especially powerful tribal sheikhs, had their own prisons to punish those they deemed deserving of punishment. They were acting like feudal landlords and the state watched and did not intervene.[15]

Can these young educated Yemeni men and women be blamed for demanding change? They had enough and wanted change desperately. They dared to dream of a country they could call their own and were inspired—inspired by the Tunisian Jasmine Revolution.

That inspiration led to three concurrent forms of youth uprisings. These took place in Sana'a, the capital of United Yemen and former capital of North Yemen; Taiz, the country's third most populated city, located in southwestern Yemen (Lower Yemen); and Aden, at that time Yemen's economic capital and former capital of the People's Democratic Republic of Yemen (South Yemen). The locations of these uprisings are significant. The following sections address them.

Youth Agency

Sana'a, 15 January 2011

As I have described elsewhere, on 14 January, the night that Tunisian President Ben Ali fled his country, a small group of activists organized a demonstration in front of the Tunisian embassy in Sana'a. The original idea was to hold it in front of the French Embassy: "We wanted to tell them [France], take your hands off the Arab world's democracy," Wameedh Shakir, a youth activist, told me in Sana'a a few weeks later.[16] They changed their destination to the Tunisian embassy—to express their support for the Tunisian "revolution" and demand change in Yemen as well. "A day later a huge demonstration started out of Sana'a University [and headed again towards the Tunisian embassy]."[17]

That demonstration consisted of 150 protesters and was organized by the student sector of the Socialist Party in Sana'a University with a small group of civil society actors.[18] Many of them were arrested and later released.[19] The limited number at the first demonstration on 15 January in Sana'a reveals something that may not be surprising: not all supported the demand for a regime change, at least not in Sana'a. More on this later.

Taiz, 11 February 2011

Another uprising took place in another city, Taiz, on 11 February 2011. Some insist this date is *the* decisive date of the Yemeni "revolution". And indeed, ten years later, when celebrations are held to honour the date of the youth "revolution", 11 February is the date some use.

The date is connected to another development in the region: Egyptian President Hosni Mubarak announced his resignation on that day. Young students celebrated his departure and organized the first sit-in strike in Taiz: "We went first to Tahrir Square and we were beaten [by security forces] and we had to move to Jamal Street and finally we withdrew to Freedom Square. It was the first sit-in demonstration in the whole republic," the coordinator of the Independent Youth of 11 February Revolution explained to me in a telephone interview.[20] Other youth and civil society activists organized demonstrations in Sana'a on the same day, for example a sit-in vigil on 3 February, but it was only in Taiz that a camp was created at this early date.[21] That camp was later burned to the ground by President Saleh's army and supporters on 29 May 2011.

The main issue at play here is the affiliation of the demonstrators with the Taiz governorate. Activists, who tend to come from Taiz more than elsewhere, would insist that this city has been a "pioneer of change, revolutions, and the national project",[22] and it was. But Taiz is also part of the middle region of Yemen (Lower Yemen of North Yemen in specialized literature), which has endured various forms of discrimination over the centuries. Its population's religious affiliation—Sunni rather than the Zaydi denomination of the Northern ruling political elite—may in fact have played a role in that discrimination. But the story is more complicated than this binary.

Back to this city's youth protesters. They insisted on being "independent". They were "sick" of the politics of political parties and were "afraid that" any political alliance would "interfere in the revolution and direct it towards partisan interests".[23] This position was translated into one of the most popular slogans of the Yemeni youth uprisings: "No partisans, no parties. Our revolution is a youth revolution." Notwithstanding their slogan, it is difficult not to notice a streak of leftist ideology in their statement.[24] But their distrust of the politics around political parties proved to be accurate. More later.

Aden, 16 February 2011

Yet another date, 16 February, was set for another Yemeni uprising, this time by a youth group called the 16 February Peaceful Youth Revolution, from the Southern part of Yemen, specifically the Aden governorate. The date marked the first death of a protester (Mohammad Ali Shaen) in the Yemeni uprising.[25]

What concerns us here is the Southern nature of this group—and more precisely, its strong bond to Aden. At first, the youth group was not politically affiliated with the Southern movement known as *al-Hirak*, a loose affiliation of regional opposition organizations and activists in the Southern provinces, which calls for an end to Northern hegemony. Aden has often been a challenge for the Southern movement: while it did not support the Northern regime, it persistently refrained from joining the *Hirak*.[26] The reasons for its mistrust of this Southern movement have to do with the colonial period and the history of the post-independent communist state.

But as with anything that involves this city's political aspirations, past or present, the nascent youth uprising became the focus of a power struggle between strong political actors in the South. In this case, two actors were competing over the control of this youth group: the *Hirak* and the Islamist Islah Party, the strongest party in the main opposition group, the Joint Meeting Parties (henceforth the JMP), a coalition of six opposition parties. The two groups agreed on a ban on holding any flags (that of unified Yemen or the Southern flag) during the demonstrations. Only after members of the old regime turned against Saleh at the end of March was the *Hirak* in a position to win over the 16 February youth group to its side: "the revolution, it was said, was hijacked. It was not a revolution anymore. It became part of the old political system."[27] Its protests and sit-in strikes became focused on "Southern" demands only.

Obviously, these conflicting dates reflect the complicated nature of the Yemeni political landscape. Yet whatever date we choose as the spark of the revolt, one thing is clear. By 28 February, the call for Saleh to step down had turned city squares into melting pots that managed to unify different groups that had otherwise stood at odds with one another.

Constraining Systematic Structures

Yemeni youth revolted in their respective cities. Their aspirations were real, sincere, and authentic. But the young people were few, and they had no wider social backing, or tribal or military cover. And they were not well organized. Those facts together created the space for the contextual structures of their regime to hijack their aspirations. Two internal factors facilitated that takeover of the youth aspirations: (a) the characteristics of the Yemeni regime, and (b) the power struggle of core elites in the Yemeni political system. The regional intervention is another important factor, but I will address it in the second volume, *Gulf Rivalry and the Yemeni Civil War*. Here I discuss these two factors and then conclude with an account of the developments that led to the hijacking of the youth uprisings.

THE YEMENI CIVIL WAR

Characteristics of the Yemeni Regime

The regime that has controlled Yemen since 1978 is ethnic in nature. The Saleh regime has depended on a sectarian/tribal/regional power base; its support was crucial for the political system as a whole to endure and survive. What concerns us here is the immediate tribal/sectarian clan: the president's Sanhan tribe. It is based at the south-southeast corner of Sana'a, Yemen's capital, and is a member of the Zaydi Qahtani Hashid tribal confederation. I explain these affiliations in the following chapters.[28]

The president's ability to survive Yemen's recurrent political upheavals since he came to power in 1978 has depended on the unwavering backing of his immediate family/clan and tribe. But while this regime has depended on the support and loyalty of a close network within its own sectarian and tribal group, it simultaneously played on the sectarian, tribal, and regional divisions within society. This exploitation of ethnic divisions within Yemen has led to a constant interplay in which different political and ethnic groups are included at the expense of others at one point, only to be faced with exclusion at another point.

Significantly, all military and security institutions were in the hands of a close network of family and clan members. To mention only the former President Saleh's direct family members: Saleh's brother Mohamed commanded the Air Force; his son Ahmed commanded the Yemen Special Forces and later the Republican Guard; and his two favoured nephews, Yehia and Ammar, were respectively the commander of the Central Security Forces, and the deputy director of the National Security Bureau.

It is no surprise that their loyalty to the regime's head and family outweighed any loyalty to an abstract concept of a nation or state. In any threat to Saleh's regime, they saw their own downfall. And they saw that protecting him would ensure the system's overall survival. So naturally, any attempt to get rid of the incumbent core elites was destined to be bloody from the outset. Adding to that, just as the youth were rising up, a significant power struggle was simmering within that close network of core elites. An open confrontation was only a matter of time; the uprisings merely accelerated it.

Power Struggle of Core Elites

Moving beyond the members of Saleh's immediate family, since 1978 the Yemeni political system has been held together by a tripartite alliance of a military and tribal nature. Think of it as a circle of two wings, connected by a circle at the nucleus: Saleh. He held the strings of power and they provided the military and tribal muscles enabling him.

The first strong ally is a member of Saleh's clan, Sanhan. He is Brigadier General Ali Mohsen al-Ahmar, then commander of the First Armoured Division and North-Western Military District. His exact relation to Saleh is not clear; some insiders told me he is Saleh's half-brother on his mother's side, while some news sources report he is the cousin of Saleh's half-brothers.

The second strong ally, the late Sheikh Abdullah al-Ahmar (no relation to Ali Mohsen), was the head of Saleh's larger tribe, the Hashid tribal confederation, at that time the most powerful one in Yemen. He was also, until he died in 2007, the Speaker of Parliament and head of Islah, Yemen's largest Sunni Islamist party. Islah was part of the ruling coalition until it broke off in 2003 and joined the opposition, the JMP.

This tripartite alliance has been the cornerstone of Saleh's rule. A leaked US diplomatic report says that it was "formed by written agreement in 1978" after his predecessor was assassinated.[29] Whether signed or informal, those who follow Yemeni affairs would agree that the two sets of allies helped Saleh come to power in 1978, and stood by him for decades. Together they ruled North Yemen and later United Yemen and shared the country's resources, spoils, and privileges.

A 2005 WikiLeaks US diplomatic report says this about their relationship:

> He [Saleh] has given both men a wide berth to run their affairs with informal armies, courts, and economic empires. Saleh often bows to their demands on issues such as anti-corruption and gun control, and makes direct payments from the treasury to the two men's tribal and military constituencies.[30]

The tripartite alliance continued for decades but started to weaken as Saleh's power and strength grew. The first cracks in the alliance showed in 1994, after Saleh, with the help of these two groups and others, won the civil war between the North and the South. His victory boosted him, and he started to become overconfident, depended more on his immediate family members, excluded his former allies, and in the process became isolated. He "stopped listening", one of his closest confidants, who asked to remain anonymous, told me.

Tension with the family of Sheikh Abdullah, especially his two sons Sadeq and Hamid, flared after their father died in 2007; meanwhile Ali Mohsen's relations with Saleh deteriorated because of his rivalry with Saleh's eldest son, Ahmed Ali. This tension was simmering, gradually eroding Saleh's strong traditional base of power. It first became visible when the Islah Party (headed by the al-Ahmar family) decided to join the opposition in the 2003 elections and became part of the JMP. It grew even clearer in 2007 when the Islah Party supported the presidential candidate running against Saleh. And it flared militarily as the tripartite alliance disintegrated and the confrontation took a Machiavellian turn during the six Sa'ada wars between 2004 and 2009. The causes of these wars, the Houthi militia rebellion, and the importance of this region will be addressed later on in this volume. What concerns us here is how it was used in this simmering power struggle.

Saleh's son Ahmed Ali and his arch-rival Ali Mohsen were assigned the task of fighting the Houthi rebels in their stronghold and power base, Sa'ada; Yemeni media reported that the two men's forces were in fact concurrently engaged in a proxy war in this very region.[31] Saleh's forces used these wars to weaken Ali Mohsen's military base; in addition, several attempts were made on his life. For instance, in 2010 a leaked diplomatic cable from the US embassy in Saudi Arabia indicated that Saudi air forces, which had started to support the Yemeni army in their attempt to quell the Houthi rebellion, had been sent the location of Ali Mohsen's headquarters as a target for an air strike. The Saudi pilots aborted the strike when they sensed something was wrong about the information they received.[32]

On another front, but similar in nature, the al-Ahmar family was pushing to remove Saleh. By 2011, Hamid, the son of Sheikh al-Ahmar, was a billionaire business tycoon, and the undisputed leader of the Islamist Islah Party. In 2009, he informed a high-level diplomat at the American embassy that he was "plotting" to remove Saleh from power:

> He claimed that he would organize popular demonstrations throughout Yemen aimed at removing President Saleh from power unless the president

"guarantees" the fairness of the 2011 parliamentary elections, forms a unity government with leaders from the Southern Movement, and removes his relatives from positions of power by December 2009.[33]

Thus, Hamid al-Ahmar was positioning himself as an alternative to Saleh, but many Yemenis saw no difference between Saleh and Hamid in their "tribal politics".[34]

One point bears emphasis here: Hamid al-Ahmar's plotting does not in any way cast doubt on the authenticity and genuine nature of the Yemeni youth uprisings. That said, no one, even the activists who spoke with me, denies that the youth received generous support, logistical and otherwise, from Hamid al-Ahmar. For example, during the early wave of anti-government protests, Hamid's Sabafon mobile network sent out messages with details of the time and place of demonstrations.[35]

This power struggle was boiling at a time when two regional conflicts were also heating up. One was in North Yemen: the Houthi rebellion in Sa'ada. The other, in the South, was a Southern secessionist movement, the *Hirak*. And when these powerful strong men and other political forces, including the Joint Meeting Parties (dominated by Hamid al-Ahmar's Islah Party), joined the youth and demanded the toppling of Saleh's regime, each did so for its own reason.

Youth Uprisings Hijacked

It is clear that these uprisings were never strong or well structured—if only to judge by the limited number of youth and civil society actors participating in them. Again, not all of them supported the demand for regime change.[36] In fact, when protesters demanded Saleh's removal in Sana'a, supporters of Saleh also went to the streets—in roughly equal numbers.

In addition, though a small group of civil society actors showed great conviction as they demanded real change and called on the president to "leave", the main opposition parties and their youth refrained at first from calling for Saleh's removal. In fact, the JMP, which was part of the political establishment, and their young members, were initially hesitant to join the protest; when they did join in on 3 February, they demanded "reform", not the removal of Saleh.[37]

It was their way to exert pressure on Saleh for more reforms and democratic concessions. They mainly wanted him not to extend his presidential mandate. They knew he could take a series of anti-democratic actions. He could change the constitution again, or hand power to his son. They also wanted a reform of the electoral system to a proportional one, a review of voter registers, which included non-existent and deceased voters, and establish a local government system with full authority.[38]

Saleh, worried about the waves of uprisings in Tunisia and Egypt, announced his plans for reforms, which he called "concessions". Rather too late, one might add. On 2 February, Saleh gave a speech in parliament, with leaders present from the government, army, and security institutions. He proposed postponing the upcoming April legislative elections to prepare for constitutional amendments, and political and electoral reforms. And he stressed that he did not intend to run for a new presidential term after his current presidency ended in 2013 and vowed not to hand over power to his son, Ahmed.[39]

These concessions were promising and the JMP took a middle ground: they joined a planned youth protest on 3 February while keeping the door ajar for negotiations with Saleh.[40] Gradually their demand for reform changed into a demand that Saleh resign. Ali Mohsen joined them later, in March.

Once the JMP, led by the Islah Party, and later Ali Mohsen, joined the youth in their sit-ins and camps, things changed dramatically. To understand that change, you have to imagine the scene in these camps of young people before that takeover happened.

Consider what happened in Taghir (Change) Square, a sprawling protest camp in the capital, Sana'a. Taghir Square was a melting pot during the first weeks of the youth uprisings; young Yemenis, men and women, from all regions of the country, with different ideological backgrounds, all came together demanding change. Tribesmen, who customarily dance with their daggers, opted to dance without them. Young men and women decided to create a joint committee and sweep the streets of the sit-in camp; housewives, unable to attend the rallies, cooked meals for the protesters. Some tents were dedicated to lectures on human and basic rights, other tents had Islamists reading the Quran, and still others chose instead to sing national songs in Arabic or songs by Ayob Tarish, a famous Yemeni singer, and dance along with the music.[41]

A platform was created that allowed different speakers to air their points of view. Women delivered speeches on these platforms and men would cheer them. Even blood feuds seemed to have less relevance during these early times. Sheikh Ahmed bin Saleh Almane'ay of the Bani Gaber tribe of Marib, a governorate 120 kilometres east of Sana'a, described it this way: "We the men of Marib cannot agree or sit with each other because of the tribal blood feuds between us. But in this square, many [people] of the Marib tribes are here; and we are sitting with each other despite our differences."[42]

"Leave" proved to be a powerful slogan; it managed to unify a variety of groups that usually stood at odds to each other. Many of the young people I spoke to in Taghir Square were sure about only one thing: Saleh has to go. They were convinced that "when he steps down, things will be better". But what happens after that? My question seemed to startle them.[43] That response revealed their lack of organization and planning.

Precisely this lack of planning and organization, and ultimately their division, created the space for others to hijack their aspirations. This became clear, as activists described it, after the 18 March massacre in what was termed the Friday of Dignity. That day, thousands of demonstrators attended the biggest rally at this square. After midday prayers ended, "dozens of men wearing civilian clothes and armed with military assault rifles converged on the rally from the south and opened fire".[44] It was the first deadly attack on demonstrators: at least forty-five protesters were killed—most of them university students and three of them children—and 200 were wounded. Saleh denied involvement, and blamed "armed" protesters for the bloodshed, but state security forces, which follow his orders, made no serious effort to stop the carnage.[45]

After this massacre, Ali Mohsen declared his support for the youth protests. He declared in a video message:

> I announce on their behalf our peaceful support and solidarity with the youths' revolution, we support their demands ... We will carry on with our duties in maintaining security and stability in the capital. Our units will be supporting our brothers in the security and armed forces. I ask God to spare Yemen any trouble.[46]

Translated into concrete steps, several tanks under General al-Ahmar assembled around the centre of the demonstration. Some commentators explained the move as "an apparent effort to protect protesters".[47] But activists who witnessed these developments saw in it the beginning of the hijacking of their "revolution". In fact, Mohsen's First Armoured Division, together with a military wing of the Islah Party, led by Hamid al-Ahmar, took over the sit-in camp.

Now limits were placed on the platform that had allowed various speakers to air their points of view: only vetted speakers were allowed up. Independent women activists were stopped from speaking. Meanwhile, female Islahi activists at the time, such as Tawakkol Karman (who was later awarded the Nobel prize for peace), and Salafi speakers, such as Abdel Majid Al Zindani, a known mentor of Osama bin Laden, monopolized the platform. A jail was set up within the square to discipline those who did not toe the line.

And force was used to segregate the men and women protesters in the square where they were sitting in. The measures started as a response to Saleh's comment denouncing any "mixing between the sexes". Women activists who opposed these measures were attacked, beaten, and defamed. Arwa Othman, a pioneer activist, was one of these women. On 16 April 2011, she insisted on participating in a mixed demonstration, along with other well-known activists, both female and male. As a result, she and eighteen of her colleagues, both male and female, were brutally attacked and beaten publicly. The attack drew sharp criticism and condemnation from many political and civil actors in Yemen but the segregation continued.[48]

Gradually, the independent activists, both female and male, were sidelined. This was a clash of two visions for the state of Yemen: a civil democratic state versus a tribal military and Islamist one. While the youth were clearly able to manifest their aspirations and agency, the regime's ethnic-based structures had the upper hand. No wonder these uprisings were eventually hijacked and, in the process, those who took over destabilized the whole system.

3 Legacies of Geography, Tribes, and Religious Beliefs

Why do ethnic groups rebel? Cederman, Wimmer, and Min suggest three possible reasons. Conflict, they say, is more likely when representatives of an ethnic group have been excluded from state power in the recent past, have more mobilizational capacity, and/or have experienced more conflict in the past.[1] All three indicators were present in the years leading to the 2015 civil war—and at the core was exclusion leading to recurring wars and instability. Of course, this state of affairs is hardly restricted to modern Yemeni history.

The 2015 civil war, as mentioned before, was one of many that Yemen experienced before and after unification in 1990. The country has had a long history of political instability—in North and South Yemen alike. It runs deep in the country's history.

This brings us to a key question: why has Yemen's political history been shaped by constant instability and wars? This question brings state formation into the picture. It requires that we acknowledge the past in a way that goes beyond socioeconomic grievances and expand them with those arising from ethnic exclusions, often shaped by resentment and fear. If we look more closely at Yemen's history, five facts will guide our discussions in the next chapters:[2]

- Great geographical Yemen—with its centralized political form and defined territory that extends north and south and includes Asir and Najran within today's Saudi Arabia—is a construct, one that exists in the historical narratives of many Yemenis, especially Northerners. But little strong historical evidence supports it.
- Only once in its ancient history and twice in its entire modern history has Yemen been united in its current geographical form.

- The narrative in modern history of a "united South" stands at odds with the historical and political reality of the area before and during British colonization. It also contradicts the reality of recurring group conflicts across the state of Southern Yemen between 1967 and 1990.
- Throughout Yemen's modern history, people in both the North and the South have often perceived the state as representing only one segment of society, an ethnic bodyguard. They see the state as alienating people in other regions, along with social and political segments of the population—with the result that key groups have often been excluded.
- The state was so fragile it was often unable to provide its population with basic services, including justice and security. The ruling elites often used the state's institutions to extract resources for their own benefit.

At the heart of these historical facts lies an interesting anomaly: Yemen as a geographical space is not congruent with Yemen as a political form. Geographical Yemen was always larger than the various ethnonationalist political forms that inhibited it concurrently. And this has been true since ancient times.

Geography was important for this incongruity and for the historical development of different political forms in the country. On the one hand, it divided the vast territories of geographical Yemen and in the process facilitated their populations' push for self-determination and independence. On the other hand, given the economic resources (or lack thereof) in different locations, geography shaped the political behaviour of tribes in different geographical settings.

And finally, the introduction of Zaydism as a religious denomination, with its unique religious political principles, was a recipe for political instability, especially in its interaction with Yemeni tribal structures and their geographical locations.

These three dimensions stand at the core of this part of Yemen's historical legacies. In the next sections I will explain this further. First, I will introduce the difference between geographical Yemen and political Yemen, and show how that difference impacted the development of different concurrent great ancient kingdoms. I will then introduce Zaydism, its different sub-movements, and its main religious beliefs and their political implications, and then describe how geography (with its topographical features) and tribal and ethnic divisions

LEGACIES OF GEOGRAPHY, TRIBES, AND RELIGIOUS BELIEFS

intersected with Zaydism, along with the extractive financial policies of Zaydi imams. To conclude the chapter, I will trace the relevance of all this history to the current Yemeni crisis.

Geographical Versus Political Yemen

Yemen can be defined in two ways. It can be:

a. a geographical space—the historical Greater Yemen اليمن الكبرى; or
b. a political form—the many political forms and states that have existed side by side concurrently across history.

The geographical space, according to famous medieval Arab and Yemeni geographers, extends over half of the Arabian Peninsula.[3] The political form corresponds to the diverse dynasties, kingdoms, and other political forms that dominated different parts of the south of the Arabian Peninsula, known as South of Arabia.

These two—the space and the form—rarely converged, and when they did, they ultimately imploded in wars. The fighting was an expression of a will to exert one's political and cultural identity—what Cederman and colleagues call an ethnonationalist identity.[4]

I am aware, of course, that nationalism is a modern phenomenon. But we must remember that the urge for an ethnos to rule itself in its own territory precedes modernity; it goes back deep into history in different parts of the world. Yemen is one such part, where the different ethnic groups found it difficult to live together. Think of them as a group of cousins stuck in a house they inherited from an ancient ancestor. Instead of working together to create a community within this house, one of them dominates and insists on breaking the wills of the others. In time, it dictates an intimidating worldview, ultimately behaves as a bully and in the process devours all the resources available. That the other cousins decide to exit the common house is only natural. That this house could have been better managed in a more equitable manner is also a possibility—but one that rarely occurred.

Some scholars use a geographical approach to explain this state of affairs, and not only in Yemen. For example, as Robert D. Kaplan tells us in his famous book *The Revenge of Geography*, geography affirms that "Tunisia and

Egypt are naturally cohesive; Libya, Yemen and Syria less so". The former, he argues, "required relatively moderate forms of autocracy to hold them together". Libya and Syria needed "more extreme varieties". And Yemen was "hard to govern at all"—a "segmentary society riven by mountains and desert, hovering between centralization and anarchy".[5]

Kaplan argued that the geographical situations of these states would reassert themselves in the outcomes of the 2011 Arab uprisings. These uprisings were a testimony to the power of communications technology, he acknowledged, but geography will ultimately triumph: "Tunisia and Egypt are age-old clusters of civilizations, whose statehoods originate in antiquity." Libya and Yemen, on the other hand, are "but vague geographies, whose statehoods were not established until the twentieth century". The first was torn between a region "always oriented toward the rich and urban civilizations of Carthage in Tunisia", and another region "always oriented toward those of Alexandria in Egypt". And "Yemen was rich and populous from antiquity forward but its many mountain kingdoms were always separate from one another." Kaplan concludes his argument with the statement that "building modern, non-tyrannical states in Libya and Yemen is proving more difficult than in Tunisia and Egypt".[6]

Kaplan's theory attracted its share of critique, with good reason.[7] Geography alone certainly does not suffice to explain the divergent outcomes of the 2011 Arab uprisings. And in Yemen, also the location of great ancient civilizations, the story is much more complicated. Most importantly, geography is not a fate that humans cannot escape or surmount. But one can say this: geography, in its intersection and interplay with other factors, such as ethnicity and religious beliefs, has played an important role in Yemen's story. This becomes clear in the ancient Yemeni kingdoms and later when Zaydism was introduced to Yemen during its Islamic period.

Ancient Greek geographers alluded to geographical Yemen as Arabia Felix and positioned it in the south of the Arabian Peninsula. Eratosthenes of Cyrene (died *c.*195 BCE), the director of the Library of Alexandria, was the first to call this space Arabia Felix. He described a fertile land, rich in fauna and dominated by four major peoples (ethne), located in four separate provinces.[8]

These ethne were Sabaeans, Minaeans, Qatabanians, and Hadrami (see Map 1). Their kingdoms existed at the same time in different parts of today's North and South Yemen.[9]

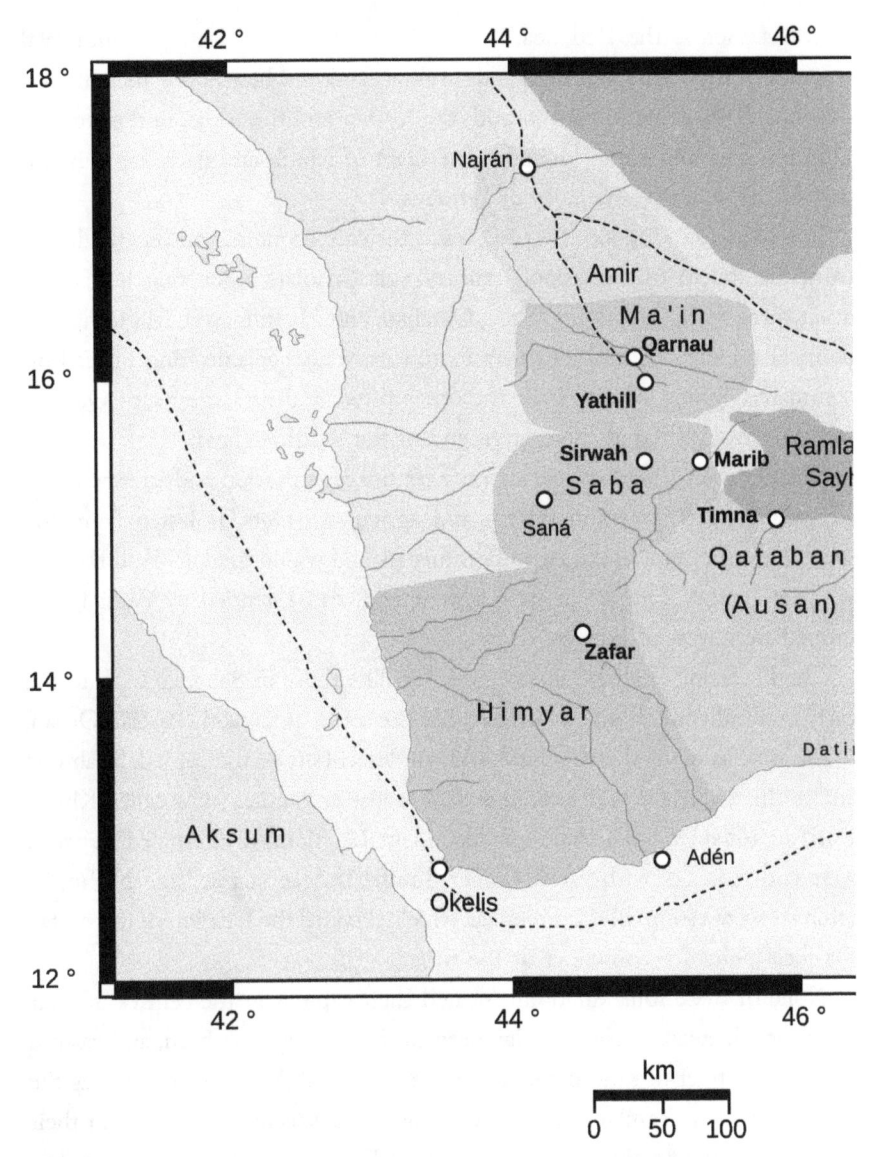

LEGACIES OF GEOGRAPHY, TRIBES, AND RELIGIOUS BELIEFS

Map 1: Ancient Yemen—Arabia Felix (adapted from Wikimedia Commons (Schreiber/Rowanwindwhistler; CC BY-SA 4.0 DEED))

The Saba kingdom was the earliest and the one most abundantly attested to in the surviving written records; its origins lie deep in the early first millennium BCE. With its capital in Marib (Mariaba), it had a sophisticated administration with monarchs assisted by an assembly of notables and heads of tribes. Across the Red Sea, it established stable and lasting commercial colonies in the Ethiopian highlands and its fame reached to the ancient civilizations. Saba is mentioned in both the Quran and the Bible, in the story of Queen Sheba and King Solomon. The Dam of Marib and its collapse is still part of the collective memory of Yemenis.

The Minaean kingdom (Maʿīn) was a thriving economic power that lasted from the fourth to the second century BCE. Scholars argue that unlike the other three major kingdoms (Saba, Qataban, and Hadramawt), Maʿīn had no political pretensions and its rulers fought no wars, concentrating instead on commerce. It was smaller than the other three, and its largest city, Qarnaw (Karna), was located at the eastern end of the Wadi Al-Jawf.

The Qataban Kingdom had a strong central organization and an exceptionally well-tended irrigation system and agriculture plots. It lasted from the seventh century BCE to the second century CE and was located at Wadi Bayḥān, with its capital, Timnaʿ, at its northern end, and extended to Wadi Ḥarīb, immediately west of Bayḥān.

The Hadramawt Kingdom's origins, just like those of Saba, go back to the early first millennium BCE. It stretched to the south as far as the Indian Ocean, to the west as far as the Ramlat Sab'atayn desert (site of the capital, Shabwat) and to the east as far as the commercial outpost of Samhar (now called Khawr Rori) in today's Oman. As an independent kingdom, it alternated between wars and alliances with various other South Arabian states. Like Maʿīn, its interests were essentially commercial, which explains the location of its capital, the focal point for commerce at the time.

None of these four kingdoms located their capitals in the centres of their territories. Instead, those cities lay deep in the western, southern, and eastern fringes of a tract of sand desert known to medieval Arab geographers as the Sayhad (modern Ramlat al-Sabʿatayn). They were specifically chosen for their proximity to the frankincense trade route.[10] Their fortunes were connected to this land trade route and its caravans, and they declined once the sea routes were established, providing a regular maritime link between the Mediterranean world, Arabia, and India. Some did adapt, including Hadramawt, which built ports to accommodate the new mode of trade routes. But in general, to quote Robert G. Hoyland: "The first century BC seems to be a turning point in the history of south Arabia, since the peoples located around the Sayhad desert,

LEGACIES OF GEOGRAPHY, TRIBES, AND RELIGIOUS BELIEFS

who had dominated the region's affairs up until this point, were now gradually overtaken by the tribes of the highlands."[11]

What interests us is the role that this region's topography and distinct community identities played in impacting its political formations. In his book *Arabia and Arabs*, Hoyland explains that role:

> The very mountainous terrain impeded the formation of a single regime, and political power was in general fragmented among the various peoples of south Arabia. Each would seem to have constituted a cult community, a human collective bound together by allegiance to a patron god and presided over by a ruler who took the title of "king" [*malik*] and sometimes "unifier" [*mukarrib*]. There were probably many other ties, such as language for example, but it is the cult and its sanctuaries that seem to play the most important role in forging the identity of each community.[12]

Significantly, all of these kingdoms were tribally based. They were named after certain tribes and in certain cases the leaders of particularly powerful tribes were able to unify the other tribes into a confederation. This led to the creation of a sophisticated system of governance, which integrated these tribes into their administration. It also created a distinction in the titles held by the kingdoms' rulers. For example—and please note this detail for its significance in certain current developments in the 2015 civil war—the head of a Sabaen *sha'b* (settled tribe) was known as *malik* (king) and the king of the dominant tribe, who was the head of the tribal confederations, took the title of *mukarrib* (unifier).

In this system, the *mukarrib* was supported by an advisory tribal council, made up of tribal and clan leaders and landowners, whom he was required to consult in the state's affairs, including taxation, land ownership, and agricultural regulations. As Sabaen kings gained more strength over their small kingdoms (tribes), a new system—the *Aqial* system—developed. It was a form of a local feudal tribal system headed by one king. The title *mukarrib* was no longer necessary.[13] I will return to these designations and their significance later in this chapter.

Finally, before concluding this part, I should mention the period when these kingdoms were united: during the Himyar Empire. Between the first century BCE and the third century CE, a power struggle ensued; a Himyarite dynasty came from Zafar, southeast of present-day Yarim (in today's Ibb governorate, see Map 1), and sought to unite all of these kingdoms in what the late renowned Yemeni historian Bafaqih called the three hundred years' war.[14]

At first, the Himyar Empire coexisted with the other kingdoms; then it took over Saba in the first century CE in a federation that eventually submerged Saba. A century later, in 200 CE, together with Hadramawt, the Himyarites divided the territory of Qataban among themselves. Eventually, the two allies turned against each other and in 300 CE, the Himyar Kingdom managed to defeat Hadramawt and include it in its territory.[15]

By the fourth century, the Himyarite kings converted to Judaism, and styled themselves as "kings of Saba and of Dhu Raydan and Hadramawt and Yamanat". Now, for the first time, South Arabia was a unified state. The king's title was very telling, though, as it reflected the geographical and ethnic (tribal) dimension of the areas conquered by the new kingdom.

Then, in the sixth century, this kingdom disintegrated. External actors played a role here: Abyssinian Ethiopians, intervening to protect Christian merchants, and Sassanid Persians, asked by a Himyarite king to expel the Ethiopians. Geographical Yemen was again divided into different regions and political forms. Some were under external control, and others were manifesting an already ingrained pattern of its history, what I term a pattern of imploding, that is, different ethne pushing for their own self-rule.

Can we take a lesson from this period? The renowned Yemeni historian Bafaqih tells us that instability was caused by the push and pull of geography and a desire for domination. Indeed: "Decentralization was a feature of government in Yemen dictated by the nature of the land, and the tendency to unity or union was another feature of it dictated by natural necessities as well. And in light of this fact, we can understand the internal wars that Yemen has witnessed."[16]

Religious Beliefs and Tribes

In the seventh century, different regions of Yemen converted to Islam. The narratives of Arab writers give the impression that Yemenis converted to Islam overnight: at the moment when the governor of Sana'a received a message

LEGACIES OF GEOGRAPHY, TRIBES, AND RELIGIOUS BELIEFS

from the Prophet Mohammed inviting him to Islam. In fact, it took at least three hundred years for Islam to be assimilated into Yemeni society.

This process was fostered by the early Islamic governors in the different regions of Sana'a, al-Janad, and Hadramawt. Yemenis of different regions became the manpower used by the rising Islamic state for its territorial expansions and conquests. And this undoubtedly left its mark on the economic welfare of these regions. Indeed, such population movements, of families and flocks leaving the Arabian Peninsula, affected all of Arabia. And in Hadramawt, they may have caused the neglect of irrigation works, resulting in the erosion of fertile lands.[17]

But in general, the relationships between the authorities of the central Islamic state and the different *wilayat* (governates) of geographical Yemen were turbulent, to say the least.

During the reign of the Umayyad dynasty in Damascus (661–750 CE) and the Abbasid dynasty in Baghdad (750–1258 CE),[18] Yemeni *wilayats* experienced severe decline, both political and economic, for two main reasons. First, because the country was so remote from the political centre, the caliphs paid scant attention to Yemen, or to its needs. Second, given this valuation, both the Umayyad and Abbasid rulers sent out to Yemen governors who ruled with force and gained a reputation for brutality. Disdaining to convey any ideological message to the Yemeni people, they focused on collecting taxes and drafting Yemeni men into the Islamic armies. This situation triggered repeated uprisings and clashes with the troops of the central authorities, leading the competing Yemeni emirates to move towards self-rule.[19]

It also prepared the ground for the Zaydi religious movement, which appealed to a dissatisfied people.

Zaydism

The legacy of Zaydism in Yemen, introduced in the northern part of North Yemen in 893, is complicated and often fraught with misunderstanding. For one thing, although it is an offshoot of Shia Islam, it is not Twelver Shia. For another, its followers are of mixed ethnicity, not just one. More generally, it cannot be understood without considering its political doctrines, the Yemeni tribal factor, and its geographical location. Despite its original emancipatory and rational principles, all this has resulted in a good deal of instability and impoverishment.

Zaydism is a religious denomination named after its founder Zayd bin Ali (died 740), a grandson of al-Husayn ibn Ali; Ali was the cousin of the Prophet of Islam, Mohammed. In their current narration and discourse on the Yemeni civil war, Houthi militia detractors, Yemeni and regional alike, often refer to followers of Zaydism as Shiites, followers of the Iranian line of Shia Islam, that is, the Twelvers, or Ithna Ashari Shia Islam. In using this term, they aim to conflate the two religious schools and turn the conflict into a religious one.

The animosity between Sunni and Shia Islam is well known and mutual. What interests us here is the accuracy of that conflation—or the lack thereof. It is in fact a false assumption. Yes, Zaydism is an offshoot of Shia Islam, it is a current of Shia tradition, but as a denomination it is distinct in its creeds and assumptions. Even recently, when I spoke with some of the protagonists in the revival of Zaydism in Saada or the Houthi movement in Yemen, they insisted that they may have been fascinated with the Iranian political project, but certainly not with its religious line of Islam.

Before explaining this point, a short introduction on the difference between the two major Islamic traditions—the Sunni and Shia—is warranted.

Originally, the difference between the two was political. Over time, however, their respective followers also came to differ on theological matters. Friction between the two sides in the early Islamic era developed from a dispute over who should become the caliph, or ruler, after the Prophet of Islam, Mohammed, died in 632.[20]

One side, known later as the Sunni, argued that this important position should be restricted to members of the Quraysh—the larger Arab tribe to which Mohammed belonged. Another side, later called the Shiite, held that only one man was eligible to become caliph—of the Hashemite clan, the tribe of Mohammad. This was Ali ibn Abi Talib, the Prophet's first cousin, and the line would include his descendants from his marriage to Fatima, the daughter of the Prophet.

This was in fact a dispute over the tribal affiliation of the successor of Mohammed; only later did it take on a religious undertone. Abd ar-Rahman ibn Khaldun, the fourteenth-century Muslim Arab sociologist and historian (b. 1332, d. Egypt 1406) offers a sociopolitical explanation for the reason why

LEGACIES OF GEOGRAPHY, TRIBES, AND RELIGIOUS BELIEFS

Mohammed's Quraishi companions insisted on choosing a caliph from among themselves: during Mohammed's lifetime, the tribe of Quraysh was the most respected in the Arabian Peninsula and enjoyed the solidarity (*assabiyya* العصبية) of other Arab tribes. The death of Mohammed could cause a rupture in their allegiance; it was important to choose someone who could command their loyalty and solidarity. This explains why, when the Quraysh tribe became weaker, and Islamic states were governed by rulers of diverse ethnic backgrounds, Sunni scholars started to provide religious edicts that legitimized opening this position to those who could ensure the loyalty and solidarity of the Muslim community, regardless of their Qurayshi ethnic background. The core issue here was legitimacy in the eyes of the Muslim community.[21]

This perception was not shared by the Shiites. To them, the position of a ruler, which they called an imam, is not a temporal one. That position is a "corner stone of religion and the basis of Islam". Thus, as Ibn Khaldun explained, the "prophet could not have delegated the appointment of the Imam to the community (*Umma*)". Instead, "he must have appointed" an imam, "someone who possesses *wilayat*—spiritual guidance—which makes him free from sin and error". In fact, Khaldun says, "the prophet did just that, and appointed Ali",[22] his cousin, but Ali was not allowed to take on that position, until he was chosen to be the fourth caliph of Islam. This is the core of the political dispute between Shiite and Sunni Islam. Over time, each tradition was further divided into different schools; Zaydism was one offshoot of Shia Islam.

What concerns us here is how Zaydism differs from the main tenets of the largest Shia movement, the Twelvers, also known as Ithna Ashari or the Imamyyah, which is followed in Iran.

The Twelvers tradition argues that the position of the imam, who is infallible and free of sin, was passed down to Ali and to his son Husayn and their sons down to the Twelfth Imam, Muhammad ibn Al-Hasan. They believe that in 874, during the Abbasid Califate, this last imam went into occultation: a state of being concealed by God. In fact, he was probably killed by his rivals.

According to the Twelvers, this hidden imam will return when God determines it to be appropriate before the day of the Judgement—and with him Jesus will also return. The Twelvers also believe in the doctrine of *Taqiyya* (fear or caution): the practice of suppressing or concealing one's beliefs through "dissimulation", as a precaution, to protect oneself and safeguard one's secrets.

Scholars see how this practice could be valuable, even necessary, for a persecuted Shiite population living in Sunni-majority areas—where they would fear external enemies, and need to conceal secret doctrines from the uninitiated.[23]

But Zaydism rejects all three of these components of the Twelvers' imamate theory: the infallibility of the imam, occultation, and the practice of *Taqiyya*.[24] In fact, the founder of Zaydism accepted the choice of the first two caliphs after the death of Mohammed, despite Ali being available; as a result, the mainstream Shiite scholars of the time rejected his teachings.[25]

Another crucial principle of Zaydism, *khuruj*, sets it apart from mainstream Shiite teachings (and Sunni teachings as well): it insists that the imam, the ruler, must be a just person, and provides a list of features that a just imam must possess. If the imam is unjust, then it is legitimate to make a formal call to allegiance (*da'wa*) and rise (*khuruj*) against oppression. Hence, the Zaydi doctrine of *khuruj* (the Arabic word for departure or exit) can be defined as openly challenging unjust authority and actively rising against illegitimate rulers and oppression.[26] More on the political ramifications of this principle later.

Sub-Movements

Zaydism, therefore, is a distinct religious school that cannot be conflated with the Shiite Twelvers denomination. What makes it unique? Yemeni scholar and poet Abdulaziz Al-Maqaleh, in his important book *Reading in the Thought of the Zaydis and the Mu'tazila: The Islamic Yemen*, tells us that its teachings combine three intellectual streams:[27]

- A Shiite stream argues that Ali, and his followers, have the right to succession.
- A Mutazili stream, a rational theological movement, is steadfast in its commitment to reason as the basis of its theological inquiry.[28]
- And a Sunni stream adopts the Hanafi jurisprudence in Islamic law.

Given this combination of the three streams, Zaydism came to be known across Islam as a school that stands in between Shiite and Sunni Islam. Significantly, and depending on the political context, the adherents of Zaydism

LEGACIES OF GEOGRAPHY, TRIBES, AND RELIGIOUS BELIEFS

have oscillated between Sunni and Shia positions in matters of theology and law.[29]

These three streams, along with the political ambitions of some Zaydi founders, were responsible for the creation of different sub-movements within Zaydism.

Scholars diverge in the number of sub-movements they see: two, three, four, or even more.[30] Each is named after its founding jurist.[31] Some explain the classification in terms of historical moments in the group's evolution in its birthplace of Kufaa, in today's Iraq. This classification tends to focus on two groups: first, the *Batriyyaa*, the dominant form of Zaydism around 704 and closest to the teachings of Zayd bin Ali; and second the *Jarudiyya*, the most extreme form of Zaydism, dominant after 802, and closest to the Twelvers in its theological positions.[32]

The two groups differed on two points: Was Ali's designation as an imam implicit or explicit? And what position did they take towards the key Twelvers' doctrines: the infallibility of the imam, occultation, and the practice of *Taqiyya*?

The *Batriyyaa* say that Ali's designation was implicit and allows for the possibility of choosing a less qualified or worthy imam as long as he rules in a just and upright manner. It also rejects the three Twelvers' doctrines. The *Jarudiyya* accept these doctrines and insist that Ali's designation was explicit. Hence, they see as apostates those who approved of the first caliphs before Ali.[33]

What interests us are those Zaydi subgroups that have been more influential in Yemen. And here, two points of classification are used to distinguish between the subgroups:

a. its position on the choice of the imam and his pedigree; and
b. the social classes it addresses.

Using this classification, two poles become visible: the *Hadawiya* and the *Mutarrifiyya*. In between these two stand three subgroups: the *Batriyyaa*, *Salihiyya*, and the *Sulaymaniyah*. These three are considered to be fairly close in their teachings, with minor differences. I will focus on the two poles.

The *Hadawiya*: Most Zaydi Yemenis are Hadawis.[34] The movement is named after the first Zaydi imam, Imam al-Hadi (Yehia bin al-Husayn al-Qasim, d. 911), who introduced Zaydism to Yemen in 893. Born in Hijaz, in today's Saudi Arabia, he was invited to Saada in the north of North Yemen to mediate between quarrelling tribes. But the tribes rejected his insistence on applying Islamic law, Shari'a, so he returned home. Three years later, he returned—and became the first Zaydi ruler of the Yemeni highlands in the Northern area. Saada became his capital and permanent base of military expansion.[35]

Just like the founder of Zaydism, al-Hadi was a Hashemite: a descendant of the family of the Prophet of Islam, through the marriage of Ali (cousin of Mohammed) and Fatima (daughter of Mohammed). This focus on descent became the cornerstone of his political project.

He acknowledged the doctrinal principle of *khuruj*: openly challenging an unjust authority or ruler. But he restricted the call for such a challenge to those who had the Hashemite pedigree. The imam, he claimed, is a supreme leader of the community, and the legal authority; therefore, the right of a person to be an imam and call for rebellion should be restricted to the descendants of Ali and Fatima. In making this claim, he introduced a new principle, one that had not been stated by Zayd bin Ali, the founder of Zaydism. Zayd had accepted the rule of the first two caliphs, who were not Hashemite.[36]

Al-Hadi also added an obedience clause that would prove detrimental to political developments in the North of Yemen. Muslims should follow the "qualified imam", he said. They should accept his call to wage war, migrate with him in waging war, and provide him with money and resources. They must obey him, and are forbidden to disobey him. Those who do not join him in this "holy mission" are deviants from Islam, and cursed. The imam has a right to destroy them, if they should fight him. But if they do not fight him and choose instead to not join his call, they should be banished, expelled, and their testimony invalidated. And Muslims are obliged to be their enemies.[37]

This new edict by al-Hadi was another decree that contradicted the teaching of Zayd, the Zaydi founder, and logically was inconsistent with the very principle of *khuruj*. But we have to understand these decrees through the prism of his political ambition. They were meant to establish a religious justification for his political project and force the spirited Yemenis in northern areas to follow him and accept his authority.

LEGACIES OF GEOGRAPHY, TRIBES, AND RELIGIOUS BELIEFS

The *Mutarrifiyya* Zaydis disagreed with al-Hadi, especially with his insistence on the "blood right to rule" of the Hashemites. In response, decades after he died, they introduced one of the most emancipatory Zaydi movements in the history of Yemen. Mutarrif bin Amr Al Shihabi (d. after 1067) started the movement, which was strongly shaped by the rational philosophy of the Mutazilites. Zayd bin Ali Mutarrif came from a tribal background and introduced his teaching at a time when the relatives of al-Hadi were fighting over the imamate in different areas of northern North Yemen. It was also a time of power struggles between different dynastic political forms, affiliated with diverse Muslim sects and denominations, and tribal leaders exercising control over their areas.[38]

The *Mutarrifiyya* introduced a different theory on the imamate: it opened the right to be an imam to any qualified Muslim regardless of his blood line or colour, or tribal, Arab, or non-Arab ethnicity. It also insisted that the imam should be chosen by consultation among those in the Muslim community. And it changed the concept of *khuruj* to one of a peaceful *hijrah* migration. So, instead of carrying arms and fighting one's oppressors or other unjust people, it is more prudent to leave one's area and move to tribally protected areas, called *hijars*, to teach one's religion and live in peace. The idea was to "create the ideal society" but also to protect themselves from the wrath of their detractors, because they adopted the most philosophical and argumentative Mutazilite ideas.[39]

Most importantly, this school introduced a different definition of the "House of the Prophet": it is not the blood line that makes a person part of that house, it is their following of the Prophet's religion and his teachings. "Honour", therefore, is not related to a person's blood line, nor is it the family relationship to the Prophet that makes a person honourable (called *sayyid*, which literally means master, as became the custom in North Yemen). Honour is based on human deeds, knowledge, piety, and behaviour toward others. This definition of honour "challenged the idea of the unconditional superiority of the Prophet's family, the main principle of the Zaydi Hadawi Imamate theory".[40]

These teachings, revolutionary in themselves, appealed to the simple tribesmen and the weakest and most vulnerable in the tribal society of Northern Yemen. And they strongly contradicted the tribal customs that were based on a rigid social hierarchy and pride in one's blood line. They also called up the wrath of the Hashemite imams, who worked closely with the tribal sheikhs to control their areas. Followers of the *Mutarrifiyya* were accused of being heretics for denying the privileged status of the Prophet's family. They were persecuted, their *hijrahs* and villages were destroyed, their women and children were enslaved, and their books were burned. By the fifteenth century, they had been eradicated.[41]

Geographical, Tribal Divisions of Zaydi Followers

This background on Zaydism may seem complicated and perhaps even irrelevant. It does, however, reveal a lot about the complicated history of Yemen. Earlier I talked about the difference between geographical Yemen and the political forms that occupied this space. The introduction of Zaydism in the tenth century only added another form to these political units and shaped the political, social, and economic developments of the North of Yemen. The traumas and group grievances of what is now termed Lower Yemen are related to this factor. Geography and the tribal structures of Northern Yemen are yet again crucial to these developments.

Scholars working on North Yemen often refer to a geographical classification of Upper and Lower Yemen (see Map 2, designed by Brinkley Messick of Columbia University, and Map 3 of modern Yemen for the locations of the areas mentioned within the two regions); both are also mentioned by Yemeni writers and scholars, past and present. Significantly, and just as in the ancient kingdoms of Yemen, in this classification geography coincides with ethnic divisions, only during this period it took on a religious and tribal tone.

Upper Yemen stands opposed to Lower Yemen, Paul Dresch tells us,[43] and that is accurate.

Upper Yemen, the land of the Hamdan and Khawlan tribes, is Zaydi. For centuries, its farming tribes supplied the manpower for the military campaigns of the Zaydi imams against rival Zaydi imams, and against outside invaders such as the Ottomans, and also for wars of conquest against other dynasties, sultanates, and emirates in geographical Yemen. Most importantly, against Lower Yemen. The relationship between the tribes and the Zaydi

LEGACIES OF GEOGRAPHY, TRIBES, AND RELIGIOUS BELIEFS

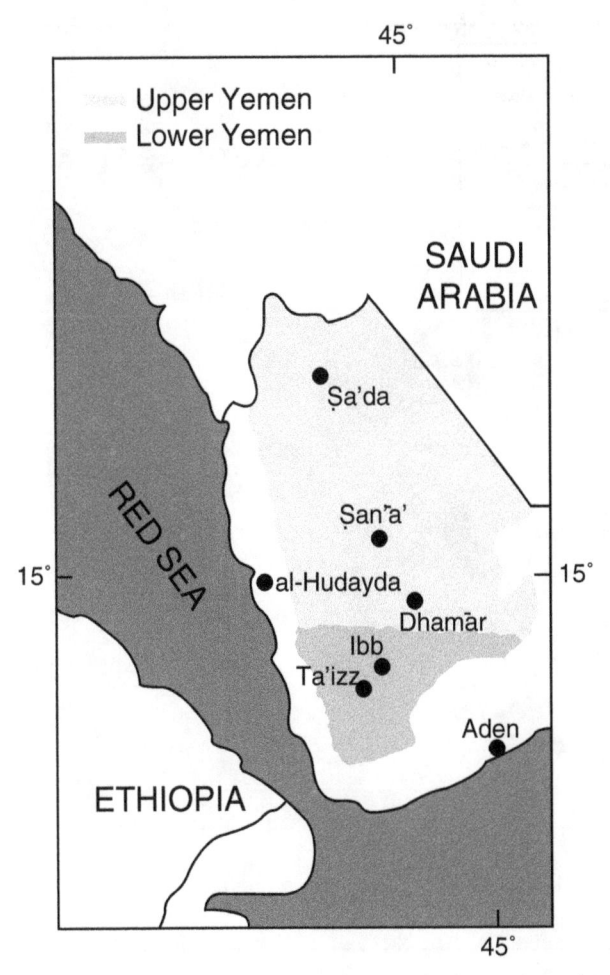

Map 2: Upper and Lower Yemen (creator Brinkley Messick)[42]

imams was often fraught with tension and conflict; they never really trusted each other. The region was unruly, always difficult to govern. Upper Yemen is located on the highland plateau that stretches from Najran in the north down to the Sumara pass south of Yarim and includes all the major Zaydi centres of learning: Saada, Hajjah, Amran, Sana'a, and Dhamar. The topography is less fertile and resources are scarce. Compared to Lower Yemen, it looks arid.[44]

Lower Yemen is populated by settled peasants of the Madhhiki tribes: Sunni Shafi' Muslims. This mountainous region, which includes Ibb and Taiz,

65

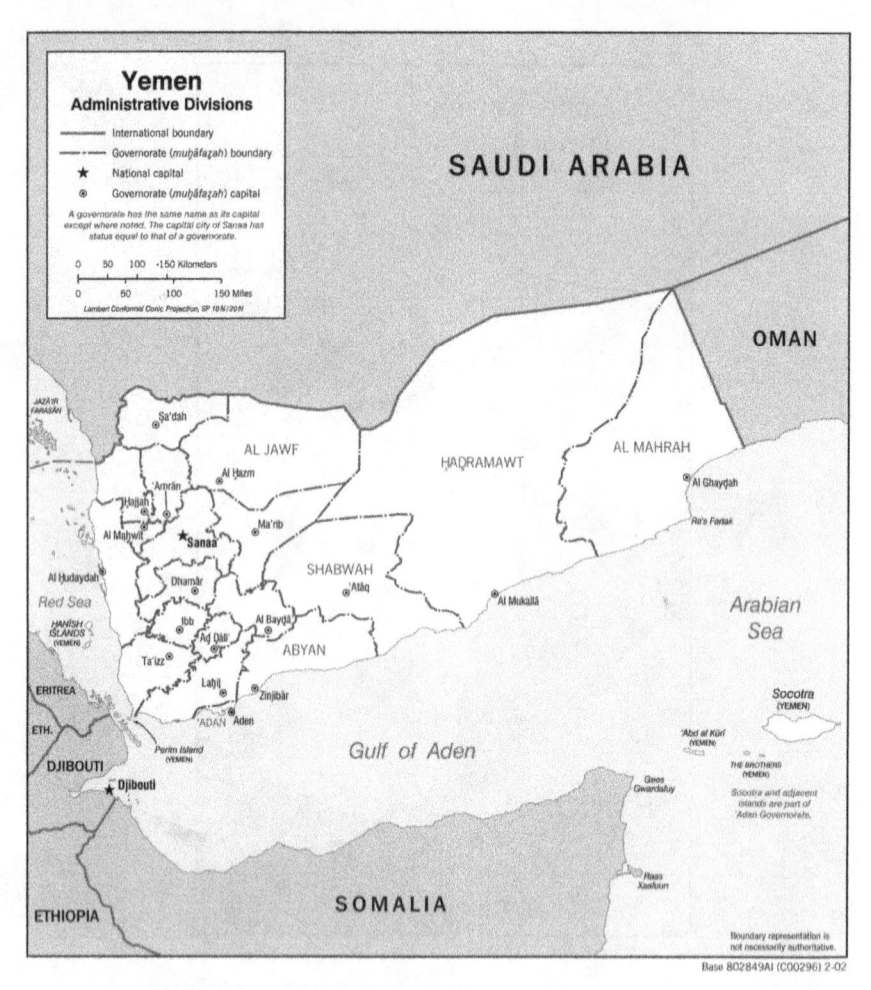

Map 3: Governorates and districts of modern Yemen (Public Domain—Library of Congress: https://lccn.loc.gov/2005625554)

is the most fertile region and the richest agricultural area in North Yemen. Here tax gathering was possible, and so was share cropping. Social affairs were best described as relations between landlords and peasants. Sunni dynasties, such as the Rasulids (1229–1454) and Tahirids (1454–1539), were centred in this region, while the Zaydi imams dominated in Upper Yemen.[45] When this region fell under the control of Zaydi imams, it often suffered. More on this later.

LEGACIES OF GEOGRAPHY, TRIBES, AND RELIGIOUS BELIEFS

Of course, Yemen includes other regions,[46] but these two regions were central in the history of Northern Yemen. They stood opposed to each other, in geography, religious denominations, tribal affiliations, and political forms. What deserves our focused attention is the tribal factor, especially in its connection to Upper Yemen.

But first, a short introduction to the tribal structure in Yemen.

Yemeni Tribal Structure

I use the definition of the tribe that Marieke Brandt offers in her highly acclaimed book *Tribes and Politics in Yemen: A History of the Houthi Conflict*. She sees the tribe as "an emic concept of social representation".[47] Emic because Yemenis describe their social structures in terms of tribal structures. It is a self-representation that reflects reality.

A tribe displays a combination of the basic characteristics that exist in Yemeni tribal structures. The first is association with a territory, a tribal area. At the same time people will use non-territorial criteria (such as *qabyalah*, a general code of conduct to which tribesmen claim to adhere) to distinguish between members and non-members. The second is a common genealogical ancestor (imagined or real) that people use to emphasize group cohesion over outside interests and internal differentiation. Third, a tribe is open to its surroundings and maintains lively relations with its tribal and non-tribal environment. And finally, Yemeni tribes are highly organized and are often represented by chieftains or sheikhs, elected from tribal families in which the office of sheikh is hereditary. The elective element means that the sheikhdom is not necessarily passed from the father to one of his male offspring, but can be transferred to any eligible, prominent, and able male of the chiefly lineage.[48] Yemeni tribes, and the tribes of southern Arabia in general, are genealogically considered Qahtani, descendants of the common ancestor Qahtan, a son of Noah. Qahtani tribes are common in southern parts of the Arabian Peninsula, especially Yemen and Oman. With very few exceptions, they are settled tribes, often working as farmers and peasants.

The Qahtani affiliation stands opposite to the Adnani genealogical affiliation. They regard themselves as descendants of Adnan, a son of Ismail, and are more predominant in Saudi Arabia, some parts of Oman, and most of the other Gulf states. They have a diversity of lifestyles; some are nomads. Mohammad is considered an Adnani Arab of the Bani Hashem clan of the Quraysh tribe. His descendants are considered Adnani.[49]

Why is this worth mentioning? Because those who adhere to Zaydism in Upper Yemen are divided into these two ethnic categories and they occupy different places in society.

The Qahtanis are the Yemeni tribes of Upper Yemen, who embraced Zaydism in the tenth century. They include the tribes of Hamdan (divided into two confederations, Hashid and Bakil) and Khawlan. Historically, they, and especially the Hamdani tribes, have provided the manpower for the Zaydi imams in their *khuruj* wars. But they often rebelled as well against the imams and their oppressive regimes.

The Hashemite Adnanis, called *Sadah* (Masters), are those who claim to be the descendants of the Prophet of Islam, from the Hashemite clan of the Quraysh tribe. They arrived in Yemen in the tenth century with al-Hadi, the first Zaydi imam, and constituted a closed class called *Sadah*. Because their origin, in genealogical terms, is not Qahtani, in Yemen they are still seen as an immigrant community. Thus, they are considered a weak group that needs protection—but simultaneously are attributed a superior status. Their marriage patterns, based on patrilineality and endogamy, have enabled them to survive as a coherent descent group among Yemeni Qahtanis. They apply endogamy stringently to their females: they are only allowed to marry a male *Sadah*. Meanwhile, their men are allowed to marry tribal women, and the children of those marriages are considered *sayyid*. For a millennium, the *Sadah* have held the positions of the imams, as well as leadership positions in government administration and the military. Over the centuries, their rule was often fragile, and confined to Upper Yemen, except for some temporary expansions of their sphere of influence.[50]

Hence, when we talk about Zaydism in Yemen, we have to distinguish between two ethnic groups, Qahtanis and Adnanis, both attached to the same geographical location: Upper Yemen. While their relationships have often been tense, they did unite in the imams' war campaigns. When they did so, Lower Yemen often suffered the consequences, but so did Upper Yemen; this point is important. The following section explains why.

LEGACIES OF GEOGRAPHY, TRIBES, AND RELIGIOUS BELIEFS

Politics of Impoverishment

Yemeni historians tell us of many Zaydi statelets and imams and the history can be rather confusing. Simply put, there have been many statelets and imams. For the sake of simplicity, I suggest we focus on three Zaydi imams and their statelets. The first started with the arrival of Imam al-Hadi, and with him Zaydism, in the tenth century. The second started in the sixteenth century with the reign of Imam al-Mansur al-Qasim, who fought and defeated the first Ottoman imperial governors. And the third started with the Imam Yehia Hamid al-Din in the early twentieth century; he also fought the Ottomans during their second encroachment in North Yemen.

They all share what Robert D. Burrowes calls "the politics of primitive unification"; by this he means "an evolving state [that] seeks to establish sovereignty over a territory and the people or the nation it contains".[51] They all tried to expand their territories from Saada, using the Zaydi religious call for *khuruj*. And in their eyes, it was a form of a holy war: a *jihad*.

Al-Hadi failed in his attempt to expand Zaydi territory and died restricted to Saada in Upper Yemen. In 1598, al-Qasim succeeded for a while in changing the political geography of Yemen. His dynasty amassed unprecedented power and territory after they drove out the Ottoman Turks in 1635. His son even managed, in 1632, to reach Mecca in today's Saudi Arabia, only to be pushed back by the Ottomans.[52]

The Qasimis reached their peak during the reign of Al Mutawakkil al-Qasim (r.1644–1676), who expanded his territory as far as Dhofar in the east (in today's Oman), Aden in the South, and Asir and Najran in the North. He also conquered Lower Yemen. During this period, the Qasimis were behaving like kings and in some respects their rule resembled a state. They designed systems for administration, tax collection, and jurisprudence, but never fully developed them.[53]

Decades later, specifically starting from 1682,[54] united geographical Yemen fell into the pattern of imploding: Northern and Southern regions pushing for self-rule and separation. The will to exert one's political and cultural identity—an ethnonationalist identity—was stronger than the will to unify. The extractive and religious policies of the victorious imams were the main factors in their loss of control.

Finally, Yehia Hamid al-Din also sought to create a dynastic kingdom. In the early 1900s, he succeeded in uniting the divided tribes of Northern Yemen and launched a military campaign against the Ottoman rulers. The confrontation ended in 1911 when the Ottomans were forced to sign a treaty recognizing his authority over most of North Yemen. After signing the treaty, he moved away from the Zaydi principle of *khuruj* to a monarchical form of rule and in 1918 declared himself head of the Mutawakkilite kingdom in what is now North Yemen. He conquered Lower Yemen and Tihama, but lost Asir and Najran in a war against Ibn Saud (founder of modern Saudi Arabia), another king pursuing his own "policy of primitive unification". And he was never able to extend his authority into southern Arabia (the modern south of Yemen). His kingdom was primordial and theocratic. It was shrewd and isolationist in its regional and international politics, but it was still an embryo of a state.[55] It was overthrown in a military coup in 1962 and replaced by a republic.

In the centuries between these three political situations, Upper Yemen suffered from constant instability.

Why? Abdullah Al-Baradouni, the great Yemeni poet and writer, in his famous book *The Republican Yemen* اليمن الكبرى, describes the problem: too many Hashemite imams, from different "houses", each believing he, along with his house, was the most suitable to be imam.[56]

The principle of *khuruj* proved to be a toxic one in its combination with Upper Yemen's tribal structures, as several imams, each claiming to be the rightful imam fighting an unjust one, sought the support of various tribal leaders. Together they fought for the spoils of power.[57]

The imams depended on the strong tribal religious affinity of Upper Yemen with the house of the Prophet of Islam.[58] But their relationships with the tribes were anything but harmonious. Mistrust was mutual. The imams did not trust the tribes, with their independent streak and their relaxed attitude towards Islamic law. And the tribes pushed to maintain their independence against the brutal politics of the imamate, and revolted against any imam who tried to extend his authority to their tribal territories. The result of all these dynamics was that their territories were impoverished again and again, especially because of the type of punishments the imams used against rebellious tribes: they targeted their tribal livelihood, destroying their farms, uprooting their grapes and crops, and killing their livestock.[59]

LEGACIES OF GEOGRAPHY, TRIBES, AND RELIGIOUS BELIEFS

The imams' mistrust of their tribal allies led them to develop increasingly violent means to "subordinate" the tribes. The Mutawakkilite Kingdom used two such techniques. The first was the hostage system. They held the sons and brothers of tribal leaders (sheikhs) as hostages in the capital, Sana'a. If a tribe attempted to oppose the imam's authority, its hostages were killed. Second, following the old principle of "divide and rule", they deliberately created conflicts and wars between the tribes, playing them off against one another.[60]

Yemeni historian Ali Mohammed Zayd emphasizes that the areas with the most cohesive tribal structures were those with the fewest resources and most marginal agricultural production; he sees this situation as in fact man-made. Their constant wars ranged from petty wars among local tribes to much bigger ones involving different actors, both local and external. Eventually some tribes that had been stable shifted into Bedouin lifestyles.[61]

In general, though, Zayd argues, the social organization during the imamate period was strongly influenced by a "process of impoverishment" that the imams inflicted on the population—in both Upper and Lower Yemen. Drawing on primary sources, he gives examples of how one twelfth-century imam funded his statelet:[62]

1. *Right* حق: the zakat was prescribed in accordance with Islamic law, and applied to crops, and animals such as sheep, cows, camels, etc., and bees. But in a clear infringement of the Islamic practice of jurisprudence, the rulers took this zakat by force from those who were unable to pay.
2. *A vow and charity* نذر وصدقة: These were donations that supporters had to give in order to "draw closer to God and to the Imam". But some gave these donations for less glorified reasons. In return for their donations, they hoped to be given the right to care for and supervise certain areas, or to recruit fighters for war and then receive a portion of the booty (الفيء). Or they hoped to collect the fines being levied for the imam.
3. *The spoils* الفيء: warriors were given one-fifth of what they looted from the property of the imam's opponents during war, whether these opponents were local or regional.

Several indirect sources of income included:[63]

1. *Hospitality—Althaifa* الضيفة: This meant bearing the expenses of the imam and supporting his entourage and fighters when he came to visit the tribes. This burden was so heavy that some tribes would rebel in order to avoid hosting the imam and his fighters. Other populations would send him money so he would not come to their area and demand their "hospitality". This practice was not restricted to the imam and his entourage. It was imposed by anyone undertaking a mission on behalf of the imam.
2. *Punishments* العقائب: financial penalties imposed on those judged to have committed a sin. The penalties were not used to bring justice to the person who had been wronged. The imam pocketed the sum and the aggrieved party received nothing to compensate for the material or moral damage they incurred.
3. *Levy contractors:* The easiest way for the imam to amass a levy was to contract with certain people, usually tribal leaders and notables, to collect specific sums from certain areas. This helped to impoverish the population, because collectors exploited the practice and increased the levies to profit personally.
4. *War financing:* Another form of levy arose when the imam was mobilizing to fight a major battle; he would summon the tribes and ask them to pay a sum for expenses and supplies.

These extractive methods combined with constant imamate *khuruj*: fighting between imams, between competing dynasties, often of different denominations, and between tribes. All this, in combination, led to the slow but deep process of impoverishment that Zayd describes.

I said before that both Upper and Lower Yemen suffered from this situation. This is important to remember. But we must acknowledge that Lower Yemen suffered even more. Here, the religious component was important. In fact, just as the followers of the Zaydi *Mutarrifiyya* school were persecuted, accused of being heretics, a similar fate awaited the Shafiite of Lower Yemen, especially during the Qasimi period.

Bernard Haykel tells us that that some imams, specifically Al Mutawakkil al-Qasim, considered the Shafii populations in Lower Yemen and in the

LEGACIES OF GEOGRAPHY, TRIBES, AND RELIGIOUS BELIEFS

southern regions of Lahj, Aden, and Abyan to be infidels for two reasons. First, they had close links with the Ottomans and cooperated with them. Hence, they were seen as collaborators with an enemy "whose adherence to Islam was at best tenuous". Second, their Sunni *Ash'ari* theological interpretation of Islam was perceived as "incorrect". So, they were *Kuffar ta'wil*, i.e. infidels by interpretation.[64]

This statement, which was disputed by other Zaydi scholars and even members of the Al Mutawakkil family, had important political and economic ramifications. On the one hand, it justified the continuous war effort in these regions even after the Ottomans were expelled in 1635. The wars were considered to be *jihad*: religious. This enabled the imams to "press into service tribal conscripts and impose special taxes in support of the war effort".[65] As a result, the Shafiite territories were considered part of the "house of war" (*dar al Harb*), that is, legitimate targets of attack. On the other hand, after a conquest it gave the imam discretionary powers over whether to expropriate their lands as war booty and to consider these as conquered lands, taxed at a higher rate of land tax (*kharaj*). It was during this period, Haykel tells us, that the practice began "of granting the land holdings to those fighting in the Imam's support".[66]

The practice has a name in today's Yemen: *Naga'il* (نقائل). Literally, it means a species of a plant that has been introduced into a region or area, whether intentionally or not. In Yemeni historical narratives, it refers to Upper Yemeni tribal sheikhs or *sayyids*, whom the imams sent or moved to Lower Yemen; they were granted control over the areas, and then settled and dominated them. The practice started during the Qasimi reign and continued during different imamate regimes that followed.[67]

Paul Dresch confirms that many families of the tribal leaders (sheikhs) of Northern descent, who are often considerable landowners, trace their migration into Lower Yemen or the western mountains to the Qasimi period. Those who remained in the North also gained control of land beyond their own territory.[68] And the Yemeni historian Hussein al Sayaghi reminds us that once the Qasimi imamate weakened, several tribes spread and moved to Lower Yemen and "even became its kings".[69]

Naqa'il was practised in at least three situations recorded in historical narratives.[70] The first is rebellions in Lower Yemen. If the population in Taiz or Ibb rebelled, the imam would send his armies, based on the Hashid and Bakil tribes, to quell the rebellion. The area would be considered an area of invasion, and through these troops/tribesmen, the imam could exert his influence. The second situation was tribal rebellion. If Northern tribes of Upper Yemen rebelled and besieged Sana'a, the imam would send them to the South and give them free hand to loot. The third case is economic migration. Because Lower Yemen was considered the most fertile area, it was also seen as the best destination for those fleeing starvation and the economic hardship of Upper Yemen. There is in fact a *Zamil*, a genre of Yemeni folk poetry, that says: "If you are fleeing death, there is no escaping death. But if you are fleeing hunger, go down to the plains of Ibn Naji."[71]

Relevance Today

"The past is never dead. It's not even past." This famous quote by William Faulkner in *Requiem for a Nun* captures the Yemeni dilemma, briefly and eloquently.

Yemeni history is not simply history. It is not a chapter in a book that can be interpreted from different perspectives: safely tucked into the past, looked at from afar, and reminisced over with mixed feelings. No. It is a wound. Bare. Raw. Painful. And certainly not dead. It is still alive and kicking. It is being used, retold, and narrated by different actors in many conflicts. And it remains a source of group grievances into the present.

This explains why it was necessary to go back deep into this history. Without recognizing the difference between Yemen as a geographical form and Yemen as a political form, we will continue to go around in circles. Yemen was always diverse: diverse in its distinct regions, diverse in its ethne. And it could have been united into one single political form despite the geographical barriers. The push for unification is not unique in the history of nations. It is normal in the rise and fall of ancient dynasties and kingdoms elsewhere. But here, unification was repeatedly imposed with a streak of brutal domination and hence it met with what I call the "pattern of imploding". This happened because those diverse ethne felt subjugated, unrepresented, and exploited. As I said at the beginning of this chapter, had the bully behaved differently, the cousins would not have felt it necessary to leave their ancestor's house.

LEGACIES OF GEOGRAPHY, TRIBES, AND RELIGIOUS BELIEFS

The historians of ancient Yemen tell us that diverse kingdoms of different ethne existed concurrently. They also tell us that these kingdoms functioned rather well when they used some form of confederation and integrated the tribal structure into their system. They needed some form of decentralized government if they were to function. We see that the push for unification led to a 300-year war, after which that great kingdom just disintegrated, by the sixth century. We also see that the ancient civilizations that populated and enriched the south of Arabia began to decline for several reasons, the most important being economic: their land trade route and its caravans—their lifeline—were replaced by sea routes, and a regular maritime link was established between the Mediterranean world, Arabia, and India. The 300 years of war certainly did not help.

In other words, by the time the Islamic period started, geographical Yemen was in a state of decline. Today there is a trendy narrative, especially on social media, that blames Yemen's decline on Islam, as a religion and as a civilization. I would argue instead that introducing Islam to geographical Yemen only exacerbated an already difficult situation. The Yemenis did what many do today when they face political disorder and lack of economic opportunities: they migrated. Because they were skilled fighters, they became a cherished source of manpower for the Islamic state wars of conquest. They were lured by the possibility of new life and a share of the booty.

But as people migrated, they left their home areas unattended, and their once fertile lands eroded away, as in the case of Hadramawt. The extractive policies of the central Islamic states—the Umayyad caliphate in Damascus and the Abbasid dynasty in Baghdad—certainly aided the decline of geographical Yemen. And given Yemen's remoteness from the centres of power, it became the scene of competing emirates, often following different religious sects, and acting on behalf of regional powers.

Then Zaydism entered the scene. There is no nice way of saying this. Zaydism was not good for the stability and formation of solid states in Yemen—specifically North Yemen. It is certainly an emancipatory religious tradition when the *Mutazilite* influence is strongest, as we have seen with the *Mutarrifiyya* and to a lesser degree the *Batriyyaa* sub-movements. But mainstream Zaydism in its *Hadawiya* version planted a seed of instability. The political ramifications of its *khuruj* principle, restrictions of the imamate to

Adnani Hashemite descendants, coupled with the arid geographical location of the Qahtani tribes in Upper Yemen, created a toxic formula that led the tribes to constantly call for revolt against the imams.

This history has shaped Yemeni politics up to the present and the Zaydi legacy left its imprint on the current conflict in at least three important ways. These are the nature of the ruling elites, and the ongoing narratives about two issues: group grievances and "racial" exclusion.

Core Ruling Elites

The legacy of Zaydism, both geography and tribe, shaped the nature of the core ruling elites in North Yemen. In the areas ruled by Zaydi imams, the core ruling elites came from the Adnani Hashemite social group. They monopolized the most important political and military positions. The North Yemeni Republic that overthrew the imamate regime in 1962 merely changed the Zaydi ethnicity of the ruling elites: instead of the elites being Adnani Hashemites, Qahatani tribal Zaydis were now in charge. And that continued until 2012. Former president Saleh and his clan belong to this tribal Zaydi group.

The Houthi leadership, who today control most of North Yemen, belong to the Hashemite Adnani line of descendants, and they follow the Hadawiya version of Zaydism. Although their movement grew out of their grievances about being excluded by the Republic and the encroachment of Salafi Wahabbi Islam, the literature and rhetoric of the Hadawiya systematically seek to revive the two key principles: Khuruj and the restriction of the imamate to Adnani Hashemite descendants. Since coming to power, they have filled the key positions in the state with Yemenis of Hashemite ancestry. But one cannot fail to notice that today, the most important positions in the state are filled by Houthi family members and Hashemites from the Saada region, the traditional power base of the Houthi militia. More on this in Chapter Seven.

Group Grievances

The division between Upper Yemen and Lower Yemen in North Yemen became engrained—and not merely because of physical features of the geography or the settled nature of the tribes in Lower Yemen. Nor can we point only to

LEGACIES OF GEOGRAPHY, TRIBES, AND RELIGIOUS BELIEFS

the oppressive extractive policies imposed for successive centuries by the imams. As explained before, Upper Yemen also experienced centuries of the imams' policies that impoverished their region. And the deep wound that still exists in its people's collective memory results from the religious justifications for oppressing these Sunni Shafite regions. Branding them as "heretics" made them subject to forms of looting and oppression that were often applied to the "infidels" in the Islamic code of conduct for wars. Finally, the practice of *Naga'il (نقايل)* caused further injury, as the region's population still see those tribal leaders as "foreign": an ongoing reminder of their subjugation and humiliation. The 1962 overthrow of the imamate regime was supposed to be a fresh opportunity to start a new chapter in the relations between the two regions. In fact, it was acknowledged in the First Constitutional Declaration of 30 October 1962. It did address citizens' rights but restricted itself to two statements. It would abolish "racist discrimination", and treat "all Yemenis as equal before the law" (Article 1.2), in a reference to the Northern society's closed class system. It also committed to the "eradication of hatred between Zaydis and Shafiis" (Article 1.3). This was the first and only time in the history of the Republic that these issues were addressed officially. But then the Republic was hijacked by a tribal military alliance and those who insisted on dealing with these group grievances were assassinated, silenced, or co-opted. More in Chapter Five.

This history of antagonism was not forgotten during the youth uprisings of 2011. For example, when Saleh's security forces attacked the student protesters, they called them *Logloughi* لغلغي, a vulgar reference to the population of Lower Yemen. And this history is clearly remembered in the vindictive and punitive ways that Saleh and later the Houthis have been treating Taiz during the civil war.

Rise of Racial Exclusion

The Houthi revival of the Zaydi Hadawiya tradition and its promotion of Hashemite superiority based on their bloodline led to the rise of a counter movement, one that is equally parochial and racist. Established in 2017 by a group of youth activists, mainly living outside of Yemen, it calls itself the Yemeni Nationalist Movement—Al Aqial Movement. It uses the symbols of the ancient Yemeni kingdoms, especially the Himyarite Kingdom, such as the Caribou and its ancient language script خط المسند. And its members embrace the titles used in the ancient kingdoms, such as *mukarrib*, "unifier", and Qiel, a tribal or clan leader (plural Aqial, hence the movement's name). It considers Yemeni Zaydi Adnani Hashemites to be outsiders, not "real" Yemenis, who should go back where they came from: Hijaz, in today's Saudi Arabia. And it emphasizes the Qahtani blood line of Yemenis. It has many followers online.

Do you see how the past is not dead yet? It is still alive with its painfully raw group grievances. But the past is also being exploited, retold, and narrated to score points in today's conflict. It is important to remember that not all Yemeni Hashemite Zaydis are supporters of the Houthi movement. In fact, many members of this social group have taken clear positions against this militia and paid with their lives for their stance. And yet, in today's conflictual situation, a person's blood has become a marker, in the eyes of both the Houthi militia and followers of the Aqial movement.

These narratives of racial exclusion should not be treated lightly. When combined with religious zealotry, they lead to forms of ethnic cleansing. For example, since the beginning of the civil war, massacres of Hashemite families, and mutilation of their bodies, have been reported in different areas. Examples are numerous, such as the massacres of Alramimah and Aljunaid families in Taiz after it fell under Sunni Islamist control in 2015. Houthi propaganda has skilfully used the massacres, and is still doing so today, on the anniversary of these killings, to mobilize support among Zaydis, and more specifically Hashemites.

***

I will conclude this section by addressing two final relevant elements: the tribal factor and the role of external actors.

Throughout Yemeni history, the tribal factor has often been used to argue against what some have termed the "modern trappings" of the state. Some scholars looking at this conflictual history jump to the conclusion that perhaps the "state" is a "foreign form" that should not be "imposed on Yemenis".[72] For example, alluding to the tribal nature of Yemen, Brian O'Neill argues that the international community should bypass the government and create an

LEGACIES OF GEOGRAPHY, TRIBES, AND RELIGIOUS BELIEFS

arrangement based on decentralized negotiations between tribal and regional leaders. The state, he maintains, is not necessary for Yemen to function:

> Contrary to some views, admitting that the modern Western state is not a feasible model for Yemen is not a patronizing idea. The political system of decentralization and negotiation in Yemen existed for a millennium before the Treaty of Westphalia; it didn't need modern trappings.[73]

What should concern us in this argument is not the patronizing tone—and it is clearly patronizing if not neo-colonial. The trouble is, it misses the core of Yemen's problem. Looking at the history of the country, we see that instability resulted from the tension between regimes that were unable to win the loyalty of their overall populations because they exploited ethnic and religious identities in order to survive and gain politically, and then to extract even more resources. This political pattern holds true in the Zaydi chapter of Yemeni history just as in its modern history. It led to the exclusion of large segments of the Yemeni population—and, not surprisingly, they developed grievances.[74]

The resistance of tribes in Upper Yemen to the central authority had more to do with the type of authority they had to submit to and endure over a millennium. Their ability to organize and provide for their tribal areas and population shows clearly that they were left with no other option but to survive and protect themselves. We have seen that the imams never trusted the tribes and treated them as lions that had to be tamed. And they tamed them using a combination of impoverishment and punishment, and lucrative incentives.

So why should the tribes trust those in authority? The Yemeni imams' statelets did not even behave like a Leviathan in the Hobbesian sense. They acted more like the Greek mythical creature the Manticore: a bloodthirsty monster with the "head of a blue-eyed man, the auburn body of a lion and the stinging tail of a scorpion". This creature "had an insatiable appetite for human flesh. After using its blistering speed to chase down its prey, the beast was said to slash at them with its claws or sting them with its tail before devouring them bones and all."[75]

What Yemen can clearly do without is not the "modern trappings" of a state. No, what it needs to leave behind is the type of extractive and exploitative authority that the people never trusted.

Another pattern that has persisted throughout the history of geographical Yemen has to do with the role of external actors in its internal affairs. That is, the external actors that had a lasting impact on Yemeni politics and states of affairs were often regional. All too often, histories of the Middle East and North Africa are focused on the colonial period. What happened before that does not attract as much interest.

North Yemen's history provides us an interesting example here: it was never colonized by a European colonizer, though some regions were controlled by dynasties acting on behalf of regional powers in Egypt, Persia, and Ethiopia. And later, when the Ottomans tried to control North Yemen, Upper Yemen considered them imperial colonizers and Lower Yemen considered them liberators. That difference in reactions is telling. But it also resulted in the differences in administrative strength and competence in these two regions. The South of Arabia, what we today call South Yemen, is another story. Its sultanates and emirates often resisted encroachment by the Zaydi imams and later were colonized or under one form or another of protectorate. The legacy of this colonization/protectorate also influenced its divergent stages of state formation. The next three chapters will explain this further.

4 The Narrative Dilemma

Narratives about the past often have more to do with the present than with what actually happened in the past. Specifically, in conflict contexts, the past is not only a matter of interpretation. It is a battlefield, brought into the present, that parties to the conflict use to score points as they push for an account, a perspective that will let them express their grievances. It gives meaning to their suffering, to their pain, to the present day they endure, and to their insistence that their version of history, only their version of history, can bring justice in their present. It is important to acknowledge that when they do that, they are not intentionally ignoring "what actually happened". Facts are often of little relevance here. It is their perception of what happened and how it shaped their lives that produces the narratives.

We cannot escape this narrative dilemma when dealing with these chapters of the Yemeni past. On the one hand, the legacies of Ottoman imperialism and British colonization are significant, not least because of how they have impacted present-day Yemen's political crisis and the country's divergent stages of state formation. But the ways they are being remembered vary significantly from one segment of today's Yemen to another. The group grievances of the present day reflect the ways they narrate the past.

Kevin Alexander Davis tells us this in his ethnographic master's thesis: "for many of the southerners I spoke with, the British occupation was symbolic of modernization and prosperity."[1] His thesis, with the title "From Collective Memory to Nationalism: Historical Remembrance in Aden", was based on fieldwork and interviews conducted in Aden in 2013.

The people he interviewed spoke of the British era with nostalgia. They saw it as a positive and prosperous time.

To the ears of the unsuspecting postmodern/postcolonial student or researcher, this may sound like heresy. But his findings in fact confirm a similar finding I observed in my fieldwork in Aden and in my interviews with some Southerner elites before and after 2014. Before you jump to conclusions, these elites were anything but collaborators.

Consider the words of Wafa Alsayed Abu Bakr, at that time a member of the Socialist Party's Political Bureau and the head of the women's sector in Aden Governance. In an in-depth interview on the issue of gender, she talked about the Southern experience across history, and had this to say on the British colonial experience:

> With all due respect, British colonialism, as much as it has flaws, has advantages. Colonialism as colonialism is rejected, but the transfer of life experience lived by these people, who are also colonialists, is considered a positive phenomenon. We in Aden, it is in our nature to be able to adapt to all circumstances. So, when colonialism came, it transferred to us the ways people communicated and operated, and the excellent administrative work that we are missing now. It ... opened schools for us, and that was an unusual move for us: education, health, simple jobs; companies that began to operate within the framework of the port of Aden. The port itself gave [us] an extraordinary step up, the entrance and exit of foreigners in and out of the country. The coastal areas had an exchange of cultures and civilizations. This was an unusual experience in the south, so we were able to coexist with all people, Aden, this small city, in which there are Christians, Muslims and Jews, in all their colours, Buddhists ... and Persians. We did not have any animosity towards others.[2]

Her positive recollections, to my astonishment, were repeated by many others, including women activists and freedom fighters, such as the late Radya Ihasn Allah, who was active in fighting British colonization and put on trial and imprisoned as a result. Despite the strong sentiments Ihasn Allah expressed as she described the struggle against British colonization, she could not conceal a streak of nostalgia in describing Aden during this imperial period. A great centre of modernity, she told me, stood proudly opposite to what she called the "Bedouin protectorates":

> Aden, this was a big state, civilized, the people there were different. If only you knew how many newspapers, societies, writers, movie theatres we had in Aden. Aden was equivalent to the biggest Arab capitals, with the

exception of Cairo. But everything, everything was there, even female artists ... we had everything in Aden. Aden was something else; they killed her. Now it is the height of backwardness, you saw it, garbage.[3]

Davis argues that the Adenis' collective memories of colonial and socialist times as well as the "hardships encountered since unification in 1990" have helped them to identify as "Southern". "Northerners" as a category, he tells us, are viewed as "tribal, backwards and unable to administer a modern and civil state". On the other hand, "Southerners", in the context of Aden, are viewed as "cosmopolitan, urban, and progressive".[4]

In my research, I encountered three types of collective recollections about British colonization. One brings up the past to denounce the situation in unified Yemen while highlighting the law and order of the socialist time. A second uses it to denounce both unified Yemen and the socialist South. Ms Abu Bakr, who was part of the political order that existed in the postcolonial period, exemplifies the first. Ms Ihasn Allah, who belonged to the political group that lost power to the socialists, exemplifies the second. In other words, while both agree on being distinct from the "Northerners", they see different subgroups within their category of "Southerners".

This brings us to the third category. People in this category denounce both British colonization and the socialist order that came after it; they insist the South had its own long historical and political formation, separate from the "Southerners". If the Southerners "want their state back", they say, a state that "did not last [even] 20 years", then those in this group "want our own state, *Al-Mahra and Soqatrate Sultante*, which is several hundred years old".[5] This statement was made to me by Sheikh Brigadier General Ali Salem Al-Huraizi Al-Mahri, a prominent leader in Al-Mahra province and a founder of the General Council of the people of Al-Mahra and Socotra Governorates, speaking in 2021 in Muscat, Oman.

This type of construction of the past has been a constant in Yemen's history, among people in both North and South. There is always truth in what is being said. But not entirely. Nor is it completely innocent. It is a narrative meant to highlight grievances of the past and at the same time address demands about how to shape the present.

Most crucially, when it concerns what we today call South Yemen, that construction has involved more than a nostalgic feeling about a past that was necessarily more complicated than these recollections tell us. It goes directly to what is being termed "South Yemen" itself.

Paul Dresch alludes to this matter-of-factly in his 2000 book *A History of Modern Yemen*:

> For those with the patience to read sources thoroughly, recent nomenclature ("South Yemen", "the Arab South") proves anyway more labile than advertised. The shifts may be fun to track but they are not worth a lot of arm-waving. Yemenis know where Yemen is and one must simplify in some degree to write history.[6]

This was an eloquent way to avoid stating something that should be obvious to the student of Yemen past and present.

The South Arabian identity is a British construction. The South of "Yemen" was born out of a pan-Arab ideology that fascinated many in the region, in the entire MENA region. And this is surely worth mentioning especially as Yemenis do disagree about where Yemen is. Perhaps that was precisely Dresch's point.

In the previous chapter, I showed that the distinction between geographical Yemen and political Yemen is crucial to our understanding of the current crisis there. The former was united twice during efforts to expand and dominate: during the Himyarite Kingdom period (fourth century CE) and the Qasimi imamate (seventeenth century CE). Before, in between, and after these two historical landmarks, geographical Yemen was often inhabited by different political units (kingdoms, dynasties, and so on) concurrently existing alongside each other. And sometimes it was controlled by outside powers, such as Persians, Ethiopians, and Egyptians.

While most of the populations in geographical Yemen were descended from the Qahtani line, they were nevertheless diverse in their identities and ethnicities. This diversity was shaped by more than a presumed or imagined bloodline: it was shaped by geography, the nature of the people, modes of life, religious denomination, shared background—and shared grievances.

Ahmed Alahssab explains this complexity with great nuance in his 2019 book *Power Identity in Yemen: The Controversy of Politics and History*. He describes three levels of markers that shaped the political identity of power in Yemen and produced complex and intersecting group grievances: sectarian, regional, and tribal (clan).[7]

THE NARRATIVE DILEMMA

The sectarian (doctrinal) level divides the country into two groups, Zaydi and Shafiis. The main grievances here revolve around the continuous Zaydi control of power.

The tribal (clan) level divides Yemenis into Qahtanis and Adnani Hashemites. The grievances here stem from the Hashemite control of power for the last eleven centuries.

The regional geographical level is the most complex of these levels. Simply stated, it branches into several regional binaries. In the first binary the North stands opposed to the South; and Hadramawt is positioned against all of the rest of Yemen. But this simple binary of North and South is divided into further binaries. In the North, Lower Yemen is positioned versus Upper Yemen; and to a lesser extent the Tihamis (from Tihama) are seen versus the Jabaliah or people of the mountains. This is the name that the people of the western coastal areas, the Tihamis, give to the Upper Yemenis. In the South, Hadramawt stands opposite the whole of the South; the South is positioned against the Ad-Dali governorate in today's southwestern Yemen; and the Adenis (from Aden) stand contrasted to the Bedouins (meaning all of the Southerners). Alahssab did not include another binary in the South that is worth mentioning: Al-Mahra and Soqatra versus Hadramawt and the rest of the South.

In each of the above regional binaries, the first party accuses the second of possessing and controlling power, and all share a collective grievance against the control of Upper Yemen; hence it is called the "the holy centre المركز المقدس" or "God's plateau - هضبة ربنا".[8] This regional geographical level often intersects with other tribal and sectarian dimensions. This will be further explained in Chapter Five.

You may wonder why I am mentioning these important levels of group grievances, which go directly to today's lines of division in the Yemeni crisis, in a chapter dealing with the legacies of Ottoman and British imperialism and colonization. The reason is simple: they existed before the Ottomans arrived in the North of Yemen, and they existed before Britain colonized the South. This is important to understand. They were not created by either of the empires but were certainly exploited for their benefit and control.

Above all, the ways their legacies are being narrated and remembered are connected to these three levels of identity markers and grievances. So, just as we have seen with the recollections above about British colonial times, a similar pattern tends to emerge when North Yemenis recall the Ottoman period. People in Lower Yemen, the Sunni Shafii, are more likely to look more kindly at the Ottoman legacy. Those in Upper Yemen, the Zaydi, are less likely to. And this statement is just the simplest version of a complex picture.

Consider the divergent reactions to an event on 12 March 2022 in Sana'a, the Yemeni capital: the Houthi militia destroyed a memorial to the Turkish soldiers who died in Yemen during the Ottoman period. A prominent landmark in the vicinity of the Ottoman-style Ministry of Defence complex, the memorial was inaugurated on 11 January 2011 by former Turkish president Abdullah Gul, on a visit to Yemen. It was intended to replace an earlier monument the Ottomans built during their second campaign in the North of Yemen that was destroyed after they withdrew.[9]

The demolition took place at a time when Turkey and Israel were attempting to mend their fractured ties. At first, some Houthi supporters writing on social media used this as an excuse to explain the destruction. And the action did take place after Israel's President Issac Herzog was received in Ankara on 9 March 2022 by his counterpart President Recep Tayyip Erdoğan. It was the first visit to Turkey by an Israeli head of state since 2007.[10]

In a tweet, Houthi Deputy Foreign Minister Hussein al-Azzi first tried to explain the demolition as an individual action caused by a technical mistake and engineers' miscalculations. But he took pains to emphasize the great history of Turkey and its people.[11] Thirty minutes later, he changed course with a tweet of a different nature. Gone was any attempt at justification. Instead, he provided a reminder of the Ottoman history in Yemen from his perspective:

> In fact, no one should resent the demolition of this monument because in reality it is not necessary and it reminds us of the negative side of the history of the two brotherly peoples, namely the side of blood, wars and great pain. On the other hand, it also provokes the feelings of the honorable Yemeni families who sacrificed for their country in that era of history; so, I suggest better alternatives.[12]

These alternatives were never elaborated on; but the controversy did not end with this tweet.

Several intellectuals, who are known for their affiliation with the Sunni Islamist Islah Party, and who, not coincidentally, are mostly from Taiz (Lower Yemen), responded by insisting that the Houthi militia were trying to erase the Islamic Ottoman chapter from Yemeni history.

The Yemeni researcher and writer Nabil al-Bukiri remarked in an interview that "The Houthi group's demolition of the Turkish memorial in Sana'a ... is a result of the long history of hostility and conflict between the Zaydis and the Ottoman Empire." He added that this step indicates that the "the group still has the same old [Zaydi] hostility to Turkey, drawing on the history of its ancient conflict with the Ottoman Empire".[13]

Yassin al-Tamimi, another journalist and political analyst, represents a current within the Islah Party, which rejects the Houthi takeover of North Yemen and, and at the same time, Saudi and Emirati involvement in Yemeni affairs. He had this to say about the demolition:

> The demolition of the Turkish memorial is part of an agenda aimed at severing the nation's legacy and serving a regional sectarian agenda. It is similar to the killing of Yemenis as [if they were] Zionists and Americans, [a role] this group [the Houthi Militia] has been practicing since some regional players decided to use it to defeat the February 11, 2011 national democratic project of change.[14]

The Ottoman legacy in Yemen's history is huge, he insists, and it remains in Yemen today. It cannot be erased by such an action, for the Ottomans left other imprints, too:

> There are mosques full of the remembrance of God, lofty buildings, avenues, bridges, foods, vocabulary, customs and traditions. [If the Houthis reject this heritage], then they should impose a new form of clothing for their women and change people's habits and their civilized lifestyle in the most important cities of Yemen (Sana'a).[15]

I said it was not surprising that those cited for opposing the demolition come from Taiz. It is based on an observation I made during my fieldwork between 2006 and 2008 for another research project, which took me to Syria, Kuwait, and Yemen. I used the phrase "old and traditional in a modern package": "Often, the affiliations of sectarian, tribal, religious, regional, or cliental groups in Arab states have taken a modern political shape, especially in the structural form of political parties or associations and blocks in states where political parties are prohibited."[16] In other words, this is old wine in new bottles.

Hence, in Syria, the Alawites could capture power only because they controlled two key state institutions: the Ba'ath Party and the army. In Kuwait, the Islamist movement in its Muslim Brotherhood and Salafi factions has found a strong footing in the tribal areas, which have long resented their secondary position in the state's power structure.

Similarly, Lower Yemen was often more receptive to radical ideologies calling for change or reform. Whichever ideology was the current trend—pan-Arabism, socialism, or Islamism—Lower Yemen was at the forefront in embracing it. We may interpret this receptiveness as a way of expressing regional grievances and the aspiration to change a form of domination that the group saw itself as having endured for too long. It is no coincidence, therefore, that Sunni Islamist movements in North Yemen found a stronghold in this region in the 1980s before they started to seek one in other areas. More on the nuances of this story and the role of external factors later in this volume.

But a word of caution: do not fall into the essentialist perspective. Yes, the rejection of this demolition intersects with the sectarian and regional dimensions. But these identities are generally fluid and changing. They tend to assert or reassert themselves depending on the situation and circumstances, and in conflict situations. It is the grievances that are constantly expressed in the subtext and that rarely dissolve.

A personal story may be illuminating. When the war started in September 2014 (the date when the Houthi militia took over Sana'a), a close family member asked me whether we were "Zaydi Shia" or "Sunni Shafii". I was tempted to say "Sushi", as our family combines the heritages of both Upper and Lower Yemen and with them the two Zaydi and Sunni religious traditions. But the very fact that the question was even asked shows how fluid and changing such categories can be. And it shows how many are not even aware of them. In fact, before the war, this family member always gave the logical and clear answer of "Yemeni nationality", without a moment of hesitation. Luckily this clear answer remains today.

If we expand the pool of examples, it may be interesting to note that some of the strongest resistance to the Houthi advancement in Taiz was located in the Jahmaliya الجحملية district, which lies on the slopes of Saber Mountain, overlooking the city of Taiz and the Cairo Citadel. Nabil al-Bukiri, mentioned previously, told me that the "origins of the population there are *from above, from the Zaydi areas*".[17] They came with Imam Hamid al-Din in 1918, when he made Taiz his capital.

Taiz, al-Bukiri emphasizes, dissolves these identities, i.e. upper and lower Yemeni identities, and creates a single identity: "cities always create their own identity and the city that has best integrated [its diverse population] is Taiz and also Aden to a large extent". Hence, although he acknowledges that some of the population in the Jahmaliya district fought on the side of the Houthis, the majority fought the militia—"without mercy".[18]

That said, the very fact that al-Bukiri mentioned the origins of this district's population shows how relevant they remain.

If we go back to the example of the Turkish monument's demolition, some of the strongest denunciations came from Yemenis of Zaydi heritage. The harsh words of Ambassador Abdulwahab Alamrani are a case in point. The son of the famous late mufti of the Yemen Republic (unified Yemen), he is known in his own right for his famous travel writings. His father, Mohammed bin Ismail Alamrani, is descended from Zaydi judges, a social class that has traditionally been part of the imamate political order. But he belongs to the Shawkani school of Zaydism, which rejects the Zaydi Hadawi school and has historically sought to align it with the Sunni tradition of Islam.[19]

Using very strong language, Alamrani accused the Houthi militia of being followers of the Jarudiyya school of Zaydism, the most extreme form of Zaydism, and closest to the Twelvers in its theological positions.[20] Here is his statement:

> The demolition of the memorial to the Ottoman martyrs at the hands of the backward Zaidi Jarudiyya should be considered a crime, and it will not pass. Eight years of eroding Yemeni identity suffice for Yemenis.[21]

"The Ottomans are often accused unjustly of being 'occupiers'," he declared. Further, "This accusation is being promoted by Yemenis, taught in schools, and encouraged by ignorance and regional and Egyptian influence." They have been repeating the fallacy that the Ottomans were colonizers, "when the real colonizers in fact, are the political Hashemites, who came from Quraysh".

Then he embarked on a passionate defence of Ottoman rule in North Yemen, similar to those about the era of British colonization in the South which I cited at the beginning of this chapter: they built educational and vocational colleges and roads, provided medicine for free, and started newspapers, and the country witnessed an industrial renaissance. They even started a railroad between Sana'a and Hodeida, though it was never finished.[22] All of this legacy, he tells us, was destroyed by Imam Yehia when he took power officially in 1918. His account was later published on various Yemeni websites critical of the Houthi militia.[23]

Clearly, these recollections tell us more about the present than about what actually happened in the past. And this was precisely my reason for applying the approach of critical realism used here. It captures the complexities of reality shaped by narratives and perceptions and makes it possible to make sense of the divergent and contradictory narratives of the different Yemeni warring factions. But it also recognizes that there is a real world that exists independently of our beliefs and constructions.[24]

That real world has shaped what is happening today. There are surely positive but also negative sides of the Ottoman and British eras. Most importantly, their legacies, while complex and perhaps contradictory, have shaped divergent Yemeni state formations, engrained certain patterns of state–society relations that limited the state's ability to exert power and authority, and constructed certain identities that are still felt today in the Yemeni conflict. I explain this further in the next two chapters.

5 Legacies of Ottoman Imperialism

Most of the MENA region was incorporated into the Ottoman Empire in a process of conquest and expansion that started in 1514 (in Mosul in today's Iraq) and ended in 1574 (in Tunisia). Only Oman, Morocco, and Mauritania escaped that imperial control. Sudan did not experience direct Ottoman rule but came under Egyptian rule in 1820, when the latter was nominally part of the Ottoman Empire.[1]

The regions of what constitutes today's Iraq were difficult to control because it was part of the Safavid Empire (today's Iran). It took a while until the Ottomans could exert their control entirely. They occupied Mosul in 1514, then Baghdad in 1535 and Basra a couple of years later, only to lose the two regions again to the Iranians in 1623. In 1639, after a powerful campaign that lasted for a year, they again captured the whole of Iraq and the two empires signed a treaty defining the boundaries between them.[2]

Libya and Yemen were even more difficult to control. Facing resistance in their first attempt to control these regions in the sixteenth century, the Ottomans left, and then returned in the nineteenth century. More on Yemen later.

As the Ottomans captured areas, they divided them into vilayets (provinces). These constituted major segments of the expansive Ottoman Empire from the sixteenth century onward and grew in importance in the nineteenth century as Ottoman "holdings" in Europe were lost to independence movements.[3] Significantly, in the nineteenth century the boundaries of the vilayets were used as the boundaries for the areas colonized by European powers: British, French, and Italian.

In the past, historians, especially in the West, tended to deal with Ottoman imperialism in the MENA region from a religious perspective. The argument they used was rather simplistic: since the Ottomans were Muslims, and large segments of the populations in the MENA region were of Islamic faith, the Ottoman imperialism was "welcome" if not "tolerated". This is an absurd argument that would never have been made in a European context. The Germans were Christians during the two world wars. Did that fact make their territorial expansions in Europe, also populated by Christians, any less problematic?

Even Majid Khadduri, a renowned American–Iraqi authority on Middle Eastern studies, did not avoid this narrative in his first book in 1963, *Modern Libya: A Study in Political Development*. He said:

> The Ottoman sultans governed Libya as they governed other Arab lands, not as Turkish rulers but as Muslim Caliphs, and their Islamic policy made their subjects, regardless of whether they were Turks or Arabs, feel at home under their rule.[4]

This narrative is contradicted by historians, old and new, who offer a more complex picture. For one thing, to take Libya as an example, some Libyan historians, such as the late Bazamah, describe the Ottomans as "occupiers", whose interest in controlling the region was driven by imperial strategic and economic interests.[5] The Ottomans took over Cyrenaica in 1517 and Tripolitania in 1551, and they reoccupied the two regions, along with Fezzan, in 1835. Their strategy for control combined a mixture of oppressive and soft methods. In general, as the late renowned professor Cherif Bassiouni explains, "historical record documents the disproportionate use of military force by Ottoman governors against the 'native' Arab-Berber population, involving occasional acts of terror combined with diplomacy designed to play various tribes against each other".[6]

That said, Libya's three distinct regions had different relations with the empire, which found it difficult to control the area. Fezzan, which was historically independent, and ruled by a dynasty, had long resisted the Ottomans' attempts to subjugate it, refusing to pay an annual tribute/payment in the form of slaves and gold. The Ottoman presence in Cyrenaica was very weak and it faced revolts in the first Ottoman period, then left it to the control of the Senussi dynastic order in the second. But during that second period of imperial control, they focused their attention and reforms on Tripolitania and its coastal areas, due to their rich resources.[7]

And even here some Libyan historians, such as al-Zawi in 1930, had only harsh words for their conduct:

> The rule of the Turks in Tripoli lasted for 403 years, during which time they did not establish enough schools for the needs of its people, nor did they establish railways, or organized mail. The era of the Turks in Tripoli during its length was not related to knowledge nor to construction. They left our country as they entered, leaving us to reap what they sowed for us. And they shall have with God a recompense for what they used to do.[8]

One may attribute al-Zawi's negative portrayal of Ottoman rule to the rise of pan- Arab/nationalist sentiments. And there is an element of truth in this. But some Libyan scholars insist that this conclusion misses the point, especially because of his religious Islamic orientation. Rather, they argue, his writings were "a description of the Libyan situation under the Ottoman rule".[9]

As you can see, we can strongly dispute Majid Khadurri's argument that "the [Ottoman] Islamic policy made their subjects, regardless of whether they were Turks or Arabs, feel at home under their rule". We need only look at the actual historical records of that period.

The intention here, however, is not to portray the Ottomans as villains. That would be anyway inaccurate and would certainly not capture the complexity of this great empire. Rather, my aim here is to show that though the "religious" dimension was important for the purpose of legitimizing Ottoman control, it was less of a factor in decisions about territorial expansions in the MENA region. We are dealing with an imperial power, one that sought to control land and sea routes, and amass resources and power. And just like other European empires in that historical period, it moved beyond its borders and sought to enlarge and increase its wealth and territory.

It is also important to recognize that four hundred years of imperial rule cannot be treated as a footnote as some do when examining the history and state formation of countries in the MENA region. The Ottomans did leave an important legacy, and elements of it do explain the political and state tradition in the region.

State Formation in the MENA Region

From the areas controlled by the Ottomans, only Tunisia and Egypt were countries with clear state forms. Egypt was controlled by the Mamluks, a dynasty of former military slaves based in the capital Cairo from 1250 to 1517.[10] In addition to greater Syria (which includes today's Syria, Lebanon, Israel, Palestinian territories, and parts of Jordan), it also controlled parts of the Arabian Peninsula, including Yemen in some periods (especially Tihama and Aden) and Cyrenaica in today's Libya. Once the Ottomans conquered Egypt in 1517, it, and greater Syria, were relegated to the status of provinces.

Tunisia, under the rule of the Hafsids, an Amazigh (Berber) dynasty based in the capital Tunis from 1229 to 1574, controlled part of Eastern Algeria and expanded its authority to northern Morocco and Spain during some periods. It fought the Turkish forces and to do so even entered into a military alliance with the Knights Hospitaller, a Catholic military order based on the Mediterranean islands of Rhodes and Malta, which controlled Tripolitania between 1530 and 1551. It finally succumbed to Ottoman supremacy in 1574 and was turned into a province, in the process losing its territory in Algeria.[11]

Aside from Egypt and Tunisia, the other parts of the MENA region were controlled by small dynasties, tribal clans, or independent states, such as Morocco and Oman. In the areas that were incorporated into the empire, the Ottoman state tradition had a lasting impact. It shaped the structure and behaviour of the successor states, their state–society relations, and the role of the military in their political systems. Each of these points deserves further explanation.

Structure and Behaviour of the Successor States

Ergun Özbdun tells us that the Ottoman state tradition influenced the structure and behaviour of the successor states in three ways.

First, it lacked a nation-state tradition. The Ottoman Empire, created and ruled by an Osman dynasty that moved in from the Anatolian highlands in 1290, was a multinational, multiethnic, multireligious, and multisectarian state. It was not a nation state. And it ruled its areas as such. Only in the middle of the nineteenth century, with the Tanzimat reforms of 1839 and 1876, did it try to push for a concept of Ottoman nation and citizenship. But those reforms came too late to leave a real impact. In fact, with the exception of

Tunisia and Egypt, the legitimacy of the nation state within the successor states was always under strain from three sources: Arab nationalism, Islam, and the substate ethnic and sectarian divisions.[12]

Second, the Ottoman state had more capacity to accumulate and use political power. The core political institutions of the empire were strongly centralized and bureaucratic. Of course, its total capacity to penetrate, extract, and regulate varied, depending on whether or not the central Ottoman government could establish its authority in the area. Its state apparatuses, at least in the areas where it could exert control, had greater capacity to concentrate and expand political power, unhampered by established class interests.[13]

Third, it lacked any representative institutions. The same factors that made it possible to concentrate and expand political power in the empire also prevented the growth of any democratic institutions. The empire was a bureaucratic one and it had no representative tradition until the last quarter of the nineteenth century. The Ottoman government had an established custom to convene an assembly of leading civil, military, and religious officials to discuss important matters of policy, particularly in times of stress. This body, the "general assembly" or alternatively the "consultative assembly", was not at all representative. Similarly, the Grand Council of Justice, created in 1838, which functioned as a de facto legislature, was also an appointed body. Some attempts were made to introduce representative-elective elements at the level of local government and later at the level of central government, but these proved short lived.[14]

State–Society Relations

As described above, the Ottoman Empire was not a nation state. Religion was used as the primary tool of personal identification, and was institutionalized in the millet system.[15] This, as my own research has shown, reflected directly on state–society relations.

The millet system organized the population of the empire on the basis of religion, rather than territory or language. Before the Tanzimat reforms of the late nineteenth century, people in the empire were not considered citizens. They were members of religious communities. Accordingly, the system was composed of religious communities, each of which had its own internal organization controlled by a religious hierarchy.[16]

Under the millet system in regions such as greater Syria, recognized religious groups, such as Christians, were organized into relatively self-contained autonomous communities. Each was directed by a religious leader, each had its own religious laws and customs, and each took on various social and administrative functions, including deciding on issues of marriage and divorce.[17] The result of this system was the creation of uneven and divisive hierarchies: one within the Empire, one between the communities, and one within the "recognized" communities.

Looking more closely at the Ottoman policies we see that they fostered the hegemony of Sunni elites over non-Sunnis and non-Muslims while keeping religious, sectarian, and denominational divisions intact. Very tellingly, the systems of family law adopted during that period simply mirrored the division of these societies. Hence, three key elements of family law during the Ottoman period reflected Ottoman rule:[18]

- Sunni jurisprudence took precedence over that of non-Sunni Muslims.
- Society was fragmented along religious, denominational, and sectarian lines, as each community had its own family law.
- And tribes had autonomy as their customary laws, called *al Orf*, regulated their family affairs.

Ironically, while modern Turkey, which inherited the Ottoman Empire after the latter collapsed, embraces a civil family law, the family laws in most MENA societies today (with the exception of Tunisia) reflect features mentioned above. The religious nature of family law perpetuates the social fragmentation within each society. It has kept society divided, hindering intermarriage between Sunnis and Shiites, Christians, Muslims, and Jews, superior tribes and inferior tribes, and so on. In the process, it has sabotaged the development of a national identity. One may argue that the state–society relations in many countries of the region remain hostage to this legacy. The individual is not a citizen. Rather she or he is primarily and foremost a member of an ethnic group.

In 2019, the UNDP came to a similar conclusion in its Arab Human Development Report with the title "Leaving No One Behind: Towards Inclusive Citizenship". "Arab states' constitutions affirm equality before the law", it said. In reality, however, "diverse policies, politics and social dynamics define how citizenship is implemented and experienced in practice"; as a result, they produce what the UNDP termed "differentiated citizenship" or "different grades of citizenship" depending on the rights and privileges that a citizen enjoys.

Differentiated citizenship is based on identities, group identities, determined by religion, gender, race, ethnicity, and class. It extends both vertically and horizontally, where unequal treatment and exclusion are practised in state–citizen relations and citizen–citizen relations.[19]

The Role of the Military

When discussing the impact of the Ottoman period on the MENA region, Benjamin MacQueen explained that the role of the Ottoman military left a significant legacy. It was not just confined to the way the institution was organized, but also impacted "how it saw its role in politics and as a vehicle for change, by force if necessary".[20]

The military was a central institution for the functioning of the empire as a whole. Succession to the throne was deeply embedded in the military and often involved the use of violence. The throne did not automatically pass from the monarch to the eldest son. Rather, the sultan's sons were sent to the various provinces of the empire, where they received military and political education, and acted as governors. On the occasion of the sultan's death, each of the sons would engage in a contest for the throne, with the victor claiming the position. Starting with the reign of Sultan Mehmet II (1451–1481), the victor would order the execution of all his brothers—an act of fratricide that was institutionalized until the seventeenth century.[21]

As the tradition of fratricide ended, the challenges to the authority and rule of the sultan came from the royal household and from the military—which grew more powerful in the later period of the Ottoman Empire. Significantly, the role of the military in sponsoring political and economic reforms "established a pattern whereby regional militaries have continued to intervene in politics since independence".[22]

State Formation in Yemen

> There was a special policy that Sultan Hamid [r. 1876–1909] pursued toward distant regions [of the empire], such as Iraq and Yemen, and that one could term a colonial policy. Sultan Hamid, who fully understood that the people

of these areas could not be administered like those living in the other parts of the empire and according to the same law and modes [of governance], had accepted an administrative system that was in accordance with the capabilities of the local population.

(Tahsin Pasha, First Secretary of Sultan Abdülhamid II, 1938)[23]

Yemen's strategic position at the southern tip of the Arabian Peninsula brought the Ottomans to its shores. It was vital for protecting the Ottoman Empire's southern borders, and the safety of the holy cities in al-Hijaz, as well as controlling both the Red and Arabian Seas.[24] As a result, Istanbul launched two military campaigns to take over Yemen (or rather parts of it), in the mid-1500s and again in the mid-1800s.

The first Ottoman era extended for nearly a century, from 1538 to 1635; the second lasted nearly half a century, from 1872 to 1918, and was mainly concentrated in parts of North Yemen. South Yemen in the nineteenth century was either colonized or under protectorate arrangements by Britain. Both periods were marked by persistent Zaydi uprisings and tribal wars.[25]

General Background

In 1517, when Sultan Selim I conquered the Mamluks in Egypt, the Mamluks' "holdings", including those in Yemen, were automatically considered part of the empire. Not surprisingly, the Mamluks of Tihama (Zabid) and Lower Yemen (Ta'iz) acknowledged Ottoman authority; the Zaydi imams did not, and the Ottomans had to force Aden to capitulate. They considered Aden to be vitally important because of the Portuguese presence in the Red Sea and Indian Ocean. Despite their initial success in capturing parts of Upper Yemen, especially Sana'a, they were driven out and were forced to relocate to the Tihama region, operating from Mocha (famous in the seventeenth century for its coffee trade). By 1538, the Ottomans had a hold in the country, but Upper Yemen remained in the hands of the Zaydi imams.[26]

As Aden declined in importance, so did Ottoman rule in this first period. By 1635, the Qasimi Zaydi imams, supported by the northern tribes, had expelled the Ottomans, and now had a short-lived expansion, when their tribes moved into much of southern Arabia. As the Qasimi imams fought over power, greater geographical Yemen was again ruled by diverse dynasties.

Tihama, Asir, and the South of Arabia were declared independent and reverted to being ruled by local authorities.[27]

Although the Zaydis lost their dominance in most of greater geographical Yemen, the Ottomans were not tempted to capture it again. But now another phenomenon forced them to re-evaluate their position: the rise of the Wahhabi movement in the heart of the Arabian Peninsula and its territorial expansion, which targeted, among other places, the holy cities of Mecca and Medina. They turned to the governor of Egypt, Mohammad Ali Pasha, to subdue the movement.

He proved to be all too successful in crushing it and expanded his authority over the whole of Arabia, including towns along the western coast of North Yemen (Hodeida, Zabid, and Mucha). London was worried about Ali Basha's success in helping Istanbul, fearing that he might pose a serious threat to their interests and position in India. So, in January 1839, the British seized Aden. And Istanbul was worried about his rising star. Together with other European powers, he was pushed to withdraw his forces from Arabia, including the Yemeni areas, in 1840.[28]

Muhammad Ali's withdrawal marked the beginning of the second phase of Ottoman reign in North Yemen. Some scholars argue that the empire returned in order to pursue its claim to sovereignty, which it based on its sixteenth-century conquest of the country.[29] Others explain that the Ottomans were invited to return. Some Yemeni notables—tired of the chaos, and the sectarian and tribal wars and constant competition between Zaydi imams that tore their region apart over a century and a half—invited the Ottomans to enter the capital Sana'a. They accepted readily, keen as they were on confronting the mounting British authority in the Arabian Peninsula, determined to compensate for their territorial losses in Europe, and never losing sight of Yemen's strategic maritime position in the Red Sea after the opening of the Suez Canal in 1869.[30]

But all of that hardly made it easier for the Ottomans to capture the North. In fact, they confronted "immense difficulties" in controlling all of the Northern territory, literally fighting their way from one area to another. Even when they managed to get one area to "acknowledge Turkish authority", another would start a rebellion. The situation deteriorated further starting from 1892, when a series of uprisings and revolts began. In 1911, the Ottomans finally conceded and agreed to sign a peace treaty, the Da'an treaty, with the Qasimi Zaydi Imam Yehia, recognizing him as the imam of North Yemen.[31]

The Sectarian Factor

There is no doubt that both sides have strong feelings about the two Ottoman periods in Yemen. From the perspective of Yemenis from Upper Yemen, they were invaders. From the perspective of Yemenis from Lower Yemen, they were liberators, or at least the lesser of two evils, the Zaydi imams being the greater evil.

On the other hand, from the perspective of the Turks, their experience in North Yemen amounted to a trauma. Yemen was labelled "the grave of the sons of Anatolia". Soldiers sent to Yemen took with them the cloths for their burial, and they sang a folk song with the title *Yemen Türküsü*. "Yemen lands are so rugged," they sang. "Those who go never return. Why?"

Two indicators point to the decisive role that the sectarian/religious factor played in shaping relations between the Ottomans and North Yemen. The first is the way the Sunni Ottomans' walis—governors—treated the Zaydis; they perceived them as "non-Muslims", or at best members of a deviant sect. The Yemeni historian al-Wasa'i, who lived during this period, wrote:

> Because the Turks were Ajam [foreigners who do not speak Arabic], and they did not understand what Zaydism means, and that it is just a denomination just like other [Islamic] denominations … the Turks, as a result of their ignorance, thought that they were not Muslims.[32]

The Zaydi Imam Yehia, who raised the banner against the Ottomans during their second reign, voiced this grievance in a letter to the Ottoman sultan in 1907; he protested that the Turkish governors kept "describing Yemenis [Zaydis] as 'Kharijites'[33] and 'Rafidhite'[34] *and perhaps as not even followers of Mohammad's religion*".[35]

Turkish disdain of Zaydism was translated into outright persecution; starting in 1876, the Ottoman provincial governor began to target and imprison Zaydi religious scholars. The Yemeni Zaydis reciprocated with contempt and accusations of religious "laxity" and "infidelity". Al-Wasa'i, himself a Zaydi scholar, derided the Turkish government for "failing to follow the Shari'a and implementing corporal punishments"; and for its "dependence on fallacious laws and inclinations".[36] Imam Yehia, for his part, rallied the support of the tribes by accusing the Turks of being "outside the realm of the Islamic religion" and of failing to enforce the Islamic Shari'a.[37] These accusations were in fact a protest against the secular reforms the Ottomans introduced to the juridical system.

The second indicator that suggests sectarian differences were at play in the political developments in North Yemen during this period is the position the tribes took towards the Zaydi imam's call to revolt. According to the historian Salim, at this time the tribes could be divided into two groups: (a) Zaydi tribes who responded to the imam's call for revolt because of their sectarian affinity and the imam's promise to share the loot and spoils of war; and (b) Shafite tribes who joined the imam's revolt as a protest against the Ottomans' mismanagement and high taxes.

But not all of the Yemeni Shafite population in Lower Yemen joined the rebellion. Salim wrote that people in the rural agricultural areas (Lower Yemen) did not heed the imam's call to revolt; they were reluctant to join in any kind of war. He also indicated elsewhere that the imam had no supporters in the non-Zaydi areas.[38]

Divergent State Capacities and Role of Traditional Leaders

In general, as explained above, the Ottoman state tradition had a lasting impact in the MENA region and shaped the structure and behaviour of the successor states, their state–society relations, and the role of the military in their political systems. Contextualizing this legacy within the particular Yemeni case, three main outcomes become clear. These revolve around regional variations in capacity to rule, the roles given to traditional rulers, and the manipulating of sectarian differences.

Regional Divergence in State and Administrative Capacities

While the Ottomans ruled, North Yemen was divided into four districts (*sanjaks*): Sana'a, Hodeida, Ta'iz, and Asir. In general, the Ottomans were able to rule and control Lower Yemen but were less successful in Upper Yemen, especially its tribal areas and Saada. It was an extension of the pattern that we have seen in the past and reflected on the administrative structures created earlier: the ability to introduce some reforms; build certain infrastructure, courts, and roads; and extract taxes and resources. This was not the case in so many parts of Upper Yemen, except for Sana'a.[39]

That said, even in the areas they controlled, the Ottomans were not able to implement any of the reforms they introduced in other "difficult" provinces. They tried to carry out censuses, introduce land registration, implement conscription, and establish a secular court system, but simply could not, anywhere in the province of Yemen.[40]

Reinforcing the Role of Traditional Leaders Via Indirect Rule

North Yemen was one of the peripheral "provinces" and very difficult to control. As a result, Istanbul adapted its policies to suit the local context and, in the process, institutionalized their view of the "different" Yemenis as "savages" and "backwards", people who could not be ruled or treated as "civilized". Instead, it opted for a form of indirect rule, which was described as "suitable".

In his meticulously researched book, based on Ottoman archives and communications, Thomas Kuehn remarked that, starting in the 1870s, the Ottomans' power struggles with the local communities pushed them to elaborate a form of governance based on institutionalizing and reproducing difference. This went beyond emphasizing the cultural inferiority and hence the differences in the local population. Rather, they institutionalized their practices by adapting modes of taxation, the traditional/religious judicial system, and local military recruitment to what was described as the customs and dispositions of the local people. Significantly, they also translated this into a policy of co-opting elite figures, the *Sadah*, tribal sheikhs, lords (feudal rulers in Lower Yemen) and judges (*Qadis*), who were integrated in the provinces, and served as administrators, on the administrative councils and in the judiciary.[41]

These local leaders were tasked with actually collecting taxes in the system of *tevzi*: a tax collection system based on apportionment. In this system, the government determined a specific tax burden for a particular fiscal unit, say a village, but left to local leaders the task of apportioning the tax burden and collecting the taxes. The local leaders were then allowed to assume the role of tax collectors, and to serve as administrators, judges, gendarmerie officers, and members of administrative councils. But the government had lower expectations for them than for leaders in other contexts. From the perspective of the Ottoman central government, the bargain was that these local leaders did not have to "deliver" as much in return; instead, in exchange for the influence they wielded in their newly acquired positions, they would ensure the loyalty of the local population. One can argue that this policy was an extension of Zaydi imams' policies; they had often worked with the traditional leaders to ensure their control. Similarly, Ottoman officials resorted to what they termed "ancient customs", by taking hostages from rebellious tribes to ensure their loyalty.[42]

Ensuring the loyalty of the local population was not the only outcome of the indirect Ottoman rule. It also institutionalized a system of corruption. Local officials found every opportunity to extort funds (15–20% more than legal levies) from the local inhabitants. Given how peripheral and geographically remote Yemen was, these local leaders were secure in the knowledge that the central government was "too far away to catch up with them".[43]

Perpetuating a System of Sectarian Difference

The Ottoman policies towards the Zaydi imams and their areas differed according to the positions of the governors. Some governors insisted on a policy of outright coercion; others treated the tribes and regions according to their degree of loyalty to Istanbul, rather than their sectarian affiliations. But as the Yemeni rebellions grew stronger, various officials, bureaucrats, and military officers pursued sectarian policies in order to contain and control the influence of the Zaydi imams. For instance, in order to "gradually remove the sect of Zaydism from the minds of children", a state-sponsored primary education system pushed to hire teachers from among the Shafi'i population of the Hodeida and Taiz areas.[44]

Sectarian differences became visibly clear in the 1911 peace treaty, the Da'an treaty, between the Turks and Imam Yehia. In the treaty, the imam accepted Ottoman jurisdiction over defence and foreign policy. Internally, however, North Yemen was divided into two spheres of influence: one run by Imam Yehia and the other by the Turks. Imam Yehia, accordingly, had jurisdiction over the Zaydi tribes and areas, while the Turks were in charge of the Sunni areas and the appointment of their judges and governors.[45]

Salim commented on this treaty:

> The treaty paid special attention to the Zaydis because they were the ones with special situations and special [sectarian] demands; and, therefore, these provisions were included as a means to regulate this special situation. The rest of the Yemeni areas, which are inhabited by non-Zaydis [Sunni Shafites], were only demanding some reforms from the Ottomans and a reduction in taxes, and these were also mentioned clearly in the treaty.[46]

In other words, the Sunni areas acknowledged both the "religious" and "political" authority of the Sunni Ottomans as long as they would moderate their heavy taxes and reform some of their ways, but the Zaydi areas acknowledged only the "political" authority of the Turks—provided that the Turks recognized their sectarian demands. The difference between the two groups' demands highlighted the sectarian dilemma within Northern Yemeni society, which became even more apparent after the collapse of the Ottoman Empire in 1918 when Imam Yehia extended his authority over the Lower Yemen areas.

6 Legacies of Colonization

The Ottoman period left profound legacies for the political landscape of the MENA region and these became intertwined with diverse patterns of colonial authority as well as local forms of political organization. Together, these phenomena shaped the political formation of the MENA region.[1] Just as the Ottomans had co-opted local leaders and dynasties, so did the colonial powers. They exploited the internal divisions and group grievances within societies they controlled. The specific ways they managed the region differed from one area to another. They adapted their methods to the local setting, population, and colonial interests. This legacy, together with that of the Ottomans, has left its mark on the region and its states.

All of the MENA countries are new states which gained their independence in the last century. The region is composed of seventeen states: the seven states of the Arabian Peninsula (Bahrain, Kuwait, Qatar, Oman, Saudi Arabia, the United Arab Emirates, and Yemen); the countries of North Africa (Algeria, Egypt, Libya, Morocco, and Tunisia), plus Jordan, Iraq, Lebanon, Syria, and Sudan.[2]

While all are newly independent states, they vary in their capacities as states: an outcome of the differences in their formation as states and bureaucratic development during the Ottoman and colonial periods. Apart from some regions of Saudi Arabia and North Yemen, they all experienced decades of European rule: either direct rule or various forms of protectorates starting in the nineteenth century. Colonial activity was heightened between the two world wars. It was during this period that the former Ottoman Arab territories were divided, and the political map of the MENA region was drawn, with the creation of its modern states.[3]

State Formation in the MENA Region

From the nineteenth century on, France and Britain started to encroach on the periphery of the Ottoman Empire. But the Europeans advanced in the MENA region long before they actually colonized it. Nazih Ayubi described this as a process that stretched from the sixteenth century to the nineteenth, as the Ottoman Empire was incorporated into the capitalist world economy. At the same time, as Bahgat Korany highlighted, the empire was integrated into Europe's state system and came to recognize the principles of Europe's inter-state order. Most importantly, as Lisa Anderson emphasized, the immediate threat from European military and economic power compelled the Ottomans, along with the rulers of Egypt, Tunisia, and Morocco, to undertake a course of "defensive modernization". That is, they undertook reforms designed to lend their domain the appearance and to some extent the reality of European-style statehood: they restructured their militaries, established standing armies, reformed the administration of their provinces, reorganized tax collection, and relied more on staff with technical expertise.[4]

But this defensive modernization came to a startled halt when the European powers colonized Egypt, Tunisia, and Morocco (Britain in 1882, and France in 1881 and 1912 respectively), and the Ottoman Empire was dismantled after World War I. The provinces constituting the Arab region were divided among Britain and France: Britain was to control what later became Palestine/Israel, Transjordan, and Iraq, in addition to Egypt and the Gulf sheikhdoms; and France was given the mandates of what became later Lebanon and Syria, in addition to Algeria, Tunisia, and Morocco. Furthermore, Italy colonized Libya, and Spain chewed at parts of Morocco.

But only three were "official" colonies: French Algeria, Italian Libya, and Britain in the southern Yemeni city of Aden. The rest were under various forms of protectorates or mandates. Regardless of whether control was direct or indirect, it was the colonial powers that "dictated the political arrangements across the regions".[5]

Their political styles varied. British colonialism emphasized economic concerns and relied as much as possible on indirect rule, whereas French colonialism was more obsessed with cultural links and what it termed its *mission civilisatrice*.[6] But their policies diverged from one area to another within their domain of influence with different consequences for the formation of states.

For example, Charrad tells us that the different strategies used by the French colonial power in the North African countries (Algeria, Morocco, and Tunisia) had consequences for the "degree of political centralization, the strength of tribal solidarities, and the legal system of each country". Hence, depending on the characteristics of each of its Maghribi colonies, France pursued differentiated policies.[7]

Furthermore, in Egypt and Tunisia, European colonizers retained the local dynasties that were previously representatives of the Ottoman sultan and maintained and accelerated their earlier efforts at reforms to strengthen the state administration. Thus, as Anderson puts it,

> although the immediate beneficiaries of the state formation and administrative development changed dramatically, as local powerholders gave way to European rulers, the process of the administrative growth and reform itself was marked by considerable continuity.[8]

In the Persian/Arabian Gulf, Britain's main concern was maintaining its access to India, so it signed antipiracy treaties with locally powerful families, thus elevating them to the status of rulers.[9] These local rulers had an invested interest in seeking the protection of Britain to guarantee their survival against: (a) Ottoman imperialism, as in the case of Kuwait; (b) Saudi territorial advancements; and (c) internal rivalry threats, as in the case of Sultanate of Oman.

Over the years, Britain played a decisive role in protecting these local leaders, sustaining their leadership, while controlling the area indirectly. That is, they left the social order intact and unchallenged but dictated the terms of their foreign policies. Britain also literally charted the borders of what would later be called the Gulf countries (Bahrain, Kuwait, Qatar, Oman, and the United Arab Emirates), sometimes to the detriment of the local leaders themselves. Saudi Arabia, never colonized, was able to establish by sheer force a territorial reality that took over a large chunk of the Arabian Peninsula.

Britain acknowledged this in the way it charted the borders of the Gulf countries. Nevertheless, both Britain and the local leaders had an interest in keeping and fostering their political and economic ties.

For Libya, Algeria, and greater Syria, however, colonization was very disruptive. In Libya, for example, the Italians dismantled the existing Ottoman bureaucracy, military and financial establishment and imposed an entirely Italian administration. When Libya gained independence after World War II, it had virtually no experienced local bureaucrats and little by way of a state, modern or otherwise. The same can be said about Algeria, which France colonized deeply from 1830 to 1962, and the fertile crescent (greater Syria), which it controlled from 1923 to 1943. There, repeated changes in the administrative policies of the mandates and frequent efforts to "isolate, aid, and protect favoured communities", such as the Christians in Lebanon and Alawites in Syria, "contributed to the administrative instability and exacerbated the discontinuity" of the European rule in the region.[10]

In all of these colonies, and regardless of the type of administration, the local population actively cooperated and participated with the colonial powers. The colonizer could not have existed and endured without the "cooperation" of local leaders or threatened communities: people long disadvantaged within their own societies. This pattern can also be discerned during the Ottoman period, when the Shafii and Jewish communities in North Yemen cooperated[11] with the Ottomans as an expression of their frustration at the harsh and discriminatory policies of the Zaydi imams. The Southern case will clearly highlight this point later in this chapter.

Overall, then, the colonial experience led to four key consequences for the formation of states in MENA.

1. Arab countries came to independence with widely varying levels of administrative strength and competence. Egypt and Tunisia were the only two countries that had effectively established a national bureaucracy with control over the national territory by the time they became independent. The rest had not developed much capacity to thoroughly administer the territory, to force a military monopoly, or to extract resources.[12]

2. The institutionalization and consolidation of territorial states with borders. It is important to understand that the administrative boundaries of the Ottoman Empire became the lines that the colonial powers used to define their boundaries. MacQueen confirms this: "The most direct manifestation of European control was the territorial definition of the new political entities, each of which would form the modern-day states of the MENA region. This was not purely artificial, with Ottoman policies of centralized bureaucracy around major urban areas as well as deeper historical communities, helping to provide the logic for these new polities."[13]
3. In some areas, however, colonial interests led the colonial powers to carve out specific countries from the Ottoman Empire: Iraq, Jordan, Lebanon, Palestine, and Syria. The state systems in these countries were literally created by the colonial powers.[14] Some of the enduring conflicts in the region, such as the Israeli–Palestinian conflict and the Kurdish question, are an outcome of this period. The boundaries of these new states were rarely congruent with indigenous social formations or economic systems. The arbitrary borders left many of the states with heterogeneous and partial social structures and economies. For example, new borders deprived the tribes in Jordan of their traditional markets. And geographical and ethnic units were divided among the new states; this was the case for the Kurds.[15]
4. Along with carving out newly shaped states, the colonial powers also pushed to unite Ottoman provinces into states that had not existed in that unified form. Libya and Iraq are examples. South Yemen is another. This is one of the most important and lasting legacies of the colonial period.

State Formation in Yemen

Our period of occupation did the country little permanent good, for all the selfless work of many devoted Englishmen and so many good intentions. Whatever the rights and wrongs of the way we left, whatever was to come after us, the time for us to be there was over. And if we were to go, it was better not to linger on.[16]

"We left without glory but without disaster." That was the opinion of Sir Humphrey Trevelyan, the last British High Commissioner of the Federation of South Arabia, quoted above. And to some extent he only saw half of the glass. Britain's withdrawal on 20 November 1967 from the Federation of the South of Arabia, later named the South of Yemen, was not forced and not the result of military or political pressure, though the security situation had certainly deteriorated. The decision to leave Aden after 130 years of colonial control had already been made in 1964. The withdrawal itself was certainly conducted without glory.[17]

He and the commander-in-chief simply left. They were seen off at the airport by senior officers of the "Arab army and police and by Arab civil servants". "No indigenous president or prime minister was present to raise the newly designated national flag, nor was any royal personage in attendance to welcome a new member of the commonwealth of nations." The military band, true to the spirit of the moment, played "Fings Ain't Wot They Used T'Be".[18]

Still, things could have been worse. In his memoir, Trevelyan reminds his readers how dire the situation looked at the time. Indeed, the possibility of disaster was hardly far-fetched:

> When one remembers the position in the last week of June with Crater [a district in Aden] under siege ... the Arab army in a state of near-mutiny, a hundred British soldiers and civilians virtual hostages up-country, another hundred British officials in the power of the Arab Forces at Ittihad (the federal capital), and the British commercial community scattered throughout the colony, one realises how near we were to calamity.[19]

So, they left without glory and with limited catastrophe, at least from the perspective of the colonial authorities.

But seen from the perspective of what was yet to come, the seed of disaster was already planted. That seed was the division that has haunted the area known then as the South of Arabia, later the South of Yemen, later again the People's Democratic Republic of Yemen, and now the southern movements. It was during a specific period of British rule that the seeds of this division were sowed.

Significantly, the seeds of division were not the result of Britain's famous divide-and-rule policy. In fact, it was the reverse: its colonial officers' insistence on unification, on creating a united South of Arabia, when there was no basis for it, and no indigenous social, economic, or political formations or structures that could justify such unity. Disparate political units, with different histories of state formation, were pushed to enter into a federation. Britain had two reasons: it needed an orderly withdrawal from the South of Arabia, and it wanted to counter Nasser's pan-Arabism with its very own ideology—hence unification.

It achieved neither: the withdrawal was certainly not orderly and given the British obsession with Nasser, it handed South Arabia to the Soviet Union as if served on a plate. In the process, a construction of South Arabian identity took place. The Southern problem today has its roots in this period. In the next sections I explain this further. First comes a general background on the colonization of Aden, followed by a section that presents the divergent state and administrative capacities of the South Arabian units. A final section will highlight how the construction of South Arabian identity took place.

General Background

When Britain colonized the port of Aden in 1829, it came to a Yemen that was fragmented geographically. North Yemen was under Ottoman control and in certain regions, especially Upper Yemen, politically unstable.

South of Arabia (as it was called at the time) was not haunted by sectarian division as was the case in the North. Its populations were, and are, mostly Sunnis with some segments following Sufism. Regional division was and remains a feature. At the time, it was divided into Aden, a port near the intersection of the Red Sea and the Indian Ocean, and the Hinterland, composed of twenty-four sultanates and sheikhdoms, each ruled by a sultan, sheikh, or semi-feudal lord.

British policies reinforced this state of social and political reality, only to reverse course in the middle of the twentieth century when Britain decided that unifying Aden and the Hinterland might ensure its survival in the face of a pan-Arab wave. Ironically, the British-manufactured unification created a new political entity, one whose parts did not trust each other, and did not share a "Yemeni" identity. This is the real legacy of British colonial role: imposing a unity on units that did not really want to be part of it.

Britain had two interests in South of Arabia. First, it was intent on stopping competing regional powers from threatening its Indian trade route. One such was Egypt's Mohammad Ali, who overcame the Wahhabi movement in the Arabian Peninsula, took over Syria, and turned against his Ottoman suzerain in 1832. And Britain needed the strategically important port of Aden as a location for coaling stations for its steam-powered commercial fleet. As a result, its aim was to capture Aden and ensure its authority in the area. The so-called Hinterland was not significant for its own strategic value; Britain seized and connected it in a protectorate form of relationship mainly to create a buffer zone around Aden.[20]

British imperial control of these protectorates of the Hinterland was designed to keep out other powers (Ottomans, Persians, French, Italians, Ibn Saud, and the North Yemeni imam). There was no need to control or develop these areas; indeed, any attempt to do so at the time would have jeopardized the goodwill of the rulers.

Decades later, in 1869, the building of the Suez Canal further amplified Aden's importance. Control of Aden's port made it possible to control all the shipping passing in and out of the Red Sea. Then oil was discovered in the Middle East, and the Royal Navy decided to switch from coal to oil. And Aden became a crucial base for the Allied war effort during World War II. All these developments highlighted Aden's crucial location as an outpost of the British Empire, and necessitated its maintenance.[21]

Colonial policies toward Aden and the surrounding sheikdoms and sultanates reflected the differing value Britain placed on each one. It left untouched the status quo in the Hinterland, with its convoluted constitutional and political legacy, and it turned Aden into a bustling economic centre and established both constitutional and bureaucratic order.

Britain fortified Aden and the area surrounding it, and concentrated all its economic activities there, allowing commercial interests to establish a major infrastructure to service the shipping industry. Small-scale industrial activity and commerce developed, turning the city into a prosperous colony. Education, combined with fairly functional media and rights to association, fostered a sizeable and influential middle class. This segment of Southern society, organized in the form of political parties and labour unions, began to participate in politics and later spearheaded an opposition movement against British colonization.[22]

Conversely, the Hinterland received scant attention from British authorities. It was left to the rule of local sultans and sheikhs and emirs with whom Britain signed protection treaties starting in 1886. In return for an annual salary and military protection, the local rulers pledged to relinquish foreign policy-making to the British and to refrain from direct contact with external powers. The protectorates were constitutionally separate from the Aden Colony and were politically and economically diverse as a result of tribal segmentation and local autonomy.[23]

The colonial power took it upon itself to delineate the borders of its spheres of influence with its rival power in this region, the Ottomans. Hence, between January 1902 and May 1904, an Anglo-Turkish committee undertook the task of demarcating the two nations' areas of influence and in 1914 they signed a treaty. This agreement awarded the Hadramawt Province to the British; it saw the political units and tribes as part of the British sphere of influence and called them British protectorates, and it effectively demarcated the boundaries separating these protectorates from North Yemen. Given that the two foreign powers enjoyed only nominal authority in these tribal areas, this action was truly imprudent: British control extended barely 10 kilometres beyond Aden City while the Turks' influence in Yemen was limited to those territories where they could establish garrisons. The Egyptian historian Farouq Abatha commented on the agreement: "this theoretical division [of borders] ignored the fact that much of the areas within the spheres of influence of the two powers were ruled by Arab rulers and Arab tribes."[24]

Divergent State and Administrative Capacities

The British–Ottoman demarcation of spheres of influence did not mark any significant departure from Britain's policy towards what it termed the Hinterland. Hence, Aden was the focus of all its modernization efforts; the sultanates and tribal regions of the Hinterland were left to their own local structures and continued to vary widely in their internal structures, economic resources, legal practices, and treaty relationships with Britain. They were divided into two geographical/political units: the Western and Eastern Protectorates. The next section explains the institutional framework of these units further.

Aden Colony

"The Crown Colony of Aden" was part of British India from 1839 until 1937, when the Order in Council of 28 September 1936 was adopted and turned it into a Crown colony. It followed the lines of basic legislation for British colonies, i.e. the basic legislation was enacted by the Crown, but the Ordinary legislation, specific to the colony, was enacted locally in the form of "Ordinances enacted by the Governor of the Colony of Aden".[25] The governor, later given the title of high commissioner, was assisted by two councils, one executive and one legislative.

The Executive Council had a purely advisory function, consisting of the chief secretary, the attorney general, and other appointed persons. Under the 1962 constitution, the title of governor was changed to High Commissioner for Aden and the Protectorate of South Arabia. Provisions were made for the appointment of two deputy high commissioners. His assent was required for all legislation and he had certain reserved powers and exclusive control of the public service and the police. The Executive Council was also replaced by a Council of Ministers which consisted of "not less than seven Ministers who are members of the Legislative Council, one of whom is styled Chief Minister, and the Attorney General who is an ex officio member".[26]

The first Legislative Council was established in Aden Colony in 1947. Elections were held at the end of 1955 for the first time and four of the nine non-official seats were filled by elected members. The council was reorganized in 1959 to include twelve elected members, six nominated members, and five ex officio members. The governor, who had formerly presided over the council, was replaced by a speaker. At the 1959 elections, twelve elected members of the Legislative Council were elected from five constituencies. The franchise qualifications required that voters be adult males and be British subjects born in Aden, or British subjects or protected persons (inhabitants of the Protectorate) who had resided in Aden for not less than two of the three years preceding registration. Voters were also required to have property ownership or a minimum monthly income. These ownership and financial requirements were struck down by the 1962 constitution.[27]

The local government consisted of three bodies. Aden Municipality, an autonomous body which collected its own revenue, mainly from rates and taxes, had a council of fourteen elected and six nominated members. Sheikh

LEGACIES OF COLONIZATION

Othman Township Authority comprised four nominated and six elected members. And Little Aden Township contained six nominated members. The two township authorities were autonomous but collected taxes and fees on behalf of the central government.[28]

The system of law that prevailed in Aden was similar in its essentials to those that existed in other British colonies. The colonial legal and judicial system, with its system of supreme, divisional, and magistrates' courts, tried all cases of legal infringement, and heard them in English. Only in matters pertaining to marriage, divorce, and inheritance did Islamic stipulations remain in force. Legal pluralism was a feature of the legal system. Religious minorities in Aden, such as Jews and Hindus, had their separate religious courts to resolve their family disputes.[29]

As mentioned earlier, the Aden Colony had a bustling civil society. Starting from 1945, political parties were active and thriving. By 1957, there were twenty-four registered trade unions in Aden Colony, with a total membership of about 12,000.[30] Most of these workers came from the protectorates or from North Yemen. These will play an important role in the developments that took place, on which more later.

Western and Eastern Aden Protectorates

Compared to the orderly and thriving Aden Colony, the "Hinterland" was a world of contradiction, and with the possible exception of the Lahji Sultanate in Western Aden Protectorate and two sultanates in Hadramawt, few of its political units had much capacity and infrastructure. Nothing can better illustrate the complexity of these units than a look at how the British handbook of Aden classified the "Hinterland" and its types of Protectorate States:[31]

The first category was settled areas close to Aden with considerable incomes from cotton and agricultural produce (Lahij, Fadhli, and Lower Yafa).

Second, tribal areas were divided into three types, depending on their relationship with the British authorities. The first type was areas that "cooperated ... fairly well" with the authorities, including Al Amiri (Dhala), Wahidi, Audhali, Beihan, and Upper Aulaqi. In the second type of area, "cooperation is slight and local conditions of insecurity obstruct administration and progress"; these were Lower Aulaqi, Haushabi, and Dathina. The third type was described in the handbook as "'wild Tribal areas' where government has not entered and where there is no formal local authority". These areas were Radfan (in Dhala), Halmain, Upper Yafa, the Illah Tribes, Mahra, and parts of Upper Aulaqi.

The third category was Hadramawt, with its more socially advanced Qaiti and Kathiri sultanates.

For administrative purposes, these "types" of protectorate "states" were divided into two major units: the Western and Eastern Aden protectorates. The two diverged considerably in their development and state formation.

The Western Aden Protectorate (WAP) was in general less advanced than the Eastern. It consisted of a large number of sultanates and sheikhdoms that varied in size and level of administrative and structural capacity. It was divided into five areas for advisory purposes, with an adviser stationed in each area: northeastern (Beihan, Upper Aulaqi Sultanate, Upper Aulaqi Sheikhdom); southeastern (Audhali Sultanate, Lower Aulaqi Sultanate, Dathina Confederation); central (Fadhli Sultanate, Lower Yafa Sultanate); southwestern (Sultanate of Lahej, Haushabi Sultanate, Aqrabi Sheikhdom, and Alawi Sheikhdom); and northwestern (Emirate of Dhala, Sha'ib Sheikhdom, Maflahi Sheikhdom, Radfan Sheikhdom).[32]

The WAP included small units with which the British had not concluded any advisory treaty, and in some cases, such as the Radfan, not even a protectorate treaty. This happened because the British administration believed that separate treaties with small units would perpetuate the excessive fragmentation of the WAP, a situation they were trying to eliminate.[33]

The most developed unit in the WAP was the Sultanate of Lahej, which bordered the Colony of Aden. It had its own constitution, and administrative and judicial structures. As a sultanate, it was divided into the capital and four districts, each headed by a *na'ib* (deputy, a title used for the provincial governor in both protectorates). Lahej also had a more advanced judicial organization than the other states in the Western Protectorate. Shari'a courts had been in existence for considerably longer, and the administration of justice was regulated by a decree of 2 April 1949, which was based on Egyptian prototypes.[34]

In the other states of the WAP, varying degrees of administrative organization and central authority could be discerned. In general, the pattern was to subdivide the states into several districts, each headed by a *qa'im* (a district director). In many of the states there was only one *na'ib* (deputy) who was the head of the central administration, and several had state councils. Shari'a judges' (*Qadis'*) courts existed in most of the states, but these were outdated and did not have criminal jurisdiction, which was in the hands of customary law judges.[35]

Eastern Aden Protectorate (EAP) was a category by itself. Liebesny tells us that the Eastern Protectorate stood in strong contrast to the Western. Its cultural contacts, and the commercial and remittances ties, with India, Indonesia, and Malaya gave the cities and towns of the Hadramawt a diversity and fascination of their own. Harold Ingrams, the First Political Officer at the Aden protectorate, in his 1936 report on Hadramawt, described the intermarriage between Hadhrami men and Malay and Javanese wives and how this affected the languages spoken there, Malay and Swahili among them. He also reported that old Semitic languages had been, and still were, only spoken in Al-Mahra, and that a distinct Mahari language had been spoken in the sultanate up to the present.[36]

The Protectorate included the two "best organized states", both of them dynastic: the Qu'aiti state of Shihr and Mukalla was created in the early nineteenth century, and the Kathiri State of Say'un in the late fifteenth century. Both had advisory treaties with the British. The Mahra Sultanate of Qishn and Socotra (a dynastic sultanate created in the sixteenth century) in the east, and the Wahidi Sultanate in the west, also had advisory treaties, but they remained the least developed within the Protectorate, especially the very remote Mahra Sultanate.[37]

The Qu'aiti and Kathiri sultanates had complete administrative organizations of their own; the British advisers played less of a direct administrative role and more of a guiding one than in the Western Protectorate. The Qu'aiti state was the largest, wealthiest, and most thoroughly organized. Its capital was Mukalla, the residence of the sultan, and the seat of the British resident adviser for the EAP. Assistant advisers were stationed at Say'un and in the Wahidi sultanates. Mukalla had its own budget and levied its own taxes. The city administration handled such problems as water supply and roads. Taxes collected by local administration went directly to the municipality attached to it.[38]

The Qu'aiti state had developed a court system that involved two sets of courts on the intermediate level but not on the lowest or highest one. The lowest courts—Local Council Courts created in 1952 for more efficiency—had jurisdiction in petty civil and criminal cases and were administered using the "customs" that prevailed "in the area over which the court exercises jurisdiction, provided that such custom is not contrary to justice, morality or order".[39] All civil and personal status cases were tried by Shari'a judges. The Court of the Chief Qadi in Mukalla handled all appeals and jurisdiction in murder cases. Tribal courts also existed, along with a commercial court in Mukalla. Despite the prevalence of the Shari'a law of the Shafi'i jurisprudence, the sultan enacted a number of decrees that dealt with areas of the substantive law, both civil and criminal.[40]

The Kathiri state, by contrast, was smaller, less wealthy, and slower in its development. It was, as Liebesny argues, in many ways "administratively a microcosm to the Qu'aiti macrocosm". It was headed by a sultan, with the central executive establishment headed by a state secretary, who was aided by an administrative inspector. Deputies and directors were assigned to provinces; town councils were established and village councils in other places. A state council was presided over by the sultan and consisted of official and unofficial members, among them the state secretary, the administrative inspector, a Shari'a expert, the president of the Town Council, and the British assistant adviser.[41]

The Construction of South Arabian Identity

Thus far, I have focused on the different political forms of the units within the two protectorates. In contrast, Aden Colony was a world apart. The divergent political, economic, and social forms in these units were matched by policies that were specifically designed to keep the "Hinterland" under control without much intervention. It was seen as merely a buffer zone to protect Aden—Britain's second most treasured colony—from any incursion or disturbance.

Sir Richard Beaumont, in his famous confidential memo "lessons learned from South Arabia", explained what went wrong with these British policies:

> Though there were Protectorate treaties designed to prevent interference with Aden in particular, the general attitude of the Government of India was to confine itself to so much involvement, and no more, in the Protectorate as to keep the territory quiet enough for Aden to get along in peace.[42]

LEGACIES OF COLONIZATION

This decentralized system did not foster state building in the Hinterland, except in the Hadhrami sultanates, which were historically more developed. On the whole, the Hinterland remained separate from Aden, politically, economically, socially, and culturally. In return, Adenis also saw it as "foreign" and treated its peoples as "aliens" in the city.

Only after World War II did Britain reverse its policy and begin to interfere actively in the Hinterland while proposing constitutional rule and elections in Aden. It also started to take systematic measures to set up an efficient administrative system that would connect the Hinterland to Aden.[43]

The reason for this change of policies was geopolitical, as Sir Richard Beaumont explained:

> In the 1950s—mainly, paradoxically, after the advent of Nasser [Egyptian President and champion of pan-Arab ideology], the evacuation of the Canal Zone, and eventually after Suez [Egyptian nationalization of the Suez Canal]—there was an energetic British reversal of earlier policy of non-involvement in the Hinterland of the Western Aden Protectorate—though not in the Eastern Aden Protectorate. A forward policy developed, abortively at the beginning of the decade and more energetically and successfully at the end of the decade, despite tribal and Yemeni [Zaydi imam] reactions against it. Some Protectorate treaties were signed as recently as this period.[44]

The Forward Policy and Birth of the Federation "Idea"

The "forward policy" was a preparation for the British withdrawal from the region and the colony's independence. It involved constitutional reforms, along with development of the political, social, and economic sectors and the creation of a strong self-sustaining government. Its creators saw it as a "prelude to an attenuated form of self-government ... [because] the region required a period of formal British tutelage prior to independence". Then, "After the demission of authority, Britain's impact would still be evident in the form of the institutions and ideology which had been implanted."[45]

Instead of preparing the ground for institutional reforms in the three parts of South Arabia, as logic would have dictated, a federation was suggested. On the one hand, the Zaydi imams (Yehia and his son Ahmed after him) in Sana'a continued to claim their territorial rights in the WAP. This was met with much fear and resistance by the rulers of the various sultanates and sheikhdoms, who energetically pushed for deeper relations with Britain. On the other hand, Saudi Arabia, similar to Zaydi Yemen, ever the territorial expansionist kingdom, was pushing for territorial claims in the EAP—which the sultanates there resisted. But the most important factor, which really threw the dice in favour of federation, was the popularity of the pan-Arabism ideology.

At the time, the Arab world was in the grip of a pan-Arabist ideology championed by Egypt. It was first introduced in the nineteenth century by Syrian and Lebanese Christians, who had a secular conception of a political community in which they could participate on an equal footing in the Muslim Ottoman Empire. Later, from the 1950s to 1970s, Nasserite Egypt championed the ideology both politically and militarily. Pan-Arabism maintained that the boundaries that set out Arab states were artificial, having been imposed on the region by colonial powers, and it held to the view that a "national Arab bond" brought together all those inhabiting the region who speak the Arabic language. Therefore, it aspired to unite Arab countries into one state. The unification between Egypt and Syria in 1958, which lasted only three years, was a failed attempt to translate this ideology into reality. During the Nasserite era, Egypt advocated a policy of financing and supporting Arab nationalist groups in the region, enabling some of them to stage military coups and assume power in what it considered to be "reactionary monarchies", in the process destabilizing Arab political systems. The ideology, and with it Egypt's President Nasser, proved to be a thorn in the side of British colonial interests.

Relations between Britain and Egypt were very tense for three reasons. First, Egypt had nationalized its Suez Canal, which led to a failed military campaign against Cairo by Britain, France, and Israel. Second, Egypt was deepening its relations with the Soviet Union, and third, Nasser and his brand of pan-Arabism were very popular in the region, including the Arabian Peninsula. However, as Robert MacNamara explains, between July 1958 and September 1962 an Anglo-Egyptian rapprochement could be observed, as Nasser and the British interests aligned over opposition to the growing communist influence in post-revolutionary Iraq (Nasser preferred the pan-Arab Baathists). This period saw the settlement of financial issues arising from Suez and cooperation over the withdrawal of British forces from Jordan (1958) and over the Iraqi threat to Kuwait (1961).[46]

It was during this period, specifically in 1958, at the height of the Cold War, that the idea of federation was suggested. The idea was that Britain would champion pan-Arabism in order to gain favour in the region and stop communist encroachment. Sir William Luce, the Governor of Aden from 13 July 1956 to 23 October 1960, was the first to suggest the idea of a federation, in a memo to London:[47]

> By fighting Arab Nationalism, we shall facilitate Russian Expansion. If we could rely on Aden as a secure base from which to resist the Russian advance in the Arabian Peninsula and the Red Sea area, that would be a very strong argument for entrenching ourselves here indefinitely. But, as it is, Arab ambitions constitute the more immediate threat to our position and by resisting them indefinitely we shall present Russia with the simplest means of furthering her own aims. Our aim should rather be to enlist Arab nationalism against Russian expansionism.[48]

Indeed, federation became attractive:

> a federal government would be politically placed in a better position to deal with rebels in the Protectorate than the Aden Government. Rebels could not be persuaded to fight a federal Arab government as easily as they were induced to fight an alien non-Arab government.[49]

At this stage, the focus was to create a federation of the sultanates and sheikhdoms of the WAP. On 11 February 1959, a federation of six states in the Western Protectorate, called the Federation of Arab Emirates of the South, was inaugurated, and the United Kingdom signed a Treaty of Friendship and Protection with the new federation.

Several years later, the idea took further shape as other states joined the federation, which in 1962 was renamed the Federation of South Arabia.[50] But by now the relationship between London and Cairo was becoming adversarial. On 26 September 1962, a coup d'état by Yemeni military officers—trained in Egypt—toppled the Zaydi imamate regime in North Yemen.

The coup was engineered by Egypt and its choice of the date, 26 September, was not arbitrary. It was meant to obscure a Syrian celebration of the first anniversary of the failed Egyptian–Syrian unification. The United Arab

Republic had been dissolved by a Syrian military coup on 28 September 1961, and the event was supposed to be hugely celebrated in Syria.[51]

That said, the Yemeni officers who led the military coup—members of the Free Officers Movement—were genuinely opposed to the archaic theocratic nature of the imamate regime. Egypt's obvious role in the coup, especially in its swift deployment of troops to Yemen, was deemed by Saudi Arabia to be a direct threat. It responded by providing military support to the toppled Yemeni royal family.[52] The regional contest between Egypt and Saudi Arabia quickly became a proxy civil war between republicans and royalists in Yemen. Britain was on the side of the royalists and Saudi Arabia, and Egypt quickly regained its position as Britain's arch enemy.

Now federation became an acute priority for Britain, to enable an orderly transfer of power in the South of Arabia. It was at this period that Aden, despite its fierce refusal to join the federation, was strong-armed into doing so; what made it possible was a change in the pool of those eligible to vote.

In his meticulously researched chapter on this period, John Ducker tells us that the democratic institutions in Aden had made it possible for the population to express their opposition:

> The debate about the merger in Aden, which had a free press and fully accepted rights of public assembly, was intense and led to some clashes between demonstrators and the police. The democratic institutions and the judicial system in Aden both permitted the expression of opposition to the merger and made it difficult, even at this stage, to prevent intimidation of officials, jurors and politicians. Despite the opposition, however, the elections in Aden produced a majority of those entitled to vote in favour of the merger, though those who thought the franchise should have been wider predictably denounced this result.[53]

Understanding Aden's demographic structure is important to understanding this vote. When Aden was colonized in 1839 it was composed of two fishing villages with a total population of less than 1,000. Over the years, as it expanded and became an active commercial and maritime hub, the population increased, drawing migrants from the surrounding areas. By 1950, the population had reached about 100,000 through immigration from the Protectorate, and North Yemen (especially Lower Yemen), Somaliland, and India.[54]

LEGACIES OF COLONIZATION

The list of those entitled to vote in Aden was widened to include adult males born in Aden, Protected Persons (inhabitants of the Protectorate), and those who had resided in Aden for at least two of the three years before they registered to vote.[55] Naturally this shaped the results of the elections. Of those who voted, more were people who originally came from the Protectorate and North Yemen than were those calling themselves "Adenis". On 18 January 1963, Aden was included in the Federation of South Arabia and became the twelfth state of the federation. That did not mean that the Adeni government was convinced of being included and its participation in the federation council and negotiations over the terms of independence were often marred with impasse and disagreement.[56]

The EAP, specifically the Kathiri and Qaiti Sultanates, were not involved in these plans and at first were discouraged from joining. Later, when they were asked to join, they rejected the invitation: the tribal nature of the federation was not tenable, and the federation was "too weak", to use the words of the Kathiri sultan. Most importantly, the proposed plan for institutional representation in the Federal Council, with a voting system for a future federation that would include the Eastern Aden Protectorate, put the EAP (and Aden as well) at the mercy of a majoritarian vote by the WAP (twenty-eight representatives for Aden, eighty-five representatives for WAP, and thirty-six representatives for EAP).[57]

The British colonial policy pushing federation was indeed hasty, artificial, and not based on any really solid social or political foundations. Even the creators of this "forward policy" were aware of what it really entailed. One of its co-authors, Sir Kennedy Trevaskis, who in 1951 became the advisor for the West Aden Protectorate, commented that the policy's main task was "to construct 'states' out of the loosest and most fluid tribal considerations imaginable".[58] From his perspective the difficulty was two-fold.

One difficulty entailed bringing together states with a variety of forms. And this state building would in no way be easy in the South Arabian context:

> [T]here was so much that was unusual or anomalous to comprehend—the distinction between states with advisory treaties and those without; between rulers who ruled and those that did not; the differing degrees in which advice and control were employed in different states; the intricate web of feuds and rivalries in which every state, tribe, or clan seemed to be enmeshed;

and, brooding over the whole battlefield of conflict and confusion, the dark continuing shadow of the Yemen's claim to South Arabia.[59]

The second difficulty was in convincing the leaders of the Western Aden Confederate's states to come together and concede their power:

> At the root of our difficulties was the Rulers' total aversion to what we meant by federation. What they had pictured was some kind of Arab League which would meet every now and again and take decisions by consensus. What they had never dreamed possible was that we should lure them into an organisation where they would have to surrender some of their powers and subordinate themselves to the orders of others.[60]

So, if this was clear enough to this political officer, why did colonial Britain nevertheless push for this federation? Sir Richard Beaumont explained it this way in his famous confidential memo "Lessons learned from South Arabia", lessons which were used later in the successful unification of the United Arab Emirates:

> We knew that decolonisation was imminent. We did not want to leave fragmentation. It was untidy. It represented a poor colonial legacy. Some of the better Federal Rulers, though anxious not to proceed without assurance of continued British backing, thought the time for greater unity had come.[61]

And yes, there was a "strong social and economic case" for abolishing divisions within the Protectorate. Especially as any "worthwhile investment could only be attracted on any normal basis, if the unit were larger than any contemporary individual State". But it was the enthusiastic insistence of "highly intelligent, but limited and nineteenth century-type, individuals like Trevaskis", who pushed for federation. They "thought that their mission in life included bringing about good government and development ... and [i]n the later 1950s, these latter-day imperialists also saw themselves as building a barrier against Nasser. Inevitably, immersed in parishes within what was itself a small parish, the perspective was often distorted."[62]

One gets the sense that a decision was made and it had to be followed despite the doubts, objections, and ramifications. Two structural factors played an important role in making it possible. The first was the frequent and rapid change of those in charge in the colony, i.e. "the non-Arabist, frequently changing and largely administrative Colonial Service in Aden", which "did not match the limited but active intelligence and the drive of most of the Protectorate Service up-country".[63]

The second was a lack of communication between the colony and London, compounded by lack of knowledge about the South of Arabia among politicians in London. With so little ability to judge the feasibility of these plans, those in favour of them had the upper hand. In the words of Beaumont:

> There was practically no interchange between the Colonial Service in the field and the Colonial Office at home, and little or no first-hand knowledge of the Protectorate among politicians and public here [in London]. In the absence of basic knowledge in London, the flaws which were with other factors to prove fatal—the unrepresentative and lethargic character of many Protectorate Rulers, the factional hostilities and jealousies, the hostile Yemeni reaction and its ability to make itself effective, the mercenary nature of many Protectorate Arabs, the deep resentment of Adenis, the power of Yemenis in Aden to disrupt and so on—were so little known here that the confident asseverations of Trevaskis and others both dominated consideration and fooled policy makers in London.[64]

Internal politics in London also played a role in weakening the relations between Britain and the Federation leaders. When the Labour Party came to power in October 1964, it appointed a new colonial secretary, Anthony Greenwood, who was sympathetic towards South Arabian nationalists, and less so towards what Beaumont called "our friends"—i.e. the Federation's leaders. Labour was pushing for an end to colonization and a focus on Britain's deteriorating internal economic situation. Federation leaders assumed that the new colonial secretary "was hostile to them" and in fact, he "left them with the impression, through his manifest interest in free elections and so on, that they were dealing with a government which either did not understand, or was not prepared to work within, what they regarded as the power realities in South Arabia. The Federation's opponents were ready to reinforce such feelings."[65]

As you can see, the British colonial decision-making process, its context and those involved in it, together shaped what one can only describe as a messy picture: complicated, laced with strong personalities, lack of communication, and uninformed decisions. In the process, they facilitated the construction of a South Arabian identity: one that concealed very complex realities and distinct identities.

Now, what if we look at the other side of the coin and ask why the populations inside South Arabia did not reject these plans? Here the picture becomes even more complicated. For one thing, they did reject these plans. But the tide of pan-Arabism was stronger.

South Arabian Political Landscape

The South Arabian political landscape can be described as confusing, but that is just a mirror of the diversity of Southern political forms and identities. If we ignore for a moment those Adeni officials, protectorates' sultans, sheikhs, and emirs who had a vested interest in working with the British colonial administration, we are justified in asking: why did the independence movements (the plural sense is deliberate) accept what took place?

In this section I will sketch an answer based on a research project I conducted in 1994, supported by interviews in a fieldwork study in 2006 with men and women who participated in the independence struggle against Britain and/or were residents of Aden. Together with new sources, and archival material I have recently accessed, a complex picture emerges.[66]

Initially the independence movements in Aden and within the protectorates were peaceful, and conducted in cooperation with Britain, and people sensed that this cooperation would bring a better deal to the new state once it was established. Adenis aspired to an Aden with a separate status, similar to that of Singapore. The Hadhrami independence movement was pushing for its own unity and state. Over time, the movements were divided into two major currents: one called for separate political forms and the other for unity.

One: Independence Movements Calling for Separate Political Forms for Aden or for States Within the Protectorates

Developed in the 1940s, these movements were seeking independence either for Aden or for states within the Hinterland. Unification with other South Arabian units or with North Yemen was not on their agenda. Two types of organizations serve as examples here.

The Adeni Society. Created on 23 June 1949, it promoted the slogan "Aden for the Adenis", and was popular among Adenis, especially among the upper and upper-middle class. It called for Aden's independence and identified the Adenis as those "original inhabitants and foreigners, who were born and settled in Aden, and who were of different nationalities and religions".[67] It was conscious of the changing demographic structure in the colony and demanded that Aden be closed to those coming from the protectorates and North Yemen. It also called for the expulsion of "workers residing in Aden belonging to this category, and only allow those, who have obtained an Aden birth certificate, to stay". Most of those workers were of Indian, Pakistani, and Somali descent.[68]

Adenis calling for their own independence looked down at the various peoples in the Hinterland as "different worlds and societies" and as "closed societies".[69] They, especially those of Arab ancestry, tended to "think themselves superior to the people of the Hinterland".[70]

The National Party—Hadhrami Unity. Created in 1945, this group called for Hadramawt independence and unity. It demanded reform of the Hadhrami administrative situation in the area and wanted the "foreign" administrative staff replaced with a local one. The movement became a threat to both the authority of the sultans and the presence of the British Protectorate, and was prohibited after clashes in Mukalla in 1950.[71]

Two: Independence Movements Calling for Southern Unification or Pan-Arab Unity

This current developed in the 1950s, swept by the pan-Arab ideological wave that spread across the region. Interestingly, it was not concerned with Yemeni unification per se, neither in a local sense of the South of Arabia, nor in a larger sense of a Yemeni unification that would bring together the North and South of Yemen. It saw unity in either case as a step toward something greater: Arab unity from "the ocean to the Gulf"—namely, unity of the MENA region as a whole.

This passion was expressed by Radya Ihasn Allah, who was a member of the Supreme Committee of the People's Socialist Party (PSP) and actively participated in the nationalist independence movement: "We were struggling for an Arab unity. [Our idea was] first we liberate ourselves from the colonial power, and then create an Arab unity. The slogan of 'Yemen unity' only came later, when [northern] Yemeni refuges came to Aden", fleeing the imam's regime.[72]

It was also reiterated by one leading and respected nationalist figure within the Hadhrami independence movement, who confided to me in a private meeting that the idea of joining with Aden in one state only "came later" as a result of the pan-Arab movement; their "initial idea was gaining independence for Hadhramaut".[73]

Within this current we see two types of organizations.

Some called only for South Arabian unity and opposed a Yemeni unification. The South Arabia League is one such organization. It was created in 1950 out of a coalition of three local independent movements: the Hadhrami Unity mentioned above, the Al Aulaqi movement (which called for the independence and unity of its region in Shabwa), and the Lahji movement, led by its sultan, who actively opposed British advisory treaties. The League featured diversity in its social structure and constituency and was popular inside the protectorates and Aden, but especially in Shabwa, Lahj, Abyan, and Hadramawt. (Please note these regional affiliations. They are important for future conflicts.)

It called for the end of British colonization, while engaging in the institutional measures suggested by British authorities. It demanded that "Aden and the Aden Protectorate be unified and that all treaties with the United Kingdom be terminated" and it opposed the Federation of South Arabia, which it described as a "loose and fictitious federation established to divert the people from their aspirations for an immediate transfer of sovereignty rights to the people".[74]

Though its rhetoric emphasized "the belief in Arab unity and comprehensive unity", it was in fact not at all keen on unification with Yemen. Again, if unity were achieved, it was only a step toward the greater unity. Its Secretary General Shikhan Al Hibshi expressed this in no uncertain terms:

> The league supports the idea of uniting the two countries South Arabia and Yemen, not on the basis of the South's dependency and subordination to Yemen, nor on its being part of it, or that the Arabs of the south belong to the Yemeni race. [It is based] rather on [them being] two neighbouring Arab countries. In fact, the League does not theoretically endorse the principle that the south must unite with Yemen first and foremost, no matter what the existing regime in Yemen is.[75]

Even after the end of the Zaydi imamate regime in 1962, the League, which received direct diplomatic and financial support from Saudi Arabia,[76] remained one of the most vocal movements that warned against the push for unity with what it called "Yemen".

It also highlighted the intimidation that the pan-Arab nationalist sentiments were causing, making it hard for those who did not want unification to express their views. For example, when meeting with the UN Fact-Finding Special Delegation on Aden,[77] in Cairo, in March 1967, the League's President Mohammed Ali Al Jifri suggested that the delegation's sessions with the Southerners should be "confidential". He also suggested that it visit all parts of the South and "not just Aden, which has around 80 thousand citizens of the Yemen Arab Republic, who are primarily loyal to Yemen".[78]

The second type of group in this category called for pan-Arab unity. Allied with Egyptian pan-Arab ideology and/or the Arab Nationalist Movement (ANM), these movements were divided even though they called for unity, and competed for power against each other. Here the two most important were the PSP, which merged in 1964 with the Liberation Organization and in 1965 became the Front for the Liberation of South Yemen (FLOSY), and the National Liberation Front for Occupied South Yemen (NLF).

The PSP was founded in July 1962. Its base and origins were in Aden Colony and in the labour movement of Aden, especially with the Aden Trade Union Congress (ATUC), which was strongly influenced by Yemeni workers. The president of the party, Mr Abdullah Asnag, was Secretary General of the ATUC. It was created to provide the Adeni labour unions with a political voice in the independence negotiations. The party was shaped by the pan-Arab ideology, had strong relations with Nasser's Egypt, and adopted the slogan "unity, freedom, socialism".[79] It featured the unity of Yemen in its programme and constitution, and again saw that unity as the necessary first step toward Arab unity:

> The region of Yemen is part of the Arab Nation, and the Arab nation of Yemen is part of the Arab nation, and the liberation of the natural Yemeni region from colonization and reactionary [governance] and its unification on a democratic socialist basis is the practical way to contribute to the unification of the Arab nation in one Arab nation.[80]

THE YEMENI CIVIL WAR

The PSP was opposed to the federation of South Arabia, and had several demands: British forces should evacuate, the Legislative Council and the Supreme Council of the Federation should be dissolved, and free and general elections should be held throughout "South Yemen" (Aden and Emirates) on the basis of universal adult franchise. And it should have self-determination in accordance with the charter of the United Nations.[81]

The PSP believed that engaging in a non-violent political struggle was the best means to achieve independence. Because of the rising star of the National Liberation Front for Occupied South Yemen (NLF), which espoused violence as a means to gain independence, in July 1964 the PSP entered into a coalition with the South Arabian League and strong leaders (tribal and former sultans) from Abyan, Lahj, and Shabwa, who were opposed to British colonization. (Again, please note the regional composition of these organizations which are relevant to the Yemeni conflict today.) The coalition was called the Liberation Movement. In 1965, Egypt forced it to enter into a coalition with the NLF in what was called Front for the Liberation of South Yemen (FLOSY). Egypt was worried about the NLF's independent streak and the NLF initially complied but did not activate its membership in FLOSY. The scene was divided between the two movements, and the Federation and its sultans.[82]

The National Liberation Front for Occupied South Yemen (NLF) originated in the Southern branch of a pan-Arab movement, the ANM. Created in the 1950s by Palestinian students at the American University of Beirut and led by George Habash, it aimed to promote the Palestinian cause and achieve Arab unity. It had members and branches in most Arab countries and started to operate in Aden from the mid-1950s. When the Yemen Arab Republic was declared, many Southern ANM members moved to the North to support it militarily. The Republican North provided a base from which ANM members from the North and the South coordinated their work together. The common enemies were the royalists in the North and the colonial power in the South. And at the time, the backer was Egypt. It was not surprising, therefore, that the creation of the NLF took place in Sana'a on 23 February 1963. Over a thousand people from South Arabia, in addition to representatives of the ANM, the main movement, joined together and announced the establishment of the National Liberation Front for Occupied South Yemen (NLF).[83]

Unlike FLOSY, the NLF, whose leaders came from the Protectorate with a few from the North, recruited from their own regional areas, and their movement grew especially among the tribal areas. Significantly, it created what it called the Formation of the Tribes (تشكيل القبائل), mostly drawn from Dhala, which was allocated half of the seats of the leadership at that time. They also recruited from the Yafa tribes. They used a strategy of entryism: recruiting actively in both the Federal Arab Army and the security sector. In Aden, they competed with FLOSY to attract members of the labour unions.[84]

From its inception, following the method of the Algerian independence movement, the NLF used military violence against the British colonial authorities and the Federation as its "strategy" for liberation. It argued that the struggle "was not a struggle of political elections, and in its deciding form, is not a struggle of strikes and demonstrations alone"; further, "it is in the end ... a battle of stubborn armed struggle, in which there is neither leniency nor truce, a battle of blood and heroism in which there is no retreat or compromise".[85]

At first, the ideology of pan-Arabism shaped the movement's vision. The same rhetoric used by FLOSY was reiterated here as well. Yemen, North and South, is one unit—i.e. the Yemeni region—and it is part of the larger Arab nation. But it is worth mentioning that it extended the definition of "natural Yemen" to include both North and South, in addition to the "whole of the south Arabian Peninsula", from "Aden to Bahrain including Muscat and Oman". The "struggle against the separation in the south is part of the struggle for the sake of the comprehensive Arab unity" and should also extend to an end of "colonization in the Arabian Gulf" and the rule of "local reactionary forces".[86]

Originally hostile to communism, the movement took a stark turn to the left in 1965, in its first organizational conference in Beirut. Its charter sought to blend pan-Arabism with "scientific socialism". It declared that the struggle now was against "British colonization", "feudal" local leaders, and "bourgeois independence"; its core was "class struggle". In reality the shift mirrored those of its umbrella organization, the ANM, its gradual distancing from Nasser's Egypt, and most significantly a power struggle within the ranks of the NLF between pro-Nasser and pro-ANM currents. By 1967, the NLF was acting independently from Egypt, and criticizing the latter for both its hegemony in North Yemen and its rapprochement with Saudi Arabia.[87]

Concluding Remarks

I did say that the South of Arabia political landscape can be confusing. What concerns us is how the nature of independent movements changed over time. It began with movements calling for separate political independent forms for Aden and for states within the protectorates, especially in Hadramawt: those regions that indeed had a viable basis for separate political statehood. It moved toward demanding Arab unity, using the unification of the North and the South as the first step to an Arab nation, united from "the ocean to the Gulf". The latter genre was connected, financed, and in some cases created, by regional actors.

Also significant is how this change in the nature of the movement ran in the same vein with the British idea of federation and its construction of one South Arabian identity, albeit with an added Yemeni component.

The call for unity was somehow the motto of the era, repeated without much reflection on whether it actually made sense. Britain used it in its obsession with Nasser's appeal in the region, and the final genre of independence movements truly believed in it. And together they shaped a legacy that would haunt the South up to the present.

This is the legacy of Britain's colonization of the South. Granted, an important part of that legacy is the diversity of institutional bases, and of administrative and state capacities in Aden and the sultanates, sheikhdoms, and emirates in the Western and Eastern protectorates. But the real legacy is its construction of a Southern Arabian identity, glossing over the legitimate aspirations of those political units that did have a solid basis for independent statehood. And insisting instead on an "idea" because it suited the zeitgeist of the region.

The "idea" was faulty from its outset. Pan-Arabism ignored the diversity of local realities. Despite the shared common language and historical bonds, each country in the region clearly had its own unique social and cultural character; moreover, some populations within the region did not even speak Arabic, or even consider themselves Arabs. As much as the idea was sentimentally appealing, it did not materialize, for the simple reason that it had no basis for its realization. This was manifested in the first attempt for unification between Egypt and Syria in 1958, the United Arab Republic, which dissolved after less than three years. And as charismatic as President Nasser was and as loved by enthusiastic masses, the core of his project was personalized authoritarian popularism. That project did not allow for the creation of independent states with institutional frameworks that could channel the divergent local realities, or for states that would respect their citizens as equal before the law.

So, if we look back at the South Arabian scene, the popularity of this ideology glossed over complex diverse local realities; ironically those same diverse realities shaped the various independence movements, in their regional and tribal affiliations, and the ways their members were recruited based on personal loyalties. In fact, if you look closer, you will see these regional and tribal affiliations being mirrored in the constant fighting that was yet to come before and after Southern independence.

In other words, the same pattern mentioned elsewhere—"old and traditional in a modern package"—repeated itself in the Southern context. Again, I have seen this pattern in my fieldwork in Yemen, Syria, and Kuwait, where "the affiliations of sectarian, tribal, religious, regional, or cliental groups in Arab states have taken a modern political shape, especially in the structural form of political parties or associations and blocks in states where political parties are prohibited".[88]

This pattern manifested itself from the moment Britain announced its intention to withdraw from South Arabia in 1964. The declaration, while necessary, only accelerated the power struggle between these movements. It turned that struggle into an undeclared civil war and later into an open one. And Britain, against the advice of the UN special mission on Aden, literally handed over power to the leftist NLF on a platter, excluding the other movements, simply because the NLF took an increasingly hostile stance towards Egypt. As a result, the British felt compelled to favour the NLF as its successor rather than to hand over control to the second main power in the South, the Egyptian-supported FLOSY.[89] As one British officer wrote in a 23 March 1967 memo:

> [T]he NLF are opposed to Egyptian policy and show more effectiveness as terrorists than FLOSY. The NLF's weakness is that it has no political leadership of note. But I have myself idly wondered whether, if we were forced to have any dealings with the extremists, the NLF do not have more

to deliver—or at least more to withhold from the Egyptians—than the craven Asnag and the entirely negative Makkawi [leaders of FLOSY].[90]

On 29 November 1967, Great Britain and the representatives of NLF concluded independence negotiations, issuing a "Memorandum of Agreed Points Relating to Independence for South Arabia", which became effective the following day. According to this agreement, the new Republic would be established by the National Front (NLF), which was recognized as the "representatives of the peoples of the territory of the Republic".[91]

Once in control, the NLF made its intentions unmistakable, declaring itself "the leader of the revolution and the supreme authority" and "the only political organization in the country". It promised to take on "the task of creating an ideological and pioneer party capable of assuming the tasks of the next phase and of leading the people to realize their promising future".[92] In other words, the NLF considered itself the sole legitimate representative of the people of South Yemen and was determined to set up a socialist regime.[93] But the seeds of division were already planted. In fact, the very name of the new Republic indicated the power struggle that lay ahead.

On the eve of independence, heated discussions took place between the NLF leaders about the name of the new state. One participant, Haidar Abu Bakr al Attas, the former first prime minister of United Yemen, who also served as prime minister (1985–1986) and chairman (1986–1990) in the Southern PDRY, tells us that the leaders naturally rejected the name of the Federation of South Arabia because of its ties to the colonial power. Two names were suggested: the Federal State of Aden and the Federal State of Hadramawt. The hardcore NLF pan-Arabists opposed both alternatives and insisted on including the word Yemen in the name. The compromise was to include the adjective South to Yemen. Hence it was called the People's Republic of Southern Yemen: the name mentioned in the "Memorandum of Agreed Points". Later, in 1970, after yet another power struggle, the name was changed to People's Democratic Republic of Yemen (PDRY)—and thus was sealed the victory of the communist current in the movement.[94]

7 The Cunning State and the Politics of Survival

Meet Radhya al-Mutawakel, the chairwoman of the Mwatana Organization for Human Rights, created in 2007. Her work entails documenting the violations committed by all parties to the conflict in Yemen. Not an easy task given that she insists on living in Yemen. She was engaged with the conflict even before the war started and she has an inside perspective, especially through her work as a member of the Technical Preparatory Committee for the Comprehensive National Dialogue Conference (created in July 2012), until she resigned with a colleague in January 2013.

When I asked her about the causes of the conflict, she had an interesting way of articulating the answer:

> The Yemeni civil war is not a genie that suddenly came out of the lamp … [As if] Yemen was in peace and everything was going well and all of a sudden, the war started! This is the biggest lie we tell ourselves. The anomalies, even if we put the extended historical anomalies aside, started from the moment the political settlement took place after the 2011 revolution. I believe the transitional period (2012–2014) was a big opportunity and it had all the ingredients that could have given Yemen an opportunity to move forward … but the government was very corrupt. Very corrupt.[1]

The 2015 Yemeni civil war was certainly not a genie that appeared out of nowhere. It is one of many wars, in North, South, and United Yemen. And it was surely expected, at least by those who follow Yemen closely.[2]

What should interest us in al-Mutawakel's answer is the two dimensions she mentioned: the "extended historical anomalies" *and* the role of the government, i.e. the role of the state. The two are crucial if we are to understand

Yemeni predicaments and the type of state formations the country has experienced.

But by now, alert readers must have realized that we are talking about divergent state formations for multiple Yemen(s). We are not even talking about two state formations for two Yemen(s), North and South. The divergence goes deeper and is related to the two legacies, addressed in the previous chapters, that played a central role in this state of affairs.

To review, these are legacies of geography, religious beliefs, and tribes. Together they highlight three important historical facts. One, Yemen as a geographical space (North and South) was always larger than the different ethnonationalist political forms that inhabited it concurrently. Two, the political dogmas of Zaydism, introduced in North Yemen in 893 CE, and the ethnic affiliations of its followers, planted seeds of recurrent instability. Three, although the imamate policy of impoverishment and oppression had been used against Zaydi populations, it had a greater impact on the populations in Lower Yemen. The division between Upper Yemen and Lower Yemen in North Yemen started in the tenth century and the religious justifications used to take over these Sunni Shafite regions left deep wounds in the collective memory of their populations.

And consider the legacies of external interferences in both North and South. In North Yemen, the Ottoman Empire left three impacts. It left a regional divergence in state and administrative capacities between Lower Yemen and Upper Yemen. It ingrained the role of traditional leaders (*Sadah*, tribal sheikhs, lords, and jurists) through the Ottoman practice of indirect rule. And it perpetuated a system of sectarian difference between Lower and Upper Yemen.

In what became South Yemen, the British left two major impacts as it colonized Aden in 1839 and created protectorate relations with the sultanates and statelets in the south of Arabia. As the Ottomans had in the North, it left behind a regional divergence in the state formations and administrative capacities of Aden, compared to the Eastern and Western protectorates. And significantly, it literally constructed South Arabia as a political unit as a means to counter Nasser's pan-Arabism, without any foundational basis for such unity. The Southern independent movements were divided between those calling for separate political states for Aden or protectorate units, those calling only for South Arabian unity, and those that insisted on pan-Arab unity. All those calling for unity saw it as a step towards something greater: the unity of the whole Arab MENA region. And yet, even when these movements were emphatically calling for unity, they were divided among themselves, shaped by regional and tribal affiliations, and recruitment methods based on personal, regional, and tribal loyalties. These divisions remain relevant today.

These are the legacies inherited from the past in Yemen, both North and South. We cannot understand their impact on Yemen without considering the role of the state. I cannot emphasize enough how important that role was in bringing Yemen to the fragmented situation we see today. The divisions within society, the group grievances, and the fragility of the state were cemented, perpetuated, and recreated by the conduct of the state: the independent and modern state, whether in North, South, or United Yemen.

Before elaborating further, some theoretical reflections on the role of state and group grievances in leading to rebellion and civil war.

Theoretical Deliberations

In political science, state fragility is often attributed to the conduct of the state itself. In their famous volume *Why Nations Fail*, Daron Acemoğlu and James A. Robinson argue that nations fail because of the way in which state institutions behave, economically and politically:

> Nations fail because their extractive economic institutions do not create the incentive needed for people to save, invest and innovate. Extractive political institutions support these economic institutions by cementing the power of those who benefit from extraction. Extractive economic and political institutions, though their details vary under different circumstances, are always at the root of this failure.[3]

In other words, regardless of the context, what makes the difference is the conduct of the state and the elites in power. And that conduct is in itself a pattern that leads to state fragility. Defined by the Fragile State Index, a fragile state exhibits specific features: loss of physical control of its territory or a monopoly on the legitimate use of force; erosion of legitimate authority to make collective decisions; an inability to provide reasonable public services; and an inability to interact with other states as a full member of the international community.

Significantly, among the twelve indicators that measure fragility, two consistently rank near the top in almost all the states in the index: uneven development, and the criminalizing or delegitimizing of the state. The first suggests that "inequality within states—and not merely poverty—increases instability"; and the second occurs "when state institutions are regarded as corrupt, illegal, or ineffective". In such conditions, "people often shift their allegiances to other leaders—opposition parties, warlords, ethnic nationalists, clergy, or rebel forces".[4]

Uneven development suggests a preferential treatment of specific regions and a bias towards others and is related to the conduct of the state and its ethnic nature. The actions of the state often lead it to become delegitimized; in turn both citizens and foreign actors challenge its authority.

A 2015 study by David Carment and colleagues, with the title "Towards a Theory of Fragile State Transitions: Evidence from Yemen, Bangladesh and Laos", argued that for those states mired at the bottom of the fragility list, such as Yemen, challenges to authority have been the primary factor keeping it trapped in extreme fragility. For stability to develop, they argue, the best strategy is interventions that will bolster authority structures.[5] This bolstering of authority structures is certainly an important strategy. But it is not enough. More is needed. And the authors stated this indirectly, adding that they know "at least intuitively" that "authority challenges do not simply arise out of thin air. They are based on *perceived injustices* and *legitimate grievances* and arise in many cases as a result of a misdistribution of resources" (italics added).[6]

Addressing the "perceived injustices and legitimate grievances" is the second part of the equation in any strategy to end fragility and allow stability to take root. And perceived injustices and grievances are core to understanding Yemen's recurring political conflicts, and the wars and instability in North, South, and United Yemen. This argument is strongly supported by a 2013 study, conducted by Cederman, Gleditsch, and Buhug, which led them to argue that "group-level inequality and grievances matter for conflict".[7] Their finding, which may not be surprising to those working on qualitative case studies of ethnic violence, seems to stand at odds with much of the contemporary literature on "within-state conflict". As they argue, such studies have often tended to "brush aside ethnic grievances in favour of materialist interpretations that highlight individual economic incentives, natural resources, and state weakness, while overlooking the fundamental importance of group-level mechanisms".[8]

The crucial contribution of their study is the quantitative support it provides for the relevance of group grievances caused by what they call "horizontal inequality": group inequality. They developed this concept by considering political, economic, social, and cultural dimensions. Specifically, they found that political horizontal inequalities can block or limit access to central decision-making authority within the state (political exclusion). The economic dimension taps the distribution of income between groups. The dimension of social horizontal inequality primarily measures groups' uneven social access, for example to education and societal status. Finally, the cultural aspect captures group-level inequalities with respect to cultural policies and symbols, including traditional holidays and religious rights.[9]

At this point, it should be emphasized that the aim here is not to problematize ethnic diversity, be it sectarian, tribal, or regional. And as I explained in the Introduction, it is important to avoid essentialist fallacies and tropes. Most people have multiple identities, and these are sometimes in flux, with new identities emerging and old ones disappearing, especially in times of crisis.[10] The personal story of "sushi" I told in Chapter Four testifies to this awareness. However, when these ethnic group identities become the basis for political mobilization, competition, and conflict, they become relevant to our study.[11] This is the case in the Yemeni conflict, where group identities—ethnonationalist—have played an important role not only in challenging the authority of the state, but also in denying its legitimacy and, in some cases, its right to exist in its current form.

Again, as in the case of the state's manipulation and exploitation of Yemen's tribal structures, the state's role in exploiting Yemeni group identities is central to the creation of these conflicts. Some of these group identities have existed throughout Yemen's history. However, their political significance in relation to their group grievances has been heightened by the role of the state. Thus, ethnic diversity does not in itself lead to violence.

What does lead to conflict is the grievances connected to the actions of the state and to people's experiences of exclusion. In other words, as Cederman,

Gleditsch, and Buhug noted, ethnic conflict results from specific ethno-political configurations of power, rather than from ethnic diversity per se.[12]

I suggest, therefore, looking at the "ethnonationalist" claims to the state and its power as the key to understanding the Yemeni case. Using the words of the 2013 study,

> civil wars by definition do not merely confront individuals or groups with each other, but primarily feature the state and a specific incumbent government against one or more organized opposition actors. Thus, the state should be seen as both as a protagonist and a prize worth fighting over in internal conflict processes.[13]

In short, collectively felt grievances result from structural inequalities caused by the state's biased actions and its extractive policies that benefit specific groups within society. Inequality creates tensions between ethnic groups, which can be exploited for ethnonationalist mobilization and may lead to violent conflict under specific conditions.

How does all of the above relate to the Yemeni crisis?

Yemen's recurrent instability and wars can be explained by the pattern described above. The role of the state and its manipulation of ethnic identities are central to the country's volatility and fragility.

Given the complexity of the Yemeni story and its multiple "states" and "core elites", I will first consider Yemeni instability across its modern history in North, South, and United Yemen. In the section that follows, I will describe the pattern of the cunning state, by defining the concept of the Yemeni cunning state, and then explaining its ethnic features, and its role in producing and cementing group grievances. I will provide three examples: the policies of the imamate; the overlapping group grievances in the South; and the Saada grievances and Houthi rebellion.

But first, a brief look at instability in Yemen.

A Brief Description of Yemeni Instability

I said before that the current civil war in Yemen is not the first. It is one of many. The modern histories of North, South, and United Yemen testify to this state of affairs.

THE CUNNING STATE AND THE POLITICS OF SURVIVAL

North Yemen

The end of Ottoman rule did not bring stability. The Mutawakkilite Kingdom under the Hamid al-Din family—Yehia and then his son Ahmed—ruled between 1911 and 1961. Theocratic, socially conservative, and isolationist at its core, it aspired nevertheless to expand its territory. This led to a war with the Saudi king, Abdel Aziz bin Saud, over the Asir, Jizan, and Najran regions and Hodeida; Saud won, and in 1934 he and Yehia signed the Taif Treaty. It bore witness to Imam Yehia's constant territorial claims over Aden and the Western protectorates, and his support for some tribes in Aden. This support resulted in military confrontations with Britain, which led Britain to use air force campaigns. Yehia also signed a treaty with Britain in 1934 but it left the demarcation of borders to the future.[14]

Internally, Yehia continued his politics of impoverishment, and he brutally subdued repeated revolts by the Northern tribes, in different regions. Coups were attempted and failed three times: in 1948, 1955, and 1961. Imam Yehia was killed in the 1948 attempt and Imam Ahmed survived one in 1961. A fourth attempt in 1962 led to the creation of the Yemen Arab Republic (North Yemen). It was followed by a civil war from 1962 to 1967 between republicans and royalists. As is true in the current civil war, each party to the conflict was supported by a regional patron. The republicans were supported by Nasser's Egypt, and the royalists by Saudi Arabia. The republicans won the war after the Egyptian forces withdrew. Then the Zaydi Qahtani tribal military rose to become the political elite, and North Yemen was co-opted as a satellite state of Saudi Arabia.

After the war, a republican system based on the tribal military asserted itself, but stability was not in sight. In the following decade, between 1967 and 1977, three presidents resigned and two were assassinated. President Saleh took power between 1978 and 1990.[15] He became the president of United Yemen from 1990 until he was forced to resign in 2012.

South Yemen

In South Yemen, the 1967 independence of the People's Republic of Southern Yemen was heralded by a civil war between supporters of the FLOSY and those of the NLF. Fighting took a regional and tribal shape. The NLF won, and massive numbers of people moved; some left the country. Once in power, the NLF used coercive and oppressive methods to ensure that its authority remained unchallenged. They applied them from the moment they took control and long after 1978 when the Front changed its name to the Yemeni Socialist Party; this was the result of the NLF's merger with three leftist parties including the Northern Yemeni Popular Unity Party. At first, the NLF was content to ban other political parties and vigorously censor the press, but it became much more repressive in 1969 after the first power struggle within its ranks. By then, it was ordering mass arrests and had established special courts to track down "anti-state activities". The party also took action to ensure that both the state administration and the army faithfully adhered to Marxist ideology. Thus, it systematically removed all public figures and senior army representatives seen to sympathize with the defeated "right wing" and "petty-bourgeois traitors".[16]

In addition, the NLF neutralized social groups they considered a threat to their established order, in a "policy of undermining clan, tribal, and regional loyalties by emphasizing instead the need for class loyalty".[17] They abolished traditional sheikhdoms and feverishly pursued tribalism, denouncing it as synonymous with feudalism. The result was atrocities: "village headmen, who owned no more than anyone else, were murdered by the state as 'feudal landlords', and in later years a person was as likely to be 'disappeared' for tribalism as for other sins."[18]

They never got the outcome they intended. The most obvious feature of South Yemen's one-party system was its constant internal conflict, shaped by regional and tribal loyalties. The fissures between competing factions of the party's elite often led to power struggles. In fact, between 1967 and 1986, five presidents alternated in office; three were removed by force, two were killed. These power struggles came to a climax in the 1986 civil war. Its ferocity shocked the region. The feuding factions within the Socialist Party ultimately split over their tribal and home origins.

United Yemen

Before the 1990 Yemeni unification, the two countries had engaged in two wars with each other, in 1972 and 1979. The South supported a guerrilla war by Northern Marxist guerillas, members of the Yemeni Popular Unity Party, mentioned before. It raged along the borders of the two countries, in Lower Yemen, until the end of the 1980s.

Many factors led to the ill-prepared unification. With the end of the Cold War, the Soviet Union would no longer patronize the South. The 1986 Southern civil war had caused great economic devastation. The discovery of oil along the joint border raised the possibility of a new war between the two countries. And the leaders in both North and South were determined to press for unity. The Republic of Yemen (RoY), founded on 22 May 1990, introduced political pluralism for the first time in Yemen's recent history. After unification, forty-six political parties emerged and soon the first free parliamentary elections were held: truly a phenomenon in the Arabian Peninsula![19]

Perhaps not surprising, the unification project did not succeed in integrating the two systems into a functional new entity with sound institutions. Instead, the country was sleepwalking into the civil war of 1994 as both the Northern and Southern leaders were preparing for the worst-case scenario, setting up fallback strategies and contingency plans for expected conflicts. President Saleh took deliberate measures to undermine the Southern leadership, reviving tribal and regional feuds within the South. A campaign of assassinations targeted Socialist Party leaders and critical Northern national figures.[20] Each side sought to build up its own military capabilities, in the process hindering any possibility of unifying the two armies. They also cultivated external support, persistently thwarting the development of independent political forces, and corrupted attempts by Yemen's nascent civil society to enter into Yemeni politics. Then, during the Second Gulf War in 1990, Yemen sided with Iraq in its occupation of Kuwait, putting economic pressure on its state and earning it both regional and international wrath.[21]

The 1994 civil war was inevitable, if only to determine the outcome of the power struggle between the two leaders: President Ali Abdullah Saleh in the North, and Vice President Ali Salim al-Baid in the South. The once voluntary unification was now unification by force—with some Southern populations seeing the North as an occupier.[22]

United Yemen was not immune from further conflicts. In addition to the rise of Southern movements, demanding either reform or secession, six rounds of wars occurred in Saada, the birthplace of the Zaydi tradition and the Houthi movement. They began in 2004 and ended in 2010. More than 250,000 people have been displaced; the number of casualties is unknown.[23]

Then in 2011, the youth uprisings took place and the rest is history.

The Pattern

Stability has been rare in Yemeni history. Some are quick to blame the tribal composition, and the sectarian and regional dividing lines. But I hope that by now my main argument in this volume is clear: in itself, ethnic plurality is not a problem. What matters is how the state has been treating its diverse societal segments. Throughout Yemen's history, the state—North, South, or United—has never been just or fair. It has consistently catered to the interests of a few to the exclusion of others. It has played on ethnic divisions, cemented them, and extracted resources in a manner that engrained regional/group inequality and plundered the country's resources. It has often acted with the attitude of "winner takes all", leaving large segments of society excluded and angry. The state was cunning and its role made the difference between stability and instability, unity and division, and peace and civil wars.

The term "cunning state" was first used in 2003 by Shalini Randeria, an Indian professor of anthropology and sociology, to refer to states that "capitalize on their perceived weakness in order to render themselves unaccountable both to their citizens and to international institutions".[24]

I suggest we modify this term to fit the Yemeni context: I define the cunning state as a state run by ethnic core elites, who exploit the ethnic divisions of their own society, and constantly engage in the politics of survival, with the goal of perpetuating their grip on power.

A state may inherit difficult legacies, like those described in the previous chapters, and yet develop a government that values inclusion, rule of law, and transparency. That did not happen in Yemen and has yet to happen there. The features of the cunning state brought Yemen to the point where it is today. One key feature is its politics of survival, which I define, in a Machiavellian sense, as undertaking whatever is necessary to survive in the shifting sands of politics.[25] Other features include the way it has constantly manipulated ethnic identities, playing and depending on them, and extracted resources for its own co-optative survival methods.

The civil war was just a given: an expected outcome. And today, the actors in its conflict are engaged in a similar pattern of divisive tactics to ensure the cunning state will survive. The type of the state and its actions set the stage for a political pattern of far-reaching consequences. I argue that the behaviour of the cunning state set the stage for the combination of state fragility and group grievances in Yemen and that if Yemen is to have sustainable peace, it must change that behaviour and address these grievances.

In the next section I explain the ethnic nature of the state. Chapter Eight highlights its role in producing group grievances with three concrete examples that stand at the core of today's civil war.

An Ethnically Structured State

The cunning state is a state run by ethnic core elites. In Chapter One, I distinguished between two types of states in the Arab MENA region, each with its respective state formation:

- Countries of old states and old societies. These are characterized by a long tradition of centralized state apparatus and the existence of a strong national identity. This group includes Egypt, Tunisia, and to a lesser extent Morocco.
- Countries of new states and old societies. These are characterized by the youth of their states, the lack of a coherent national identity, and the division of society along tribal, religious sectarian, linguistic, and/or regional lines. The Arabian Peninsula countries, Syria, and Libya are examples of this group.

In states shaped by ethnic features, such as Libya, Syria, Bahrain, and Yemen, the ruling elites were shaped by ethnic markers. They depended on a traditional power base: the sectarian, tribal, religious, and/or regional groups from which their political elites originate, or on which they depend, and whose support is vital if the political system as a whole is to endure and survive.

Remember the case of Egypt and Syria during the Arab uprisings mentioned in Chapter One. In Egypt, former President Hosni Mubarak and his sons were just a family that could be pushed to step down from power without shaking up the entire system.

In Syria, by contrast, Syrian President Bashar al-Assad was not just an individual. Were he to step down, his clan, controlling the senior positions in the army, security, and state institutions, would have been targeted by extension. The Syrian army was not a "national" army. It acted as an ethnic bodyguard of the president and his clan. In his demise, it saw its own downfall.

Similarly, the ethnic markers of the ruling elites and their dependence on a traditional power base have constituted a pattern in Yemeni history, in North, South, and United Yemen and even in today's fragmented political scene. The next sections explain.

North Yemen

During the imamate regimes, the core elite came from the Zaydi Adnani Hashemite group, as described in Chapter Three. They monopolized the main positions in their competing concurrent primordial statelets in the north of North Yemen and later during the Mutawakkilite Kingdom (1911–1962). In the Republic (1962–1990), by contrast, the core elite were replaced by Zaydi Qahtani tribal and military leaders (see Figure 7.1). The Zaydi factor remained constant. What changed was the tribal affiliation. Though other social groups participated in the wider circle of power, the crucial point is who held the strings: who had authority over the government and its extractive institutions.

Core elites of Immamte regimes: **Zaydi Hashemites**

Core elites of Republic regime: **Zaydi Qahtanis**

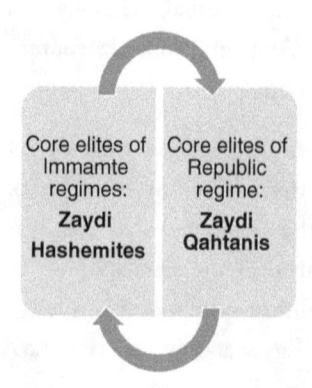

Figure 7.1: Zaydi core elites remained a constant in the Imamate Statelets, the Mutawakkilite Kingdom, and the Northern Republic. What changed was their tribal affiliation

The social stratification among the Northern tribes determined which groups were included in the political system.

At the top of the social hierarchy stood the Hashemites, the *Sadah*. Their assumed bloodline as descendants of the Prophet Mohammed allowed them to establish themselves as a higher and closed "class". Not all *Sadah* are Zaydis. Those who follow the Sunni denomination were often deprived of the political privileges enjoyed by their Zaydi counterparts.[26] Directly below the *Sadah* are the "judges"—*Qadis*; these are often Zaydi who are descendants of the Qahtani tribe. They gain their position by attaining a high level of religious education. Membership in the "judges" stratum is not hereditary, as the Yemeni sociologist Qaid al-Sharjabi tells us. It depends entirely on the individual's level of knowledge of religious topics and Islamic law. But many *Qadis*—judges—still ensure that their sons get the necessary qualifications to sustain that status and so certain *Qadi* families have become known as such.[27] Both strata were, and still are, considered *Hijrah*: they are still protected by the tribes and harming them is prohibited.[28]

The third stratum was the tribal sheikhs, leaders of the Zaydi Qahtani tribes, followed by their tribesmen. Here an egalitarian type of relations used to dominate. Traditionally, sheikhs were accountable to their constituents: they were elected for their mediation skills and ability to represent the tribe's interests. A sheikh was often regarded as a first among equals, rather than an absolute ruler. Over time, however, and due to the state's policies of divide and rule, patronage, and co-optation,[29] this type of relationship has changed dramatically, setting these sheikhs apart—a privileged strata divorced from the harsh reality of their tribesmen.

Other groups were considered weak, protected like the *Sadah* and *Qadis*, but considered of lower social status. They were not allowed to own property or bear arms. These included persons working in specific craft and vocational professions, such as butchers, barbers, drummers, and employees of the hamams, the public baths. They also included the Yemeni Jews, a persecuted religious minority that has now disappeared.[30]

At the bottom of the social ladder stand the Black Yemenis, who have endured discrimination into the present. In Yemen, they are called Al Khadam (servants). They are the descendants of Ethiopian soldiers who came to Yemen in the sixth century. They have to serve the tribe, and are considered an

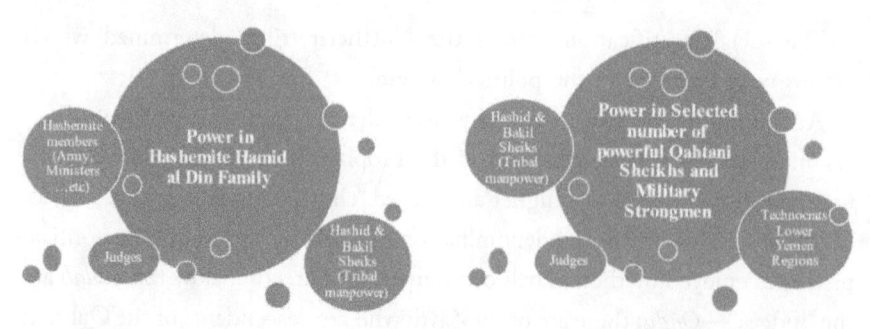

Figure 7.2: Core strata groups' relations to power in Mutawakkilite Kingdom (left) and Republic (right)

untouchable caste. That is, they are allowed no social interaction with other Yemenis, even eating with them; they must marry within their own stratum, and they are forced to bury their dead in a separate cemetery.

This social stratification was strong before the Republic was instituted and gradually weakened over the decades. Where it has held on strongly, as in the Saada region, it had important ramifications especially in the spread of some forms of Sunni Islam. More on this later.

In general, however, two strata remained constant in both regimes, the imamate and the republican (see Figure 7.2). The judges were instrumental in both regimes as influential members of the power structure; and tribal sheikhs of the two confederations, Hashid and Bakil, were sought for their military manpower. This dependence, however, did not translate into a trusting relationship.

South Yemen

Chapter Four, on the legacy of British colonization, may have debunked a widely held assumption: namely, because of the socialist system of the PDRY (1986–1990), tribal and ethnic factors were less important; they were eradicated by the socialist regime's combination of penetrative (social engineering) and coercive (oppressive) methods. The research prism used may have clouded the fragmented reality of the South of Arabia. The South was and is still many souths.

In fact, what happened was that these policies only kept the traditional structures in check; this was evident in their quick rise once unification took place in 1990. It was evident also in the fact that traditional identities were crucial for the competing factions of the ruling elites to survive during their repeated power struggles. From the start, tribal and regional affiliations shaped the PDRY power structure; they explain why, in every power struggle, the elites fought across tribal and regional lines.

This feature was an extension of the protracted scene before independence. Remember that the Shabwa and Abyan affiliations were strongly represented in FLOSY, the front that fought against the NLF once independence was declared. In addition, the tribal and regional affiliations of the Federation Army, before independence, were mainly from the Shabwa (Alwaliq) tribes and Abyan. Hadramawt had its own army.[31]

Because the Alwaliqi tribes participated in the Federation Army, they were considered "reactionary" and "collaborators". In contrast, individual leaders from Abyan were often represented in the highest structures of the army and the Socialist Party. Adenis were considered petite bourgeoisie collaborators; from the outset they were excluded and many of their best-known personalities either fled or were persecuted.

At the same time, the recruitment strategy of the NLF led to two outcomes: a higher proportional representation of the tribes from Dhala, Radfan, and Yafa; and a recruitment practice based on personal loyalties. That is, NLF leaders recruited from their own regions/tribes, and these men owed their loyalty to their leaders, not to the state.

Once in power, the NLF, and later the Socialist Party, had a policy of using a regional quota for recruiting members of the military and security apparatus. Interestingly, young Hadhrami men were less inclined to join these sectors. They often left, migrated abroad, and pursued their own economic ambitions.[32] Those Hadhramis with political ambitions joined the Socialist Party. They found strength in choosing to join one wing of the party rather than others during the constant power struggles. As those struggles increased, men from Dhala, Radfan, and Yafa gained more control in the army, to the exclusion of those from Abyan and Shabwa.

Hence the power structure was made up of leaders coming from specific regions, with a stronger representation from Dhala, Radfan, and Yafa, and each had his loyal traditional power base (see Figure 7.3). Every time they fought, they fought over these regional/tribal identities.

THE YEMENI CIVIL WAR

Figure 7.3: Regional/tribal representation in the traditional power base of the Socialist Party/army

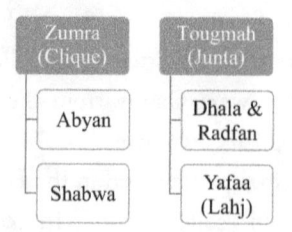

Figure 7.4: The regional/tribal affiliations of the Zumra and Tougmah, the two fighting factions in the 1986 Southern civil war

The 1986 civil war had a tribal and regional character. The winning faction was composed of groups from Radfan, Dhala, Yafa, and individuals from Hadramawt. The defeated factions were from Abyan and Shabwa.[33] This division solidified, and became engrained in the Southern political landscape after unification and even more after the youth uprisings. It was especially potent between those who wanted to separate from the North and those who wanted to federate with it. It is expressed in the two popular expressions—Zumra الزمرة (Clique) and Tougmah الطغمة (Junta)—used to refer to the two fighting groups of 1986.[34] Figure 7.4 shows their regional/tribal affiliations.

United Yemen

When North and South united in 1990, the new configuration was ushered in with much hope. The key idea was power sharing. A five-member presidential council was created, intended to bring in a specific power equation. It adhered to a geographic balance: three members from North Yemen (a member of the tribal military, a judge, and a technocrat) and two from South Yemen.[35] The Southern members belonged to the victorious party in the 1986 Southern civil war (people from Dhala, Yafa, and Hadramawt).

THE CUNNING STATE AND THE POLITICS OF SURVIVAL

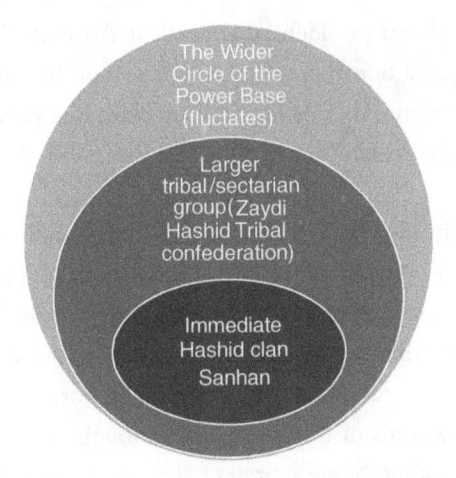

Figure 7.5: Traditional power base of President Saleh's regime

But the hope evaporated and with it any opportunity to build a new state, as President Salah adopted the politics of survival (more later in the chapter on the role of the state). The 1994 civil war concentrated power in the hands of Saleh's inner circle, members of his Sanhan tribe, located at the south-southeast corner of Sana'a, the capital of Yemen. When Saleh came to power in 1978, he systematically appointed close relatives and members of his tribe to key command positions, thus ensuring the loyalty of the army and the security apparatus. His clan's grip on those two institutions continued after the civil war of 1994 but increasingly favoured his direct family members. Figure 7.5 depicts the power structure that continued until 2012, when Saleh was forced to step down.

Post-2015 Political Elites

The 2015 civil war fragmented the political scene in Yemen beyond recognition. Now the landscape is filled with parties to the conflict who have overlapping group identities, and are driven by grievances, combined with warlords and militia, supported by regional patrons, all acting with a form of realism devoid of responsibility. Think of it as different local and regional power centres, each favouring specific groups based on ideological, regional, tribal, and sectarian affiliations.

The newly appointed presidential council of April 2022 reveals the fragmentation of the coalition that is fighting the Houthi militia. Pressured by Saudi Arabia, President Abdrabbuh Mansur Hadi delegated his power to an eight-member presidential council and dismissed his deputy Ali Mohsen al-Ahmar.[36]

The council is headed by Dr Rashad al-Alimi, a military security man, a former member of Saleh's ruling party, the People's General Conference. Dr al-Alimi comes from Taiz (Lower Yemen), a first in all of Yemen's modern history. He has no tribal affiliation. Those choosing the composition of the council deliberately sought equal representation of North and South but could not avoid including seeds of implosion. They brought in members who stand at odds with each other. Some represent the Southern Transitional Council (with a strong representation from Dhala and Yafa) who seek to have the South secede. Others, allied with Hadi (Abyan and Shabwa), insist on unification. Also brought in were powerful military, tribal, and Islamist (Salafi) leaders, a nephew of former President Saleh, supported by the United Emirates. The Islamist Islah Party was also included but was seriously weakened after its patron, Ali Mohsen al-Ahmar, was dismissed. It did not take long for military confrontations to emerge between two different factions of the council, the Islah Party and the Southern Transitional Council, in August 2022. Not surprisingly, this occurred in Shabwa.

The fragmentation and power struggle within the presidential council in the South is countered by an ethnic sectarian concentration of power in the hands of the Houthi militia, in their three wings, missionary (الدعوي), military, and political. Here we see a monopoly on power in the hands of the Hashemites of Saada but with a preference for the Houthi family, followed by the Hashemites of other regions. A third layer of the power base is grounded in sectarian Zaydi solidarity (*assabiyya* العصبية). A tribal solidarity constitutes the fourth layer of the power structure; this includes selected members of the Saada tribal confederation, Khawlan bin Amer. Those in this tribal category are not pursuing a religious sectarian agenda. Instead, they have used the conflict to address pre-existing grievances towards and feuds with the Saleh regime; among other things, the regime has constantly used a divide-and-rule policy within the Khawlan bin Amer confederation as a means to weaken strong tribal leaders. Perhaps because of this, the core group of the Houthi

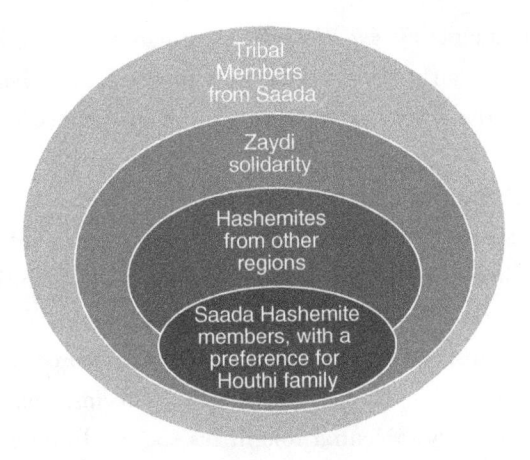

[Diagram: nested ellipses labeled from outer to inner:
- Tribal Members from Saada
- Zaydi solidarity
- Hashemites from other regions
- Saada Hashemite members, with a preference for Houthi family]

Figure 7.6: Traditional power base of Houthi militia

militia hardly trust their tribal members, who are inclined to switch loyalties, if they think that doing so will serve their interests.[37]

Here, please notice a key difference between the traditional power base of the Saleh regime and that of the Houthi militia since it took power. Although both are based on family and clan loyalty, and both are Zaydi, the Saleh regime was not ideological. It was purely Machiavellian. It saw no value in Zaydism as a religious affiliation. In fact, in the late 1970s, this regime recognized that working with Sunni Islamist movements would help it survive; so, with the generous support of Saudi Arabia, it allowed the Islamists to establish religious educational institutions all over the Republic. These preached a form of religious Islamist ideology that was hostile to the non-Sunni Islamic tradition, including the Zaydi tradition.

This is not the case with the Houthi militia. It is ideological to the core. Four elements constitute the crux of its ideological political project: Zaydi solidarity; its Hashemite pedigree;[38] its insistence on *Wilaya* (guardianship/rulership),[39] the Prophet's specific designation of Ali as his successor in 632; and the role of *A'lam Al Huda*, which literally means Guidance Luminaries. This expression is used to allow designated leaders of the Houthi family to take on a guardianship role. And some of the more ideological Houthis use it as an extension of the *Wilaya* concept itself.[40] That is, the historical *Wilaya*, naming Ali as the successor of Mohammed, is tied to the Houthi leadership role as *A'lam Al Huda*. This tie is reminiscent of the Islamist political project in Iran: the Khomeini *Wilayat Al Faqih* (Guardianship of the Islamic Jurists) designates religious jurists as the guardians of the Iranian Islamic Republic until the Mahdi, the absent imam, returns from his occultation (see Chapter Three).[41]

Bernard Haykel argues that the concept of *A'lam Al Huda* allows the Houthi movement to bring in the idea of an imamate regime in a different disguise, that is a "super imam whose role is more encompassing than that of a traditional Zaydi imam". The movement rejects traditional Islamic sciences (scholarship) and insists that the Quran is the only source that contains all that Muslims need to implement the necessary reforms; therefore the *Alam Al Huda* (singular) plays a central role in his society. Through his lead, "the community is able to apprehend the Quran and establish the order that God has decreed for mankind".[42]

These four elements constitute an uncompromising ideological core that sets it apart from the Saleh Zaydi tribal regime and from mainstream Zaydi tradition.

8 The Role of the Cunning State

Ethnic plurality, as I said earlier, should not be seen as a problem in itself. What matters is how the state treats the diverse segments of the society. This is the crux of the matter. In the previous chapters I have shown that Yemen has had three lines of division: sectarian (doctrinal), tribal (clan) level, and regional/geographical.

I argue that the state's conduct has been crucial in cementing these lines of division and producing overlapping group grievances (see Figure 8.1). Going back to the definition of the cunning state, the key actors are the ethnic core elites, who deliberately exploit the ethnic division of their own society and constantly engage in the politics of survival, with the goal of maintaining their

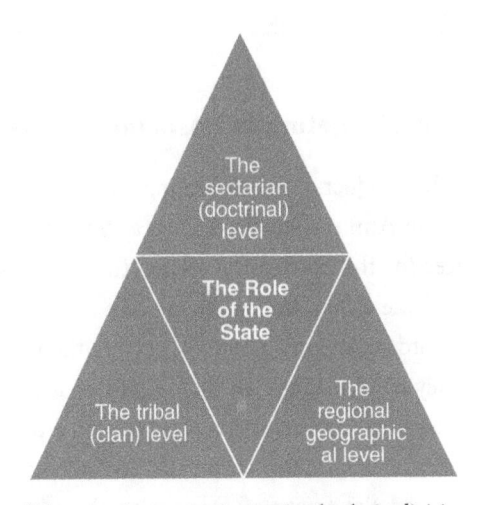

Figure 8.1: Role of the state in cementing societal ethnic divisions and overlapping group grievances

grip on power. This behaviour has fostered overlapping group grievances, which have been the source of Yemen's recurring wars and instability.

One point is crucial to acknowledge: the various statelets, kingdoms, imamates, sultanates, and modern states that are part of Yemen's history did not invent the lines of ethnic plurality I discussed above. Instead, they were a product of the divergence between greater geographical Yemen and the political forms that inhabited it. One factor has been a constant in the history of Yemen: the elites have constantly rejected the right of these political forms to exist separately. In every era we can see a political player acting on religious dogmas (e.g. the Zaydi), ideological beliefs (e.g. pan-Arabism and socialism), and/or the leader's personal ambitious (e.g. former President Saleh) and insisting on uniting Yemen by force. Had that player introduced fair and inclusive policies, unity may have endured.

Add to that the reality that, once in power, the state or statelet, whether primordial or modern, adopted what I call a "mentality of revenge" in its treatment of those who did not toe the line, along with a greedy extractive policy that allowed some segments of society to flourish to the exclusion of others. Overall, then, it was the conduct of the state that produced the various ethnonationalist groups, with experiences of grievance and humiliation that often led them to seek revenge.

Consider these examples from different historical periods. They stand at the core of today's Yemeni civil war.

Example One: Ethnic Targeting of Hashemite Strata

My example here is the conduct of the two ruling imams—Imam Yehia Hamid al-Din and then his son Ahmed—towards the Zaydi tribes and Lower Yemen and the consequences for the Hashemite strata after the 1962 coup.

The imams treated the tribes as lions that had to be tamed, always using a combination of rewards and punishments to ensure their subjugation rather than their loyalty. They needed them for their continuous military campaigns, to subdue other tribes, or to fight rivals to their personal power. But they did not trust them and had to constantly keep them in a weaker position. In fact, once Imam Yehia signed the treaty of Daan with the Ottomans, he turned against the tribes that had supported him and fought on his side. In reality, he was trying to establish sovereignty over his newly established kingdom. Starting from 1919, imamate and tribal forces fought battles in central regions and in the environs outside Sana'a. Yehia experienced a string of victories, including those over the Al-Maqatirah tribe in 1920, over the Hashid tribes in 1922, and over tribes from Al-Jawf in 1925.[1]

After these victories, the imams revived what the Ottomans called an "ancient custom". Each tribe was obliged to send representatives that the imam would hold as hostages. For example, Hashid sheikhs handed over two hostages to the imam as a guarantee they would not rebel against him. If a hostage died, the tribe was obliged to replace him. If a tribe attempted to oppose the imam's authority, its hostages were killed.[2]

And sometimes the imams violated customary tribal laws, which guarantee the safety of a persecuted person, once a tribal figure has pledged it. This was the case in the late 1950s, when Imam Ahmed executed the father and brother of Sheikh Abdullah al-Ahmar, the paramount sheikh of the Hashid tribal confederation. Their areas were ransacked, houses destroyed, and property stolen.

Another technique the two imams used followed the old principle of "divide and rule": by deliberately creating conflicts and wars between the tribes, they played them off against one another. Later on, the Saleh regime picked up this technique.

In contrast, the imams offered a reward, in the form of monthly financial stipends, to the sheikhs of the Hashid and Bakil confederations. They also recruited Zaydi tribesmen as soldiers and then relocated them to the agricultural areas of Lower Yemen whose inhabitants had to provide them with free food and shelter. Tellingly, those Zaydi tribesmen were called *Mujahedeen*: fighters for a holy war. Finally, to reward those who supported them against rivals, the imams allowed tribal warriors to enter any insurgent city for three days to loot and plunder. This occurred, for example, in 1948 in Sana'a after Yemeni reformers tried to overthrow Imam Yehia.[3]

Group grievances were a fact of life. Mohammed Ahmed Noman, the former Northern prime minister and foreign minister after the overthrow of the imamate, was one of the most vocal Yemeni politicians calling for the rights of those in Lower Yemen (he came from Taiz). In his 1965 book *The Stakeholders in Yemen* (الأطراف المعنية في اليمن), he criticized the tendency of

Yemeni political elites in the new Republic to block any discussion about the sectarian grievances of Lower Yemen, out of their fear that opening such chapters of Yemeni history would only lead to division. He reminded his readers about the Yemeni Union, a leading Northern political organization created in 1951, which called first for reform and later changed into an oppositional organization demanding an end to the imamate regime; it had been open about these issues before 1962. He cited one of its reports on the period between 26 July 1957 and 3 September 1961, which highlighted the separation and distance between Northern regions—leading to a situation where "reformers" in each region did not even "know the conditions of their compatriots in the area where the others live". The report emphasized the divergent forms of regional grievances:

> The problems that the citizen suffers from in Taiz and Ibb (Lower Yemen), for example, are other than those in Sana'a or Tihama. Consequently, the enlightened people had different reactions to the situation … for the enlightened in Taiz, for example, are hypersensitive to the grievances of the peasants, enduring [the controlling presence of] the soldier and the sheriffs; and the enlightened in Sana'a are annoyed by the intellectual repression due to religious and dynastic fanaticism.[4]

Mr Noman was a passionate advocate for the grievances of Lower Yemen, and that passion cost him his life: he was assassinated in Beirut in 1974. But while I agree with his assessment on the different nature of the grievances in Lower Yemen and Upper Yemen, I would also emphasize that the Zaydi regions too were often subject to exploitation and destruction. This is important if we are to understand the dynamics that developed after the imamate regime was overthrown.

In his memoir, Judge Abdul Rahman al-Eryani, the second president of the Northern Republic (1967–1974), recounted how his father, who considered himself loyal to Imam Yehia, was outraged at the plundering behaviour of the imam's army:

> In 1911, Imam Yehia sent an army to discipline some tribes. The army passed the city of Yarim, which is a quiet Zaydi city and loyal to Imam Yehia. So, it opened its doors to the Imam's army, proud of it as an army

struggling to liberate Yemen from the Ottoman authority. But the army, whose members were barbaric tribesmen, was horrified by what they saw in the homes of the citizens who hosted them, of belongings and money that they were not used to, so they plundered everything they could get their hands on; they even cut off the ears of women to take the earrings they had on them.[5]

When the father protested to the imam in a letter, the imam answered expressing his "understanding" of his protest. But he gave no compensation. The perpetrators were not punished. Impunity was the norm.[6]

This conduct of the imamate regime came to haunt the Hashemite stratum as a whole. In fact, once that regime was overthrown, the Hashemite stratum was specifically targeted as a group by the Zaydi Qahtani tribal stratum (Upper Yemen) and the leftist revolutionary elements from Taiz (Lower Yemen). This occurred even though a large segment of those who participated in the reform movement and the coup to overthrow Imam Ahmed were themselves Hashemites.

Why did republicans target the Hashemites between 1962 and 1967? We may find an answer if we consider the role of emotions in ethnic violence. In his groundbreaking 2002 volume *Understanding Ethnic Violence: Fear, Hatred, and Resentment in Twentieth-Century Eastern Europe*, Roger D. Peterson provides a coherent explanation of how emotions play a role in ethnic violence. In his attempt to explain ethnic violence in Eastern Europe, Petersen addresses the motivation driving individuals to commit, participate in, or support violent or punitive actions against ethnic others. An emotions-based approach defines emotion as a "mechanism facilitating individual action to satisfy an identified desire/concern".[7] It shows how emotions, caused by the conduct of the state or of core elites, lead to actions that concern us.

Emotions lead to actions to meet situational challenges in two ways.[8] One: they raise the saliency of one desire/concern over others. The assumption here is that all individuals strongly and commonly desire a few basic things: safety, wealth, and status or self-esteem. Emotions help them select among competing desires. Two: an emotion heightens both the cognitive and physical capabilities necessary to respond to the situational challenge.

Peterson uses the metaphor of a switch. An emotion acts as a switch, creating the compulsion to meet one environmental demand above all others. Four emotions—fear, hatred, resentment, and rage—are important here. Fear orients the individual to take action, fight or flight, to meet a threat. Fear is therefore instrumental because it produces actions that directly meet a pressing concern in the form of threat. Hatred prepares the individual to act on historical grievances. Resentment prepares the individual to address discrepancies in status or self-esteem. Rage is an emotion that often drives the individual toward self-destructive actions.[9]

This approach can explain the actions of republicans in targeting the Hashemites between 1962 and 1967. Resentment among those who had endured exploitation, humiliation, and violence at the hands of the imamate regimes since the tenth century was instrumental in the events that took place after the coup. Here the structural changes that resulted from the overthrow of the Mutawakkilite Kingdom eliminated constraints and fear and produced an opportunity both to commit aggression against the Hashemite group, perceived as farthest up the ethnic status hierarchy, and to attempt to subordinate the group through violence.[10]

Executions of the "men of the imam" first targeted members of Hamid al-Din family, then members of the imamate regime and his ministers, then the Hashemites as a group. They were indiscriminately targeted, mostly without any due process or trials; their heads, cut off, would be displayed with their turbans (a sign of their status) in Tahrir Square.[11]

The following story is often told to highlight the sweeping indiscriminate nature of this violence. A Yemeni Hashemite was in prison in Sana'a for some petty charges. He was brought to the execution square with other Yemeni Hashemites, of the Hamid al-Din family. One soldier noted that the man was in prison for a different charge. When he told his superior, the answer was, "Execute him, he is already here!"[12]

Whether or not this event actually occurred, one point is above dispute: many Yemeni Hashemites were killed and executed for no crime other than their bloodline. And what is cynical about this type of violence is that it was in fact instigated by a deliberate decision to frame the conflict before the coup took place as one between "Hashemites and Qahtanis". Not surprisingly, the leaders who pushed for this framing, to the chagrin of others, came from Lower Yemen.[13]

Example Two: Southern Group Grievances

The example above highlights how the actions of the state and core elites fuel division, hatred, and ethnic violence. By the same token, the actions of core elites in the South paved the way for the atrocities of 1986 and this trauma paved the way for the victory of the Saleh regime in the 1994 civil war—another trauma in the collective memory of some Southern regions (the choice of "some" is deliberate).

Political violence among groups within a state (which includes civil wars, riots, and internal ethnic conflicts) have core characteristics, Roger Petersen and Sarah Zuckerman tell us. And these go beyond structural variables, such as economic inequality, imbalances in military force, and access to political institutions. The latter variables are certainly linked to the outbreak, length, and ultimate resolution of this violence. But in themselves, they do not capture or address several salient and core qualities of political violence. Therefore, Petersen and Zuckerman suggest seven key characteristics of such violence:[14]

1. *Recognizable actors and actions:* Ethnic groups, political parties, insurgent groups, leaders, etc. are committing specific, purposeful, and blameworthy actions.
2. *Violence* often takes place among groups with long-term relations.
3. *Elements of domination and subordination:* These are introduced into group relations through violence.
4. *Intensity of experience:* Repressive actions, desecrations, killings, and bombings often produce intense new experiences that disrupt normal life.
5. *Distortion of cognitive processes:* "Intense experiences during and after violence often trigger mechanisms that distort information collection and belief formation."
6. *Elevated preferences:* The violence transforms and heightens specific preferences, specifically "the desire for flight, retaliation, and vengeance".
7. *Changing intensity of preferences:* During "hurting stalemates"[15] or in the post-violence period, conflict parties are likely to want to "move on with their lives". Continuing violence or the desire to punish the opponent may fade at this stage.

THE YEMENI CIVIL WAR

Using the first features, Petersen and Zuckerman bring in the conception of anger in political violence. They say that anger is closely tied to one's cognitive appraisal that one has been the target of a harmful action, committed by an individual or group that is to be blamed for the sustained harm. In instances of political violence, the harmful action usually involves identifiable actors (ethnic groups, political parties, insurgent groups, leaders) and their actions can be named, often exacerbating violent conflict. The action tendency of anger is toward pursuing measures of punishment against those perceived as having committed the harmful action.[16]

Recall please the tragic events of the 1986 civil war between the different factions of core elites in the socialist state of the South. How did these events lead to the ethnic cleansing that took place in the two weeks that followed? This seems to be a typical case of political violence among groups within a state, described above. I said earlier that it had a tribal and regional character; that is, it had recognizable actors and groups. The winning faction was from Dhala and Yafa and individuals from Hadramawt. The defeated faction came from Abyan and Shabwa.[17]

The conflict between these regions did not spring out of nowhere. It started, as I've described, with the competing factions within the independence movements, and continued during the socialist regime. Repeated power struggles were often shaped by ideological differences between dogmatic factions and more pragmatic ones. But when fighting took place, the regional and tribal affiliations of these factions decided the outcome. The two regions, Dhala and Abyan, often stood opposed to each other.

The 1986 civil war was the epicentre of these conflicts, with two identifiable powerful individuals. Each had his regional and tribal base, each enjoyed the support of other powerful leaders with their respective regions, each enjoyed the loyalty of specific security and army sectors, and each distributed arms to their people. President Ali Nasr Mohammed, whose regional/tribal base is Abyan, had the support of Shabwa. And Vice President and Interior Minister, Ali Antar, whose regional/tribal base is Dhala, enjoyed the support of Lahj (Yafa) and Radfan. As usual, the leaders from Hadramawt were divided between these two factions.[18] There was another central ideologist figure in this conflict, namely Abdel Fatah Ismail, allied with Ali Antar, but he came from Taiz, North Yemen, and did not have a tribal or regional backing. He was easier to kill. These core elites were all members of the politburo of the Socialist Party.

The fighting started when the president invited his opponents to a meeting of the politburo on 13 January 1986. None of the politburo members who were known for their support of the president showed up. Only the Ali Antar faction was present. A personal bodyguard of the president entered the room and started to shoot at them, in the process killing Ali Antar and several other members of his faction.[19]

Hasan Abdallah, a Southern analyst and witness to these events, points out the fatal mistake here: the president's faction was too impatient to declare victory. A statement was broadcast on the radio in the afternoon declaring that his government had foiled a coup attempt and "liquidated" those involved, naming each of those who were either killed or fled from the scene. The naming of three of them, including Ali Antar, all from the Dhala region, led to a chain of events, which culminated in ethnic cleansing. Abdallah recounts, "Once the statement was heard the whole army moved to Aden, because it was all from Dhala. You killed their leaders, ok, let's move."[20]

The atrocities that followed were horrific to a level never seen before. A person would be killed point blank, on the spot, based on the regional affiliation in his identity card. Members fighting for a certain group would be gathered in containers and buried alive. An estimated 13,000 deaths resulted from twelve days of indiscriminate fighting.[21]

The 1986 Southern civil war shocked the Southern state and its society; South Yemen had never experienced such trauma. Ali al-Sarraf, an Iraqi journalist, who researched this period in the South over several years and had extensive relationships with its political elites, describes this shock:

> The state of astonishment that afflicted the society made the party unable to push the citizens to overcome their negative attitude towards work. And somehow the country was experiencing a cold kind of despair, frustration, and general indifference, until it no longer mattered to the great majority of the citizens who had won and who had been defeated, who was right and who was wrong.[22]

That state of shock dealt a blow to the Socialist Party and even led some to question the very essence of their society. A female member of the Socialist

Party Politburo and later a member of parliament in United Yemen told me this in Aden in 2006:

> The blow was fatal to the Yemeni Socialist Party. ... We lost many cadres of the Yemeni Socialist Party, which the party had trained over twenty years. The 1986 war killed them. People felt that this war and the killing was between brothers, they used to eat from one plate, that one person would come to kill his brother, or a comrade would kill his comrade. I mean, there was something wrong with us, people began to feel that there was something wrong with our faith, and that the reason [this happened] was spiritual and religious [because of the lack of religious practice the party had imposed, their society was punished].[23]

Similar to what happened after the first civil war between the Southern independence movements, the defeated faction of Abyan and Shabwa were displaced and persecuted, and thousands fled to the North. And many military *liwas* moved to the North (a *liwa* is roughly equivalent to a brigade. It is made up of 1,500 to 3,000 men and under 50 tanks).[24] Abdrabbuh Mansur Hadi, who was president of Yemen from 2012 to 2022, was a field marshal from Abyan in the South, from the defeated faction. He moved to the North and united seven of these Southern *liwas*, in what were later called the Brigades of Unity, as a protégée of Northern President Saleh. These brigades were instrumental in supporting Saleh in the 1994 civil war: another trauma in the Southern consciousness.

The Politics of Survival and the 1994 Civil War

Survival has been the main concern of the Yemeni ethnic core elites: in the North, in the South, and in United Yemen. But former president Saleh was a master of the politics of survival.

In using the word "survival" here, I point to the ruling elites' need to undertake whatever they deem necessary to keep their hold on power and to survive in the moving sands of Yemeni politics. The term indicates the core elites' "shifting alliances with various political and social groups and their allocation and channelling of resources to these groups to ensure their hold on power and to survive in a hostile political environment".[25]

THE ROLE OF THE CUNNING STATE

Very often this allocation and channelling of resources takes the form of regional, sectarian, and tribal favouritism. Yemeni core elites juggle multiple different and sometimes competing interests, and simultaneously direct these strategies to the ultimate aim of this politics: staying in power. This feature is not particular to Yemen and is common to other Arab authoritarian regimes. The ethnic character of the core elites, however, is what separates countries such as Yemen from countries such as Egypt.

In addition to their shifting alliances, the Yemeni elites have employed other strategies of survival. What concerns us here is how they exploited the phenomenon of political Islam, by endorsing certain Islamist groups rather than others and forging political alliances with them. The main aim of this strategy has always been political: to deploy the support of these Islamist groups as a means of legitimizing the regime's rule in a religious sense and/or delegitimizing that of its rivals. The tactic has also been instrumental in undermining rival Islamist groups that pose a real challenge to the state's leadership, and sidelining, or even gaining the reluctant support of, other political groups that fear the rise of political Islam in their societies.[26]

In the Yemeni case, the instrumentalizing of the Islamist card was facilitated and supported by the tripartite alliance, mentioned in Chapter Two, between Saleh, his clan's military strongman, Ali Mohsen al-Ahmar, and the late Sheikh Abdullah al-Ahmar, the paramount sheikh of the Hashid tribal confederation.

During the Cold War, and working closely with Saudi Arabia, Northern President Saleh made use of the phenomenon of political Islam. He aimed to combat the leftist ideology exported from socialist South Yemen, which found a foothold in Lower Yemen, and culminated in a guerrilla war started by their Northern ally, the leftist Northern National Liberation Front.

The tripartite allies also worked together in exporting Yemeni fighters to Afghanistan to fight the Soviet Union. A US security report explained it this way:

> Osama bin Laden, whose family hails from the Hadramout region of the eastern Yemeni hinterland, commanded a small group of Arab volunteers under the leadership of Abdullah Azzam in the Islamist insurgency against the Soviets through the 1980s. Yemenis formed one of the largest contingents

THE YEMENI CIVIL WAR

within bin Laden's Arab volunteer force in Afghanistan, which meant that by 1989, a sizable number of battle-hardened Yemenis returned home looking for a new purpose.[27]

These fighters were then commonly called the "Afghan Arabs"; today we know them as Al-Qaeda fighters. They would prove useful during the 1994 civil war. Ali Mohsen al-Ahmar has enjoyed very close relations (including marriage relations) with some leaders of these Afghan Arabs.

When unification took place in 1990, President Saleh continued to apply the same methods that had enabled him to hold on to power in the North.[28] He "treated the South according to the principles of Northern politics, making inroads into Southern groups (from socialist leaders to tribal sheikhs and former sultans who fled the country after independence) through personal contacts, appointments, and subvention".[29] Added to the corrupting effects of these methods, the burgeoning rivalry between Saleh's ruling party, the General People's Congress (GPC), and the Southern Yemeni Socialist Party became fierce competition after unification. Soon each side sought aggressively to establish its power base at the expense of the other.[30]

Notice that the Southern leadership that agreed to unification with North Yemen was the victorious faction of the Southern 1986 civil war. The faction that lost and fled to the North, with its military brigades, became President Saleh's bargaining chip in his power struggle with his Southern vice president Ali Salem al-Beidh.

The reasons behind the war are not our concern here; what matters is that the 1994 civil war was not only fought between the North and the South. It was also fought along the Southern factional lines that developed during the 1986 civil war. In other words, the Northern tripartite alliance (whose core was in clans and tribes), and the Islamist actors, in addition to the military wing of the defeated Southern faction of 1986, mainly from Abyan and Shabwa, would prove instrumental in the victory of Saleh's side in the 1994 civil war (see Figure 8.2). Three specific points are crucial here: The al-Ahmar tribal base allowed him to command more than 100,000 armed tribesmen; they had been active in fighting against the South in the 1979 border war, and in the Islamic Front, a coalition of tribal and Islamist forces that fought against the leftist National Democratic Front militia in Lower Yemen during

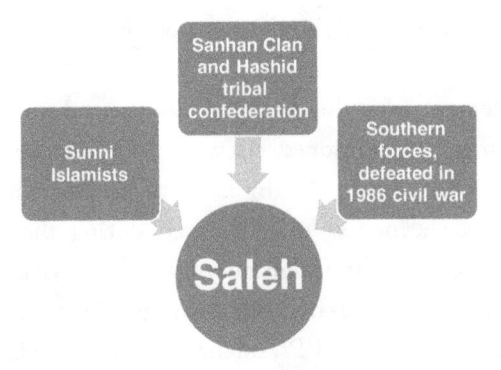

Figure 8.2: The factions that supported President Saleh in the 1994 civil war

the 1980s. Al-Ahmar joined the president in the civil war out of tribal solidarity; the president's Sanhan tribe is part of the al-Ahmar Hashid confederation. In addition, al-Ahmar deeply mistrusted the socialist regime, calling it communist, and secular, which is a slur within the Northern context. He also had much to lose if the Southern side were to win the power struggle: the Southern vice president and his allies persistently tried to disarm the tribes, to limit the tribal institution's influence in politics, and to abolish any form of military power outside the army.

The Islamists, in both their political and military wings, were also allies for Saleh and his clan strongman Ali Mohsen al-Ahmar. They were the most vocal element opposing Yemeni unification before it came about in May 1990, and justified their stance on religious grounds. When they failed to prevent unification, they decided to organize themselves into a political party. On 13 September 1990, they formed the Yemeni Reform Grouping (Islah), a broad coalition that brought Muslim Brothers and Salafi members together under the tribal leadership of Sheikh al-Ahmar. As the political crisis developed, the Islah Party sided with Saleh, who used it to further isolate the Socialist Party and its leadership. Another wing that also supported President Saleh was the militant Yemeni jihadists (Afghan Arabs) who had fought in Afghanistan and came back to Yemen, headed by Sheikh Tareq al-Fathli, leader of the al-Fathl tribe of the Southern province of Abyan. They militantly opposed the Southern leadership because of its socialist ideology, and were accused of masterminding several assassinations against leaders of the Socialist Party. The Salafi wing of the Islah Party supported these jihadists and incorporated them into high executive positions in the president's party, the GPC.

The third element was the defeated Southern leaders of the 1986 Southern civil war. As mentioned elsewhere, these leaders, based in the Southern regions of Abyan and Shabwa, fled to the North after their defeat in 1986. Given the atrocities that occurred during the war, this camp carried personal reasons for vengeance against the victorious Southern leadership led by Ali Salem al-Beidh (the vice president of unified Yemen). During the war they supported President Saleh with their army brigades, called "Brigades of Unity". From their perspective, the 1994 civil war was an opportunity to get back at those who had defeated, persecuted, and humiliated them in 1986.[31] These three tribal, ideological, and regional forces were instrumental in deciding the outcome of the war in President Saleh's favour.

If the 1986 civil war left a scar and traumatized the South, the 1994 civil war created another layer of grievances and trauma in the collective memories of some Southern regions. And the actions the victorious side took during and after the end of the war left a painful mark shaped by resentment, fear, and discontent. That mark is still alive today.

In 2006, I interviewed several Southern witnesses who lived through the siege of Aden, which started in mid-May and ended on 4 July. They showed signs of trauma as they recollected the 1994 civil war's events and its aftermath. Some interviewees expressed their deep resentment at the way the Yemeni authorities instrumentalized some religious leaders among the Salafi and Muslim Brothers: they declared that those fighting for Southern secession were infidels, which ultimately meant that their lives, families, and possessions were open targets for killing and looting.[32]

These testimonies are supported by the religious terms in which the war was framed. In Northerners' newspapers it was called the Ridda War (War of Apostasy).[33] And religious leaders kept denouncing the "separatists" publicly as apostates seeking to undermine Islam. As such, in the media and newspapers they declared them to be fair targets for killing.[34]

Fear, panic, resentment, and bitterness were the dominant emotions these interviewees expressed to me. The indiscriminate attacks and shelling into crowded districts of Aden, the destruction of water installations, the cutting of telephones and electricity, and the anarchy, chaos, and looting[35] that took place only manifested a revenge mentality. One human rights report on the conditions in the South after 7 July 1994, tells of looting and plundering of "private homes, public institutions, companies, individuals, places of worship, museums, schools, universities, service facilities, newspapers, and hospitals, under the eyes of the defeated or victorious military authorities".[36]

This report describes a situation of systematic persecution, the "displacement, expulsion and prosecution of hundreds of citizens (civilians and military); the arrest of hundreds of citizens, and the liquidation and disappearance of others. The expulsion and robbery of dozens of citizens of their homes and jobs."[37] Compounding this revenge mentality was a religious zealousness and vengeance. A number of mosques, graves, and Islamic (Sufi) shrines were demolished in both Aden and Hadramawt governorates.[38]

Systematic measures were taken to re-Islamize the South. Interviewees who lived through this period told of Islamists attacking women in Aden who did not wear the veil. Others described younger people in the South being systematically recruited to the ideologies of Islah and Salafism, and children accusing their parents of being "unbelievers", describing their parents' marriage as "void" because it was "contracted during the Party's era". Still others described how the education system in Southern provinces was overhauled: teachers were dismissed in favour of new groups of Islamist teachers—who made sure to disseminate their ideology—and several facilities in Aden received written instructions "not to hire women" and to "hire men instead".[39]

The events of the 1994 civil war have been constantly used in the narratives of Northern oppression.[40] They are still alive in Southern memory and have caused deep fissures between the South and the North while reinforcing the lines of divisions within the South itself.

The Saleh regime came out of the war thinking that a unity that took place by mutual consent could be imposed by force. The participation of the Southern "Brigades of Unity" in the civil war provided a way to legitimize a narrative that framed the war as a secessionist attempt. The appointment of Abdrabbuh Mansur Hadi as vice president was meant to counter the image of a unity imposed on the South. But that was futile. Subsequent actions by the core elites only reinforced the conviction of a unity imposed by force. The plundering of Southern lands, dividing them among key clan and tribal allies of Saleh, the mass early retirement of thousands of Southern army officers (who fought on the side of secession), and the perception of some Southerners that the North was deliberately attempting to change its demographic structure:[41] these all contributed to the rise of a Southern movement, first demanding reform and later secession.

Example Three: Saada Group Grievances

A 2020 paper on peace building in the MENA region points out why the conflicts prevalent in the region have erupted. The key is an accumulation of many unaddressed grievances, including injustice, inequality, and the exclusion of some segments of the population. These conflicts are of a "fluid type"; they "have no easily defined front lines", or "clear beginning or end". They are "refracted across space and time; and engage multiple state and nonstate actors, domestically, regionally, and often globally".[42] The paper describes the "conflict traps" in these cycles of violence. Those traps "cannot be escaped until their underlying dynamics are addressed".[43]

The six Saada wars between 2004 and 2010 can be described as "conflict traps" caused by an "accumulation of unaddressed grievances, including injustice, inequality, and the exclusion of some segments of the population". They can be traced to the troubled relations between the two Zaydi ethnic groups mentioned earlier since the tenth century and essentially to the role of the core elites since then. In modern history, several factors were instrumental in causing these conflict traps: the role of the state, core elites' power struggles, and the social structure of Yemeni Zaydi society, in addition to the role of regional neighbours.[44]

The starting point of these group grievances can be traced to the 1962–1967 Northern civil war, mentioned before. On the one hand, Zaydi Adnani Hashemites, who monopolized power for more than a thousand years in the areas they controlled in the north of North Yemen, lost their power to the Zaydi Qahtani tribal sheikhs. On the other hand, the civil war unleashed a dramatic escalation of violence, with deliberate revenge ethnic targeting of the Hashemites as a group in the areas controlled by the republicans.

What took place after that shaped the future. The regional context is important to understand these developments. As in today's war, each party to the conflict had a regional patron. The royalists—the Zaydi Hashemites—were supported by Saudi Arabia; the republicans were backed by Egypt. Both patrons were fighting a proxy war on the soil of North Yemen. Egypt was trying to export its pan-Arabism ideology and in the process destabilize its arch enemy, Saudi Arabia. And the latter looked at the Egyptian forces on its borders and saw an existential national security threat. It used the protracted war to bleed and weaken its regional rival.

Once they lost interest in the conflict, each for its own reasons, the war eventually ended. Egypt came to regret its involvement in what it termed "Our Vietnam". The Egyptian conventional military was ill prepared to defeat a guerrilla insurgency launched by royalist tribal fighters used to Yemen's mountainous terrain.

But it was Egypt's humiliating defeat in the Arab–Israeli Six-Day War of 1967 that ended its involvement in Yemen. In August 1967, Saudi Arabia and Egypt signed an agreement in Khartoum that called for a "complete withdrawal of Egyptian forces, an end of Saudi assistance to the royalists, and for Yemen's political future to be decided by the Yemenis themselves".[45] Ironically, neither the republicans nor the royalists took part in the negotiations that led to the agreement.[46] And both parties rejected it.

The royalist forces, based in Saada, led by Imam al-Badr (the son of Imam Ahmed) saw a chance to regain power. They launched a major offensive in early December 1967, engaging more than 50,000 tribesmen, but it failed, given desertions, a lack of supplies, and the fierce resistance of republican troops. Significantly, the Saudis, no longer driven by regional competition, lost interest in the war and ended all aid to Yemen by March 1968. By then, the republicans were receiving external support from the Soviet Union and were able to regain ground.[47]

But the closer relationship between republicans and the Soviet Union was short lived. Power struggles within the republican side led it to eliminate its left-wing elements, most of whom came from Lower Yemen, and to consolidate the conservative tribal groups. Judge Abdul Rahman al-Eryani stood firmly against the ethnic targeting of Hashemites and the framing of the conflict as one between the Hashemites and Qahtani, calling it "racist" and "divisive"; he became president of the Republic.[48] In 1970, Saudi Arabia brokered a compromise. Republicans guaranteed representation for the imam's supporters, and the royalists, pressured by the Kingdom, agreed to remove Imam al-Badr and his family from power.[49]

But the Hashemites' political representation in the system did not translate into actual power, or into trusting relationships. In fact, once it gained power, and engaged in a cycle of power struggles, the conservative tribal military wing had the upper hand and by the time President Saleh came to power in 1978, the Hashemite representation was diminished and sidelined. Fears that a political imamate agenda might arise again remained engrained within the republican political system. Those tribes and groups with familial or social ties to the imamate regime in Saada and in North Yemen were punished.[50]

The Cold War and its proxy regional actors provided another source of conflict. This time it targeted the Zaydi religious tradition itself. It added another deep layer of grievances, this time of a sectarian nature.

One reason why Saudi Arabia pressured its former allies to accept the compromise and later dropped them altogether was the independence of South Yemen. By now the Marxist tendencies in South Yemen had become clear and the new regime was intent on exporting its revolution to the rest of the Arabian Peninsula. It found an ally in North Yemen in the form of the National Democratic Front (NDF), created by the leftist elements that had been excluded from the political arena under President al-Iryani.

At first, the movement was little more than a deeply frustrated leftist block (mostly from Lower Yemen) in the conservative North Yemen society, but given their socialist orientation they bonded naturally with the Marxist regime in South Yemen. A guerrilla war was launched in Lower Yemen. That crucial action moderated Saudi Arabia's position towards the North. In fact, while the conservative monarchy in Riyadh saw the republican character of the Northern Yemen Arab Republic (YAR) political system as a potential challenge, it also welcomed the YAR as a potential buffer to the Marxist regime in the Southern PDRY.[51]

With the support of Saudi Arabia and their generous financial backing, North Yemeni presidents worked with various Sunni Islamist groups to find ways to counter communism. By 1982, the state had finally crushed the armed leftist group, with the help of the Muslim Brotherhood's affiliated militia known as the Islamic Front.[52]

It was within this context of the Cold War that the Northern regime, especially the tripartite alliance of the Saleh regime, although culturally Zaydis themselves, managed to build a parallel educational infrastructure all over North Yemen, designed to disseminate Sunni forms of Islamist ideologies. And these were extremist to the core and from the outset hostile to Zaydi Islamic tradition.

The regime built two forms of parallel Islamic infrastructures between 1974 and 2001: Scholastic institutes (*ma'ahid 'ilmiya*) of the Muslim Brotherhood and Salafi institutions.[53] Because they played a significant role in creating sectarian strife and division in Yemeni society, we need to look more closely at these two educational structures.

Scholastic institutes (*ma'ahid 'ilmiya*) were controlled by the Muslim Brotherhood. This modern Islamist movement propagates an exclusionary religious political ideology, seeking state political power as a means to transform existing societies into more puritanical Islamist ones.[54]

The first institute was established in the Zaydi-dominated Khawlan region north of Sana'a in 1972. The numbers of theological institutes grew rapidly, from 500 in 1982 to 1,200 in 2002, operating in North and South Yemen, with some 600,000 students. They covered all stages of primary and secondary education and hosted some 13% of the total public school student population. They provided food and boarding facilities to male students from remote areas. Although administratively and financially independent from the Education Ministry, they received huge amounts of funding from a range of sources, including the North Yemen state, the Saudi government, and private donors. Given their political function, "the Yemeni state", according to a former Yemeni official, "was at one point spending six times more per student" at these institutes than at public schools. The institutes became a key recruitment tool of the Muslim Brotherhood. The curricula invariably followed hard-line teachings close to those of Salafism.[55]

The schools, along with summer camps for male students, placed great emphasis on the concepts of *dawa* (Islamic proselytizing), and *jihad* (used in the military sense), and also focused on Sunni concepts such as obedience to the ruler. Individuals from Egypt, Sudan, and elsewhere who had been exiled for belonging to the Muslim Brotherhood were accepted as students, teachers, and administrators.

Significantly, and despite the state's support, graduates of these religious schools were not accepted into public and private universities. They were, however, allowed to enter the High Institute for Teachers and earn a primary school teaching degree. As a result, the institutes' extremist ideology was extended to the public schools via their former students, who disproportionately became teachers. The scholastic institutes were shut down in 2001 after the government decided to centralize the public education sector following the October 2000 attack on the USS *Cole* in Aden's port and the beginning of the US war on terror.[56]

Salafi institutions promoted Salafi Islam. This is a fundamentalist reading of Sunni Islam that seeks to implement Islam as it was observed during the Medina time of Muhammad and his *salafs* (companions, followers, and forefathers—hence the adjective Salafi). It emerged in a coherent form in the thirteenth century through the writings of Ibn Taymiyyah, a controversial religious scholar. His ideas were revived in the eighteenth century through various movements including the Wahhabi movement in the Arabian Peninsula. Starting in the late 1960s, during the reign of the Saudi King Faisal (1964–1975), it became mainstreamed, using oil money.[57]

The first Salafist institute in Yemen was founded in 1979 by Sheikh Muqbil bin Hadi al-Wadi'i, widely recognized as the founder of Salafism in Yemen. He set up an institute, Dar al-Hadith, in the village of Damaj, in the lands of his tribe in Saada Province, the heartland of Zaydism. To counter the anger of traditional Zaydi authorities, he sought and received tribal guarantees of protection. Dar al-Hadith became one of the most important Salafi centres in Yemen, attracting students not only from across Yemen but also from Africa, the Americas, Indonesia, Western Europe, and Arab countries, mainly Egypt and Algeria. Like the Muslim Brotherhood's scholastic institutes, it offered accommodation and food to some students. Al-Wadi'i's students soon founded their own institutes on similar lines, in other regions such as Marib, Dhamar, and Aden. Until January 2014, when the Houthi militia was finally able to close the institute and expel its residents, Dar al-Hadith in Damaj hosted a multinational community (Yemeni and foreigners) with roughly 15,000 residents.[58]

THE ROLE OF THE CUNNING STATE

The Saudis had an influence in these institutes for three reasons: (a) most of the teaching cadre had studied at universities in Saudi Arabia; (b) the teaching material relied heavily on Saudi textbooks, especially the writings of known Saudi Salafists (Ibn Baz, Ibn 'Uthaymin, al-Fawzan, al-Lahaydan, and Rabi' al-Madkhali); and (c) financial support came from Saudi preachers close to Saudi Arabia's ruling family, including al-Madkhali himself.[59]

Again, the state protected these institutes, and did not interfere in either their teaching or their extremist curricula. It persistently ignored the complaints of Zaydis in Saada and elsewhere, though the Salafis consider them to be an aberrant sect. The institutes continued to work and were encouraged and financed by Saudi and Yemeni business figures, by the Islah Party (Yemeni Reform Grouping), and even by the Ministry of Religious Guidance (Irshad), controlled by Wahhabi Salafis.[60]

State Success in Promoting Sunni Islamism

The state was successful in mainstreaming the ideology and religious teachings of these Sunni Islamist movements. But this success was hardly arbitrary. Three factors explain the rapid spread of these forms of Sunni Islamism in Zaydi areas and Lower Yemen: the grievances of the Lower Yemen region combined with the social structure of Zaydi society; the utility of Sunni Islamism for legitimizing the regime; and the politics of educational impoverishment combined with the grievances of tribespeople.

Group Grievances and Social Structure

Remember the pattern I described in Chapter Four? I called it "old and traditional in a modern package". I have observed this pattern in Syria, Kuwait, Yemen, and countries of the Arabian Peninsula. When social groups—whether sectarian, tribal, religious, or regional—find themselves excluded and discriminated against within their own society and the state system, they often find a means of countering this inferior position by joining revisionist and radical ideologies, parties, or associations. It is no coincidence that Saudi Shiite minorities were overwhelmingly members of clandestine pan-Arab and leftist movements in the 1960s and 1970s; then, after 1979, some joined the ideology of political Islam led by Khomeini in the Islamic revolution in Iran.

By the same token, Lower Yemen was often more receptive to radical ideologies calling for change or reform. Whichever ideology was the trend at the moment—pan-Arabism, socialism, or Islamism—Lower Yemen was at the forefront in embracing it. As I've said, we can interpret this as a means of expressing the regional grievances and the aspiration to change a form of domination they feel they have endured for so long. It is no coincidence, therefore, that Sunni Islamist movements in North Yemen found a stronghold in this region in the 1980s before they started to seek power in other areas.

It is also no surprise that Salafism in its Saudi Wahhabi form found a strong footing in Zaydi tribal areas. Of course, it was clearly promoted by both Saudi Arabia and the Northern Yemeni political regime. But the rigid stratification of the Zaydi tribal social structure, which I described earlier, created a welcome for an ideology that preaches that all "believing Muslims" are equal regardless of blood, colour, or social status. It was easier to recruit disgruntled members of Zaydi regions who were considered to be of "lower" status within their own society.

Consider the biography of al-Wadi'i, who built Dar al-Hadith in Saada. He was a Zaydi religious teacher, a Qahtani Zaydi from the Wada'a tribe in Saada. His father was a peasant farmer of tribal origin. He began Zaydi studies at the al-Hadi Mosque in Saada city after a short stay in Saudi Arabia. But because of his humble tribal origins, he tells us in his biography, he was rejected and not taken seriously by the local Zaydi Hashemite scholars (*Sadah*). In traditional Northern society, knowledge and learning (*ilm*) is usually the monopoly of the sons of the *Sadah* and the judges. In the 1950s, he left and settled in Saudi Arabia, where he became a Salafist. His shift from Zaydism to Salafism and his founding of his own teaching centre in his own tribal hometown look to be a "kind of social revenge", to use the words of Laurent Bonnefoy. Al-Wadi'i became a vocal opponent of the Zaydi doctrine that distinguishes between the descendants of Hashemite and other Qahtani tribesmen.[61]

Shelagh Weir tells us in her book *A Tribal Order: Politics and Law in the Mountains of Yemen* that during the 1970s and 1980s, certain segments from the Saada region and Razih in the north of North Yemen converted to Wahhabism, "while living and studying in Saudi Arabia" or "while fighting

THE ROLE OF THE CUNNING STATE

with the *Mujahidin* against the Russians in Afghanistan". Starting from the mid-1980s, leaders of this religious movement began to "propagate their beliefs through lesson circles, mosques, and colleges in their native *bilads* [hometowns] in explicit opposition to Zaydism".[62] She pointed out how remarkable it was that this Sunni Wahhabi movement flourished in the birthplace and heartlands of Zaydism. And she was spot on in explaining the reason:

> This was largely because it tapped a hitherto dormant resentment of key tenets of Zaydi doctrine still manifest there—especially the *sayyid* [Hashemite] claim to religious authority and social superiority on the grounds of religious descent, which Wahhabis felt contravened Islamic ideals by promoting inequality.[63]

Weir gives an example of Razih, a district of the Saada governorate. She explains that the most public and active converts to Wahhabism in the region were young men from tribal and butchering families. Struggling to find work and pay for the costs of marriage, and traditionally subordinate to their elders and "betters", they were "attracted to Islah [Muslim Brotherhood] (which they equated with Wahhabism) by its welfare program, and to Wahhabism by its egalitarianism".[64]

Young men in the area were not the only ones to resent the existing social stratification and *Sadah* claim of superiority. Many Razih sheikhs also supported Wahhabi Sunnism for two reasons. On the one hand, they resented their unequal marriage relations with the *sayyids*. They were often humiliatingly rejected when they asked to marry *Sharifahs*, women of Hashemite blood. On the other hand, they saw a political opportunity: they hoped that the pro-sheikh and anti-*Sadah* thrust of these ideologies would strengthen their position and bring material benefits. That had already happened among the sheikhs in the Saada region.[65]

Usefulness for Regime's Legitimacy

The state's politics of survival played an important role in spreading the ideology of Sunni political Islam and favouring its Salafi reading of Islam. I said earlier that the Northern Yemeni political elites and later those who won after the 1994 civil war have masterfully exploited the phenomenon of political Islam, endorsing certain Islamist groups rather than others and forging political alliances with them. The main aim of this strategy is political: deploy the support of these Islamist groups to legitimize the regime's rule in a religious sense and/or delegitimize its rivals. The regime thus exploited Islamism along with the three strong figures of the tripartite alliance in Yemen.

Undoubtedly the regime worked closely with Saudi Arabia in promoting Sunni Islamist movements within the regional and international contexts of the Cold War. The external factor (international and regional) aimed to counter the Soviet Union and the spread of communism in the region. But another important dimension is a question about the regime's very "legitimacy".

Unlike the Zaydi tradition and its doctrinal principle of *khuruj*, which called on its adherents to "openly challenge an unjust authority and actively rise against illegitimate rulers and oppression", the form of Salafism supported by the Saleh regime and the tripartite alliance preached exactly the opposite.

There are several types of Salafism.[66] What concerns us is the one called the purists, or the quietists, or *as-salafiya al-'ilmiya*, which is roughly translated as academic Salafism. This strand focuses on propagation, purification, and education. They view politics as a diversion that encourages deviance. Within Muslim-majority societies, they ask their followers to obey the state's political leader in order not to commit *fitna*: creating discord and chaos.[67]

Given the political implications of the purist quietist strand of Salafism, it was actively promoted by the tripartite alliance "inside" Yemen. It called on its followers to abstain from politics and focus on proselytizing. It frowned on political party activity, promoted the Sunni concept of obedience to the ruler or leader of a community, and strongly opposed jihadists on the basis that *jihad* was only to be waged on the orders of the ruler.[68]

Naturally, if a ruler were to decide that *jihad* in the military sense were necessary, these followers should oblige. We saw this when the regime's tripartite alliance exploitatively called on its Islamist followers to fight the leftist NLF in Lower Yemen in the 1970s, the Soviet Union in Afghanistan in the 1980s, and Southern "infidel socialists" in the 1994 civil war.

We also saw it when the regime pointed to "Islamist threats" in the Southern regions and growing instability in order to 'reiterate the fundamental value of the regime' to the United States and its allies in the war on terror after the 9/11 terrorist attacks.[69]

Educational Impoverishment

Shelagh Weir made an interesting point about this group in Zaydi areas who embraced the ideology of political Islam and Sunni Wahhabism and their reading of Islam. Yes, these Sunni Islamist movements attracted them because of their welfare programmes and egalitarianism. But they also credited their "education" for their "conversion". She explains:

> In contrast to their mostly illiterate fathers, who had depended on religious specialists for guidance, they had attended the first secondary schools (which opened in Razih in the 1980s) and had studied the Sunni texts then flooding Yemen and formed their own opinions. One convert explained: "we could read books the imams had forbidden and disparaged before the revolution. They prevented access to the 'truth' in order to maintain other people's inferiority".[70]

Yet another dimension helps explain how these forms of Sunni Islamism made such strong inroads in rural tribal areas. Both before and after 1962, the imams and then the tribal sheikhs were wary of any form of modern secular education that might lead to Yemenis' emancipation. This explains why the Ottomans found it difficult to introduce schools and mandatory education in the north of North Yemen. Plenty of evidence shows that the imams' policy was hardly arbitrary: it was a deliberate strategy that tapped into the politics of impoverishment (described in Chapter Three). Alas, here, it had both an educational and intellectual dimension.

Consider the case of Imam Yehia Hamid al-Din (r. 1904–1948). He was opposed to anyone introducing forms of modern education and curricula in his areas of influence. Such education, he stressed, contradicts religious values and poses a threat to the security of the "homeland". It could allow "external powers" and modernists to interfere and have destabilizing effects.[71]

In reality, this stance ensured his authoritarian grip on his subjects and protected his theocratic legitimacy. Hence, once he signed the Da'an Agreement with the Ottomans in 1911, he dismantled the educational infrastructures that had been built in the main cities: separate primary schools for boys and girls, along with secondary schools, vocational institutes, and a teachers' academy. He closed the only school for girls the Ottomans built before they departed. The tribes raided the Ottoman *Irshad* primary schools and destroyed them. In their place were erected two types of traditional religious schools: one for children in urban centres and another for a selected few to fill certain ranks and jobs in the primordial kingdom.[72]

In the first, children's education was restricted mostly to reading, writing, Islamic laws, and Arabic literature. Little was done to advance science and the arts. Although by the 1940s compulsory education was instituted, in general, the schools offered only minimal religious education and not all children were included.[73]

The second form of education, offered in religious centres and mosque circles, was an additional level of learning focused on language, Islamic law, and religious studies. It prepared a selected few from wealthy families for the positions of judges, clerks, and other functionaries. Three schools were built in Sana'a, including one for orphans.[74] These aimed to prepare for a clerical cadre but were still poorly equipped. This author's father, who, as a bright orphan, studied in the orphans' school in the early 1940s, recalled a dearth of teaching materials and curricula, despite the best efforts of the existing Egyptian, Iraqi, and Yemeni teachers. For example, on the subjects of history and geography, the curricula contained no more than "ten pages".[75]

This isolation, this deliberate policy of keeping the population ignorant, and clamping down on any modern school built in Taiz and Hodeida by reformers—including members of his family—was one more way Yahia could extend his authoritarian control. Mohammed Ahmed Zabarah explains the imam's emphasis on religious education as an attempt "to lessen spiritually subversive influences from abroad". Sadiq Mohammed Al Safwany explains that "the imam authorities believed that ignorant people were easier to rule and lead".[76] And as Juliette Honvault and Talal al-Rashoud put it, the state's "regulation of these schools, through the control of their numbers, location, and the selection of teachers and curricula, provided a basis upon which they built part of their authority".[77]

This isolationist system continued during the reign of Imam Ahmed (1948–1962) and might have changed during the time of his son al-Badr, if he had been given the chance. But Yemeni reformers from all strata of society were fed up watching Yemen fail to embrace the reforms and modernization that were spreading elsewhere in the MENA region, and the military coup of 1962 put an end to the imamate regime.

Ironically, the social group that took over, the tribal sheikhs, were also not so keen on educating their tribesmen and discouraged their learning beyond secondary school. Marieke Brandt makes an important distinction between tribal sheikhs and their tribesmen. Although the Republic promised to abolish social inequality and birth right privileges and to more equitably distribute political power, economic resources, and development, the reality was anything but fair and just. A patrimonial structure emerged in which political power was bound to persons, rather than to institutions.[78]

Northern Yemen's *Sadah* hegemony was replaced with the hegemony of the tribal sheikhs, who now, for the first time in Yemen's history, were able to shake off their former *Sadah* overlords and become part of the government itself. Significantly, this rise of tribal leaders in national politics did not translate into the empowerment of their tribes or tribesmen:

> The few thousands who have been included via their Shaykhs in the state's military or administration were (and are) by far outnumbered by millions of simple people whose economic situation and living conditions were and remained dire.[79]

These dire conditions were also connected to a deliberate politics of educational impoverishment, similar to those of Imam Yehia. According to a member of an influential tribal sheikh family in a Zaydi region, who asked to remain anonymous, these tribal leaders were often in areas aligned with Saleh's ruling party, the GPC. They often blamed the tribesmen's lack of education on infrastructure and poor teacher preparation, but in reality, it was a deliberate strategy.

Again, the fear here was that modern education might emancipate their tribesmen and weaken the strength of their traditional loyalty. Young tribesmen who sought a high school education or more were systematically discouraged. Along with discouraging further education in tribal areas, the GPC had a selective educational strategy: it reserved its scholarships for sons of tribal sheikhs.[80] Thus it kept intact the rigid social stratification in these tribal areas.

When the Sunni Islamist Islah Party started to operate in rural areas, it found a fertile ground for its ideological teachings. Two factors made it popular. First, the sheikhs allowed them to build their educational infrastructure because of their perceived "religious nature". Second, the socially marginalized groups—including butchers, barbers, and Yemeni blacks—found in Islah's education a means of social mobility and became enthusiastic supporters of its ideology.[81]

By the late 1990s, President Saleh had turned against his Islah and Salafi allies—and the Islah educational infrastructure became unwelcome in many tribal areas. Later, tribesmen who were alienated from their leaders, as described above, were easily recruited by the Houthi militia.

Thus three factors, in combination—the grievances of Lower Yemen combined with the social structure of Zaydi society; the utility of Sunni Islamism for the regime's legitimacy; and educational impoverishment—changed the religious demographics of Yemen and added another source of conflict to Yemeni society.

Social cohesion was the first victim of the dogmatic re-Islamization process. Salafi doctrines divided society. One Salafi principle was especially problematic. *Al-wala' wa-l-bara*, loyalty and disavowal,[82] called on believers to be openly hostile to polytheists, proclaim their hatred of them, and prohibit any kind of friendly association with them. This has broken families along sectarian lines. Brothers shun their own brothers, shrinking from the very idea of eating or celebrating with them. Daughters and sons reject their own parents, calling them non-believers who live in *Jahiliat* (ignorance) because they watch TV or listen to music.[83] But that is not all.

Zaydi Religious Revival and the Birth of the Houthi Militia

The encroachment of Salafi Islam and the Muslim Brotherhood ideology was bound to face resistance from the Zaydis. This came in two forms. The first had a religious revivalist dimension and led to the creation of what was called the Believing Youth Forum in Saada, only to be overtaken by the Houthi family and its supporters.[84] The other was political, mobilized through the creation of two parties in 1990: Al-Haq and the Union of Popular Forces. It sought to articulate Hashemite group grievances. Inadvertently, this resistance combined with Saleh's politics of survival, especially as he turned against his former clan allies and Sunni Islamist allies. Together, these trends led to the rise of the Houthi militia, named after the family of Badreddun al-Houthi, a Zaydi Hashemite religious leader in the Saada region.

THE ROLE OF THE CUNNING STATE

Zaydi adherents struggled to adapt to the encroachment of Salafism in their own heartland. By the early 1980s, they had become limited to study circles in mosques, especially in the Imam al-Hadi Mosque in Saada and the Great Mosque in Sana'a. Zaydi-populated regions, such as Dhamar, were gradually converted to Sunni Islam and by 2010 few mosques were teaching Zaydi Islam. But in Saada, anger was mounting among traditional Zaydi elders, who were mostly Hashemites,[85] and young Zaydi Qahtani followers, who were students of Hashemite religious teachers.

A Zaydi revival movement began in Saada. It started in 1990 in a room with eight students in the Al-Hamazat region and by 1995 it had flourished into religious camps hosting some 15,000 students. It spread into other governorates (Amran, Hijjah, Al-Mahwit, and Dhamar) and even into Shafi'i-dominated areas such as Ibb and Taiz.[86]

But this aspiration for a Zaydi religious revival was not shared by all Zaydi traditional leaders and families. In fact, Zaydi religious scholars were divided on the issue and what it would mean for the imamate concept and the role of the *Sadah*.

Among the Hashemite scholars, two positions emerged; one strongly supported revivalism and another shied away from it. Badreddin al-Houthi (1926–2010), the patriarch of the Houthi family and an influential contemporary Zaydi scholar, belonged to the first current and became one of its most recognizable leaders in Saada. Significantly, he never renounced publicly the principle of *Sadah* supremacy and right to authority. Instead, he differentiated between two types of government. One was an *imamah*, which should be held by a member of the *Sadah*; he stressed that this was the right form of government. The second was an *ihtisab*, led by an administrator who applies Islamic law but does not have the authority to make law or independent reasoning (*ijtihad*). The latter could be elected and could also be a non-*sayyid* descendant, as long as he is God-fearing. Clearly, from his perspective, the *Muhtasib* would be the exception, just a substitute for an imam when no imam or qualified *Sadah* is available.[87] Many scholars saw this distinction as artificial, just a matter of semantics; they saw he meant it as a form of *Taqiyya*,[88] an act of self-protection from the Saleh regime.

Another position was a quietist Zaydi form that rejected the *Sadah* claim to leadership. Majid al-Din al Muayydi (1913–2007), one of the most influential and respected contemporary Zaydi scholars, belonged to this current. He tried to reconcile the Zaydi doctrine with republicanism. He renounced the *Sadah* claim to leadership (*shart al-batnayn*), and argued that the conditions of Zaydi political doctrine, which restrict legitimate rule to the *Sadah*, are only valid under certain historical circumstances which are no longer present. Hence, political leadership was a right vested in the community at large. And anyone elected by the people becomes a legitimate ruler regardless of his blood descent. He formulated this position in a statement that was signed by a group of influential Zaydi religious scholars and published on 12 November 1990. He was also among the few Zaydi Hashemite scholars who advocated marriage between tribesmen and Hashemite women. Conservative Hashemite Zaydi scholars criticized him for diluting Zaydi doctrines and also for remaining silent in the face of the increasing onslaught against Zaydism.[89] Al Muayydi was not alone in his position. Zaydi religious leaders and established Hashemite families in Sana'a were also wary of the revivalist movement, fearing it would stoke a backlash against them by the Saleh regime.

Finally, in the Saada region, another current was instrumental in creating the revivalist movement. The groups who were driving the movement are Qahtani descendants and thus resentful of the Salafi encroachment in their regions and attacks on their religious tradition. At the same time, they were critical of the *Sadah* right to authority. Mohammed Azzan, a founding member of the Believing Youth Forum in Saada, belonged to this group. He engaged in a scholarly debate on the imamate theory in Zaydism and disapproved of any group's right to leadership based only on their blood line. For example, in a tract with the title *Imamate Theory in Zaydism*, he argues that in contemporary times, the imamate is "subject to positive laws (human made) for governing and can be modified and altered according to what is commensurate with the interests of the peoples and their circumstances".[90]

The above notwithstanding, all of these currents within the Zaydi population resented the rise of Salafi Islam and Muslim Brotherhood ideology, and of their dogmatic and ideological attacks against Zaydism.

In Saada, this grievance was particularly acute; people often speak of it in connection with the actions of the newly created Republic of 1962 and the encroachment of Salafism and the Muslim Brotherhood in the Saada region.

In 2020, Mohammed Azzan,[91] mentioned above, explained it to me like this: the "1962 revolution ended the imamate as a political regime and replaced it with a republic". The act was "political", and was understandable given the imamate's shortcomings. But after that, the focus turned against the Zaydi heritage itself. These Islamist movements, i.e. the Muslim Brotherhood and Salafi preachers, started to "turn the issue into a religious one: an assault against Zaydism itself". The religious institutes of the Muslim Brotherhood were promoting an ideology that "stood at odds with Zaydism"; and the Salafi preachers in Saada, "coming from Saudi Arabia", were "criminalizing Zaydism, labeling it as deviant". It was an "external invasion" and people realized they had to confront it. Thus Zaydis had to "come together to protect what they consider part of their religious and historical identity". Smiling at the irony, he insisted that "If it were not for this religious invasion, Zaydism would have died".[92]

The beginning of the Zaydi religious revival movement can be traced back to the mid-1980s. The timing coincides with the 1979 success of the Iranian Islamic Revolution in toppling the shah's regime. As a revolutionary state, which adopted a political form of Shia Islam, Iran set itself up as an outspoken leader for the contemporary Islamic world. It portrayed itself as an Islamic model that other Islamic countries should emulate. It also attacked the Islamic credentials of its neighbouring Gulf countries, specifically Saudi Arabia, and sought to export its revolution and to destabilize these regimes in the process.[93]

In Saada, people became aware of the 1979 Iranian revolution via the radio; television was not yet available in the region. They also read newspapers and magazines, which often arrived months after publication. The Zaydi population in the region enthusiastically hailed the Iranian revolution and engaged in pro-revolution demonstrations—which the government met with a wave of arrests.[94] The allegiance was political, I must emphasize, not religious. It was a response to the revisionist Khomeini political project of the new Islamic Republic. Azzan explains it this way:

> Of course, most Arabs and Muslims were sympathetic to the Iranian revolution, but the Zaydis in particular felt that they shared a common denominator with Iran, even if it was not identical. Because Iran used to call for ideas

that in the general framework were similar or close to what the Zaydis had. Particularly as the Zaydis felt that everybody conspired against them, including their own state. They felt unjustly treated and looked for anything that could preserve what they had.[95]

During the 1980s, and despite the ongoing Iran–Iraq war (1980–1988), the Islamic Republic started to export its revolution and Yemen was one of its targets. The targeting during this period took a cultural dimension; Iran communicated through its embassy with religious leaders, sheikhs, and civil society actors in all of Yemen's social segments, including the Zaydis. Invitations to visit Iran, and later on scholarships for Yemeni students, became part of this cultural outreach specifically to Zaydi Yemenis.

Again, and this point was repeated by several Houthi political leaders I interviewed, the Saada Zaydi fascination with Iran was more about its political project than about its Jaafari Twelvers religious tradition. For example, Mohammed Azzan recalls his 1986 visit to Iran with Zaydi colleagues among a delegation of young Yemeni leaders. At the time, he said, they were "young and extremist" and very much conscious of the doctrinal differences between their Zaydi tradition and the Iranian Jaafari denomination. This awareness was so strong that they refrained from praying with their Iranian counterparts and "engaged in heated discussions with them".[96]

By the same token, when members of the Houthi family developed relations with the religious seminaries (*hawza*) in Qom in Iran and with those in Najaf in Iraq, they were not converted to the Iranian Twelver Imami Shiism. The Houthi family patriarch Badreddin al-Houthi (1926–2010), a Zaydi scholar, and his son, Hussein al-Houthi (1959–2004), the founder of the movement and its militia, visited Iran after the 1994 civil war. The father went into exile after an attempt on his life. But as Haykel confirms, "there is no evidence that either [of them] converted to Twelver Imami Shiism … it is clear that al-Houthi was concerned about the preservation of the Zaydi heritage and community and was seeking ways to revive its political and religious fortunes".[97]

In fact, as a well-known Zaydi insider, with close connections to the Houthi movement, told me in 2021, the doctrinal divergence was so strong that the hard-line Twelvers scholars did not welcome Badreddin al-Houthi's teaching of Zaydism in the religious seminaries of Qum in Iran. He was harassed and his house was raided, so he returned to Yemen.[98] It was indeed the radical political ideology of the Islamic Revolution and its strong emphasis on "social justice, liberation and resistance to western hegemony and exploitation" that found resonance among this group and the aggrieved population in the underdeveloped and neglected Saada region.[99]

By now readers may be asking how an underfunded and isolated religious revival turned into a flourishing movement, and then changed into a military militia and culminated in six wars with the Yemeni state. How, indeed?

To answer this question, we have to consider two facts. First, the state played a role in encouraging this revival movement as a tool in the power struggle between Saleh and his former clan ally Ali Mohsen al-Ahmar. Second, the founder of the Houthi militia, Hussein al-Houthi (1959–2004), became radicalized. The first set of events allowed the movement to flourish unhindered and the second radicalized it and turned it in a militant direction.

Role of the State

The victory of President Saleh and his allies in the 1994 civil war was a defining political turn. Up until then the tripartite alliance, together with Sunni Islamist groups, had worked well for Saleh and his allies. Many within the military–intelligence–security apparatus who fought to defeat South Yemen in the 1994 civil war formed a base of support around Saleh's presidency. Interspersed within them were the mujahideen fighters returning from Afghanistan. Sunni Islamists were rewarded with positions throughout the Yemeni security and intelligence apparatus. Ali Mohsen al-Ahmar was the leading figure of this group and was properly rewarded with abundant military funding and control over several provinces: Saada, Hodeida, Hajjah, Amran, and Mahwit. In these regions he had more influence than the local governors.[100]

However, the tripartite alliance started to crack in the latter half of the 1990s. Saleh became overconfident, depended more on his immediate family members, and gradually started to exclude his former allies.

To weaken those former allies, he turned to an established survival strategy: he shifted his alliance to include other political and social groups, channelling resources to them as a means to counter and weaken his competitors. This time, the idea was to weaken the Sunni Islamist Islah Party with its patrons, the two al-Ahmars, using other religious movements, most importantly the quietist Salafis, who preached obedience to his rule, and the Zaydis.[101]

Saleh was cautious when he approached the Zaydi revival movement, aware of the potential that he could revive the *khuruj* principle or an imamate form of government.

Mohammed Azzan, quoted above, described the first time that he and colleagues from the Believing Youth Forum met with President Saleh in 1997. Saleh summoned them from Saada. At the time, "competing religious movements [Sunnis] were spreading negative propaganda against them". Saleh wanted to meet them in person. During this meeting, Azzan acknowledged, "one of us asked President Saleh to support our movement". Saleh replied that he was "the president of all Yemenis and could not stand by a particular movement". But then he said, "The field is before you, and you can prove your presence." He then gave an order to pay a monthly stipend of 400,000 Yemeni riyals (20 riyals at the time were equivalent to one dollar) to the Believing Youth. This tacit approval sent the message that their educational camps were working "not far from the eyes of the state".[102]

In a similar vein, Saleh started to engage with and support the political Hashemite Zaydi wing, represented by the two parties Al-Haq and the Union of Popular Forces. Zayd al-Dhari, himself a Zaydi Hashemite politician, was the mediator between the two sides. It was clear to everyone that Saleh was trying to undermine the Islah Party and their military and tribal patrons. He explained this to me in 2021:

> Saleh began to break up the [tripartite] alliance between him and these [old allies]. He took several measures in that direction. He removed those members of his ruling party—the People's General Congress—who were loyal to the Muslim Brotherhood [Islah Party]; and he undermined the Islah Party's candidates in the 1997 parliamentary elections. ... He was looking for alternatives to the Muslim Brotherhood to fill the void in the structure of the state. Religiously, those that could fill this void were the Zaydis, Sufis and Salafis. He turned to the Hashemites as an alternative. I mean, the Hashemites were part of the state, in its social fabric and in its functional fabric, but he wanted ... to enhance their role ... because the Muslim Brothers were the opposite of the Zaydis, and the Hashemites were targeted by the Muslim Brothers.[103]

From the perspective of some leadership members of the Zayidi Hashemite political parties, especially the Al-Haq Party, this signified an opportunity. Al-Dhari recounted:

> We were aware of the breakdown of the Saleh alliance and we [some within the leadership of Al-Haq] thought we could build a form of alliance with the regime of Ali Abdullah Saleh, in order to restore a comfortable environment for our political activity as well as our activity on the level of religious ideas [revivalist religious schools].[104]

Despite a hiccup in the relations between the two sides, when Al-Haq sided with the South in the 1994 civil war, the rapprochement continued in the late 1990s at the height of the tripartite falling out.

Al-Dhari repeated a conversation he claims he had with Saleh in November 1999. He told him the country was facing a threat: the struggle with the Saudi Wahhabis and Iranian Twelvers. It threatens Yemen's identity, he said, and, as president, Saleh was responsible for protecting this identity. This would entail reviving the Yemeni religious schools, in their Zaydi, Shafii, and Sufi denominations.[105] The president's response was similar to what he said to Azzan and his colleagues in the Believing Youth movement: "As president he wants stability and stability means a balance between all actors." He promised to signal his tacit approval to those Yemeni merchants who wanted to support these schools but would refrain from more for fear of the state's reprisal.[106]

Saleh did not confine his politics of survival only to the political support of Zaydi groups. In both the US war on terror and later the Saada wars, he saw opportunities to weaken his rivals.

Saleh faced enormous pressure from the United States after the 2000 bombing of the USS *Cole* and the 9/11 terrorist attacks. Washington demanded that Yemen "crack down on al Qaeda operatives and their protectors in Yemen, both within and beyond the bounds of the state".[107]

Fearful that the United States would take unilateral military action in Yemen and tempted by the large amounts of counterterrorism aid being channelled from Washington, President Saleh saw an opportunity to further marginalize his old guard and meanwhile cement his family's grip on power. He was preparing a succession plan that would see the next generation of Saleh men at the helm. To do so, he created new and distinct security agencies run by selected family members—the strongmen of the old guard—under the tutelage of the United States.[108]

He also sought to reform all security agencies to counter the heavy jihadist penetration of the Political Security Organization (PSO), a roughly 150,000-strong state security and intelligence agency controlled by Ali Mohsen.

Saleh's use of the politics of survival was not lost on his former ally Ali Mohsen, who watched nervously as his power base flattened and the members of his loyal old guard were replaced, one by one, by Saleh's closest family members.[109]

This was the context within which President Saleh used the six successive Saada wars to weaken Mohsen's strong military base. Mohsen was the commander of the 1st Armoured Division and the Northwestern Military District, which included Saada. Saleh charged Mohsen and his own son, Ahmed, with the task of combating the Houthi rebellion. That rebellion started in 2004 and continued until 2009, in six consecutive wars. Yemeni media reported that the two men's forces were in fact concurrently engaged in a proxy war in this very region.[110] The fact that the war continued despite repeated declarations of truce indicated that Saleh and Mohsen had differing opinions towards the war and that Saleh's forces used these wars to weaken Mohsen's base.[111]

But why did the Saada wars start in the first place? Here Hussein al-Houthi played a crucial role.

Radicalization of Hussein al-Houthi

Hussein al-Houthi (1959–2004) was the eldest son of Baddredin al-Houthi. A charismatic Zaydi religious leader, he had a wide religious and tribal backing in Northern Yemen's mountainous region. The Houthi movement took his family name after he was killed in the first Saada war in 2004. In comparison to the established Hashemite families and Zaydi scholars in Sana'a, his family represented a distinct group of Zaydi Hashemites. As provincial *sayyids* drawn mostly from the Saada region, they were consistently persecuted by the republican government in Sana'a, especially during the Saleh era. This was not an experience shared by the *sayyids* of Sana'a. Yes, they did lose power after 1962, but after the Saudi-brokered deal of 1970, most kept their properties and held positions in the judiciary and public administration and in business.[112]

Hussein did have a traditional Zaydi religious education. But over time, like other fundamentalists before him, he came to reject this tradition. He contended that it created a barrier between the believers and the direct and uncorrupted message of the Quran—the only authentic source of knowledge. His oral lessons, delivered in classical Arabic and colloquial Yemeni, became—and remain—the ideological and credal basis of the Houthi movement. These oral lessons were transcribed and collected in a 2,129-page document that can be found online. It is called the *Malazim* (Fascicles).[113]

His position towards the Zaydi tradition and his emphasis on the Quran as the only source of learning have been translated into concrete policies today in the Houthi-controlled areas. In a complete contradiction to traditional Zaydism and its philosophical roots, these policies recognize only the Quran as sacred, reject all other books in the entire Islamic heritage, and insist that all other learning and human literature may tarnish the purity of the faith. Zaydi study centres were closed, and traditional Zaydi religious authorities sidelined; the Houthi Islamist ideology has been systematically spread by the Ministry of Religious Endowments, and by revised school curricula. Cultural lessons are mandatory for many groups in Yemen: imams, public sector workers, and conscripts heading for the front lines, along with head teachers of schools for females, and women who recite the Quran in household rituals.[114]

Significantly, they attach the Quran to the descendants of Mohammed, setting them apart as a higher category of leaders, supreme and holy. This point has been repeatedly emphasized in Houthi rhetoric and propaganda. It was also documented in a famous pact signed in 2012 by Houthi leaders and some famous Zaydi scholars. It was meant to bridge the differences between the two sides. Entitled the Intellectual and Cultural Charter, it insisted that the only approach to guidance, salvation, and safety involves holding to two forces: "The Book of God [Quran] ... the source of guidance and light. And ... the family of the Messenger of God, the guides of the nation, and the companions [counterparts] of the book."[115]

Hussein al-Houthi continues to be called the Speaking Quran (*Quran Natiq*) and his *Malazim* are core to the ideological indoctrination measures of today's Houthi movement today; the way they are taught and spread makes them even more relevant to the movement than the Quran itself. This system of indoctrination reminds one of the strategies the Sunni Islamists used once they came to power. The Houthi movement, we have heard repeatedly, imitated the methods of the Muslim Brotherhood institutions in Yemen.

Hussein al-Houthi has become a cult figure, portrayed and used by the movement as a holy figure, in a manner that reminds one of the holiness attached in the Shia tradition to Hassan and Hussein, the murdered grandsons of the Prophet of Islam. That he was killed in the first Saada war only adds to this aura. He is the "Martyr leader" (*al-shahid al-qaid*), the "Quran's Companion" (*Qarin al-Quran*). Songs (*anashied*) have been dedicated to him. One famous song has the title "The Martyr of Quran". It is played by a male band, dedicated to him only, called the Martyr Leader Band (*Firqat al-shahid al-qaid*).[116]

Hussein al-Houthi's story is one of radicalization. It reminds one of other radical Islamists, such as Sayyid Qutb (1906–1966), the leader of the Egyptian Muslim Brotherhood, who was radicalized, among other experiences, in Egyptian prisons and became the father of Jihadi Sunni Islamism. The story of Qutb's Yemeni Zaydi counterpart is equally complicated.

Hussain was once a rising political aspirant in Yemen, and a member of the Yemeni parliament for the Al-Haqq Islamic party between 1993 and 1997. In fact, my interviewees, both supporters and detractors, acknowledge that when he started his political career, he was hopeful that the political opening produced by the 1990 Yemeni unification would allow him to advocate for his region and for Zaydi Hashemites within the system. In fact, as Marieke Brandt tells us, he was influenced by one of his teachers, who maintained that there are two acceptable ways of practising Zaydi *khuruj*, through *force* or *elections* (my emphasis). In 1993, he took the position that political change should result from free elections.[117]

But when the 1994 civil war broke out, Hussein al-Houthi supported the Southern vice president Ali Salem al-Beidh. He tried to mediate as a member of a reconciliation committee. When mediation failed and war continued, he left Sana'a, defying a Saleh directive that prohibited members of parliament from leaving the capital. Once in Saada, he organized demonstrations rejecting the war. This prompted a backlash from the Saleh regime, which accused him of "supporting secession".[118]

Once the war ended, the Saleh regime retaliated. On 16 June 1994, a major military campaign was dispatched to Saada. Saleh launched a campaign of massive arrests, and destroyed the houses of Hussein al-Houthi and his father Badrredin. The two had to leave the country and landed, after a short stay in Syria, in Iran. There he was fascinated by the Khomeini revolutionary political project, as I mentioned earlier.

But he did try to engage in politics again and entered the 1997 parliamentary elections as an independent, having left the al-Haqq Party. Some say this was due to ideological differences with members of the party. Other sources, such as a WikiLeaked classified US diplomatic document, suggest that President Saleh promised al-Houthi his support in the election, "if he distanced himself from his party and aligned with the ruling GPC party". Accordingly, Hussein did just that, only to discover that he had been lured by empty promises. He soon realized that the aim was to keep him under government eyes in the capital and away from his base of support in Saada. Indeed, the president's office deliberately campaigned against Hussein—and in the 1997 parliamentary election he lost his seat to another GPC member.[119]

Disappointed, he left again, this time on a government scholarship to Sudan. His aim was to earn a master's degree and then a PhD. Bernard Haykel believes that he may have thought this academic credential would help him in a leadership role after his return. But Sudan turned out to be instrumental in further radicalizing Hussein al-Houthi. During the 1990s, it was a hotbed of Islamist movements. Khartoum's military regime was allied with the Muslim Brotherhood, and the city hosted large international gatherings and a plethora of Islamist groups and leaders, including Shiite Islamists as well as Osama bin Laden and members of Al-Qaeda. Hussein al-Houthi was exposed to many revolutionary Islamist ideologists during his stay.[120]

He obtained his master's degree in 2001 and was working on his doctoral thesis in Islamic studies when family health issues prompted him to return to Saada. His scholarship was cancelled by the government, the confidential WikiLeaks memo tells us, and he could not return to Sudan.[121]

Once back in Saada, he turned his attention to the Believing Youth educational camps. He had not played any part in founding this movement, though his brother Mohammed did, along with Mohammed Azzan. These educational summer camps proved to be very successful. Again, they followed in the steps of the ideological camps of the Scientific Institutions of the Muslim Brotherhood. They placed a heavy emphasis on artistic and sporting activities as well as a religious curriculum based on small religious books that did not touch on political or sectarian subjects but rather carried simplified religious teachings.[122] The importance of the camps, Maysaa Shuja al-Deen tells us, lies in the fact that, "for the first time, they created a young community brought together by their ideas of Zaydi identity as sons of the tribes, or Hashemites. Through this shared identity, some Zaydi figures were able to gain influence over these youth."[123] It also played a role in allowing Zaydi scholars of tribal origins, such as Azzan, to have influence over these youth. This explains why several Hashemite Zaydi scholars attacked these camps in Saada.

When Hussein al-Houthi returned from Sudan, he fell into disputes with some of these leaders, including Azzan. He sought to politicize the Believing Youth in a way the founders did not appreciate. He criticized these camps "for only being an educational association, and not rising to the next necessary step of becoming a movement".[124]

By 2002, the camps were split into two sections: one following Azzan and one following Hussein al-Houthi. The latter endorsed study materials that promoted a religious political ideology—one that had been rejected by the original founders of these Believing Youth.[125]

In the years just before his death, his group began to be known as *harakat al-shi'ar* or the movement of the slogan, the shout. The slogan, which now appears on the movement's flag and is repeated by its followers in the mosques and rallies, says: "Death to America; Death to Israel; Curse the Jews; Victory to Islam". It is a twisted modification of the Khomeini slogan, "Death to America". The latter, *marg bar Amreeka* in Farsi, dates back to before the 1979 Iranian Revolution. Once used by communists, it was popularized by Ayatollah Ruhollah Khomeini, Iran's first supreme leader after the militants took over the American embassy.[126]

Some attribute Hussein's use of the "shout" to the second Palestinian Intifada, others to the US invasion of Iraq.[127] Houthi sources set the date at 17 January 2002, a year after the 9/11 attacks and the subsequent war on terror, and immediately after he returned from a visit outside Yemen. The country he visited was not specified in the sources.[128] But we can assume that the country was either Iran or Lebanon, where he had good relations with Hizballah.

THE ROLE OF THE CUNNING STATE

Once in Saada, he gave a lecture, recorded with the title "The Shout in the Face of Arrogants [*sic*]".[129] The lecture, whose transcript runs to eleven pages, was a non-stop rant, infused with anger at the United States, Israel, and the "Jews". They are launching a war against Islam and Muslims, he tells his audience. His language is laced with conspiracy theories and blatant antisemitism. He sets himself clearly in the camp of Hizballah and Iran. And he insists that Muslims have a duty to rise up against these anti-Islamic forces. The shout, he insists, is the way to stand up against them. It shows that Muslims fear no one but God.

Houthi supporters started to use the "shout" wherever they were. It started to attract the attention of the state's security agencies, especially as the Saleh regime was cooperating with the United States in its international "war on terror". Then, in 2003, the US invasion of Iraq gave Hussein al-Houthi and his "shout" the fuel he needed for his ideology. The shout became an indirect criticism of the Saleh regime, which the movement painted as a "corrupt stooge of the United States and Israel". The state's authorities took a firm stance against these chanters, arresting approximately 800 individuals throughout numerous Friday prayer gatherings, and further fuelling anti-government sentiments in Saada.

It was the shout that sparked the first Saada war in 2004. When President Saleh passed through Saada on his way to the Hajj pilgrimage in Mecca, al-Houthi "sent protesters to chant the shout outside the Saada Mosque where Saleh had stopped to pray. After prayers, the president attempted to give a speech, but was impeded by three men loudly chanting the slogan." Once back from his travels, Saleh summoned Hussein al-Houthi to Sana'a—twice. And twice al-Houthi agreed to meet Saleh but on his way to Sana'a he was intercepted by government troops, who were sent to address an unrelated tribal conflict. "Three of these troops were killed reportedly, while trying to break up a drug smuggling confrontation in the province. Saleh believed that al-Houthi was behind the death of the three soldiers. Fighting erupted."[130]

Following this incident, al-Houthi and his followers took to the mountains of Marran in Saada. Hussein al-Houthi was asked to surrender, but he refused, setting off the first armed confrontations with the Yemeni state in 2004. On 10 September 2004, after approximately ten weeks of fighting, he was killed, and his body decapitated.

The state's indiscriminate actions towards the population of Saada after this first war popularized the Houthi movement and explain how it grew in popularity.

Azzan, who fell out with al-Houthi and did not agree with his political ideology, explains it in these words:

> The war targeted everybody. It did not distinguish between a Houthi (supporter) or a believing youth. And when it targeted everybody, it mixed everything together. People felt the Houthi were not really the target. Rather, the youth, those who believe in Zaydism, the Hashemites, and the people of Saada. They started to come together and protect themselves. The brothers of Hussein al-Houthi did not fight with him in this first war. And yet they were targeted. So, when all were targeted, all came together.[131]

And the rest is history.

9 Conclusion: Yemen's Transition Towards Chaos

In Chapter Two, I asked, "Where do we start our analysis? When did this civil war start?" Those questions were not rhetorical. By now, it must be clear that this civil war was in the making long before it began. The regional rivalry and interventions, combined with the Saudi/Emirati/Iranian proxy wars, are certainly important. This will be made clear in the forthcoming volume, *Gulf Rivalry and the Yemeni Civil War*. But the Yemeni civil war would still have happened, with or without the regional rivalry. The key catalysts are still internal ones. We must all recognize this fact if we are to have sustainable peace in Yemen.

So first, a recap. What is the purpose of this project? Its starting point is the first wave of the Arab uprisings: popular protests that brought together different segments of society, frustrated by economic and political stagnation in their societies, demanding radical change, with divergent contexts and outcomes. They began in Tunisia on 16 December 2010 and spread to Egypt, Libya, Yemen, Syria, and other countries, and managed to topple the incumbent presidents of these five states.

My purpose in this project has been to understand the outcomes of the Arab uprisings. Not their democratic transitions—those didn't happen. Rather, I have sought to explain the meltdown of countries such as Yemen, Syria, and Libya.

Countries that experienced popular uprisings had a range of outcomes. Tunisia experienced a fragile (now shattered) democratization process, while Egypt reverted to a form of military authoritarianism. In these two cases, the state remained intact, albeit shaken. Other countries, such as Yemen, Syria, and Libya, experienced a meltdown of the political order, along with civil war and fragmentation. The state was torn between competing factions and groups, in the process exposing its ethnic character.

The question I pose here is straightforward: Why?

In this volume, I present the first part of my argument that the interaction between different types of state formation and regional rivalry explains differentiated reactions across different MENA countries. I focus the discussion here on a detailed consideration of the factors involved in state formation using Yemen as a case study.

I argue that the interaction between different types of state formation *and* regional rivalry can explain, respectively, the civil wars of countries such as Yemen, Syria, and Libya, and the preservation of the Bahraini system, despite its ethnic nature. Egypt and Tunisia exhibit further variants of statehood and national identity—which have enabled them to withstand the shocks their systems have been experiencing. That does not mean these two states are immune to new uprisings or to political instability. What it does mean is that the type of violence they could witness will not have an ethnic character of the type seen in Yemen, Syria, or Libya.

To explain these outcomes, I propose a framework of analysis of two interconnected levels: First, an internal level focusing on the state formation of the observed country, discussed in this volume. Second, a regional level examining the operational context within which each country is functioning, and the type of actors involved in its political affairs, to be discussed in *Gulf Rivalry and the Yemeni Civil War*.

In this framework of analysis, and across the two volumes of this project, I apply Joseph A. Maxwell's approach of critical realism. This approach captures the complexities of reality shaped by narratives and perceptions and allows me to make sense of the divergent and contradictory narratives of the different Yemeni warring factions. It combines a realist ontology with a constructivist epistemology. In other words, it recognizes that there is a real world that exists independently of our beliefs and constructions. At the same time, this approach accepts that our knowledge of this world is inevitably our own construction, created from a specific vantage point. But I insist that there is an objective world out there that can be understood and discovered. How we make sense of it may differ according to our perspectives.

CONCLUSION: YEMEN'S TRANSITION TOWARDS CHAOS

This volume is focused on the first level of analysis—the state formation—and uses Yemen as a case study. I address the second level separately in the second volume. Focusing our attention on the first level, I classify countries in the Arab MENA region according to their state formation. Simply put, I see two types of states. The first is countries that are old states and old societies. These are characterized by a long tradition of centralized state apparatus and the existence of a strong national identity. This group includes Egypt, Tunisia, and to a lesser extent Morocco.

The second is countries that are new states and old societies. These are characterized by the youth of their states, the lack of a coherent national identity, and the division of society along tribal, religious sectarian, linguistic, and regional lines. The Arabian Peninsula countries, along with Syria and Libya, are examples of this group.

The difference between these two groups of states can be seen in their types of political elite and their power base: traditional (ethnic) or cliental. This difference can explain to a great extent why it was possible for the Tunisian and Egyptian presidents to step down without bloodshed and why, in contrast, the removal of the Yemeni and Libyan presidents, and the attempt to do so in Syria, led to their countries' meltdown and the outbreak of civil wars.

The difference explains to a great extent how the army in each set of states acted towards the uprisings. In Egypt, the army is perceived as a national army. More to the point, Hosni Mubarak and his family were just a family, and as influential as they may have been, it was possible to pressure them to step down without threatening the collapse of the whole system.

On the other hand, in countries such as Syria, Libya, and Yemen, the armies were and still are based on ethnic affiliations. At the time of the uprisings, these were: in Syria the Alwaite and other minorities; in Libya the Qadhadfa, al-Warfalla, and al-Magariha tribes; and in Yemen the Sanhan clan and Hashid tribal confederation. As a result, each national army has acted as an ethnic bodyguard of the ethnic core elite. In protecting the elites, it guaranteed its own survival—and that of the overall system. In the demise of these ethnic core elites, it saw its own downfall. Naturally, getting rid of the incumbent core elites was destined to be bloody; hence the civil wars in Yemen, Syria, and Libya.

The nature of the core elites in the countries of the Arab uprisings is one part of the puzzle and is strongly tied to these countries' different paths to state formation. Which brings me to my main argument in this volume: To understand the divergent outcomes of the first waves of uprisings, we must focus our analysis back on the state itself. We must look at its formative moments and evolving processes, and understand its formation in relation to specific contextual factors.

Doing so requires an interdisciplinary approach. I have moved away from a Eurocentric focus on European and North American forms of state formation, and instead recognized that countries of the MENA region have had a variety of distinct historical and institutional experiences. I have also moved away from a postmodern fixation on colonial legacies, to include other legacies and other factors specific to the region.

Hence, to bring the state back into my contextual analysis of the MENA region required looking at the main factors that played decisive roles in shaping each state's formative moments. I showed that five factors were most important:

a. the types of social structures and the roles they play, combined with the legacy of geography;
b. religious beliefs and their impacts;
c. legacies of the Ottoman and colonial periods;
d. the role of ideologies, including pan-Arabism and pan-Islamism; and
e. the role of the political elites in the post-independence period.

In other words, my approach entailed looking at the legacies of both the past and the present, in the specific context of the MENA region.

Applied to the Yemeni context, I showed the results of three legacies.

First, legacies of geography, tribes, and religious beliefs. I described three important historical facts. One, Yemen as a geographical space (North and South) was always larger than the different ethnonationalist political forms that inhabited it concurrently. Two, the political dogmas of Zaydism, introduced in North Yemen in 893 CE, and the ethnic affiliations of its followers in the Qahatni and Adnani tribal identifications, planted the seeds of the recurrent instability that still exists today. The Houthi rebellion is connected to this dimension and to the ramifications of the 1962 Northern civil war. Three,

CONCLUSION: YEMEN'S TRANSITION TOWARDS CHAOS

although the imamate policy of impoverishment and oppression was used against Zaydi populations, it had a stronger impact on the populations in Lower Yemen. The division between Upper Yemen and Lower Yemen within North Yemen started in the tenth century and the religious justifications the imams used to take over these Sunni Shafite regions left deep wounds in the collective memory of their populations.

Second, legacies of Ottoman imperialism and British colonization. In North Yemen, the Ottoman Empire left three impacts. It left a regional divergence in state and administrative capacities between Lower Yemen and Upper Yemen. The empire's practice of indirect rule strengthened the power of traditional leaders: *Sadah*, tribal sheikhs, lords, and jurists. And it perpetuated a system of sectarian difference between Lower and Upper Yemen. In what became South Yemen, the British left two major impacts as they colonized Aden in 1839 and created protectorate relations with the sultanates and statelets in the south of Arabia. As the Ottomans had in the North, they left behind a regional divergence in state formations and administrative capacities; Aden was much more advanced, compared to the Eastern and Western protectorates. And the British constructed South Arabia as a political unit as a means to counter Nasser's pan-Arabism, without any real foundation for such unity. The Southern independence movements were divided in their demands: some called for separate political states for Aden or protectorate units; some called only for South Arabian unity; and some insisted on pan-Arab unity. All those calling for unity saw it as a step towards something greater: the unity of the whole Arab MENA region. And yet, even when these movements were emphatically calling for unity, they were divided among themselves, shaped by regional and tribal affiliations, and recruitment methods based on personal, regional, and tribal loyalties. These lines of division remain relevant today in the Yemeni civil war.

Third, legacies of the cunning state and the politics of survival. This is the legacy that most strongly shapes the present. The cunning state is a state run by ethnic core elites, who exploit the ethnic divisions of their own society, and constantly engage in the politics of survival, with the goal of perpetuating their grip on power. A state may inherit difficult legacies, like those two described above, and yet develop a government that values inclusion, the rule of law, and transparency. That did not happen in Yemen and has yet to occur there. The features of the cunning state brought Yemen to the point where it is today. One key feature is its politics of survival: the Machiavellian approach of undertaking whatever is necessary to survive in the shifting sands of politics. In order to survive, it has constantly manipulated Yemen's three lines of division: sectarian (doctrinal), tribal (clan), and regional/geographical; it has also exploited ethnic identities, playing and depending on them, and has extracted resources using methods of co-optation. After decades of this behaviour by the cunning state, Yemen had become a fragile state animated by group grievances. The civil war was a given: an expected outcome. And today, the actors in its conflict are engaged in a similar pattern of divisive tactics to ensure the cunning state will survive.

How Things Spiralled Out of Control

The Yemeni youth uprisings, as discussed in Chapter Two, were an outcome of true agency. Yemeni youth revolted in several cities. Their aspirations were real, sincere, and authentic. But the young people were few, and they had no wider social backing, or tribal or military cover. And they were not well organized. Given the structure of the regime, those facts together created the space for the core elites, tribal and military, to hijack their aspirations.

Remember, please, that at the time of the Yemeni youth uprisings, four concurrent crises were brewing and destabilizing the Yemeni political system. (1) The core elites, who have controlled Yemen over the past three decades, were engaged in a power struggle. (2) The Houthis, in the Northern region of Saada, were engaged in a rebellion which led to four wars, the last of them in 2009. (3) An independence movement in the Southern region was calling for the separation of the South. (4) And Al-Qaeda-affiliated Islamist groups were leading an insurgency within some Southern provinces. All of these crises are connected to the legacies of the past and present of Yemeni state formation discussed in this volume. All are caused by the legacy of the cunning state and its manipulation of the three lines of division in Yemen: sectarian (doctrinal), tribal (clan), and regional/geographical.

When the 2011 youth uprisings took place, some may have thought that it put all of the four concurrent crises on hold, and that the three division lines were receding and carried less meaning. But that was not the case. In

CONCLUSION: YEMEN'S TRANSITION TOWARDS CHAOS

fact, the uprisings provided an excellent opportunity for the tribal and military strongmen of Saleh's tripartite alliance to come together and get back at Saleh and push for his departure. Many anticipated that would destabilize the whole system. Fearing that Yemen would collapse and wary of another expansion of Iranian influence, the Gulf Cooperation Council introduced the Gulf Initiative,[1] which was meant to provide Saleh a safe exit from an explosive situation but without rocking the boat for Yemen or for the region.

The Gulf Initiative, and the Implementation Mechanism that was based on it, were pacts among elites. They set out an interim and transitional system of power sharing that aimed to put a temporary governance structure in place to manage the transition and (ideally) pave the way to elections and a new or revised constitutional state structure.[2] But these efforts failed to break Yemen's cycles of violence and inadvertently exacerbated ongoing conflicts, leading to another open civil war.

A closer look at the content of the Gulf Initiative, as announced on 21 April 2011, gives the impression that its main objective was to address the power struggle between the old core elites, to contain it and to protect these very strongmen. These were the very figures who had brought Yemen to the brink of collapse.

The Initiative called for Yemen's President Ali Abdullah Saleh to delegate his authority to his vice president, Abdrabbuh Mansur Hadi, and to set a ninety-day period within which Hadi would call for presidential elections. And it ensured that only one candidate would run in this election: Hadi. It also ensured that after the vice president was elected president, he would be responsible for overseeing the creation of a national unity government. In reality, it simply recycled the old regime in a new package. The national unity government was divided on a 50:50 basis between the government and the opposition. It was equally divided between Saleh's ruling party, the GPC, and its allies, and the National Council. The council included the JMP, a coalition of six political parties, the core of which is the Sunni Islamist Islah party and the Yemen Socialist Party (YSP)—and their partners.[3]

Both sides had been part of the governing regime in Yemen before and after the unification. And their main actors—the GPC, Islah, and the YSP—have been integral in causing and committing grievances and violations during

Yemen's recurrent civil wars and political conflicts, both before and after unification.

In addition, the Initiative demanded that the new president establish a constitutional committee to oversee the preparation of a new constitution, which should be submitted to a popular referendum. Once approved, a time frame for parliamentary elections was to be determined.[4]

Finally, the Initiative stipulated immunity for Saleh and his strongmen. It read: "Parliament, including the opposition, shall adopt laws granting immunity from legal and judicial prosecution to the President and those who worked with him during his time in office."[5]

Notice please that the Gulf Initiative, the one announced on 21 April 2011, deliberately excluded two key elements of Yemeni society:

- The Houthi militia were excluded, because the GCC feared Iranian influence and the Yemeni core elites insisted on excluding them.
- The Southern movement was excluded because of the legacy that included the Southern division, the 1994 civil war, and the Initiative's insistence on Yemeni unity.

Thus, from the outset, the Initiative's scope was limited; another reason for the limit was the international community's two key priorities in dealing with Yemen:[6] fear that Yemen will collapse and the focus on the international war on terror. The first priority has led to an emphasis on sustaining peace, however fragile it may be. The second priority has led to security actions, including drone attacks that have often killed civilian bystanders, and further eroded the legitimacy of the Yemeni state. In addition, the close cooperation between the Yemeni security apparatus and the United States and Gulf States in the fight against terror has made it undesirable, indeed quite risky, to pursue any real institutional reform that could undermine this alliance.[7]

By itself, the Gulf Initiative did not succeed in ending the power struggle within the core elites. The situation remained volatile and military confrontations took place. President Saleh refused to sign the Initiative, despite repeated promises to do so. He also survived an assassination attempt on 3 June 2011: a bomb was planted in a mosque within the presidential palace.[8] Thus it was hardly a surprise when tensions escalated, leading to a civil war between the strongmen of the tripartite alliance.

CONCLUSION: YEMEN'S TRANSITION TOWARDS CHAOS

To end the deadlock and defuse the tension, while addressing the shortcomings of the GCC Initiative, Jamal Benomar, the Special Adviser to the Secretary General of the United Nations, stepped in. He facilitated the "Agreement on the Implementation Mechanism for the Transition Process in Yemen in Accordance with the Initiative of the Gulf Cooperation Council". Saleh did finally sign it in Riyadh on 23 November 2011, but he required guarantees that a law would be promulgated to give him full immunity.

Hence, a law was introduced on 22 February. It provided former president Ali Abdullah Saleh a safe exit and "complete immunity from legal and judicial prosecution" in exchange for stepping down from power. Immunity was not only meant for the president. It was extended to those Yemeni officials "who have worked under the President—in state civil, military and security agencies—in connection with politically motivated acts carried out during the course of their official duties".[9] That the Immunity Law was formulated in this way reveals the desire to grant protection not only to associates of the president, but also to the rival faction within the core elites, including Vice President Hadi, and the strongman Ali Mohsen al-Ahmar, both of whom were implicated in human rights violations during their work with Saleh.[10]

The Implementation Mechanism introduced a transitional period of two phases. The first phase began with the entry into force of this Mechanism and ended with the inauguration of President Hadi, following the early presidential elections. The second phase was to last for two years; it began with the inauguration, and was to end with the holding of general elections in accordance with the new constitution and the inauguration of a new president of the Republic.[11] Those general elections and thus the inauguration of a new president never materialized. The constitution that was agreed upon during the National Dialogue was written but remained in a drawer.

Moving beyond the limits that the original Gulf Initiative had imposed on the process, the Mechanism established two institutions.

The first was the Committee on Military Affairs for Achieving Security and Stability. It had several objectives. It aimed to end the division in the armed forces and address its causes, end all the armed conflicts, ensure that the armed forces and other armed formations would return to their camps, end all armed presence in the capital Sana'a and other cities, and remove militias and irregular armed groups from the capital and other cities. Most importantly, the Committee was assigned the task of creating the "necessary conditions and tak[ing] the necessary steps to integrate the armed forces under unified, national and professional leadership in the context of the rule of law". In other words, it was assigned the task of creating a national army to replace the existing ethnically based army.[12]

The second institution was a Conference for National Dialogue. This conference was meant to address the shortcomings in the Gulf Initiative and its exclusion of the Houthi militia and the Southern movement. It also aspired to be inclusive in the real sense, involving women (who were to be represented in all participating groups), along with youth and civil society representatives as main categories in the dialogue, in addition to the political actors, political parties, and core elites who were parties to the conflict. The National Dialogue was responsible for drafting the constitution; it was also to establish a Constitutional Drafting Commission and its membership, suggest constitutional reforms, address the structure of the state and political system, and submit constitutional amendments to the Yemeni people through a referendum.

That was not all. It was also expected to address "the issue of the South in a manner conducive to a just national solution that preserves the unity, stability and security of Yemen", and examine the "various issues with a national dimension, including the causes of tension in Saada". And it was to take steps "towards building a comprehensive democratic system, including reform of the civil service, the judiciary and local governance" and steps "aimed at achieving national reconciliation and transitional justice, and measures to ensure that violations of human rights and humanitarian law do not occur in future". Finally, it was to adopt "legal and other means to strengthen the protection and rights of vulnerable groups, including children, as well as the advancement of women".[13]

These two institutions were truly ambitious (to say the least!) and provided potential solutions to Yemen's recurring instability. But they were introduced during the transitional period, so they provided seeds of volatility that further destabilized the Yemeni state.

Civil wars do occur in such transitional periods, says Barbara F. Walter, a political scientist who specializes in civil wars. She bases her position on data collected by scholars and experts on civil wars. Regimes that are moving from autocracy to a democratization process are called anocracies. The term was

CONCLUSION: YEMEN'S TRANSITION TOWARDS CHAOS

first coined in 1974 by Ted Robert Gurr, a professor at Northwestern University, who had amassed data on the traits of democratic and autocratic governments around the world. He settled on the term anocracy after debating with his team what to call such "hybrid regimes".[14]

Anocracies are regimes that are neither fully democratic nor fully autocratic. They combine a mixture of democratic and autocratic traits and practices. Among their features are "inherent qualities of instability or ineffectiveness", and they are "especially vulnerable to new political instability events, such as outbreaks of armed conflict, unexpected changes in leadership, or adverse regime changes".[15]

The features of these regimes can exacerbate the potential for conflict. Walter put it this way:

> A primary reason for revolt is that democratic transitions create new winners and losers: In the shift away from autocracy, formerly disenfranchised citizens come into new power, while those who once held privileges find themselves losing influence. Because the new government in an anocracy is often fragile, and the rule of law is still developing, the losers—former elites, opposition leaders, citizens who once enjoyed advantages—are not sure the administration will be fair, or that they will be protected. This can create genuine anxieties about the future: The losers may not be convinced of a leader's commitment to democracy; they may feel their own needs and rights are at stake. And because the government is weak, events can easily spiral out of control.[16]

Things did spiral out of control during Yemen's transitional period. Naturally, the attempt to create a national unity army encountered persistent resistance from Saleh's close relatives who controlled the army and security apparatus. The resistance to institutional reform was to be expected given that it touched on the interests and privileges of Yemeni strongmen. And the inclusion of transitional justice[17] as a primary objective in the National Dialogue backfired. The demand for "non-judiciary" justice, combined with the fear of "truth seeking", seemed to touch on a broader issue and thus brought to light the precarious situation of the transitional period and the fear of unleashing old ghosts. That broader issue was the history of human rights violations committed in both North and South Yemen before and after the unification. Then, consider how, in the tangled political history of Yemen's wars and conflicts, a victim sometimes became a perpetrator and vice versa. This still occurs today. And the fear of revenge and bloodshed in a tribal context is often mentioned as a reason for such reluctance.[18] Lack of trust among the core elites and the other political actors and parties—tribal, military, sectarian, and regional—shaped their actions.

In short, the transitional period was fraught and destabilizing. My interviewees, in their diverse backgrounds, did agree on this.

In 2020, I conducted a round of interviews as a prelude to two later rounds of interviews, along with fieldwork and archival research. I was interested in understanding the reasons behind Yemen's recent disintegration into civil war from the perspectives of those who were part of the process. Thus I conducted thirty-six online interviews between 11 June and 14 September 2020 with a variety of Yemeni stakeholders and parties to the conflict. Those interviewees include representatives of the Houthi militia (Ansar Allah) and the Southern Transitional Council, former Yemeni ministers, representatives of Yemeni civil society, and women's activists, in addition to scholars and journalists from both Yemen and the Gulf who have expertise on the conflict and its regional setting. I also tapped two former ambassadors to Yemen, one American and one British, for their knowledge of the transitional period that followed the Arab Spring. I used a variety of online tools, including Zoom, Skype, WhatsApp, and Imo. These interviews shaped some of the dimensions mentioned in this portrayal of the current conflict.[19]

If we are to pin down the reasons behind Yemen's recent disintegration into civil war, we must consider several factors repeated by these interviewees. They all alluded to the transitional period that followed the signing of the Gulf Initiative on 23 November 2011.

The interviewees described a pattern of lack of trust, old elites fearing loss of their privileges, new elites adopting the cunning state conduct of power, and all actors acting in bad faith. They listed several developments, mentioned above, that together ruined the settlement:

- President Hadi, interested in holding power, played various actors against each other.
- Former president Saleh, not willing to concede power, sabotaged the transitional period.

CONCLUSION: YEMEN'S TRANSITION TOWARDS CHAOS

- Major social and political groups were excluded from the power-sharing government, specifically the Southern movement and the Houthi militia.
- Political actors acted in bad faith; this included the Houthi leadership, which engaged in the National Dialogue Conference and meanwhile worked to derail it on the ground.
- The security sector was not reformed, and thus remained hostage to identity politics.
- President Hadi issued a federal map of Yemen without consulting with other Yemeni political and social actors, so both the Southern movement and the Houthi militia saw in the map an act of sabotage directed at their regional interests.
- Regional and international actors insisted on reproducing the same power structures and elites that had brought Yemen to the brink of collapse in the first place.
- Finally, international actors carried an attitude of "see no evil, hear no evil", turning a blind eye to the transgressions of strongmen, such as former president Saleh.[20]

The transitional period proved to be destabilizing and the process came to a halt and then collapsed when the Houthi militia, allied with troops loyal to Saleh, marched out of their Saada stronghold and took over the capital Sana'a, forcing Hadi to flee and settle in Riyadh. Houthi expansion was stopped and contained in Northern Yemen when Saudi Arabia entered the conflict on Hadi's behalf. Saleh paid with his life for having indulged in the politics of survival. He was assassinated in 2017 by his allies, the Houthis, when he tried to switch sides again. It was one switch too many.

Breaking the Yemeni Conflict Traps

These are the factors that led to the current crisis in its present form. But I do hope that by now the reader recognizes that this current crisis was brewing for a very long time. It started long ago. In the North, in the South—and in United Yemen. Unless all sides recognize and acknowledge these legacies, sustainable peace will be elusive in Yemen.

THE YEMENI CIVIL WAR

The war may end with a negotiated settlement, one between Saudi Arabia and the Houthi militia. Or a power-sharing settlement between elites, another elite pact. It may end, as most civil wars do, with a decisive military victory. It may lead to the South separating with the blessing of the Emirates. It may lead to Yemen disintegrating altogether. In all of these scenarios, one fact remains constant: instability in Yemen is rooted within. It was not created by outside forces.

In Chapter Two, I argued that the story of Yemen has often revolved around two markers: internal causes of conflict—rooted deep in history—and external interventions—exploiting these divisions for their own interests. The regional and international dimensions of the Yemeni civil war are crucial. As alluded to in Chapter Three, a pattern that has persisted throughout the history of geographical Yemen is the role that these external actors play in its internal affairs. That is, the external actors that have had a lasting impact on Yemeni politics and affairs have often been regional.

And in the recent past, in this war, the external interventions have exacerbated the conflict, and fragmented the political and military scene beyond recognition. They are not neutral: they often have stakes in the peace processes and hence often act as spoilers. The inter-state warfare and Gulf rivalry have done much damage to the country and caused great destruction. These all are facts. But the civil war in Yemen cannot only be described as a proxy war between regional actors. With or without their intervention, the war would have happened. It is one more of too many in Yemen.

At the heart of Yemeni instability is what I have termed Yemen's recurrent pattern of imploding. This derives from an elite group's will to exert their political and cultural identity—an ethnonationalist identity. And that pattern was caused by the state itself and its policies. Its source is the extractive and exploitive policies of the different statelets, imamates, and modern states acting on a diverse range of ethne who in turn felt subjugated, unrepresented, and exploited. We can think of them as a group of cousins stuck in a house they inherited from an ancient ancestor. Instead of working together to create a community within this house, one of them dominates and insists on breaking the wills of the others. In time, it dictates an intimidating worldview, ultimately behaves as a bully and in the process devours all the resources available. That the other cousins decide to exit their shared

CONCLUSION: YEMEN'S TRANSITION TOWARDS CHAOS

house is only natural. That this house could have been better managed in a fair and a more equitable manner is also a possibility—but one that has rarely occurred.

Instability in Yemen has been a result of overlapping group grievances repeatedly rising to the surface. It reflects a process of different state formations that ultimately failed to actually produce a modern state, along with core elites defined by (and at the same time exploiting) ethnic markers, perpetually fighting each other across Yemeni history. These three elements—overlapping group grievances, failed state formations, and the ethnic markers of its elites—stand at the core of the Yemeni dilemma. Understanding the conflict in this way will be crucial to any peace process and any humanitarian and development engagements. Sustainable peace in Yemen must address these three elements; it will require moving beyond a pattern of simple conflict resolution, which has so far failed to address the overlapping group grievances and historical roots of Yemen's recurrent crises.

It has to recognize that throughout the state's history, the core elites, and the state itself, have systematically perpetuated the three key divisions within the country: sectarian (doctrinal), tribal (clan level), and regional/geographical. As a result, the unequal distribution of resources has not been just a matter of priorities, policy preferences, or negligence. It is tied to historical rivalries, antagonism, and even hatred. Particular regions and areas were deliberately undermined and excluded. In other words, just as violence—like the outbreak of civil wars—evolves from an area's history and grievances, economic exclusion also carries a powerful logic.

Conflict resolution must move beyond the assumption that those fighting are driven only by material interests. People do not always act for rational reasons. They can also react out of anger: at perceived unaddressed grievances, or humiliation, or injustice. And that anger can be easily manipulated.[21]

Too often, peace processes tackling the current war in Yemen (and the region) are stuck in the "present". In other words, they seek to find solutions to the "current crises" in their present forms, and do not look farther. This approach is a bit like trying to treat the symptoms of a sickness, leaving its causes untouched. But if we are to achieve sustainable peace, we must bring our focus back to state formation. The state and its formation are key to peace making and conflict resolution for a simple reason: no one can understand today's conflicts without knowing the roots of these conflicts and their groups' grievances.[22]

Seen from this perspective, peace making should go beyond technocratic efforts to build the capacity of "strong" rather than "fragile" states. What is needed instead is larger political endeavours to transform the tainted relationships between state and society—creating what Simpson calls "civic trust".[23] In addition, various groups within society need to transform their relationships, moving from fear and hatred to trust and acceptance: only this approach can facilitate true reconciliation by recognizing previous group grievances.

This will require recognizing that an institutional setting that is designed to bring a "sustainable peace" in ethnic civil wars should avoid cementing group identities. Otherwise, it will simply lay the ground for future conflicts and become a prelude to more mini-crises.[24]

It also requires that the international community avoid the temptation to hold premature "free and fair elections" which are no guarantee of peace. In fact, researchers have found that introducing elections prematurely may contribute to further escalation of violence; it allows armed groups and their allies to effectively co-opt democratic institutions, undermining the meaningful participation and representation of ordinary citizens. In other words, if decentralization is implemented under the wrong conditions, it can lead to political and criminal armed groups capturing any existing democratic institutions.[25]

My final point might sound like wishful thinking. But it does go to the heart of Yemen's recurrent instability. Breaking apart the traps that keep Yemen in conflict will require a state that is inherently just, fair, and neutral. A state that respects the dignity and rights of its citizens. One that stands for all Yemenis in all their diversity. Realizing this state, and with it sustainable peace, requires that all Yemeni actors commit to peace. No amount of international mediation, facilitation, or intervention can help Yemen if this commitment remains elusive.

Notes

Introduction

1. Max Fisher (23 February 2022), "Word by Word and Between the Lines: A Close Look at Putin's Speech", *New York Times*, www.nytimes.com/2022/02/23/world/europe/putin-speech-russia-ukraine.html, accessed 24 February 2022.
2. For more on conventional conflict resolutions and their failure to address ethnic violence, see Elham Manea, (February 2021), "Absence of Violence or Sustainable Peace? Yemen's Road to Peace", Part One, *pm perspektive mediation*: Beiträge zur Konfliktkultur, 1, pp. 59–61.
3. The negotiations started in January in Geneva and after rounds in Vienna, they were concluded in Lausanne, Switzerland, on 2 April with an agreement on broad parameters of a nuclear deal. See Arms Control Association (February 2022), "Timeline of Nuclear Diplomacy with Iran", *Arms Control Association*, www.armscontrol.org/factsheets/Timeline-of-Nuclear-Diplomacy-With-Iran, accessed 24 February 2022.
4. *New York Times* (5 April 2015), "Iran and the Obama Doctrine: Thomas L. Friedman Interview with President Barack Obama", www.nytimes.com/2015/04/06/opinion/thomas-friedman-the-obama-doctrine-and-iran-interview.html, accessed 24 February 2022.
5. See for instance Hillary Clinton's 2011 article in *Foreign Policy* and Michael Hudson's paper on how this changing international context impacts the Middle East: Hillary Clinton (11 October 2011), "America's Pacific Century", *Foreign Policy*, https://foreignpolicy.com/2011/10/11/americas-pacific-century; Michael C. Hudson (July 2013), "Geopolitical Shifts", *Contemporary Arab Affairs*, 6(3), 458–66, www.jstor.org/stable/10.2307/48600160.
6. Joseph A. Maxwell (2011), *A Realist Approach for Qualitative Research*. Los Angeles: Sage, pp. vii–47.
7. Ibid.
8. See for example M. Olssen (1996), "Radical Constructivism and Its Failings: Anti-Realism and Individualism", *British Journal of Educational Studies*, 44(3), 275–95, https://doi.org/10.2307/3122456.
9. For example, at precisely the time when the Houthi militia took over Sana'a, Yemen, in September 2014, a hard-line member of parliament, Alireza Zakani, said: "Three Arab capitals [Baghdad, Beirut and Damascus] have today ended up in the hands of Iran and belong to the Islamic Iranian revolution", and: "Sana'a is the fourth Arab capital to join the Iranian revolution". Quoted in

International Crisis Group (13 April 2018), "Iran's Priorities in a Turbulent Middle East", *Middle East Report*, 184, p. 5, footnote 14, https://link.springer.com/chapter/10.1057/978-1-137-50675-7_3.
10. Maxwell (2011), p. 9.
11. Manea (February 2021), "Absence of Violence or Sustainable Peace? Yemen's Road to Peace", p. 61.
12. Roger D. Petersen (2002), *Understanding Ethnic Violence: Fear, Hatred, and Resentment in Twentieth-Century Eastern Europe*, Cambridge: Cambridge University Press.
13. Raymond Hinnebusch (2014), "Foreign Policy in the Middle East", in Raymond Hinnebusch and Anoushiravan Ehteshami (eds), *The Foreign Policies of Middle East States*, 2nd edn, London: Boulder, pp. 1–34.
14. On the Famous Forty see Robert D. Burrowes (Winter 2005), "The Famous Forty and Their Companions: North Yemen's First-Generation Modernists and Educational Emigrants", *Middle East Journal*, 59(1), 81–97. www.jstor.org/stable/4330098.
15. Marieke Brandt (2017), *Tribes and Politics in Yemen: A History of the Houthi Conflict*, Oxford: Oxford University Press, p. 16.
16. Ibid.
17. Ibid.
18. Adel al-Sharjabi et al. (2009), *The Palace and the Diwan: The Political Role of the Tribe in Yemen*، القصر والديوان: الدور السياسي للقبيلة في اليمن, in Arabic, Sana'a: Yemeni Observatory for Human Rights, pp. 9 and 15–17.
19. Ibid., pp. 16–17.
20. For an in-depth account of this form of co-optation policy, their political significance and impact, see Sarah Philips (2008), *Yemen's Democracy Experiment in Regional Perspective: Patronage and Pluralized Authoritarianism*, New York: Palgrave, pp. 103–11.
21. Elham Manea (21 March 2012), "Encouraging the Dissolution of the State is Not the Way to Solve Yemen's Problems", *Sada: Carnegie Endowment for International Peace*, https://carnegieendowment.org/sada/47588.
22. There is, of course, a need for more research on the impact that the internal displacement of more than 4.5 million Yemenis from their regions, some of which are tribal, has had on Yemen's tribal structures and their transformation.
23. Myra A. Waterbury (9 July 2020), "Ethnicity in International Relations", Oxford Bibliographies, DOI: 10.1093/OBO/9780199743292-013.
24. Stuart J. Kaufman (2016), "Ethnicity as a Generator of Conflict", in Karl Cordell and Stefan Wolff (eds), *The Routledge Handbook of Ethnic Conflict*, London: Routledge, p. 92.
25. Joseph Ruane and Jennifer Todd (2016), "Ethnicity and Religion", in Karl Cordell and Stefan Wolff (eds), *The Routledge Handbook of Ethnic Conflict*, London: Routledge, p. 69.
26. Stuart J. Kaufman (2016), pp. 91–101.
27. Myra A. Waterbury (9 July 2020); Stuart J. Kaufman (2016).
28. Stuart J. Kaufman (2016).

Chapter 1: The Arab Spring and its Outcomes

1. Joshua Keating (November 2011), "Who First Used the Term Arab Spring", *Foreign Policy*, https://foreignpolicy.com/2011/11/04/who-first-used-the-term-arab-spring,

accessed 21 February 2022; Joseph Massad (29 August 2012), "The 'Arab Spring' and Other American Seasons", *Al Jazeera*, https://web.archive.org/web/20120830211354/http://www.aljazeera.com/indepth/opinion/2012/08/201282972539153865.html, accessed 2 March 2022.
2. Marc Lynch (6 January 2011), "Obama's Arab Spring?", *Foreign Policy*, https://foreignpolicy.com/2011/01/06/obamas-arab-spring, accessed 21 February 2022.
3. Dieter Bednarz (25 January 2011), "Mohamed ELBaradei on Democracy in Egypt: 'There is No Turning Back Now'", *Spiegel*, www.spiegel.de/international/world/ohamed-elbaradei-on-democracy-in-egypt-there-is-no-turning-back-now-a-741322.html.
4. B. Sabry (13 January 2012), "The Origin of the Term Arab Spring", *An Arab Citizen* (Blog), http://anarabcitizen.blogspot.ca/2012/01/origin-of-term-arab-spring.html, accessed 2 March 2022; for more information on the Damascus Spring see N.N., "The Damascus Spring" (1 April 2012), *Carnegie Middle East Center*, https://carnegie-mec.org/diwan/48516?lang=en, accessed 2 March 2022.
5. Marc Lynch, "Thinking Big, Thinking New: Is the Muslim Brotherhood a Terrorist Organization or a Firewall Against Violent Extremism?", in N.N. (March 2016), *Evolving Methodologies in the Study of Islamism*, Project on Middle East Political Science, George Washington University and Carnegie Corporation of New York, p. 7.
6. Rami Khouri (18 August 2011), "Arab Spring or Revolution?", *The Globe and Mail*, www.theglobeandmail.com/opinion/arab-spring-or-revolution/article626345, accessed 2 March 2022.
7. Marc Lynch (2012), *The Arab Uprising: The Unfinished Revolutions of the New Middle East*, New York: Public Affairs, p. 9.
8. On classical definitions of revolution see for example Dale Yoder (1926), "Current Definitions of Revolution", *American Journal of Sociology*, 32(3), 433–41, www.jstor.org/stable/2765544.
9. Lynch (2012).
10. Joseph Massad (29 August 2012), "The 'Arab Spring' and Other American Seasons", *Al Jazeera*, www.aljazeera.com/opinions/2012/8/29/the-arab-spring-and-other-american-seasons, accessed 2 March 2022.
11. Rice often expressed the view during George Bush's administration that the Middle East is "badly in need of change" and that the rise of extremism in the region has its "roots in the absence of other channels for political activity or social activity or the desire for change". See the transcript of an interview with her in the *Washington Post* (25 March 2005), "Secretary of State Condoleezza Rice at *The Post*", *Washington Post*, www.washingtonpost.com/wp-dyn/articles/A2015-2005Mar25.html, accessed 3 March 2022.

The expression "New Middle East" was used in 2006 during Israel's war on Lebanon to uproot Hezbollah. To the chagrin of many in the region, Rice remarked, "What we're seeing here, in a sense, is the growing—the birth pangs of a new Middle East and whatever we do we have to be certain that we're pushing forward to the new Middle East, not going back to the old one", US Department of State Archive (21 July 2006), "Secretary Condoleezza Rice: Special Briefing on Travel to the Middle East and Europe", US Department of State Archive, https://2001-2009.state.gov/secretary/rm/2006/69331.htm, accessed 3 March 2022. The Broader Middle East and North Africa Initiative (BMENA) is an American "multilateral development and reform plan aimed at fostering economic and political liberalization

12. Interview with the Egyptian professor of modern history Asim Dasuqi, Saber Ramadan (12 May 2014), "The Sheikh of Historians, Asim Dasuqi, to Al-Wafd: 'The Arab Spring is an American Plot to Serve Israel'", in Arabic, *Al Wafd Newspaper*, صابر رمضان (12 مايو 2014)، "شيخ المؤرخين عاصم الدسوقي ل الوفد: الربيع العربي مؤامرة، أمريكية لخدمة إسرائيل"، الوفد shorturl.at/bqyKW, accessed 3 March 2022.
13. Based on a discussion with Arab intellectuals in Beirut, Lebanon, March 2022.
14. Sarah Yerkes (10 April 2018), "Journey to the Interior", *Diwan*, Carnegie Middle East Center—Carnegie Endowment for International Peace, https://carnegie-mec.org/diwan/76026.
15. Salah Aldin Al Jourchi (18 April 2008), "Tunisia: The Mining Basin's Rebellion Opens the Social File", in Arabic, Swissinfo, www.swissinfo.ch/ara/detail/content.html?cid=6592094, accessed 30 October 2012; Amnesty International (5 November 2009), "Tunisia: Releases Welcome but Repression Must End", www.amnesty.org/en/library/asset/MDE30/016/2009/en/174a9f7a-d641-4142-9d30-abed81053344/mde300162009en.html, accessed 30 October 2012.
16. N.N. (2014), "Tunisia: Breaking the Barriers to Youth Inclusion", Report, Washington, DC: World Bank Group, p. 31, http://documents.worldbank.org/curated/en/753151468312307987/Tunisia-Breaking-the-barriers-to-youth-inclusion.
17. Johan Waterbury (2013), "The Political Economy of Climate Change in the Arab Region", Arab Human Development Report: Research Paper Series, p. 29.
18. Mohamed Abdallah Youness (10 December 2015), "How Climate Change Contributed to the Conflicts in the Middle East and North Africa", World Bank Blog, https://blogs.worldbank.org/arabvoices/climate-change-conflict-mena, accessed 10 May 2022.
19. Arab Human Development Report (2009), "Challenges to Human Security in the Arab Countries", United Nations Development Programme: Regional Bureau for Arab States, p. 3; Dhavad Salehi-Isfahani (October 2010), "Human Development in the Middle East and North Africa", Arab Human Development Reports: Human Development Research Paper 2010/26, p. 10; Middle East and North Africa: Youth Facts (2007), Youth Policy, www.youthpolicy.org/mappings/regionalyouthscenes/mena/facts/#refFN15, accessed 4 March 2022; for more information on the youth bulge in the region on the eve of the Arab Spring, see also M. Chole Mulderig (2013), "An Uncertain Future: Youth Frustration and the Arab Spring", The Frederick S. Pardee Center for the Study of the Longer-Range Future, Boston University, www.bu.edu/pardee/files/2013/04/Pardee-Paper-16.pdf, accessed 4 March 2022.
20. Elham Manea (2014), "Yemen's Arab Spring: Outsmarting the Cunning State?" in Larbi Sadiki (ed.), *Routledge Handbook of the Arab Spring*, London: Routledge Studies on Middle Eastern Politics, p. 162; Jean Leca (1994), "Democratisation in the Arab World: Uncertainty, Vulnerability and Legitimacy: A Tentative Conceptualisation and Some Hypotheses", in Ghassan Salamé (ed.), *Democracy without Democrats*, London: I.B.Tauris, p. 49.
21. The second wave of uprisings in the region started in 2018 in Iraq (2018 and 2019), Sudan (2018), Algeria (2019), and Lebanon (2019).

NOTES

22. Carnegie Endowment (22 September 2010), "Kifaya: A Background", https://carnegieendowment.org/2010/09/22/kifaya-pub-54922.
23. The name of this activist is kept anonymous for obvious reasons.
24. See the background of the 6 April movement that was created out of such collaboration between young activists supporting workers' demands in Mahal al-Kubra. Michael Slackman (6 April 2008), "Day of Angry Protest Stuns Egypt", *New York Times*, www.nytimes.com/2008/04/06/world/africa/06iht-egypt.4.11708118.html, accessed 3 March 2022; and on the neo-liberal economic policies and their impact in Egypt see Joya, A. (2011), "The Egyptian Revolution: Crisis of Neoliberalism and the Potential for Democratic Politics", *Review of African Political Economy*, 38(129), p. 370; www.jstor.org/stable/23055361, accessed 3 March 2022.
25. Sami Zemni (2014), "The Roots of Tunisian Revolution", in Larb Sadiki (ed.), *Routledge Handbook of the Arab Spring*, London: Routledge Studies on Middle Eastern Politics, p. 82.
26. Raymond Hinnebusch (2015), "Change and Continuity after the Arab Uprising: The Consequences of State Formation in Arab North African States", *British Journal of Middle Eastern Studies*, 42(1), p. 12.
27. See Daniella Raz (August 2019), "Youth in Middle East and North Africa", Arab Barometer—Wave V, www.arabbarometer.org/wp-content/uploads/ABV_Youth_Report_Public-Opinion_Middle-East-North-Africa_2019-1.pdf, accessed 3 May 2022; since 2013, the number of people across the region identifying as "not religious" has risen from 8% to 13%. The rise is greatest in those under 30, among whom 18% identify as not religious, according to the research. Only Yemen saw a fall in the category. Religious leaders are losing the trust of the region's populations. In 2013, around 51% of respondents said they trusted their religious leaders to a "great" or "medium" extent. When a comparable question was asked in 2019, the number was down to 40%. The decline in trust for Islamist parties is similarly dramatic, falling from 35% in 2013, when the question was first widely asked, to 20% in 2018. BBC News, www.bbc.com/news/world-middle-east-48703377; N.N. (5 December 2019), "Arabs are Losing Faith in Religious Parties and Leaders", *The Economist*, www.economist.com/graphic-detail/2019/12/05/arabs-are-losing-faith-in-religious-parties-and-leaders?fbclid=IwAR30Wut0Fm7cRGCURTWg_xwiYk1oXJGIVci9WG9n6GjJYUssLO-qAgVTsfoI, accessed 4 February 2022.
28. Amel Grami, professor in the department of Arabic studies of the Faculty of Literatures, Arts and Humanities in Manouba, Tunisia, Zoom interview by author (8 March 2022); see also N.N. (24 January 2021), "This is the Reason: Female Tunisian Protesters File a Collective Divorce Petition", in Arabic, *Magharibi Voices*, "أصوات مغاربية"، "لهذا السبب: محتجات تونسيات يتقدمن بعريضة طلاق جماعي", shorturl.at/qxI15, accessed 8 March 2022.
29. Protests in various other forms also occurred in Algeria, the Eastern Region of Saudi Arabia, Jordan, Morocco, Mauritania, and the Sultanate of Oman.
30. Volker Perthes (2004), "Politics and Elite Change in the Arab World", in Volker Perthes (ed.), *Arab Elites: Negotiating the Politics of Change*, Colorado: Lynne Rienner, p. 5.
31. Ibid., p. 6.
32. Elham Manea (2011), *The Arab State and Women's Rights: The Trap of Authoritarian Governance (Yemen, Syria, and Kuwait)*, London: Routledge Studies in Middle Eastern Politics, p. 28.

33. Thus, the heads of the defence units, Republican Guard, military intelligence, the military security branch, the Presidential Intelligence Committee, the Bureau of Military Operations and Training, the Air Defence forces, and so on, all are fairly close relatives of al-Assad. For more information see Mahmud A. Faksh (April 1984), "The Alawi Community of Syria: A New Dominant Political Force", *Middle Eastern Studies*, 20(2), p. 153, footnote 80; Nikolaos Van Dam (1997), *The Struggle for Power in Syria: Politics and Society Under Assad and the Ba'th Party*, London: I.B.Tauris, p. 70ff.
34. Ibid.
35. Manea (2011), p. 100; Van Dam, p. 142. For instance, minorities, such as Christians, Ismailis, and Druze, are driven into the alliance by fear, just like the larger Alawite community. Indeed, the regime has encouraged and supported Sunni "societal Islamism"—that is, Islamist groups that concern themselves with changing social behaviours that conform to their world views, who call for an Islamic mode of life, refrain from politics, and ask their supporters to be loyal to the regime. This support has "raised the ire and panic of other groups", Manea (2011), p. 101. See also Hanna Batatu's landmark 1990 book *Syria's Peasantry, the Descendants of its Lesser Rural Notables, and Their Politics*. He explains how the Ba'th Party's membership and leadership changed over the decades to be dominated by members of minorities (such as Druze, Ismaili, Alawite, and Christian Orthodox peasants). As the descendants of a long-neglected and oppressed class, they found in what he called the "old Ba'th", with its "proclivity against social injustice, its censure of discrimination between the sects, and its emphasis on their Arabism rather than religion", a "qualitative break with existing conditions for their communities" and an ascent to a life of equality with all other citizens. Hanna Batatu (1990), *Syria's Peasantry, the Descendants of Its Lesser Rural Notables, and Their Politics*, Princeton: Princeton University Press, pp. 142 & 124ff.
36. Field visit by author, Syria, 2007.
37. A group is understood here as a number of people of the same generation and same social background, with a common profession, historical experience, and ideological outlook. Gamal Abdelnasser, "Egypt: Succession Politics", in Volker Perthes (ed.), *Arab Elites: Negotiating the Politics of Change*, Colorado: Lynne Rienner, pp. 118–20.
38. Gamal Abdelnasser, ibid.
39. Ahmed Youssef Ahmed (professor of political science at the Faculty of Economics and Political Science, Cairo University), interview by author (3 August 2021), Cairo, Egypt.
40. For more information on the tribal composition of core elites in Libya see Al-Hamzeh Al-Shadeedi and Nancy Ezzedine (February 2019), "Libyan Tribes in the Shadows of War and Peace", Policy Brief, Netherlands Institute of International Relations, www.clingendael.org/publication/libyan-tribes-shadow-war-and-peace, accessed 8 March 2022; and Amal S.M. Obeid (2008), "Political Elites in Libya Since 1969", in Dirk Vandewalle (ed.), *Libya Since 1969: Qadhafi's Revolution Revisited*, 1st edn, New York: Palgrave Macmillan, pp. 105–26.
41. Abdulmalik Abduljalil Al-Mekhlafi (Advisor to the President of the Republic of Yemen and former Deputy Prime Minister and Foreign Minister), interview by author (15 August 2021), Cairo, Egypt.
42. For more on developing trends in the study of state formation see Tuong Vu (2010), "Studying the State through State Formation", *World Politics*, 62(1), 148–75, www.jstor.org/stable/40646194.

NOTES

43. Illiya Harik (1987), "The Origins of the Arab State System", in Ghassan Salamé (ed.), *The Foundation of the Arab State*, London: Croom Helm, p. 19ff; Ghassan Salamé (1987), "Introduction", in Ghassan Salamé (ed.), *The Foundation of the Arab State*, London: Croom Helm, p. 5.
44. Nazih N. Ayubi (2006), *Over-Stating the Arab State: Politics and Society in the Middle East*, 3rd edn, London: I.B.Tauris, p. 86.
45. Benjamin MacQueen (2018), *An Introduction to Middle East Politics*, 2nd edn, London: Sage, p. 45.
46. See Manea (2011), pp. 19–22.
47. See Almusif Wannas (2014), *The Libyan Character: The Trinity of the Tribe, the Booty, and the Victory*, الشخصية الليبية: ثلاثية القبيلة والغنيمة والغلبة, in Arabic, *Tunis Mediterranean Publisher*. Dirk Vandewalle (2008), *Libya Since 1969: Qadhafi's Revolution Revisited*, 1st edn, New York: Palgrave Macmillan; Aziz Sameh (1969), *The Ottoman Turks in North Africa*, الأتراك العثمانيون في إفريقيا الشمالية, in Arabic, Translated from Turkish by Abdelsalm Adham, Beirut: Dar Lebanon.

    Mohammed Yousef el-Magariaf (2017), Libya Between the Past and Present: Pages of Political History, ليبيا بين الماضي والحاضر: صفحات من التاريخ السياسي, in Arabic, Part One, 2nd edn, Oxford: Center for Libyan Studies.
48. See Elham Manea (2005), *Regional Politics of the Gulf*, London: Saqi Books; Elham Manea (2001), *Regional Politics in the Developing World: The Case of the Arabian Peninsula*, PhD Thesis, Zurich University.
49. Peter Calvert, in "the international rules of the game", affirms that states "seek to modify the behaviour of other states by a range of inducements and threats, the orchestration of which, indeed, forms a large part of the major activity of diplomatic organization". In addition, they try to permanently change the behaviour of other states by "inducing structural changes in governments they perceive as hostile in order to make them more friendly, and by supporting governments they perceive to be friendly in a way that incurs a sense of mutual obligation". See Peter Calvert (1986), *The Foreign Policy of New States*, London: Palgrave Macmillan, p. 35.
50. Sandrina Antunes and Isabel Casisao (27 February 2018), "Introducing Realism in International Relations Theory", *International Relations*, www.e-ir.info/2018/02/27/introducing-realism-in-international-relations-theory; Scott Burchill et al. (eds) (2013), *Theories of International Relations*, 5th edn, London: Palgrave, ch. 2; Jack Synder (October 2009), "One World, Rival Theories", *Foreign Policy*, 145, 52–62, https://edisciplinas.usp.br/pluginfile.php/4245015/mod_resource/content/1/Snyder_2004.pdf.
51. Raymond Hinnebusch (2014), "Foreign Policy in the Middle East", in Raymond Hinnebusch and Anoushiravan Ehteshami (eds), *The Foreign Policies of Middle East States*, 2nd edn, London: Boulder, 2014, pp. 1–34.
52. Raymond Hinnebusch (2018), *The International Politics of the Middle East*, 2nd edn, Manchester: Manchester University Press, pp. 1–16.
53. Ibid.
54. Ibid., p. 2ff.
55. For more information on the theory of constructivism in international relations, see Scott Burchill et al. (eds), ch. 9; Jack Synder, "One World, Rival Theories"; and Maysam Behravesh (February 2011), "Constructivism: An Introduction", *International Relations*, www.e-ir.info/2011/02/03/constructivism-an-introduction.
56. Hinnebusch, *The International Politics of the Middle East*.
57. For more information on this regional intervention see Kristian Coates Ulrichsen (2013), "Bahrain's Uprising: Regional Dimensions and International Consequences",

Stability: International Journal of Security & Development, 2(1): 14, pp.1–12, DOI: http://dx.doi.org/10.5334/sta.be.
58. Bahrain has had a pattern of uprisings almost every decade in the last century. The 2011 uprisings were fuelled by several factors. The first was outrage at the capture of national resources by networks wound tightly around ruling families. At the core of this was the regime's policy of turning sea into land. Sand has actually been dug up from the sea floor and added to the coast. While this policy increased Bahrain's total area by more than 12% in forty years, the vast majority of this additional land was privatized. The consequences were staggering as fishing communities were devastated, especially with their reduced access to the coast and extreme environmental degradation. Second, the exploding population was confined to less than half the land mass, at a time when vast royal properties and local and international military facilities were off-limits to ordinary Bahrainis. This was combined with acute overcrowding and housing shortages. Third, foreign-born Sunnis were naturalized in what some see as an attempt to alter the demographic balance to reduce Shia predominance. The population has shot up, more than tripling since 2000. See Sarah Chayes and Matar Matar (13 February 2013), "Bahrain's Shifting Sands", Carnegie Endowment for International Peace, https://carnegieendowment.org/2013/02/13/bahrain-s-shifting-sands-pub-50924, accessed 3 May 2013.
59. Raymond Hinnebusch, ibid.

Chapter 2: The Yemeni Civil War and the Youth Uprisings

1. On the new forms of Yemeni studies see Laurent Bonnefoy (2021), "Revolution, War and Transformations in Yemeni Studies", *Middle East Report*, 51(301), 1–12; Isa Blumi (2021), "Speaking Above Yemenis: A Reading Beyond the Tyranny of Experts", *Global Intellectual History*, 6(6), 990–1014.
2. Maria-Louise Clausen (2015), "Understanding the Crisis in Yemen: Evaluating Competing Narratives", *The International Spectator*, 50(3), 16–29, DOI: 10.1080/03932729.2015.105370; Peter Salisbury (18 February 2015), "Yemen and the Saudi–Iranian Cold War", Chatham House: The Royal Institute of International Affairs, www.chathamhouse.org/publication/yemen-and-saudi-iranian-cold-war; Alex Vatanka (4 March 2015), "Iran's Yemen Play: What Tehran Wants—And What It Doesn't", *Foreign Affairs*; Stacey Philbrick Yadav and Marc Lynch (eds.) (2017), "Politics, Governance, and Reconstruction in Yemen", *Project on Middle East Political Science (POMEPS)*, 29, https://scholarspace.library.gwu.edu/work/fb494883w; Elisabeth Kendall (2019), "The Failing Islamic State Within the Failed State of Yemen", *Perspectives on Terrorism*, 13, 77–86.
3. *Without Restrictions* (25 April 2021), interview with Former UN Special Envoy Jamal Benomar, in Arabic, *Without Restrictions*, BBC Arabic, (بلاقيود 2021 أبريل،) حوار مع المبعوث، الأممي الأسبق لليمن جمال بن عمر، الجزيرة، (24) www.youtube.com/watch?v=9ibZtcOkvbE, accessed 20 April 2022.
4. Elham Manea (February 2021), p. 61.
5. *Al Jazeera* (26 March 2015), "Saudi and Arab Allies Bomb Houthi Positions in Yemen", *Al Jazeera*, www.aljazeera.com/news/2015/3/26/saudi-and-arab-allies-bomb-houthi-positions-in-yemen, accessed 21 April 2022.

NOTES

6. For more information on the Houthi militia's takeover see April Longley Alley (22 December 2014), "Yemen's Houthi Takeover", *Middle East Institute*, www.mei.edu/publications/yemens-houthi-takeover, accessed 21 April 2022.
7. Asher Orkaby (April 2019), "Yemen: A Civil War Centuries in the Making", *Origins: Current Events in Historical Perspective*, https://origins.osu.edu/article/yemen-civil-war-houthi-humanitarian-crisis-arabia-zaydi?language_content_entity=en, accessed 21 April 2022.
8. Jamal Benomar (the first UN Special Envoy for Yemen), Zoom interview by author (23 August 2022).
9. Raymond Hinnebusch (2015), "Change and Continuity After the Arab Uprising".
10. Majda Al Haddad, former youth activist and former school principal (20 August 2020), Zoom interview by author, New York, USA.
11. Hani Al Junaid, journalist, former youth activist, and first secretary of the student sector of the Yemeni Socialist Party at Sana'a University (27 August 2020), WhatsApp interview by author, South Korea.
12. Corruption Index 2011, Transparency International, www.transparency.org/en/cpi/2011, accessed 22 April 2022; Elham Manea (2014), "Yemen's Arab Spring", p. 162.
13. Manea, ibid., p. 163. The bicameral electoral system consists of (a) 301 members of the House of Representatives (*Majlis Annowab*), elected by plurality vote in single-member constituencies to serve six-year terms and (b) the 111 members of the Shura Council (*Majlis Alshoora*) who are appointed by the president. For an account of how Yemeni voters exercised their rights in the 2003 elections see Sheila Carapico, "How Yemen's Ruling Party Secured an Electoral Landslide", MERI Middle East Research and Information Project, 16 May 2003. Available from: www.merip.org/mero/mero051603.
14. Elham Manea (2011), *The Arab State and Women's Rights*, p. 87.
15. Fatima Al-Aghbari (4 December 2010), "Al-Jaashin: A Human Tragedy Caused by a Member of the Yemeni Shura Council", in Arabic, *Deutsche Welle*, فاطمة الأغبري (4 ديسمبر 2010)، «الجعاشن – مأساة إنسانية يتسبب فيها عضو في ،مجلس الشورى اليمني، shorturl.at/bjwE0, accessed 22 April 2022.
16. Wameedh Shakir, activist and human rights campaigner (28 February 2011), interview by author, Sana'a, Yemen, quoted in Manea (2014).
17. Ibid.
18. Alsharaea Newpaper (14 January 2012), "The Secretary of the Student Sector of the Socialist [Party] Speaks to 'The Street' about the First Statement of the Youth Revolution", سكرتير القطاع الطلابي للإشتراكي يتحدث ل»الشارع« عن البيان الأول، in Arabic, Archive Yamenat, https://yemenat.net/2012/01/88180, accessed 22 April 2022.
19. Hani Al Junaid (27 August 2020), Zoom interview by author.
20. Quoted in Manea (2014), "Yemen's Arab Spring", p. 161.
21. *Alsharaea Newspaper* (14 January 2012).
22. Olfat Al-Dubai, former youth activist and member of the NDC's Transitional Justice working group and member of the Constitution Drafting Committee (6 August 2021), interview by author, Istanbul, Turkey.
23. Quoted in Manea (2014).
24. Ibid.
25. Ibid.
26. Ibid.
27. Quoted in Manea (2014).

28. Elham Manea (2011), *The Arab State and Women's Rights*, pp. 94–97.
29. WikiLeaks (17 September 2005), 05SANAA2766_a, www.wikileaks.org/plusd/cables/05SANAA2766_a.html, accessed 26 April 2022.
30. Ibid.
31. Reuters Staff (23 September 2011), "Factbox: Key Players in Yemen Power Struggle", *Reuters*, www.reuters.com/article/us-yemen-players-idUSTRE78M3C520110923, accessed 26 April 2022; Elham Manea (19 March 2011), "Yemen Protests Have Created a Melting Pot: Hopes Have Been Raised for a Better Future, but Can They be Achieved Without Bloodshed?", *The Guardian*, www.theguardian.com/commentisfree/2011/mar/19/yemeni-protests-melting-pot, accessed 26 April 2022.
32. WikiLeaks (7 February 2010), 10RIYADH159_a, www.wikileaks.org/plusd/cables/10RIYADH159_a.html, accessed 26 April 2022.
33. WikiLeaks (31 August 2009), 09SANAA1617, www.wikileaks.org/plusd/cables/09SANAA1617_a.html, accessed 26 April 2022.
34. Elham Manea (19 March 2011).
35. Reuters staff (23 September 2011).
36. For example, reflecting in retrospect, Nadia Al Sakkaf, the respected former editor-in-chief of the *Yemen Times*, and later the information minister from 2014 to 2015, told this author that those who joined at first were more interested in reform: "at the beginning, when people took to the streets, the issue was not for them to overthrow the regime. It was a matter of rights, life, [it was about an] economic situation". She herself participated in these events. Nadia Al Saqaf, former editor-in-chief of *Yemen Times* and former information minister, Zoom interview by author (26 August 2020), United Kingdom.
37. N.N. (27 August 2011), "Yemeni Youth Revolution" (ثورة الشباب اليمني), in Arabic, *Elsyasi*, available from: www.elsyasi.com/article_detail.aspx?id=425.
38. Abdel Karim Sallam (6 February 2011), "The Yemeni President's Initiative… A Proactive Step on a Bumpy Road Fraught with Dangers", in Arabic, *Swissinfo Arabic*, عبدالكريم سلام، "مبادرة الرئيس اليمني.. خطوة إستباقية في طريق، وعر محفوف بالمخاطر"، سويس إنفو العربية shorturl.at/iCGMU, accessed 22 April 2022.
39. Ibid.
40. Ibid.
41. Elham Manea (19 March 2011).
42. Ibid.
43. Ibid.
44. Human Rights Watch (12 February 2013), "Yemen's Failed Response to the 'Friday of Dignity' Killings", Human Rights Watch, www.hrw.org/report/2013/02/12/unpunished-massacre/yemens-failed-response-friday-dignity-killings.
45. Ibid.
46. Radio Free Europe (21 March 2011), "Split Emerges in Yemen's Armed Forces as Top Commanders Defect", www.rferl.org/a/yemen_protests_generals_resign_sanaa/2344825.html.
47. Ibid.
48. Elham Manea (2014), "The Significance of Gender in Arab-Spring Transitional Justice", in Kirsten Fisher and Robert Stewart (eds), *Transitional Justice and the Arab Spring*, London: Routledge Studies on Middle Eastern Politics, p. 161.

NOTES

Chapter 3: Legacies of Geography, Tribes, and Religious Beliefs

1. Lars-Erik Cederman, Andreas Wimmer, and Brian Min (January 2010), "Why Do Ethnic Groups Rebel? New Data and Analysis", *World Politics*, 62(1), p. 88.
2. Elham Manea (6 July 2021), "Absence of Violence or Sustainable Peace? Yemen's Pathway Forward", MAP Middle East and Asia Project on Transitional Justice, Middle East Institute, www.mei.edu/publications/absence-violence-or-sustainable-peace-yemens-pathway-forward.
3. Throughout history, the space has been referred to as Greater Yemen. The famous tenth-century Yemeni geographer Al Hamdani and the thirteenth-century Muslim Roman geographer Yaqut al-Hamawi insist that it includes almost half of the Arabian Peninsula: today's Yemen, Sultanate of Oman, Asir and Najran, and deep into the heart of today's Saudi Arabia. Yaqut al-Hamawi, *Mu'jam ul-Buldān* معجم البلدان, in Arabic, Volume Five, Beirut: Dar Sader, pp. 447–48; Abu Muhammad al-Hasan al-Hamdani, *Sifat Jazīrat al 'Arab* صفة جزيرة العرب, in Arabic, commented on by Mohammed bin Ali Alakwa'a (1990), pp. 90–91. It should be mentioned that the idea of "great Yemen" was also promoted by Yemeni Zaydi geographers before the 1962 military coup in the North of Yemen, which overthrew the Zaydi Kingdom. And their writings were promoted after the 1990 Yemeni unification; see for example the book of Hussein Bin Ali Alwaisi (first published in Cairo in 1962), *Greater Yemen* اليمن الكبرى, in Arabic, Volume One, Sana'a: Maktabat Al Irshad, 1991, pp. 20–21.
4. Cederman, Wimmer and Min (January 2010).
5. Robert D. Kaplan (2012), *The Revenge of Geography*, New York: Random House, pp. xxi–xxii.
6. Ibid., p. 301.
7. See for example Ron Johnston (2013), "*The Revenge of Geography: What the Map Tells Us About Coming Conflicts and the Battle against Fate*, Robert D. Kaplan, New York: Random House, 2012"; *The AAG Review of Books*, 1(1), 1–3, DOI: 10.1080/2325548X.2013.785741.
8. Alessandro de Maigret (1996), *Arabia Felix: An Exploration of the Archaeological History of Yemen*, London: Stacey International, p. 26; Robert G. Hoyland (2001), *Arabia and the Arabs: From the Bronze Age to the Coming of Islam*, London and New York: Routledge, p. 40.
9. De Maigret (1996), 213–25; Hoyland, pp. 36–43; W.L. Ochsenwald, Robert Bertram Serjeant, Mahmud Ali Ghul, and Alfred Felix L. Beeston (30 April 2020), "History of Arabia", *Encyclopaedia Britannica*, www.britannica.com/topic/history-of-Arabia-31558, accessed 24 May 2022.
10. Ochsenwald, Serjeant, Ghul, and Beeston.
11. Hoyland, pp. 41ff.
12. Ibid., p. 36.
13. De Maigret (1996)(, pp. 200–02; Mohammed Abdulqader Alfaqih (1987), *On Arabia Felix: Short Historical Studies* دراسات تاريخية قصيرة في العربية السعيدة, Sana'a: Yemeni Centre for Studies and Research, pp. 44–47, 162; Elham Manea (1998), "La tribu et l'Etat au Yémen", in Mondher Kilani (ed.), *Islam et changement social*, Lausanne: Editions Payot, pp. 205–18 ; Fathel Abu Gahnem (1990), *The Tribe and the State in Yemen* القبيلة والدولة في اليمن, in Arabic, Cairo: Dar Almanar, pp. 65–66; Al Shargaby, Kaid, 1983, *Al Sharaih Al Igtimaiaah Al taqlidiah Fi Al Mugtamaa Al Yamani* الشرائح الاجتماعية التقليدية في المجتمع اليمني, [The Traditional Social Strata in the

Yemeni Society], in Arabic, Beirut: Dar Al Hadath, pp. 55–56; Mohammed Yahia Al-Hadad (1986), *The General History of Yemen: History of Yemen Before Islam* التاريخ العام لليمني: تاريخ اليمن قبل الإسلام, Part One, in Arabic, Beirut: Al Madina Publications, 155–58; Jawad Ali (1993), *The Detailed History of the Arabs Before Islam* في المفصل تاريخ العرب قبل الإسلام, in Arabic, 2nd edn, no publisher, pp. 70–71.

14. Alfaqih (1987), p. 162.
15. Alfaqih (1987), pp. 43ff; de Maigret (1996), pp. 227–37; Hoyland (2001), pp. 45ff.
16. Alfaqih (1987), p. 45.
17. G.R. Smith (1990), "Yemenite History: Problems and Misconceptions", *Proceedings of the Seminar for Arabian Studies*, 20, pp. 134ff, www.jstor.org/stable/41223264; Ochsenwald, Serjeant, Ghul, and Beeston.
18. This caliphate had started to disintegrate earlier. In fact, the year 945 marked the beginning of a century-long period in which much of the empire was ruled by local dynasties, who nominally acknowledged the religious authority of the Abbasid. It was officially destroyed in 1258 by the Mongols. Britannica (5 March 2020), "Abbasid caliphate", Encyclopaedia Britannica, www.britannica.com/topic/Abbasid-caliphate.
19. Manea (2005), 18–19; Abdulaziz Al-Maqaleh (1982), *A Review of the Thought of Zaydism and Mutazilah: The Islamic Yemen*, قراءة في فكر الزيدية والمعتزلة: اليمن الإسلامي, in Arabic, Beirut: Dar al-Auda, pp. 51–84, 111ff.
20. Manea (2005), *Regional Politics of the Gulf*, p. 17.
21. Abd ar-Raḥman ibn Khaldun (first published in 1377), *The Introduction of Ibn Khaldun*, مقدمة إبن خلدون, Checked and Prepared by Hamed Ahmed Altaher (2004), in Arabic, Cairo: Dar Al Fagr lil Turath, pp. 244–50.
22. Ibid., pp. 250–51.
23. Etan Kohlberg and Amin Ehteshami (2020), *In Praise of the Few: Studies in Shi'i Thought and History*, Amin Ehteshami (ed.), Leiden: Brill, pp. 266–67; Najam Haider (2014), *Shi'i Islam: An Introduction*, Cambridge: Cambridge University Press, ch. 5; A.J. Newman (4 September 2019), "Twelver Shi'a", *Encyclopedia Britannica*, www.britannica.com/topic/Twelver-Shia.
24. Maysaa Shuja al-Deen (2016), *Radicalization of Zaydi Refrom Attempts*, Master's thesis, Cairo: The American University, pp. 6–10.
25. Muhammad al-Shahrastani (d. 1153 CE), *Kitāb al-Milal wa al-Nihal* كتاب الملل والنحل [The Book of Sects and Creeds], in Arabic, checked and prepared by Amir Ali Muhanna and Ali Hassan Faoud (1993), 3rd edn, Beirut: Dar El-Marefah, pp. 180–81.
26. Marieke Brandt (2017), *Tribes and Politics in Yemen: A History of the Houthi Conflict*, Oxford: Oxford University Press, pp. 41, 101; Paul Dresch (1993), *Tribes, Government and History in Yemen*, Oxford: Clarendon Press, Oxford University Press, p. 161; Bernard Haykel (2003), *Revival and Reform in Islam: The Legacy of Muhammad al-Shawkani*, Cambridge: Cambridge University Press, pp. 6–7.
27. Abdulaziz Al-Maqaleh (1982), pp. 15–70.
28. For more on this movement see Racha el-Omari (2016), "The Mu'tazilite Movement (I): The Origins of the Mu'tazila", in Sabine Schmidtke (ed.), *The Oxford Handbook of Islamic Theology*, Oxford: Oxford University Press, pp. 1–12.
29. Najam Haider (2014).
30. Ibid., pp. 105–109.
31. Wilferd Madelung (1965), *Der Imam al-Qāsim ibn Ibrahim und die Glaubenslehre der Zaiditen*, Berlin: Walter De Gruyter & Co., p. 4ff; Haykel (2003), p. 8; Haider (2014),

NOTES

pp. 105–09; Maysaa Shuja al-Deen (2016), p. 7; Muhammad al-Shahrastani (d. 1153 CE), Kitāb al–Milal wa al-Nihal, pp. 183–89. Ali Mohammed Zayd (1997), Mu'tazila currents in Yemen in the sixth century Hijri, تيارات معتزلة اليمن في القرن السادس الهجري, Sana'a: The French Center for Yemeni Studies; Mohammed Yehia Azzan (30 September 2002), "A Review in the Imamate Theory in Zaydism", قراءة في نظرية الإمامة عند الزيدية, in Arabic, *Al Massar: A Periodical of the Yemeni Heritage and Research Center*, No. 9, Sana'a, shorturl.at/uOQV5, accessed 25 May 2022.

32. Haider (2014), p. 105; Haykel (2003); Madelung (1965).
33. Haider (2014), pp. 105–109; Haykel (2003); Madelung (1965).
34. Maysaa Shuja al-Deen (Yemeni senior researcher at Sana'a Center for Strategic Studies and an expert on Zaydism), Zoom interview by author (23 June 2020).
35. Maysaa Shuja al-Deen (2016), pp. 31–34; Barak A. Salmoni et al. (2010), "APPENDIX B: Zaydism: Overview and Comparison to Other Versions of Shi'ism", in *Regime and Periphery in Northern Yemen: The Huthi Phenomenon*, RAND Corporation, 2010, pp. 285–96, accessed 3 June 2022.

    Wilfred Madelung, 'Al-Hādī Ila 'l-Ḥakk', in *Encyclopaedia of Islam*, 2nd edn, edited by P. Bearman, Th. Bianquis, C.E. Bosworth, E. van Donzel, and W.P. Heinrichs (Volumes X, XI, XII), Th. Bianquis (Volumes X, XI, XII) et al. Accessed 3 June 2022.
36. Imam al-Hadi (Yehia bin al-Husayn bin al-Qasim bin Ibrahim), *The Collection of Edicts by Imam al-Hadi*, مجموع رسائل الإمام الهادي، يحيى بن الحسين بن القاسم بن إبراهيم, checked and prepared by Abdullah bin Mohammed Alshathli (2001), Imam Zayd bin Ali Cultural Institute: Saada & Amman, pp. 54–56; Maysaa Shuja al-Deen (2016); Wilfred Madelung, "Al-Hādī Ila 'l-Ḥakk"; Salmoni et al. (2010).
37. Imam al-Hadi, *The Collection of Edicts*, pp. 509–11.
38. See Ali Mohammed Zayd (1997), introduction and chs 1–4; Wilfred Madelung, "Muṭarrifiyya", in *Encyclopaedia of Islam*, 2nd edn, Bearman et al. (eds), accessed 3 June 2022.
39. Ali Mohammed Zayd (1997), pp. 69ff, 111–15; Maysaa Shuja al-Deen (2016), pp. 34–37.
40. Zayd (1997), pp. 72–80; Shuja al-Deen (2016).
41. Zayd (1997), ch. 7; Shuja al-Deen (2016); Madelung, "Muṭarrifiyya".
42. Brinkley Messick (2018), "Map of Upper and Lower Yemen", *Shari'a Scripts: A Historical Anthropology*, New York/Chichester, West Sussex: Columbia University Press, pp. ix–xii, https://doi.org/10.7312/mess17874-001.
43. Dresch (1993), p. 12.
44. Dresch (1993), p. 12ff; Haykel (2003), pp. 3–4; Maysaa Shuja al-Deen (2016); pp. 42–43; Zayd (1997), p. 149.
45. Haykel (2003); Maysaa Shuja al-Deen (2016); Dresch (1993); Brinkley Messick (2018).
46. An example is Tihama, the hot sandy plains along the coast of the Red Sea populated by a majority of Sunni Shafii Yemenis, with strong links with Africa, the Hijaz, and the wider world of the Indian Ocean. Their sea trade in port towns such as Mocha generated high revenues. See Haykel (2003), ibid. Also, for more elaborate discussion and understanding of Yemeni regional divisions, with its seven regions, see Stephen W. Day (2012), *Regionalism and Rebellion in Yemen: A Troubled National Union*, Cambridge: Cambridge University Press, pp. 47–53.
47. Brandt (2017), p. 16.
48. Ibid., pp. 17–19.
49. Manea (2005), p. 16; Brandt (2017), p. 21.
50. Brandt (2017).

51. Burrowes argued that the imams of the Hamid al-Din family—Yehia and then his son Ahmed—sought to expand the territory of their kingdom just as the kings of England and France had centuries earlier. See Robert D. Burrowes (1991), "Prelude to Unification: The Yemen Arab Republic, 1962–1990", *International Journal of Middle East Studies*, 23, p. 484; quoted in Manea (2005), p. 32.
52. Haykel (2003), p. 17; N.N. (1789), *Accounts and Extracts of the Manuscripts in the Library of the King of France*, published in Paris: under the inspection of a Committee of the Royal Academy of Sciences at Paris. Translated from the French, pp. 74–76.
53. Haykel (2003), pp. 16–17.
54. Al-Hadad (1986), Part Four, p. 95ff.
55. Manea (2005).
56. Abdullah Al-Baradouni (1983), *The Republican Yemen* اليمن الجمهوري, in Arabic, 1st edn, Damascus: The Arab Writer Printer, pp. 24ff.
57. For detailed accounts of this state of affairs see author unknown, *Yemeni Years*, in Arabic; Al Aamry, Hussain A. (1996), *One Hundred Years of Yemeni Modern History: 1748–1848* مائة عام من تاريخ اليمن الحديث, in Arabic; Damascus: Al Ahaly for Publication; Farouq O. Abatha (1979), *Ottoman Rule in Yemen: 1872–1918* الحكم العثماني في اليمن, in Arabic, 2nd edn, Beirut: Dar al-A'awda, pp. 51–68.
58. On this cultural affinity see Abdullah Al-Baradouni (1983).
59. Al-Hadad (1986), Part Four, p. 61.
60. Manea (2005), p. 33.
61. Zayd (1997), pp. 149–50.
62. Ibid., 151ff.
63. Ibid.
64. Haykel (2003), p. 38.
65. Ibid.
66. Ibid.
67. Sami Ghalib, Yemeni journalist and editor-in-chief of *Al Nidaa Newspaper*, interview by author (19 August 2021), Cairo.
68. Paul Dresch (1993), *Tribes, Government and History in Yemen*, p. 199.
69. Hussein bin Ahmed al Sayaghi (ed.) (2008), *Unknown pages from the history of Yemen and the Sana'a law* صفحات مجهولة من تاريخ اليمن وقانون صنعاء, in Arabic, third edition, Sana'a: Yemeni Center for Studies and Research, pp. 130–31.
70. In Arabic:
    إن كنت هارب من الموت فما من الموت ناج
    وإن كنت هارب من الجوع إنزل سهول إبن ناجي
71. Sami Ghalib (19 August 2021), interview.
72. Elham Manea (May 2021), *Absence of Violence*, Part Two, p. 140.
73. B. O'Neill (February 2012), "Into Nations and Tribes: Yemen and AQAP", *Carnegie Endowment: Sada*, carnegieendowment.org/sada/47279, quoted in Manea, ibid.
74. Ibid., Part Two.
75. Evan Andrews (22 August 2018), "Mythical Monsters", *History*, www.history.com/news/6-mythical-monsters, accessed 14 June 2022.

Chapter 4: The Narrative Dilemma

1. Kevin Alexander Davis (2014), "From Collective Memory to Nationalism: Historical Remembrance in Aden", Master's thesis, Washington, DC: Georgetown University, pp. 27ff.

NOTES

2. Wafa Alsayed Abu Bakr (7 October 2006), interview by author, Aden, Yemen.
3. Radya Ihasn Allah (member of the Supreme Committee of the People's Socialist Party, Secretary General of the Arab Women's Association in Aden, Outreach Officer in the Liberation Front, and independent member of the Coordination Council of Aden Governorate), interview by author, 8 October 2006, Aden. She was a social and political activist and writer, member of the Supreme Committee of the People's Socialist Party, Secretary General of the Arab Women's Association in Aden, Outreach Officer in the Liberation Front, and independent member of the Coordination Council of Aden Governorate.
4. Davis (2014), p. 16.
5. Sheikh Brigadier General Ali Salem Al-Huraizi Al-Mahri, former Undersecretary for Desert Affairs in Al-Mahra Governorate and its Border Guard Commander, interview by author (26 October 2021), Muscat, Sultanate of Oman.
6. Paul Dresch (2000), *A History of Modern Yemen*, Cambridge: Cambridge University Press, pp. xiii–xiv.
7. Ahmed Alahssab (2019), *Power Identity in Yemen: The Controversy of Politics and History*, هوية السلطة في اليمن: جدل السياسة والتاريخ, in Arabic, Beirut: Arab Center for Research & Policy Studies, p. 43ff.
8. Ibid.
9. Ossam Al Ahamadi (18 March 2022), "The Tip of the Iceberg. That is Why the Houthis Demolished the 'Turkish Monument' in the Yemeni Capital", لهذا هدم الحوثيون النصب التركي في العاصمة اليمنية..رأس جبل الجليد], in Arabic, *Alistiklat Newspaper*, www.alestiklal.net/ar/view/12692/dep-news-1647352160, accessed 22 June 2022. Saba Net (11 January 2011), "Turkish President Inaugurates the Memorial to Turkish Soldiers in Sana'a", الرئيس التركي يفتتح النصب التذكاري للجنود الأتراك بصنعاء, in Arabic, Yemeni News Agency: Saba Net, www.saba.ye/ar/news233008.htm, accessed 23 June 2022.
10. Daily Sabah with AFP (9 March 2022), "Israel's Herzog Visits Turkey, Meets Erdoğan to 'Restart' Ties", *Daily Sabah with AFP*, www.dailysabah.com/politics/diplomacy/israels-herzog-visits-turkey-meets-erdogan-to-restart-ties, accessed 22 June 2022.
11. Hussin Alezzi (@hussinalezzi5) (12 March 2022), بخصوص النصب التذكاري التركي أعتقد كان عملا فرديا بحتا والاعمال الفردية تحدث بشكل اعتيادي في جميع البلدان وفي كل زمان ومكان وهناك ايضا اختلالات فنية لم يتنبه لها المهندسون لحظة البناء إن العلاقات دائما وأبدا لا تقاس بحجر هنا أو هناك وتركيا في الواقع تاريخ عريق وشعب جميل ومحبوب لدينا https://twitter.com/hussinalezzi5/status/1502642127209123841?s=20&t=s3-OUpOm4qsXe9CjaYzb1Q, accessed 23 June 2022.
12. Ibid.
13. Ossam Al Ahamadi (18 March 2022).
14. Yaseen Al-Tamimi (@yaseentamimi68) (12 March 2022), هدم النصب التذكاري التركي جزء من أجندة ترمي الى القطع مع إرث الأمة والارتهان لأجندة طائفية إقليمية، وهو يشبه قتل اليمنيين بصفتهم صهاينة وأمريكيون، والذي تمارسه هذه الجماعة منذ أن قرر بعض اللاعبين الإقليميين استخدامها لهزيمة مشروع التغيير الوطني الديمقراطي في 11فبراير/شباط 2011. https://twitter.com/yaseentamimi68/status/1502591489951641600?s=20&t=tW-BrVe-wwZuW4ojnPqL7g, accessed 23 June 2022.
15. Yaseen Al-Tamimi (@yaseentamimi68) (12 March 2022), ليس هذا النصب وحده من يشير الى حجم الحضور العثماني التركي في تاريخنا، فهناك جوامع عامرة بذكر الله وأبنية شامخة وسبل وجسور وأطعمة ومفردات وعادات وتقاليد. على الحوثيين اذاً أن يفرضوا شكلا جديدا لملابس نسائهم وأن يغيروا من عادات الناس ونمط عيشهم المتمدن في اهم مدن اليمن(صنعاء) https://twitter.com/yaseentamimi68/status/1502591218219421703?s=20&t=tW-BrVe-wwZuW4ojnPqL7g, accessed 23 June 2022.

227

In saying "new form of clothing", he is alluding to the *sharshaf* الشرشف veiling tradition: two pieces of black cloth that cover the woman from head to toe, complemented by another one that hides the face. Worn by upper-class Turkish women, it was followed by the female members of the Hashemite families in North Yemen and became widespread among Yemenis of all social strata after 1962.

16. Manea (2011), p. 102ff.
17. Nabil al-Bukiri (Yemeni writer and activist, editor-in-chief of *Muqribat Journal*, Islah Party), interview by author (7 August 2021), Istanbul, Turkey.
18. The words he used were "killing them and dragging them in the streets", ibid.
19. See Bernard Haykael (2003), p. 10ff; Abdulaziz Al-Maqaleh (1982), p. 215ff.
20. Mentioned in Chapter Three, the Jarudiyya is the most extreme form of Zaydism, dominant after 802, and closest to the Twelvers in its theological positions.
21. Abdulwahab Alamrani (12 March 2022), "Yemen in the Ottoman Era", اليمن في العهد العثماني, in Arabic, www.facebook.com/permalink.php?story_fbid=1272893546 538914&id=100014548425572, accessed 23 June 2022.
22. Ibid.
23. See for example, Abdulwahab Alamrani (13 March 2022), "Yemen in the Ottoman Era", اليمن في العهد العثماني, *Yemen Now News*, in Arabic, https://yemennownews.com/article/1713667, accessed 23 June 2022.
24. Joseph A. Maxwell (2011), *A Realist Approach for Qualitative Research*, Los Angeles: Sage, pp. vii–47.

Chapter 5: Legacies of Ottoman Imperialism

1. André Raymond (1996), "The Ottoman Legacy in Arab Political Boundaries", in L. Carl Brown (ed.), *Imperial Legacy: The Ottoman Imprint on the Balkans and the Middle East*, New York: Columbia University Press, p. 115.
2. Ibid.
3. Ibid.
4. Majid Khadduri (1963), *Modern Libya: A Study in Political Development*, Baltimore: The Johns Hopkins Press, p. 7.
5. Muhammad Mustafa Bazamah (1968), *The City of Benghazi Throughout History*, بنغازي عبر التاريخ, in Arabic, Part One, Benghazi: Dar Libya for Publication, p. 243ff.
6. Cherif Bassiouni (ed.) (2013), *Libya: From Repression to Revolution*, Leiden, The Netherlands: Brill, p. 20 ff.
7. Theocharis N. Grigoriadis and Walied Kassem (2021), "The Regional Origins of the Libyan Conflict", *Middle East Policy*, 28(2), pp. 120–21; Mohammed Yousef el-Magariaf (2017), p. 62ff; Muhammad Mustafa Bazamah (2001), *Chapter from the History of Fezzan*, صفحات من تاريخ فزان, in Arabic, republished by the General Authority for Culture in 2018, Benghazi: The General Authority for Culture, p. 108ff; Abu Salim Abdullah bin Muhammad Al-Ayyashy, *The Ayyachian Journey (1661–1663)*, edited and presented by Saeed Al-Fadhili and Suleiman Al-Qurashi (2006), الرحلة العياشية, in Arabic, Volume One, Abu Dhabi: Dar Al Suwaidi Publishing and Distribution, p. 201.
8. Ṭahir Aḥmad al-Zawi (1930), *Explanation of the Book "Al Tithkar: The History of Western Tripoli" by Ibn Ghalboun*, "شرح لكتاب "التذكار: تاريخ طرابلس الغرب لإبن غلبون, in Arabic, Cairo: Salafi Library, p. 13.

NOTES

9. Fatih Rajab Qadara (November 2014), "The Ottoman Empire in the Traces of Sheikh Al-Taher Al-Zawi", الدولة العثمانية في آثار الشيخ الطاهر الزاوي, in Arabic, *Al-Majalla Al-Jami'a*, *4*(16), pp. 7–8.
10. For more information on the Mamluks see *Encyclopaedia Britannica* (7 April 2020), "Mamluk", *Encyclopedia Britannica*, www.britannica.com/topic/Mamluk; Doris Behrens-Abouseif, Anna Contadini, and R. Darley-Doran, "Mamlūks", in *Encyclopaedia of Islam*, 2nd edn, edited by P. Bearman, Th. Bianquis, C.E. Bosworth, E. van Donzel, W.P. Heinrichs and P.J. Bearman (Volumes X, XI, XII), accessed 5 January 2023, http://dx.doi.org/10.1163/1573-3912_islam_COM_1424.
11. For more information on this dynasty see *Encyclopaedia Britannica* (27 June 2008), "Ḥafṣid Dynasty", *Encyclopaedia Britannica*, www.britannica.com/topic/Hafsid-dynasty.
    For more information on the Hospitaller Order of the Knights of St John see Amelia Robertson Brown (2021), "Antiquarian Knights in Mediterranean Island Landscapes: The Hospitaller Order of St John and Crusading Among the Ruins of Classical Antiquity, from Medieval Rhodes to Early Modern Malta", *Journal of Medieval History*, *47*(3), 413–32, DOI: 10.1080/03044181.2021.1930446; Ṭahir Aḥmad Zawi (1930), pp. 140 ff, 153 ff.
12. Ergun Özbundun (1996), "The Continuing Ottoman Legacy and the State Tradition in the Middle East", in L. Carl Brown (ed.), pp. 139–43. For a short summary of the Tanzimat reforms see *Encyclopædia Britannica* (n.d.), "Tanzimat", *Britannica Academic*, retrieved 5 July 2022, from https://academic.eb.com/levels/collegiate/article/Tanzimat/71216. For more information on the Ottoman Empire see Donald Quataert (2005), *The Ottoman Empire, 1700–1922*, 2nd edn, Cambridge: Cambridge University Press. doi:10.1017/CBO9780511818868.
13. Benjamin MacQueen (2018), *An Introduction to Middle East Politics*, p. 13; Ergun Özbundun (1996), p. 143; Manea (2011), *The Arab State*, pp. 35–41, 68, 190–91.
14. Ergun Özbundun (1996), pp. 143–45.
15. MacQueen (2018), *An Introduction to Middle East Politics*, p. 8.
16. Manea (2011), *The Arab State*, pp. 35–41, 68, 190–91; *Encyclopedia Britannica* (2006), "Ottoman Empire", Ultimate Reference Suite, DVD; Fouad Shubat (1966), *The Organisation of Personal Status for Non-Muslims: Legislation and Judiciary in Syria and Lebanon*, تنظيم الأحوال الشخصية لغير المسلمين: التشريعات والقضاء في سوريا ولبنان, in Arabic, Damascus: The Higher Institute for Arab Studies, p. 51.
17. Manea (2011), *The Arab State*, p. 68.
18. For more information see Manea (2016), *Women and Sharia Law*, pp. 54–60.
19. UNDP (2019), Arab Human Development Report, "Leaving No One Behind: Towards Inclusive Citizenship in Arab Countries", Research Paper, p. 5.
20. MacQueen (2018), *An Introduction to Middle East Politics*, pp. 13, 18–20.
21. Ibid.
22. Ibid., p. 19.
23. Quoted in Thomas Kuehn (2011), *Empire, Islam, and Politics of Difference: Ottoman Rule in Yemen, 1849/1919*, Leiden: Brill, p. 2.
24. Farouq O. Abatha (1979), *Ottoman Rule in Yemen: 1872–1918.*, pp. 16f; *Encyclopædia Britannica* (n.d.), "History of Arabia", Britannica Academic. Retrieved 5 July 2022 from https://academic.eb.com/levels/collegiate/article/history-of-Arabia/110498.
25. Abatha, ibid, pp. 16–18, 26; Said Mustafa Salim (1984), *The Structure of Contemporary Yemen: Yemen and Imam Yihia*, 3rd edn, تكوين اليمن الحديث, in Arabic, Cairo: Madbouli Library, p. 29f.

26. Abatha (1979); Salim (1984); Britannica, "History of Arabia", ibid.; Abdol Rauh Yaccob (2012), "Yemeni Opposition to Ottoman Rule: An Overview", *Proceedings of the Seminar for Arabian Studies*, 42, 411–19, www.jstor.org/stable/41623653.
27. Manea (2011), *The Arab State*, pp. 43–46; Abatha (1979); Salim(1984); Britannica, "History of Arabia"; Yaccob (2012).
28. Manea (2011); Yaccob (2012).
29. Ibid.
30. Manea (2011); Abatha (1979), *Ottoman Rule in Yemen: 1872–1918*, pp. 83–87.
31. Manea (2011); Salim (1984), *The Structure of Contemporary Yemen*, pp. 32–33.
32. Quoted in Abatha (1979), *Ottoman Rule in Yemen: 1872–1918*, p. 133; Manea (2011), *The Arab State*.
33. Kharijites, or Secessionists, are supporters of an early Islamic movement. Originally, they supported Ali ibn Abi Talib, the cousin of Mohammad the founder of the Islamic religion, but later turned against him and recognized only the legitimacy of the first two caliphs in Islam. They launched many revolts throughout early Islamic history and were perceived as religious fanatics who disturbed the political order. For more information about this movement and its modern form Ibadism see Lawrence Ziring (1992), *The Middle East: A Political Dictionary*, Santa Barbara, California: ABC-CLIO, Inc., pp. 87–89; Manea (2005), *Regional Politics*, p. 18.
34. A degrading expression Sunnis commonly use to describe Shi'ite Muslims.
35. Letter of the Zaydi Imam Yehia to the Delegation of Mekka sent by Sultan Abdel Hameed II, October 1907, Quoted in Abd al-Was' ibn Yehia al-Wasa'i (1944), *History of Yemen: The So-Called Venue of Concerns and Sadness in Accidents and History of Yemen*, تاريخ اليمن: المسمى فرجة الهموم والحزن في حوادث وتاريخ اليمن, in Arabic, Cairo: Salafi Press, pp. 165ff. د; also cited in Manea (2011), *The Arab State*, p. 44.
36. Al-Wasa'i (1944), pp. 119, 140.
37. Ibid.
38. Salim (1984), *The Structure of Contemporary Yemen*, pp. 123–24, 144–45.
39. For more information see Caesar E. Farah (2002), *The Sultan's Yemen: Nineteenth-Century Challenges to Ottoman Rule*, London: I.B.Tauris, pp. 95–106. On the administrative division of Yemen in the second Ottoman rule, see Abatha (1979), *Ottoman Rule in Yemen: 1872–1918*, pp. 104–05.
40. Kuehn (2011), *Empire, Islam, and Politics of Difference*, pp. 91–92.
41. Ibid., pp. 94–106.
42. Ibid.
43. Caesar E. Farah (2002), pp. 65, 104.
44. Ibid., pp. 172–77.
45. Da'an Treaty, 1911, Appendix, in Salim (1984), *The Structure of Contemporary Yemen*, pp. 516–18.
46. Ibid., p. 151.

Chapter 6: Legacies of Colonization

1. MacQueen (2018), *An Introduction to Middle East Politics*, pp. 28–29.
2. Sudan is often included by the UN in the geographical definition of North Africa. Manea (2011), *The Arab State*, pp. 19ff.
3. MacQueen (2018), *An Introduction to Middle East Politics*, pp. 28ff; Manea (2011); Lisa Anderson (October 1987), "The State in the Middle East and North Africa", *Comparative Politics*, 20(1), p. 3.

NOTES

4. Manea (2011); Nazih N. Ayubi (2006), *Over-Stating the Arab State: Politics and Society in the Middle East*, London: I.B.Tauris, 3rd edn, pp. 87ff; Bahgat Korany (1987), "Alien and Besieged Yet Here to Stay: The Contradictions of the Arab Territorial State", in Ghassan Salamé (ed.), *The Foundation of the Arab State*, London: Croom Helm, p. 57; Lisa Anderson (Spring 1991), "Absolutism and the Resilience of Monarchy in the Middle East", *Political Science Quarterly*, 106(1), p. 5; Anderson (October 1987), "The State in the Middle East and North Africa", p. 5.
5. MacQueen (2018), *An Introduction to Middle East Politics* pp. 44–45.
6. Ayubi (2006), *Over-Stating the Arab State*, pp. 89 ff; Manea (2011).
7. Mounira M. Charrad (2001), *States and Women's Rights: The Making of Postcolonial Tunisia, Algeria, and Morocco*, Berkeley: University of California Press, pp. 109–10, 114–20, 131–32; Manea (2011), *The Arab State*, p. 15.
8. Anderson (October 1987), "The State in the Middle East and North Africa"; Anderson (Spring 1991), "Absolutism"; Manea (2011), *The Arab State*, pp. 19ff.
9. Anderson (Spring 1991), "Absolutism"; Manea (2011).
10. Anderson (October 1987), "The State in the Middle East and North Africa"; Manea (2011).
11. On the Zaydi imams' treatment of Yemeni Jews, and the Jews seeking the protection of the Ottomans, see Yosef Tobi (1999), *The Jews of Yemen: Studies in their History and Culture*, Leiden: Brill, chs 1, 2 and 5.
12. Anderson (October 1987), "The State in the Middle East and North Africa"; p. 6.
13. MacQueen (2018), *An Introduction to Middle East Politics*, p. 45.
14. Manea, Manea (2011), *The Arab State*, pp. 19ff.
15. Anderson (October 1987), "The State in the Middle East and North Africa".
16. Humphrey Trevelyan (1970), *The Middle East in Revolution*, first published in 1970 by Macmillan; London: Lume Books, 2019, p. 178.
17. Ibid., p. 177.
18. Peter Hinchcliffe, John T. Ducker, and Maria Holt (2006), *Without Glory in Arabia: The British Retreat from Aden*, 1st edn, London: I.B.Tauris, pp. 1–2. In Trevelyan's memoir, Trevelyan, (1970), *The Middle East in Revolution*, p. 175. "Fings Ain't Wot They Used T'Be" is the title of a song from a 1960 musical, mimicking a cockney dialect in the East End of London (https://en.wikipedia.org/wiki/Fings_Ain't_Wot_They_Used_T'Be).
19. Ibid., p. 178.
20. Elham Manea (2005), *Regional Politics of the Gulf*, pp. 28–31, 44–45, 48–50.
21. Scott Smitson (2014), "The Road to Good Intentions: British Nation-building in Aden", in K. Guttieri, V. Franke and M. Civic (eds), *Understanding Complex Military Operations: A Case Study Approach*, London: Routledge, p. 2.
22. Manea (2005), *Regional Politics*, pp. 28–31, 47–50.
23. Ibid.
24. Abatha (1979), *Ottoman Rule in Yemen: 1872–1918*, p. 337; Manea (2005), pp. 29–30.
25. Herbert J. Liebesny (Autumn 1955), "Administration and Legal Development in Arabia: Aden Colony and Protectorate", *Middle East Journal*, 9(4), pp. 385ff.
26. A/5446/Add.4 (8 October 1963), "Report of the Special Committee on the Situation with Regard to the Implementation of the Declaration on the Granting of Independence to Colonial Countries and Peoples", Aden: United Nations General Assembly, pp. 4ff; Liebesny (Autumn 1955).

27. A/5446/Add.4 (8 October 1963).; Liebesny (Autumn 1955).; R.R. Robbins (1939), "The Legal Status of Aden Colony and the Aden Protectorate", *The American Journal of International Law*, 33(4), p. 712.
28. A/5446/Add.4.
29. Manea (2011), *The Arab State*, pp. 63–64; Z.H. Kour (1981), *The History of Aden 1839–1872*, London: Frank Kass, p. 88; Warren Hastings' Act II of 1772, in Kashi Prasad Saksena (1963), *Muslim Law as Administered in India and Pakistan*, 4th edn, Lucknow: Eastern Book Company, p. 41.
30. Elham Manea (1994), *The Political Parties and Organizations in Yemen (1948–1993)*, (1993-1948) الأحزاب والتنظيمات السياسية في اليمن، in Arabic, Sana'a: Affaq for Publication; pp. 35ff; ; Response of the Secretary of State for Colonies (12 March 1957), in Hansard, Aden Colony and Protectorate, Volume 566, Column 1129, https://hansard.parliament.uk/Commons/1957-03-13/debates/dfa4677e-b23f-4ab0-bff7-e990746fffba/AdenColonyAndProtectorate#contribution-bf0724dc-ccbd-450c-b065-7f504a7e8fc1
31. John Albert Noel Brehony (2019), "Explaining the Triumph of the National Liberation Front", in Clive Jones (ed.), *Britain and State Formation in Arabia 1962–1971*, London: Routledge, p. 35.
32. Liebesny (Autumn 1955), "Administration and Legal Development in Arabia: Aden Colony and Protectorate", pp. 389–93.
33. Ibid., p. 390.
34. Ibid., p. 391
35. Ibid., p. 392.
36. Ibid.; W.H. Ingrams (1936), *Hadhramaut: A Report on the Social, Economic and Political Condition of the Hadhramaut*, London: The Colonial Office, pp. 12–13; Nora Salem Hassan bin Ma'ili (2022), *The Role of the Mahra in Resisting the Portuguese Invasion in the Sixteenth Century AD*, دور المهرة في مقاومة الغزو البرتغالي في القرن السادس عشر الميلادي, in Arabic, Al-Mahra: The Mahri Language Center for Studies and Research, pp. 22ff.
37. Liebesny (Autumn 1955), "Administration and Legal Development in Arabia: Aden Colony and Protectorate", pp. 392 ff; Ingrams, ibid., pp. 27–29; Nora Salem Hassan bin Ma'ili (2022), *The Role of the Mahra in Resisting the Portuguese Invasion in the Sixteenth Century AD*, pp. 38ff.
38. Liebesny (Autumn 1955).
39. Ibid., p. 394.
40. Ibid., pp. 394ff.
41. Ibid.
42. FCO 8/41, 1967.
43. Carapico, *Civil Society in Yemen*, p. 26; Manea (2005), pp. 48–50; Manea, field visit, Aden, October 2006.
44. FCO 8/41, 1967.
45. Scott Smitson (2014), p. 3.
46. Robert McNamara (2017), "The Nasser Factor: Anglo-Egyptian Relations and Yemen/Aden Crisis 1962–65", *Middle Eastern Studies*, 53(1), 51–68.
47. Letter 12367/58–60 of 27 March 1958 from Sir William Luce, KGMG, KBF, Governor of Aden, to Mr W.H. Corell Barnes, GB, CMG, Colonial Office (assistant under secretary of state for the colonies).
48. Ibid.
49. Ibid.

NOTES

50. The federated states were: the Emirate of Beihan, the Sultanate of Audhali, the Sultanate of Fadhli, the Emirate of Dhala (including the Quatibi), the Sheikhdom of Upper Aulaqi, the Sultanate of Lower Aulaqi, the Sultanate of Lower Yafa, the Sultanate of Lahej, the State of Dathina, the Sheikhdom of Aqrabi, and the Sultanate of Wahidi. Aden joined the Federation on 18 January 1963. Two more states, the Sheikhdom of Sha'ib and the Sultanate of Haushabi, joined on 31 March 1963.
51. Oral history narrated by Ambassador Mohammed Manea, a member of the Famous Forties in North Yemen, interviewed by the author (his daughter), in Sana'a, Yemen in 2006. On the reasons for the failed unification between Egypt and Syria see Monte Palmer (1966), "The United Arab Republic: An Assessment of Its Failure", *Middle East Journal*, 20(1), 50–67, www.jstor.org/stable/4323954; on the Famous Forties see Robert D. Burrowes (Winter 2005), "The Famous Forty and Their Companions: North Yemen's First-Generation Modernists and Educational Emigrants", *Middle East Journal*, 59(1), 81–97, www.jstor.org/stable/4330098.
52. *The Middle East and North Africa* (1997), "Yemen", General Surveys, 43rd edn, London, p. 1064.
53. John T. Ducker (2006), "Historical and Constitutional Background", in Peter Hinchcliffe, John T. Ducker, and Maria Holt (eds), *Without Glory in Arabia*, pp. 26–27.
54. FCO 8/41, 1967.
55. PRO Co 1015/2069.
56. Ducker (2006), "Historical and Constitutional Background", pp. 37–39.
57. Ibid., pp. 45ff, 49–50, 38.
58. Quoted in Smitson (2014), "The Road to Good Intentions: British Nation-building in Aden", p. 3.
59. Quoted in ibid.
60. Kennedy Trevaskis (2019), *The Deluge: Personal View of the End of Empire in the Middle East*, 1st edn, London: I.B.Tauris, p. 365.
61. FCO 8/41, 1967.
62. Ibid.
63. Ibid.
64. Ibid.
65. Ibid.
66. Field visit, Yemen, September/October 2006.
67. Manea (1994), *Political Parties and Organizations in Yemen*, pp. 47–50.
68. Ibid., p. 49.
69. Iman Mahmoud Nasser (8 October 2006), Director, Aden Institute for Micro Credit, interview by author, Aden.
70. FCO 8/41, 1967.
71. Manea (1994), *Political Parties and Organizations in Yemen*, p. 48.
72. Radya Ihasn Allah, interview by author, 8 October 2006. See note 5.
73. Interviewee asked to remain anonymous.
74. A/5446/Add.4 (8 October 1963), "Report of the Special Committee on the Situation with Regard to the Implementation of the Declaration on the Granting of Independence to Colonial Countries and Peoples", p. 9; Manea (1994), *Political Partie and Organizations in Yemens*, p. 52.
75. Cited in Manea, ibid., p. 55; Abdel Qawi Makkawi (1987), *South Yemen... Where To? The Faulty Experience and the Desired Solution*, Cairo: House of the Voice

of Lebanese Arabism, اليمن الجنوبي ... إلى أين؟ التجربة الخطأ والبديل المنشود, in Arabic, pp. 84–86.
76. FCO 8/356 1967 Saudi Arabia, see for example Record of Conversation with Ahmad Al Dini (Saudi Emissary from Kamel al-Adhan), sent 25 July 1967 from the Aden Department in the British Chancery, Jeddah, Saudi Arabia.
77. Created based on the UN General Assembly Resolution 2185 (XXI), 12 December 1966.
78. Mohammed Salim Basindawa (1989), *The Issue of Occupied South Yemen at the United Nations*, قضية الجنوب اليمني المحتل، in Arabic, Cairo: Al-Ahram Commercial Printer, pp. 374–75; Sir Richard Beaumont put the Yemeni population of Aden at 230,000 by 1965; see FCO 8/41, 1967.
79. A/5446/Add.4, (8 October 1963), "Report of the Special Committee on the Situation with Regard to the Implementation of the Declaration on the Granting of Independence to Colonial Countries and Peoples".; Manea (1994), *Political Parties and Organizations in Yemen*, pp. 63 ff; Ducker, (2006), "Historical and Constitutional Background", p. 42; Makkawi (1987), *South Yemen... Where To? The Faulty Experience and the Desired Solution* pp. 86–91; Ahmed Attia Al Massry (1988), *The Red Star Over Yemen: The Experience of the Revolution in Democratic Yemen*, النجم الأحمر فوق اليمن: تجربة الثورة في اليمن الديمقراطي, in Arabic, 3rd edn, Beirut: Institute of Arab Studies, pp. 94–100.
80. Manea (1994), *Political Parties and Organizaions in Yemen*, p. 64.
81. A/5446/Add.4, (8 October 1963), "Report of the Special Committee on the Situation with Regard to the Implementation of the Declaration on the Granting of Independence to Colonial Countries and Peoples".
82. Makkawi (1987), *South Yemen... Where To? The Faulty Experience and the Desired Solution*, pp. 103–04; Manea (1994), *Political Parties and Organizations in Yemen*, pp. 99ff.
83. Manea (1994); Makkawi (1987), pp. 144–46; Brehony (2019), "Explaining the Triumph of the National Liberation Front", p. 37; Al Massry (1988), *The Red Star Over Yemen: The Experience of the Revolution in Democratic Yemen*, pp. 108ff.
84. Manea (2005), *Regional Politics*, pp. 50–55; Manea (1994), *Political Parties and Organizations in Yemen*, pp. 71–78, 85–90; Makkawi, p. 145; Brehony, ibid., pp. 37–38; Mohammed Jamal Barout (1997), *Arab Nationalist Movement: Foundation, Evolution and Fates*, حركة القوميين العرب: النشأة، التطور، المصائر, in Arabic, Damascus: The Arabic Center for Strategic Studies, pp. 361ff.
85. Manea (1994), *Political Parties and Organizations in Yemen*, p. 75.
86. Barout (1997), *Arab Nationalist Movement: Foundation, Evolution and Fate*, pp. 355–56.
87. Barout (1997), pp. 363ff; Makkawi, (1987), *South Yemen... Where To? The Faulty Experience and the Desired*, pp. 147–53; Manea (1994), *Political Parties*, pp. 94ff.
88. Manea (2011), *The Arab State*, pp. 102ff.
89. Fred Halliday's assessment differs from mine. He argues that "on the basis of evidence so far available, the British government had no understanding with the NF until November 1967. The decision to recognize it as the successor government was taken not out of political preference but in light of the practical consideration that it was the NF which exercised power in all regions of the country not remaining under British rule." See Fred Halliday (1990), *Revolution and Foreign Policy: The Case of South Yemen 1967–1987*, Cambridge: Cambridge University Press, p. 17.
90. FCO 8/356 1967.

91. For more detail see Halliday (1990), pp. 14, 20.
92. First Statement of the NF, 30 November 1967, quoted in Al Massry (1988), *The Red Star Over Yemen: The Experience of the Revolution in Democratic Yemen*, p. 309.
93. A symbolic gesture that reflected this determination was the NF's later decision to change the name of the People's Republic of South Yemen to the People's Democratic Republic of Yemen (PDRY).
94. Interview with Haidar Abu Bakr Al Attas (20 August 2021), مقابلة مع حيدر العطاس رئيس الوزراء في جمهورية اليمن الديمقراطية الشعبية, in Arabic, *The Political Memory*, Part Two, Al Arabyia TV, minute 13; ١٥.; "Memorandum of Agreed Points Relating to Independence for South Arabia" (29 November 1967), Article Two, copy in FO 1016/772.

Chapter 7: The Cunning State and the Politics of Survival

1. Radhya al-Mutawakel (chairwoman of the Mwatana Organization for Human Rights), Zoom interview by author, 23 June 2020.
2. For example, this author warned against it in a policy brief published in September 2012 by the Norwegian Peacebuilding Resource Centre: "while political transition and the accompanying Gulf Initiative are welcome, they are likely to generate further pressures towards secession and armed rebellion unless they address the deep structural sources of state weakness". See Elham Manea (September 2012), "The Perils of the Yemeni Cunning State", Noref Report, The Norwegian Peacebuilding Resource Centre, p. 1.
3. Daron Acemoğlu and James A. Robinson (2012), *Why Nations Fail*, New York: Crown Business, p. 372.
4. Brad Amburn (22 October 2009), "The Failed States Index 2005", *Foreign Policy*, p. 4, http://foreignpolicy.com/2009/10/22/the-failed-states-index-2005.
5. David Carment, Joe Landry, Yiagadeeseen Samy and Scott Shaw (2015), "Towards a Theory of Fragile State Transitions: Evidence from Yemen, Bangladesh and Laos", *Third World Quarterly*, 36(7), p. 1328.
6. Ibid.
7. Lars-Erik Cederman, Kristian Skrede Gleditsch and Halvard Buhaug (2013), *Inequality, Grievances, and Civil War*, Cambridge: Cambridge University Press, p. 205.
8. Ibid.
9. Ibid., p. 32.
10. Stuart J. Kaufman (2016), pp. 91, 101.
11. Myra A. Waterbury (9 July 2020).
12. Andreas Wimmer, Lars-Erik Cederman, and Brian Min (2009), "Ethnic Politics and Armed Conflict: A Configurational Analysis of a New Global Data Set", *American Sociological Review*, 74(2), 319–21.
13. Cederman et al. (2013), *Inequality, Grievances, and Civil War*, p. 210.
14. Treaty of Friendship and Mutual Co-operation between the United Kingdom and the Yemen (11 February 1934), Sana'a, Yemen.
15. For more information, see Manea (2005), ch. 2.
16. For more detail, see Manea (2005), ch. 3.
17. Manea (2005); Marius Deeb (Summer 1986), "Radical Political Ideologies and Concepts of Property in Libya and South Yemen", *The Middle East Journal*, 40(3), p. 458.

18. Manea (2005); Paul K. Dresch (1995), "The Tribal Factor in the Yemeni Crisis", in Jamal S. al-Suwaidi (ed.), *The Yemen War of 1994: Causes and Consequences*, Abu Dhabi, p. 37.
19. This number eventually was halved as the democratic experience matured.
20. One example is the bombing of the house of Yehia Hussain Al-Aarashi, Northern Minister of Unity Affairs between 1986 and 1990. Yehia Hussain Al-Aarashi (Northern Minister of Unity Affairs between 1986 and 1990), Zoom interview with Al-Aarashi by author, 13 August 2022.
21. Michael C. Hudson (1995), "Bipolarity, Rational Calculation and War in Yemen", in Jamal S. al-Suwaidi (ed.), *The Yemeni War of 1994*, pp. 20–21, 22–32; Manea (2005), pp. 56–66.
22. Elham Manea (2017), "Jemen: Die Geschichte eines fragilen Staates", in Helmut Krieger and Magda Seewald (Hrsg.), *Krise, Revolte und Krieg in der arabischen Welt*, Wiener Institut für Entwicklungsfragen (VIDC): Vienna, pp. 156–58; for more information see Manea (2005), ch. 4.
23. Christopher Boucek (2010), "War in Saada: From Local Insurrection to National Challenge", *A Carnegie Paper Series*, Washington, DC: Carnegie Endowment for International Peace, https://carnegieendowment.org/files/war_in_saada.pdf.
24. See Shalini Randeria (2003), "Between Cunning States and Unaccountable International Institutions: Legal Plurality, Social Movements and Rights of Local Communities to Common Property Resources", *European Journal of Sociology*, 44(1), pp. 27–60.
25. Joel Migdal was the first to introduce the concept of the politics of survival within a Middle Eastern context. See Joel Migdal (1989), *Strong Societies and Weak States: State–Society Relations and State Capabilities in the Third World*, Princeton, NJ: Princeton University Press, ch. 6.
26. For more information on this stratum during the imamate periods see Qaid Noman al-Sharjabi (1986), *The Traditional Social Strata in Yemeni Society*, الشرائح الاجتماعية التقليدية في المجتمع اليمني, in Arabic, Sana'a: Dar Al Hadatha and Yemeni Centre for Studies and Research, p. 138ff; see also Manea (1994), *Political Parties and Organizations in Yemen*, pp. 115–18.
27. Al-Sharjabi (1986), pp. 156ff; Manea (1994).
28. Al-Sharjabi (1986), footnote (**), p. 151.
29. For more information on these policies see Marieke Brandt (2014), "Inhabiting Tribal Structures: Leadership Hierarchies in Tribal Upper Yemen", in Andre Gingrich and Siegfried Hass (eds), *Southwest Arabia Across History: Essay to the Memory of Walter Dostal*, Wien: Verlag der Österreichis Akademie der Wissenschaften, pp. 91–116.
30. Manea (1994), pp. 117–18.
31. Interview with Haidar Abu Bakr Al Attas, 13 August 2021, *The Political Memory*, in Arabic, Part One, Al Arabyia TV, minute 16:51ff.
32. Ibid.
33. Sami Ghalib, interview by author, 2010, and field visit, Yemen, 2006.
34. Former president Ali Nasr Mohammed used the expression Zumra (clique) for the first time in his first TV statement on 13 January 1986, where he announced the "thwarting of a failed coup attempt, orchestrated by the divisive coup 'Zumra clique', with the aim of seizing power, undermining the unity of the people and overturning development". See the clip of his TV announcement in the *Investigator*, 19 August 2022, ibid., minute 51:11. However, over time, the expression Zumra was used to refer to Ali Nasr Mohammed and his power base in Abyan and Shabwa

and the expression Tougmah to refer to his opponents from Dhala, Radfan, and Yafa. See the *Investigator* (26 August 2022), "The Enemies Brothers", *Al Jazeera*, الأخوة الأعداء, in Arabic, Part Two, shorturl.at/DFIU9.
35. Maysaa Shuja al-Deen (April 2021), "Presidential Councils in Yemen: Exploring Past Attempts at Power Sharing and Possibilities for the Future", Sana'a: Sana'a Center for Strategic Studies, p. 12.
36. Mohamed Ghobari and Ahmed Tolba (8 April 2022), "Yemen President Cedes Powers to Council as Saudi Arabia Pushes to End War", Reuters, www.reuters.com/world/middle-east/yemen-president-relieves-deputy-his-post-2022-04-07.
37. Ali Al Bukhaiti, former spokesperson of the Houthi Movement, follow-up Zoom interview by author (16 August 2022). On the tribal grievances and the state's divide-and-rule policy, see Marieke Brandt (2017), *Tribes and Politics in Yemen*, chs 2 and 4.
38. Al Bukhaiti, interview.
39. Akhlaq Al Shami (member of the Political Bureau of Ansar Allah and the Secretary General of the Supreme Council for Motherhood and Childhood), Zoom interview by author (1 February 2022); Bernard Haykel translates the word as rulership. In the interviews conducted by this author, it is used to mean a form of guardianship that designates the cousin of Mohammed to be the ruler. See Bernard Haykel (2022), "The Huthi Movement's Religious and Political Ideology and Its Relationship to Zaydism in Yemen", in Abdullah Hamidaddin (ed.), *The Huthi Movement in Yemen: Ideology, Ambition and Security in the Arab Gulf*, London: I.B.Tauris, p. 25.
40. Al Shami, interview.
41. For more information see Ayatollah Khomeini (1982), *Islamic Government*, 2nd edn, Rome: European Islamic Cultural Centre, pp. 32–120; and Hamid Mavani (2011), "Ayatullah Khomeini's Concept of Governance (*wilayat al-faqih*) and the Classical Shi'i Doctrine of Imamate", *Middle Eastern Studies*, 47(5), pp. 807–24.
42. Haykel (2022), "The Huthi Movement's Religious and Political Ideology and Its Relationship to Zaydism in Yemen", pp. 22–26.

Chapter 8: The Role of the Cunning State

1. Rim Mugahed (21 January 2022), "Tribes and the State in Yemen", Sana'a: Sana'a Center for Strategic Studies, p. 10.
2. Ibid.; Manea (2005), pp. 32–34.
3. Rashad Al-Alimi (n.d.), *The Tribal Judiciary in Yemeni Society*, القضاء القبلي في المجتمع اليمني, in Arabic, Sana'a, pp. 30–35; al-Sharjabi (1986), *The Traditional Social Strata in Yemeni Society*, pp. 72–75; Ahmed Kaid al-Saidy (1983), *The Yemeni Opposition Movement During the Era of Imam Yehia ibn Mohammed Hamid al-Dien*, حركة المعارضة اليمنية في عهد الإمام يحي بن محمد حميد الدين, in Arabic, Sana'a, pp. 140–42.
4. Mohammed Ahmed Noman (1965), *The Stakeholders in Yemen*, الأطراف المعنية في اليمن, in Arabic, Beirut: Publications of Al Qiban Institute, p. 18.
5. *The Memoir of the President Judge Abdul Rahman bin Yehia al-Eryani* (2013), مذكرات الرئيس القاضي عبدالرحمن بن يحي الأرياني, in Arabic, Part One: 1910–1962; pp. 62–66.
6. Ibid., pp. 65–66.
7. Roger D. Petersen (2002), *Understanding Ethnic Violence: Fear, Hatred, and Resentment in Twentieth-Century Eastern Europe*, Cambridge: Cambridge University Press, pp. 17ff.

8. Ibid.
9. Ibid., p. 17.
10. Based on the hypothesis suggested by Petersen on resentment. Ibid., p. 25.
11. See *The Memoir of Yehia al-Eryani* (2013), in Arabic, Part Two: 1962–1967; pp. 22–23; Al Bukhaiti, interview.; *The Memoir of Jarallah Omar* (leader of the Northern National Liberation Front and a member of the Politburo of the Yemeni Socialist Party) (2007), من مذكرات جار الله عمر, in Arabic, Sana'a: Yemeni Cultural Development Foundation, pp. 30–31.
12. Al Bukhaiti, interview.
13. See, for example, how Abd al-Rhaman al-Baidhani, who held the positions of vice president and prime minister after the 1962 coup, framed the conflict in series of articles published in Egypt before the coup. Abd al-Rhaman Al-Baidhani (n.d.), *The Mutawakilia Games*, الألاعيب متوكيلة, in Arabic, Collected Articles by the Yemeni Historical Library. See as well how former president al-Eryani strongly criticized this framing for its "racism" and "divisive nature" in his memoir, *The Memoir of Yehia al-Eryani* (2013) و , Part One, p. 408. Also see the memoir of Sheikh Sinan Abu Lahoum, the paramount sheikh of the Bakil tribal federation, who recounted in a matter-of-fact way a conversation he had with Qasim Ghalib, the first Yemeni educational minister. In 1961, before the coup, Mr Ghalib, who comes from Taiz, told him he met al-Baidhani in Egypt and they agreed to "change the idea [of ending the imamate regime] to Qahtani and Hashimite" because "the sectarian strife between Zaydis and Shafi'is has ended", Sheikh Sinan Abu Lahoum (2004), *The Memoir of Sinan Abu Lahoum*, in Arabic, مذكرات الشيخ سنان أبو لحوم: حقائق ووثائق عشتها, in Arabic, Part One (1943–1962), 3rd edn, Sana'a: Al Afif Cultural Institute, p. 284; also see how Mohammed Al Zubari, an icon in the Northern Yemeni reform movement and assassinated, among other reasons, for his call of reconciliation with the Hashemites, rejected this type of framing and racial targeting of the Hashemites in his novel, *Waq al Waq*. Mohammed Mahmoud Al Zubairi (2015), *Waq al Waq*, واق الواق, in Arabic, republished edition, Qatar: The Ministry of Culture, Arts and Heritage, pp. 197 ff.
14. Roger D. Petersen and Sarah Zuckerman (2010), "Anger, Violence, and Political Science", in Michael Potegal et al. (eds), *International Handbook of Anger*, New York: Springer, p. 562.
15. Zartman defines "hurting stalemate" in conflict as a situation where "parties find themselves locked in a conflict from which they cannot escalate to victory and this deadlock is painful to both of them (although not necessarily in equal degrees or for the same reasons), so they seek a way out". See I. William Zartman (2010), "Ripeness: The Hurting Stalemate and Beyond", in Paul C. Stern, *International Conflict Resolution after the Cold War*, Washington, DC: National Academy Press, p. 228.
16. Petersen and Zuckerman (2010), "Anger, Violence, and Political Science , pp. 566ff.
17. Sami Ghalib, interview; field visit, Yemen, 2006.
18. On these divisions see for instance *The Memoir of Jarallah Omar (2007)*, p. 82; Fred Halliday (1986), "Catastrophe in South Yemen: A Preliminary Assessment", *MERIP Middle East Report*, *139*, p. 39; Ali Al Sarraf (1992), *South Yemen: Political Life From Colonialism to Unity*, اليمن الجنوبي: الحياة السياسية من الاستعمار إلى الوحدة, in Arabic, UK: Riad El Rayyes Books, pp. 240ff.
19. Al Sarraf (1992), pp. 240–52.
20. *The Investigator* (19 August 2022), "*The Investigator* opens the File of the Enemy Brothers in Yemen (South Yemen) and Ali Nasr Speaks for the first time about

NOTES

the 1986 Events", المُتَحَرّي يفتح ملف صراع الأخوة الأعداء في اليمن وعلي ناصر يتحدث لأول مرة عن تفاصيل أحداث 1986, in Arabic, *The Investigator*, Al Jazeera documentary, in Arabic, minute 40ff; shorturl.at/bcnp8; For more details, see Manea (2005), ch. 3.
21. *The Investigator* (19 August 2022), minute 45ff.
22. Al Sarraf (1992), (1992), *South Yemen: Political Life From Colonialism to Unity*, p. 360.
23. Khawla Ahmed Sharaf, member of the 1993 parliament, member of the Central Committee of the Socialist Party and a former member of the party's politburo, interview by author (9 October 2006), Aden.
24. David Warburton (1995), "The Conventional War in Yemen", *The Arab Studies Journal*, 3(1), p. 24.
25. Elham Manea (2014), "Yemen's Arab Spring: Outsmarting the Cunning State?", pp. 166–67.
26. Elham Manea (2011), *The Arab State*, pp. 107–09.
27. Reva Bhalla (21 April 2011), *Islamist Militancy in a Pre- and Post-Saleh Yemen*, Global Intelligence Stratfor, https://worldview.stratfor.com/article/islamist-militancy-pre-and-post-saleh-yemen.
28. Joseph Kostiner (1996), *Yemen: The Tortuous Quest for Unity, 1990–94*, London: The Royal Institute of International Affairs, p. 27; see Manea (2005), ch. 4.
29. Kostiner (1996), p. 28; Manea (2005).
30. Kostiner (1996), p. 27.
31. Elham Manea (2011), pp. 134–37.
32. For example, the famous fatwa (religious edict) of Abul Wahhab al Dailami, which was broadcast on Radio Sana'a on 6 June 1994, and republished in the Islah newspaper, *al Sahwa* الصحوة, on 15 January 1995. Al Dailami said, among other things, "Those who fight on the side of these apostates want to raise the banner [power] of blasphemy and diminish the strength [power] of Islam. Accordingly, the scholars say, whoever rejoices in himself when the banner of unbelief is high and the power of Islam is low, then he is a hypocrite. But if he declares that and shows it, he is also an apostate." See the dispatches of the Foreign Broadcast Information Service FBIS-NEW-94-113 (13 June 1993), *Daily Report: Near East and South Asia*, p. 33; see also two articles, which cited the fatwa upon Al Dailami's death, one defending his position and the other attacking him for it. Mara'ay Hamid (29 May 2021), "Al Dailami Fatwa on the South and Unity: The Whole Story", *Scholars Forum*, فتوى الديلمي حول الجنوب والوحدة... القصة الكاملة, in Arabic, shorturl.at/APUX7; Sama Al Watan (29 May 2021), "Sama Al-Watan Publishes a Historical Account of the Mufti of Blood Abdul Wahab Al-Dailami, Known for the Fatwa Against the Sons of the South", Sama Al Watan, سماء الوطن تنشر سرد تاريخ لمفتي الدم عبدالوهاب الديلمي المعروف بفتوى استباحة أبناء الجنوب, in Arabic, https://alwatanskynews.com/post/3470.).
33. In reference to the series of military wars waged after the death of Mohammed in 632 against tribes of Arabia who reversed their allegiance and refused to pay taxes imposed by the nascent Islamic state. Their withdrawal was also framed in religious terms, despite the fact that the core of the issue was refusal to pay taxes.
34. See, for instance, the reference to the "Ridda war" in Abudlwahhab Al Rohani (6 July 1994), "The Ridda War… the Cleanest War for the Most Marvellous Unity", *22 May Newspaper*, حرب الردة...أنظف حرب لأروع وحدة, in Arabic, Issue 153, p. 3.

For the interviews with the religious leaders and their religious framing of the war see Mohamad Al Rajawy (22 June 1994), "Religious Leaders of Hajah: The Separatists are Transgressors and Should Be Fought", *22 May Newspaper*, علماء حجة: الانفصاليون بغاة يجب مقاتلتهم, in Arabic, Issue 152, p. 3.

239

35. See, for example, Reuters dispatches from Aden, William Maclean (9 June 1994), "Aden Threatened by Water Shortages, Aid Workers Say", Reuters, Aden; Mohammed Mokhashef (16 June 1994), "Fear, Panic Hit Aden after Northern Warning", Reuters, Aden; Mohammed Mokhashef (17 June 1994), "North Yemen Blasts Aden with Shells and Rockets", Reuters, Aden; Dominic Evans (10 June 1994), "Yemeni Soldiers, Civilians Loot Food Warehouse", Reuters, Aden; Dominic Evans (12 June 1994), "Yemen Ministers Seek Ways to End Aden Chaos", Reuters, Aden.
36. See Yaseen Abdul Razzaq, lawyer and member of the Arab Institute for Human Rights, (n.d.), "Report on the Human Rights Conditions in the Yemeni Republic in a Year: From 7 July 1994 to 17 July 1995", تقرير حول أوضاع حقوق الإنسان في ج.ي. خلال عام – من الناحيتين السياسية والصحفية من 7 يوليو 1994 إلى 17 يوليو 1995, in Arabic (hard copy was given to the author during her fieldwork in 2006).
37. Razzaq, p. 1.
38. Ibid.
39. Raqia Abd al-Qader Humaidan (lawyer and women's activist), interview by author (7 October 2006), Aden, Yemen; Imam Kulthom Mahmoud Nasser (President, Society for Business Women in Aden), interview by author (10 October 2006), Aden, Yemen; Afandi Abd Ra'bu Hamid (Former Assistant Professor in Biochemistry, Sana'a University and Member, Southern Opposition Movement, interview by author (20 September 2006), Bern, Switzerland; fieldwork by author in Yemen, 2006; Manea (2011), pp. 134–35.
40. Through my interviews I learned that what happened in 1994 and the branding of Southerners as "communist infidels" and the Northern regime's use of Arab Afghan clearly created a deep wound that has yet to heal. It is also used in the narration of Southern grievances by those demanding separation. Nazar Haitham (Speaker of the Southern Transitional Council), telephone interview by author (24 August 2020).
41. Interviewees told me during my fieldwork in 2006 in the South that the Northern Yemeni Sunni Shafites had been instrumental in changing the demographic structure of the Southern part of Yemen, most evident in Aden, which was flooded by migrants from Taiz city after the end of the civil war of 1994. It was not clear to me whether this process was systematically engineered by Saleh's regime, or has mainly been a natural outcome of the economic development that Aden has started to witness. This perception led to grave acts of aggression against Northerners living in Southern regions. For example, in April 2010, unknown people set fire to a building inhabited by Northerners in Lahj. The incident happened two days after a group of the secessionist movement forced a Northerner to walk naked in the street. In the same month, during riots that erupted in the Southern Hadramawt region, demonstrators set fire to hundreds of shops owned by Northerners. This trend became more systematic after the Houthi were pushed back from the South in 2015, when measures were taken to expel Northerners from the South by Al Hirak (a Southern movement established in 2007 demanding that South Yemen secede from the Republic of Yemen) and later by the Southern Transitional Council, a Southern movement calling for independence of the South in a federal state, created in 2017, which is now part of the internationally recognized Yemeni government. Nevertheless, it has been pushing for de facto separation of the South.
42. N.N. (2020), "Building for Peace: Reconstruction for Security, Equity, and Sustainable Peace in MENA", World Bank Group and German Cooperation, pp. xiii, 9–10; cited in Elham Manea (February 2021), ibid., p. 61.

NOTES

43. Ibid.
44. Admittedly, it is difficult to separate the internal context from the regional one (as the case of the religious institutes shows). However, this volume will focus on the internal causes of Saada's grievances. The second volume of this research project, *Gulf Rivalry and the Yemeni Civil War*, will focus on the role of Saudi Arabia and the 2000 Treaty of Jeddah, which demarcated the borders between Yemen and Saudi Arabia, and its impact on economic and social structures in Saada.
45. Christopher Paul, Colin P. Clarke, Beth Grill, and Molly Dunigan (2013), "Yemen, 1962–1970: Case Outcome: COIN Loss", in *Paths to Victory: Detailed Insurgency Case Studies*, RAND Corporation, pp. 259–60.
46. Khadija Al-Haisamy (1983), 1980-1962: العلاقات اليمنية السعودية , in Arabic, *Yemeni–Saudi Relations: 1962–1980*, in Arabic, Cairo, pp. 238ff.
47. Ibid.
48. See the *Memoir of Yehia al-Eryani* (2013), Part One, p. 408.
49. Paul et al. . (2013), "Yemen, 1962–1970: Case Outcome: COIN Loss".
50. See Marieke Brandt (2017), pp. 39ff; Brian M. Perkins (2017), "Yemen: Between Revolution and Regression", *Studies in Conflict & Terrorism*, 40(4), 300–17, DOI: 10.1080/1057610X.2016.1205368, p. 307.
51. See Manea (2005), chs 2 and 3; Mark N. Katz (1992), "Yemen Unity and Saudi Security", *Middle East Policy*, 1(1), p. 121; ibid.; F. Gregory Gause III (1988), "Yemeni Unity: Past and Future", *Middle East Journal*, 41(1), p. 40.
52. Maysaa Shuja al-Deen (2021), "Yemen's War-torn Rivalries for Religious Education", in Frederic Wehrey (ed.), *Islamic Institutions in Arab States: Mapping the Dynamics of Control, Co-option, and Contention*, Washington, DC: Carnegie Endowment for International Peace, p. 37.
53. Shuja al-Deen (2021).
54. The Muslim Brotherhood was founded in 1928 in Al-Ismailia in Egypt by a primary school teacher called Hasan Al Banna (1906–1949). It was inspired by Salafi Islam and European nationalist movements. It can be described as a reaction to the advance of modernity, to the national secularism of Kemal Ataturk in Turkey, and to European colonization. It propagates an ideology—a modern ideology—which seeks state political power as a means of changing and transforming existing societies. Power is only a means to an end. Its goal is a revolutionary change compelled by a vision of a puritanical society and state. See Elham Manea (2021), *The Perils of Nonviolent Islamism*, New York: Telos Press Publishing, pp. 71–81; Barry Rubin (ed.) (2007), *Political Islam I*, London: Routledge, pp. 1–44; Bassam Tibi (2012), *Islamism and Islam*, Boston: Yale University Press, pp. 1–30.
55. Al-Deen (2021), "Yemen's War-torn Rivalries for Religious Education", pp. 37–39.
56. Ibid.
57. Elham Manea (2021), *The Perils of Nonviolent Islamism*, pp. 65–66.
58. Shuja al-Deen (2021), "Yemen's War-torn Rivalries for Religious Education", pp. 39–43; Laurent Bonnefoy (2011), *Salafism in Yemen: Transnationalism and Religious Identity*, New York: Columbia University Press, pp. 151ff; Paul et al. (2013), (2013), "Yemen, 1962–1970: Case Outcome: COIN Loss", pp. 259–60.
59. Al-Deen (2021); Bonnefoy (2011), ibid.
60. Shelagh Weir (2007), *A Tribal Order: Politics and Law in the Mountains of Yemen*, Austin: University of Texas Press, p. 296; al-Deen (2021).
61. Shuja al-Deen (2021), p. 39; Laurent Bonnefoy (2008), "Salafism in Yemen: A 'Saudisation'?", in Madawi Al-Rasheed (ed.), *Kingdom without Borders: Saudi Political,*

Religious and Media Frontiers, London: Hurst, pp. 249–50; Marieke Brandt (2017), *Tribes and Politics in Yemen,* pp. 106–07.
62. Shelagh Weir (2007), *A Tribal Order: Politics and Law in the Mountains of Yemen,* p. 296.
63. Ibid.
64. Ibid.
65. Ibid., p. 297.
66. A second type is called the politicos. They use political means to propagate their ideas and put them into practice. In this way they hope to create a society where God alone has the right to legislate. They should not be confused with the political Islamists of the Muslim Brotherhood or its relatives. This second type remains Salafi to the core. The third type is the jihadis. They take a militant position, arguing that the current context calls for violence and revolution. All three factions share a common creed but offer different explanations of the contemporary world and its associated problems and thus propose different solutions. For more information, see Quintan Wiktorowicz (2006), "Anatomy of the Salafi Movement", *Studies in Conflict & Terrorism,* 29(3), 207–39; Manea (2021), *The Perils of Nonviolent Islamism,* p. 69.
67. Wiktorowicz (2006); Manea (2021).
68. Al-Deen (2021) "Yemen's War-torn Rivalries for Religious Education", pp. 39–43.
69. Isa Blumi (2011), *Chaos in Yemen,* p. 143; Manea (2014), *Yemen's Arab Spring: Outsmarting The Cunning State,* pp. 167–68; Sarah Phillips (2011), *Yemen and the Politics of Permanent Crisis,* London: The International Institute for Strategic Studies, p. 139.
70. Weir (2007), *A Tribal Order: Politics and Law in the Mountains of Yemen,* pp. 296–97.
71. Sadiq Mohammed Al Safwany (2019), "The Establishment of Yemeni Student Missions in Egypt in the 1930s", تأسيس البعثات الطلابية اليمنية في مصر في ثلاثينات القرن العشرين, in Arabic, *Arabian Humanities,* published online 3 May 2020, accessed 23 September 2022, http://journals.openedition.org/cy/5314, p. 5ff.
Adnan Abdat Nasher Abdullah (1994), *Education in the Ottoman, Imamate Royal and British Eras in Yemen to the 1962 Yemeni Revolution,* التعليم في العهد العثماني والإمامي الملكي والبريطاني في اليمن إلى الثورة اليمنية 1962م, in Arabic, Master's thesis, Amman: Jordanian University, p. 13ff; Robert D. Burrowes (Winter 2005), "The Famous Forty and Their Companions: North Yemen's First-Generation Modernists and Educational Emigrants", p. 81.
72. Al Safwany (2019), ; Adnan Abdat Nasher Abdullah (1994), pp. 22ff; Mohammed Ahmad Zabarah (1982), *Yemen: Traditionalism vs. Modernity,* New York: Praeger, p. 16.
73. Zabarah (1982).
74. Zabarah (1982), p. 17; Al Safwany (2019), "The Establishment of Yemeni Student Missions in Egypt in the 1930s"; Adnan Abdat Nasher Abdullah (1994), pp. 25ff.
75. Oral History narrated by Ambassador Mohammed Manea, member of "Famous Forties" in North Yemen, interviewed by author (his daughter), in Sana'a, Yemen in 2006.
76. Al Safwany (2019), "The Establishment of Yemeni Student Missions in Egypt in the 1930s", p. 6.
77. Juliette Honvault and Talal Al-Rashoud (2020), "Modern Education in the Arabian Peninsula: Social Dynamics and Political Issues", *CEFAS: Arabian*

NOTES

Humanities: Education in the Arabian Peninsula During the First Half of the Twentieth Century, p. 7.

78. Marieke Brandt (2019), "The War in Yemen, Bottom-up: Tribal Politics in Depth and in Motion", *British Yemeni Society Journal*, 27, 12–13.
79. Brandt (2019), p. 13.
80. Interview in person by author with a Yemeni researcher, a member of an influential tribal sheikh family, who spoke on condition of anonymity. The interview took place in 2021 but its location is not mentioned in compliance with the wish for anonymity.
81. Ibid.
82. For more information on the principle of *al-wala' wa-l-bara* الولاء والبراءة, see Benham T. Said and Hazim Fouad (eds) (2014), *Salafismus: Auf der suche nach der wahren Islam*, Freiburg: Herder Verlag, pp. 64–74.
83. In a 2008 column in the Yemeni newspaper *Al Thawra*, Al Aghbary observed the tendency of teenagers to demand from their parents and grandparents that they "go back to the right religion", Samia Abd al Majeed Al Aghbary (2008), "Sheikhs in Teenage Years", شيوخ في سنوات المراهقة, in Arabic, *Al Thawrah*, 26 March 2008.
84. Houth or Huth (in other references) is a place, a city in Amran governorate. It is used as a surname by many families in the area, including the family of Badr al-Din al-Houthi.
85. Mohammed Azzan, founding member and former Secretary General of the Believing Youth Forum, Zoom interview by author (13 August 2020); Shuja al-Deen (2021), "Yemen's War-torn Rivalries for Religious Education", pp. 46–47; Al Bukhaiti, Zoom interview.
86. Shuja al-Deen (2021), "Yemen's War-torn Rivalries for Religious Education", pp. 46ff; Azzan, interview.
87. Ahmed Naji (2022), "Ansar Allah Movement: Reviving the Lost Zaydi Imamate in Yemen", حركة أنصار الله: إحياء الإمامة الزيدية المفقودة في اليمن, in Arabic, in Abdullah Mohammed Al Taii (ed.), *Al Hawza and the State: Shiite Islam... Questions of Power, Women and Geopolitics*, الحوزة والدولة: الإسلام الشيعي... أسئلة السلطة والمرأة والجيوبولتيك, in Arabic, Amman: Friedrich Ebert Stiftung Office in Jordan, p. 142.
    Brandt (2017), *Tribes and Politics in Yemen*, pp. 114–15.
88. *Taqiyya* التقية means fear or caution in Arabic, as mentioned in Chapter Three. As a practice it means precautionary suppression or concealing of one's beliefs.
89. Brandt (2017), *Tribes and Politics in Yemen*, pp. 114ff; Mohammed Yehia Azzan (6 September 2002), "A Reading in the Imamate Theory in Zaydism", قراءة في نظيرة الإمامة عند الزيدية, in Arabic, *Al Masar Periodical*, 9, p. 39ff.
90. Azzan, 6 September 2002), "A Reading in the Imamate Theory in Zaydism", p. 40.
91. Mohammed Azzan was born in 1967 in Razah to a family in the tribe of Khawlan bin Amer. He received a solid Zaydi religious education and became known for his writings on Zaydism and its different schools. He was a founding member of the Believing Youth Forum. After a disagreement with Hussein al-Houthi, who tried to take over the movement, the forum split into two parts, one of which is the Houthi movement.
92. Azzan, Zoom interview.
93. Manea (2005), p. 108; Shahram Chubin and Charles Tripp (1988), *Iran and Iraq at War*, London, pp. 158ff.
94. Naji (2022), "Ansar Allah Movement: Reviving the Lost Zaydi Imamate in Yemen", p. 131.
95. Azzan, interview.

96. Azzan, interview.
97. Haykel (2022), "The Huthi Movement's Religious and Political Ideology and Its Relationship to Zaydism in Yemen", p. 20.
98. Zayd al-Dhari, head of the National Concord Forum and an instrumental figure in President Saleh's rapprochement with Zaydi figures in the 1990s, interview by author (29 July 2021), Cairo, Egypt.
99. Brandt (2017), *Tribes and Politics in Yemen*, p. 115; Zayd al-Dhari (29 July 2021), interview.
100. Reva Bhalla (21 April 2011), *Islamist Militancy in a Pre- and Post-Saleh Yemen*, Global Intelligence Stratfor, https://worldview.stratfor.com/article/islamist-militancy-pre-and-post-saleh-yemen.
101. Dr Abdel Karim Sallam, Yemeni analyst and journalist, interview by author (10 September 2006), Sana'a, Yemen. It is no coincidence that the 1990s witnessed the foundation of several universities and religious seminaries that follow the three religious groups. For example, Maysaa Shuja al-Deen explains that following the 1994 civil war, Saleh began to give more space to other religious schools to counterbalance and weaken those of the Salafists and the Muslim Brotherhood. After the Yemeni Congregation for Reform (Islah) left the government in 1997, the state's warming ties with the Sufis became more apparent. Sufi Sheikh Mohammad Ali Mira'i became a member of Saleh's General People's Congress, and in 2000 he founded the College of Sharia Studies in Hudayda. Salafi universities were founded in the early 1990s, such as the Al-Eman University in Sana'a, headed by Abdulmajid al-Zindani, and al Ahgaff University in Hadhramaut governorate, founded in 1994. Shuja al-Deen (2021), "Yemen's War-torn Rivalries for Religious Education", p. 41, 44.
102. Saleh Al Baydani (11 November 2018), "Muhammed Azzan: Al-Houthi Directed the Path of the "Believing Youth" to an Extremist Project", الحوثي وجه مسار الشباب المؤمن إلى مشروع متطرف, in Arabic, Al Arab.
103. Al-Dhari (29 July 2021), interview.
104. Ibid.
105. Ibid.
106. Ibid.
107. Reva Bhalla (2011).
108. Reva Bhalla tells us that Saleh's son and preferred successor, Ahmed Ali Saleh, became head of the elite Republican Guard (roughly 30,000-plus men) and Special Operations Forces. Saleh's half-brother, Mohammed Saleh al-Ahmar, was made chief of staff of the supreme commander of the Armed Forces and supervisor to the Republican Guard. Saleh's nephews—the sons of his late brother Muhammad Abdullah Saleh—were appointed to key positions. Yehia became chief of staff of the Central Security Forces and Counter-Terrorism Unit (roughly 50,000-plus men); Tariq was made commander of the Special Guard (which effectively falls under the authority of Ahmed's Republican Guard); and Ammar became principal duty director of the National Security Bureau (NSB). All of Saleh's sons, cousins, and nephews were "evenly distributed throughout the Republican Guard. Each of these agencies received a substantial amount of money as U.S. financial aid to Yemen increased from $5 million in 2006 to $155 million in 2010. This was expected to rise to $1 billion or more over the next several years, but Washington froze the first instalment in February 2011 when the protests broke out. Ahmed's Republican Guard and Special Operations Forces worked closely with U.S. military trainers in trying to develop an elite fighting force along the lines of Jordan's U.S.-trained Fursan al-Haq (Knights of Justice)." See Reva Bhalla, ibid.

NOTES

109. Bhalla (2011).
110. Reuters Staff (23 September 2011); Elham Manea (19 March 2011).
111. Manea (2011), footnote 76, p. 212.
112. Haykel (2022), "The Huthi Movement's Religious and Political Ideology and Its Relationship to Zaydism in Yemen", p. 28.
113. Haykel (2022), pp. 17–18.
114. Al-Deen (2021), p. 49; Haykel (2022).
115. The Intellectual and Cultural Charter (February 2012), الوثيقة الفكرية والثقافية.
116. Nashied Shahid Al Quran (19 March 2020), *The Band of the al-shahid al-qaid* نشيد الشهيد القائد, شهيد القرآن، فرقة الشهيد القائد, in Arabic, www.youtube.com/watch?v=0l0HvrQqRaY, accessed 28 October 2022.
117. Brandt (2017), *Tribes and Politics in Yemen*, p. 121.
118. Zayd Al Mahbashi (26 February 2022), "Reading in the Revolution of the Martyred Leader", قراءة في ثورة الشهيد القائد, in Arabic, The Presidential Yemeni Centre for Information (controlled by the Houthi Authorities), https://yemen-nic.info/news/detail.php?ID=74067, accessed 28 October 2022. A similar narration of the event was also repeated by two personalities known for their opposition to the Houthi movement. Author interviews with Ali Albukhaiti (8 June 2020), and with Mohammad Azzan.
119. WikiLeaks (19 May 2007), 07SANAA907.
120. Haykel (2022), "The Huthi Movement's Religious and Political Ideology and Its Relationship to Zaydism in Yemen", p. 20.
121. WikiLeaks (19 May 2007), 07SANAA907.
122. Mohammad Azzan confirmed this take on the summer camps: learning from the methods of the Muslim Brotherhood camps and the apolitical content of their Believing Youth summer camps. The intention, he told this author, was to awaken their Zaydi religious identity. Azzan interview.
123. Shuja al-Deen (2021), "Yemen's War-torn Rivalries for Religious Education", p. 47.
124. WikiLeaks (19 May 2007), 07SANAA907.
125. al-Deen (2021); WikiLeaks (19 May 2007), 07SANAA907.
126. Calvin Woodward and Jon Cambrell (15 June 2019), "'Death to America' Chants Live On in Iran", https://apnews.com/article/b366e2dbdec548808c7313fd06bc9118.
127. Brandt (2017), *Tribes and Politics in Yemen*, pp. 132–33; WikiLeaks (19 May 2007), 07SANAA907.
128. Al Mahbashi (26 February 2022), Reading in the Revolution of the Martyred Leader"; N.N. (23 April 2017), "How Was the Sayyd Mr. Hussein Badr Al-Din Al-Houthi Martyred", كيف إستشهد السيد حسين بدر الحوثي؟, in Arabic, www.alsomoud.com/41692, accessed 28 October 2022.
129. A transcript of this lecture can be found in a Houthi run website "A Quranic Culture", ثقافة قرآنية, https://www.thagafaqurania.com/archives/15121
130. WikiLeaks (19 May 2007), 07SANAA907.
131. Azzan, Zoom interview.

Chapter 9: Conclusion

1. See the text, "Initiative of the Gulf Cooperation Council" (issued 21 April 2011), https://osesgy.unmissions.org/gulf-cooperation-council-gcc.
2. Christine Bell (2018), "Power-Sharing, Conflict Resolution, and Women: A Global Reappraisal", *Nationalism and Ethnic Politics*, 24(1), pp. 24–26.

3. Initiative of the Gulf Cooperation Council, ibid., articles 1, 2, 4.
4. Ibid., articles 6–7.
5. Ibid., article 3.
6. For more information on this aspect see Ginny Hill, Peter Salisbury, Léonoe Northedge, and Jane Kinninmont (September 2013), "Yemen: Corruption, Capital Flight and Global Drivers of Conflict", London: A Chatham House Report; Ibrahim Sharqieh (February 2013), "A Lasting Peace? Yemen's Long Journey to National Reconciliation", Doha: Brookings Doha Center; Elham Manea (September 2012), "The Perils of Yemen's Cunning State", *A NOREF Report*, Oslo: Norwegian Peacebuilding Resource Centre.
7. Elham Manea (January 2014), "Yemen's Contentious Transitional Justice and Fragile Peace", MAP Middle East and Asia Project on Transitional Justice, *Middle East Institute*, www.mei.edu/publications/yemens-contentious-transitional-justice-and-fragile-peace.
8. Amena Bakr (26 June 2011), "Yemen's Saleh Injured by Planted Bomb", Reuters, www.reuters.com/article/uk-yemen-president-idUKTRE75P0NO20110626.
9. Law No. 1 of 2012 Concerning the Granting of Immunity from Legal and Judicial Prosecution, articles 1 and 2.
10. Interviews conducted by author in Sana'a, November 2014.
11. Text of the Implementation Mechanism for the Transition Process in Yemen in Accordance with the Initiative of the Gulf Cooperation Council (23 November 2011), article 7, https://osesgy.unmissions.org/implementation-mechanism.
12. Ibid., articles 16 and 17.
13. Ibid., articles 20 and 21.
14. Barbara F. Walter (2022), *How Civil Wars Start*, London: Penguin, p. 16.
15. Monty Marshall and Benjamin R. Cole (2014), "Global Report 2014: Conflict, Governance and State Fragility", Vienna, VA: Center for Systemic Peace, pp. 21–22.
16. Barbara F. Walter (2022), p. 17.
17. For more detailed information on the process of transitional justice in the National Dialogue Conference see Manea (January 2014).
18. Interviews by author, Sana'a, November 2013.
19. Manea (February 2021), "Absence of Violence", Part One, p. 62.
20. Manea (May 2021), "Absence of Violence", Part Two, p. 138.
21. For more on conventional conflict resolutions and their failure to address ethnic violence see Elham Manea, (February 2021), pp. 59–61.
22. Ibid.
23. Ibid.
24. Elham Manea (May 2021).
25. Abbey Steele and Livia Schubiger (2018), "Democracy and Civil War: The Case of Colombia", *Conflict Management and Peace Science*, 35(6), pp. 587–89.

Interviews

Interviews via Zoom, Skype, and Social Media Apps (Summer 2020)

1. Ali Al Bukhaiti (Former Spokesperson of the Houthi—Ansar Allah—Movement), 8 June 2020; follow-up Zoom interview, 16 August 2022.
2. Hussein Alwaday (Yemeni researcher and political analyst), 11 June 2020 .
3. Fadhl Almaghafi (Yemeni Ambassador), 11 June 2020; follow-up interview, 6 August 2020.
4. Adnan Tabatabai (Iranian analyst and co-founder and CEO of the Germany-based Center for Applied Research in Partnership with the Orient (CARPO)), 14 June 2020.
5. Markus Josef Schefer (Swiss Chief Regional Military Cooperation, UN), Skype interview, 19 June 2020.
6. Amat Al Alim Alsoswa (Yemen's Former Minister for Human Rights and Yemen's first female ambassador), 20 June 2020.
7. Gerald Feierstein (US Ambassador to Yemen from 2010 to 2013 and a distinguished senior fellow on US diplomacy at Middle East Institute and director of its Arabian Peninsula Affairs programme), 22 June 2020.
8. Radhya al-Mutawakel (chairwoman of the Mwatana Organization for Human Rights), 23 June 2020.
9. Maysaa Shuja al-Deen (Yemeni senior researcher at Sana'a Center for Strategic Studies and an expert on Zaydism), 23 June 2020.
10. Asmhan Al Aalas (Professor of Political Science at Aden University; Member of the Yemeni Women's Technical Advisory Group to the Special UN Envoy's Office in Yemen), 26 June 2020.
11. Sami Ghalib (Yemeni journalist and editor-in-chief of *Alndaa Newspaper*), 29 June 2020.
12. Maged Al-Madhaji (Executive Director and a co-founder of the Sana'a Center for Strategic Studies), 30 June 2020.

13. Jonathan Wilks CMG (British Ambassador to Qatar and former Ambassador to Yemen 2010–2011), 30 July 2020.
14. Abu Bakr Abdullah al-Qirbi (Former Yemeni Foreign Minister and Assistant Secretary General of the General People's Congress), Zoom interview, 3/4 August 2020.
15. Abdullah Al Olofi (Official Representative of the Office of Public Affairs of the Baha'is in Yemen), 6 August 2020.
16. Hisham Al-Omeisy (Yemeni conflict analyst and activist), 10 August 2020.
17. Abdulmalik Alejri (Member of the Houthi—Ansar Allah—Political Bureau, and a key member of the Houthi delegation to negotiate peace), 11 August 2020.
18. Saddam Abu Asim (Yemeni journalist and youth activist), 11 August 2020.
19. Turki al-Balushi (Omani journalist and correspondent at Bloomberg), 14 August 2020.
20. Abd al-Barry Taher (Yemeni Former Chairman of the Press Syndicate), 13 August 2020.
21. Mohammed Azzan (founding member and former Secretary General of the Believing Youth Forum), 13 August 2020.
22. Hussein al-Azzi (Houthi—Ansar Allah—Movement Deputy Foreign Minister), 17 August 2020.
23. Noman Alhodefi (President of the National Council for Minorities of Yemen, President of the Black Muhamasheen Union in Yemen, and Member of the National Authority to monitor the implementation of the outcomes of the National Dialogue Conference), 18 August 2020.
24. Antelak al-Mutawakel (Professor at Sana'a University and at Center for Gender and Development, Co-founder of the Youth Leadership Development Foundation), 18 August 2020.
25. Youth activist (anonymous), 20 August 2020.
26. Majda al-Haddad (former youth activist and former school principal), 20 August 2020.
27. Ahmad Omar bin Fareed (Head of the Foreign Relations Office of the Southern Transitional Council, and the official representative of the Council in the European Union countries), 24 August 2020.
28. Wameedh Shakir (activist and human rights campaigner), 24 August 2020.
29. Haitham Nazar (Speaker of the Southern Transitional Council), 24 August 2020.
30. Houria Mashhour (former Human Rights Minister of Yemen), 25 August 2020.
31. Amr al-Bidh (Special Representative of the President for Foreign Affairs at Southern Transitional Council (STC)), 25 August 2020.
32. Nadia al-Saqaf (former Editor-in-Chief of *Yemen Times* and former Information Minister), 26 August 2020.
33. Hani al-Junaid (journalist, former youth activist, and first secretary of the student sector of the Yemeni Socialist Party at Sana'a University), 27 August 2020.
34. Muna Luqman (Yemeni activist, peace builder, founder of the organization Food4Humanity, and co-founder of the Women in Solidarity Network), 31 August 2020.

INTERVIEWS

35. Ahmed Mohammed Luqman (Former Yemeni Minister of the Ministry of Civil Service and Insurance and Former Director General of the Arab Labour Organization), 3 September 2020.
36. Saba Hamzah (Yemeni poet-scholar, author, and educator focused on social justice), 14 September 2020.
37. Ahmed Nagi (former non-resident scholar at the Malcolm H. Kerr Carnegie Middle East Center in Beirut, Yemen), 12 June 2020.

Interviews in Egypt, Cairo (July–August 2021)

38. Bilqis Abu-Osba (Professor of Political Science at Sana'a University and former Vice President of the Supreme National Authority for Combating Corruption), 25 July 2021.
39. Mohammed Abulahoum (Chairman of the Justice and Building Party in Yemen and Leading Sheikh of Bakil Tribal Confederation), 27 June 2021.
40. Khaldoon Bakahail (Senior Strategic Advisor and Coordinator for Yemen Programme, Geneva Centre for Security Sector Governance), 26 June 2021.
41. Muna Luqman (Yemeni activist, peace builder, founder of the organization Food4Humanity, and co-founder of the Women in Solidarity Network), 28 July 2021.
42. Abdul Rahman Omar al-Saqqaf (Secretary General of the Yemeni Socialist Party), 29 July 2021.
43. Zayd al-Dhari (head of the National Concord Forum and an instrumental figure in President Saleh's rapprochement with Zaydi figures in the 1990s), 29 July 2021.
44. Ezzat Ibrahim (editor-in-chief of *Al-Ahram Weekly*), 1 August 2021.
45. Ahmed Youssef Ahmed (Professor of Political Science at Cairo University with a focus on Yemen and Arabian Peninsula), 3 August 2021.
46. Nabil Abdel-Fattah (a scholar specializing in the affairs of Islamic groups at the Al-Ahram Center for Political and Strategic Studies), 4 August 2021.
47. Hassan Abu Talib (advisor to Al-Ahram Center for Political and Strategic Studies and a member of Egyptian Center for Strategic Studies), 14 August 2021.
48. Abdulmalik Abduljalil al-Mekhlafi (advisor to the president of the Republic of Yemen and former Deputy Prime Minister and Foreign Minister), 15 August 2021.
49. Rashad al-Alimi)Chairman of the Yemeni Presidential Leadership Council since 7 April 2022 and influential member of the People's General Congress), 18 August 2021.
50. Major General Mohsen Kharsouf (Major General in Yemeni National Army and Former Head of the Moral Guidance Department), 17 August 2021.
51. Major General Major General Mohammad Refaat Qumsan (former advisor to the Egyptian Prime Minister for Elections), 16 August 2021.
52. Sami Ghalib (Yemeni journalist and editor-in-chief of *Al Nidaa* newspaper), 19 August 2021.

53. Maggie Michael (investigative journalist at the International Consortium of Investigative Journalists based in Cairo), 19 August 2021.
54. Ahad Yassen (journalist and a Yemeni youth civil society activist from Aden), 19 August 2021.

Interviews in Turkey, Istanbul (August 2021)

55. Yaseen al-Tamimi (Yemeni journalist and political analyst, Islah Party), 6 August 2021.
56. Olfat al-Dubai (former youth activist and member of the NDC's Transitional Justice working group and member of the Constitution Drafting Committee), 6 August 2021.
57. Arif al-Sarmi (Yemeni political journalist and anchor of a talk show at Almahriah TV), 7 August 2021.
58. Nabil al-Bukiri (Yemeni writer and activist, editor-in-chief of *Muqribat Journal*, Islah Party), 7 August 2021.
59. Abdel Salam Mohammed (Head of the Abaad Center for Studies and Research, Islah), 8 August 2021.
60. Major General Abdo Hussein al-Tareb (Interior Minister April 2012–October 2014), 8 August 2021.
61. Turan Kışlakçı (Turkish journalist and the director of TRT Al Arabiya), 9 August 2021.
62. Sakher al-Wajih (Member of the Yemeni Parliament, Minister of Finance 2012–June 2014 and former Governor of Hodeida Governorate), 9 August 2021.
63. Mutahar Safari (Yemeni analyst), 9 August 2021.
64. Shawki Alkadhi (Member of the House of Representatives of the Islah Party), 10 August 2021.
65. Brigadier Ali al-Anissi (former Director of the Bureau of National Security and Presidential Office), 10 August 2021.
66. Salah Batis (member of the Yemeni Shura Council, and vice-chairman of the National Authority for Monitoring the Implementation of the National Dialogue Conference's outputs and Chairman of the Shura Council of the Yemen Tribes Alliance), 10 August 2021.
67. Amat Salam Alhaj (Founder and Director of Abductees Mothers Association), 12 August 2021.
68. Maysaa Shuja al-Deen (Yemeni senior researcher at Sana'a Center for Strategic Studies and an expert on Zaydism) and Mustapha Noman (former Yemeni Ambassador and deputy foreign minister), informal dinners 10/11 August 2021.
69. Brigadier General Askar Zoail (military attaché at the Embassy of the Republic of Yemen in Turkey, Officer of the First Armored Division, who supported the Yemeni youth revolution and Spokesman for the Commander of the First Armored Division, Major General Ali Mohsen al-Ahmar), 12 August 2021.

INTERVIEWS

Interviews in Muscat and Salalah, Sultanate of Oman (October 2021)

70. Abdulmalik Alejri (Member of the Houthi—Ansar Allah—Political Bureau, and a key member of the Houthi delegation to negotiate peace), 14 October 2021.
71. Abdullah Albadi (Omani Ambassador to Yemen until 2013), 15 October 2021.
72. Saeed al-Mahry (Omani Interlocutor on Salalah and Al-Mahra), 16/17 October 2021.
73. Sheikh Khalifa al-Harthy (Omani Foreign Ministry Undersecretary for Diplomatic Affairs), 21 October 2021.
74. Mohammed Abdusalam (Official Spokesman for the Houthi—Ansar Allah—movement, head of the Yemeni national delegation), 22 October 2021.
75. Sheikh Brigadier General Ali Salem al-Huraizi al-Mahri (former Undersecretary for Desert Affairs in Al-Mahra Governorate and its Border Guard Commander), 26 October 2021.
76. Sharifa al-Yahyai (Former Omani Minister of Social Development and a Professor at Sultan Qaboos University), 24 October 2021.
77. Salem Abdullah Belhaf (the official spokesperson for Al-Mahra Peaceful Sit-in Committee), 26 October 2021.

Zoom Interviews (October 2021–August 2022)

78. Nevin Massad (Professor of Political Science at Cairo University and a member of the National Council for Human Rights; expert on Iranian affairs), 1 October 2021.
79. Saeed al-Qumairi (Professor at Hadramawt University and the Executive Manager of Mehri Center for Studies and Research), 18 October 2021.
80. Halima Jahaf (member of Houthi—Ansar Allah—Political Bureau movement and head of the Gender Center at Sana'a University), 20 October 2021.
81. Yasin Aktay (deputy chairman of the Justice and Development Party and head of the Turkish Group of Inter-Parliamentarian Union), 6 September 2021.
82. Joke Buringa (former employee at the Dutch Ministry of Foreign Affairs specializing in Arabian Peninsula regional security, energy security, and bilateral economic relations), 9 September 2021.
83. Abdulkhaleq Abdulla (Emirati Professor of Political Science at United Arab Emirates University and non-resident fellow at the Arab Gulf States Institute in Washington), 9 September 2021.
84. Akhlaq al-Shami (Member of the Houthi—Ansar Allah—Political Bureau and the Secretary General of the Supreme Council for Motherhood and Childhood), 1 November 2021.
85. Tohid Assadi (Iranian analyst, Tehran University), informal interview, 10 January 2022.

86. Sir John Jenkins (British Director for the Middle East and North Africa in the FCO between 2007 and 2009 and Ambassador to the Kingdom of Saudi Arabia from June 2012 to January 2015), 25 February 2022.
87. Amel Grami (Tunisian professor in the department of Arabic studies of the Faculty of Literatures, Arts and Humanities in Manouba), 8 March 2022.
88. Mustapha Noman (former Yemeni Ambassador and deputy foreign minister), 11 August 2022.
89. Yehia Hussain al-Aarashi (Northern Minister of Unity Affairs between 1986 and 1990), 13 August 2022.
90. Jamal Benomar (Former UN Special Envoy for Yemen), 23 August 2022.

Cited Interviews from Previous Research Projects

91. Wameedh Shakir (activist, human rights campaigner, and gender expert), 28 February 2011, Sana'a, Yemen.
92. Wafa Alsayed Abu Bakr (Member of the Socialist Party Political Bureau), 7 October 2006, Aden, Yemen.
93. Raqia Abd al-Qader Humaidan (lawyer and women's activist), 7 October 2006, Aden, Yemen.
94. Radya Ihasn Allah (member of the Supreme Committee of the People's Socialist Party, Secretary General of the Arab Women's Association in Aden, Outreach Officer in the Liberation Front, and independent member of the Coordination Council of Aden Governorate), 8 October 2006, Aden, Yemen.
95. Iman Mahmoud Nasser (Head of Aden Institute for Micro Credit), 8 October 2006, Aden, Yemen.
96. Khawla Ahmed Sharaf (member of the 1993 Yemeni parliament, member of the Socialist Party Central Committee, and a former member of the party's politburo), 9 October 2006.
97. Imam Kulthom Mahmoud Nasser (President, Society for Business Women in Aden), 10 October 2006, Aden, Yemen.
98. Dr Abdel Karim Sallam (Yemeni political analyst and journalist), 10 September 2006, Sana'a, Yemen.
99. Afandi Abd Ra'bu Hamid (former Professor in Biochemistry, Sana'a University and Member of the Southern Movement), 20 September 2006, Bern, Switzerland.

Bibliography

Archives

Records of Yemen 1798–1960
The Arabian Gulf Digital Archives
Yemen National Digital Archive
Foreign Broadcast Information Service (FBIS)

References in Arabic

Abatha, F. O. *Ottoman Rule in Yemen: 1872–1918* الحكم العثماني في اليمن (2nd ed.). (Beirut: Dar al-A'awda, 1979).

Alahssab, A. *Power Identity in Yemen: The Controversy of Politics and History* هوية السلطة في اليمن: جدل السياسة والتاريخ. (Beirut: Arab Center for Research & Policy Studies, 1979).

Al-Alimi, R. *The Tribal Judiciary in Yemeni Society* القضاء القبلي في المجتمع اليمني. (Sana'a, n.n.).

Ali, J. *The Detailed History of the Arabs Before Islam* المفصل في تاريخ العرب قبل الإسلام (2nd ed.). (No publisher, 1993).

Al-Ayyashy, A. S. A. b. M. *The Ayyachian Journey (1661–1663)* الرحلة العياشية (Vol. 1). (Abu Dhabi: Dar Al Suwaidi Publishing and Distribution, 2006).

Azzan, M. Y. 'A Review in the Imamate Theory in Zaydism' قراءة في نظرية الإمامة عند الزيدية. *Al Massar: A Periodical of the Yemeni Heritage and Research Center*, (9), (Sana'a, 30 September 2002).

Alfaqih, M. A. *On Arabia Felix: Short Historical Studies* في العربية السعيدة: دراسات تاريخية قصيرة. (Sana'a: Yemeni Centre for Studies and Research, 1987).

Alwaisi, H. B. A. *Greater Yemen* اليمن الكبرى (Vol. 1). (Sana'a: Maktabat Al Irshad, 1991).

Abu Ghanem, F. A. A. *The Tribe and State in Yemen* القبيلة والدولة في اليمن. (Cairo: Dar Al Manar, 1990).

Abu Lahoum, S. *The Memoir of Sinan Abu Lahoum* مذكرات الشيخ سنان أبو لحوم: حقائق ووثائق عشتها (3rd ed., Part One: 1943–1962). (Sana'a: Al Afif Cultural Institute, 2004).

Al-Baradouni, A. *The Republican Yemen* اليمن الجمهوري (1st ed.). (Damascus: The Arab Writer Printer, 1983).

Al-Baidhani, A. R. *The Mutawakilia Games* ألاعيب متوكيلة. Collected Articles by the Yemeni Historical Library. (n.d.).

Barout, M. J. *Arab Nationalist Movement: Foundation, Evolution and Fates* حركة القوميين العرب: النشأة، التطور، المصائر. (Damascus: The Arabic Center for Strategic Studies, 1997).

Basindawa, M. S. (1989). *The Issue of Occupied South Yemen at the United Nations* قضية الجنوب اليمني المحتل. (Cairo: Al-Ahram Commercial Printer, 1989).

Al-Eryani, A. R. b. Y. *The Memoir of the President Judge Abdul Rahman bin Yehia al-Eryani* مذكرات الرئيس القاضي عبدالرحمن بن يحي الأرياني (Part One: 1910–1962) [Part Two: 1962–1967]. (Sana'a, 2013).

Al-Hamawi, Y. *Mu'jam ul-Buldān* معجم البلدان (Vol. 5). (Beirut: Dar Sader, n.d.).

Al-Hamdani, A. M. *Sifat Jazīrat al 'Arab* صفة جزيرة العرب. (M. bin A. Alakwa'a, Ed.), 1990.

Haisamy, K. al. *Yemeni–Saudi Relations: 1962–1980* العلاقات اليمنية -السعودية. (Cairo, 1983).

Al Aamry, H. A. *One Hundred Years of Yemeni Modern History: 1748–1848* مائة عام من تاريخ اليمن الحديث. (Damascus: Al Ahaly for Publication, 1996).

El-Magariaf, M. Y. *Libya Between the Past and Present: Pages of Political History* ليبيا بين الماضي والحاضر : صفحات من التاريخ السياسي (Part One, 2nd ed.). (Oxford: Center for Libyan Studies, 2017).

bin Ma'ili, N. S. H. *The Role of the Mahra in Resisting the Portuguese Invasion in the Sixteenth Century AD* دور المهرة في مقاومة الغزو البرتغالي في القرن السادس عشر الميلادي. (Al-Mahra: The Mahri Language Center for Studies and Research, 2022).

Al-Maqaleh, A. *A Review of the Thought of Zaydism and Mutazilah: The Islamic Yemen* قراءة في فكر الزيدية والمعتزلة: اليمن الإسلامي. (Beirut: Dar al-Auda, 1982).

Manea, E. *The Political Parties and Organizations in Yemen (1948–1993)* الأحزاب والتنظيمات السياسية في اليمن (1948–1993). (Sana'a: Affaq for Publication, 1994).

Makkawi, A. Q. (1987). *South Yemen... Where To? The Faulty Experience and the Desired Solution* اليمن الجنوبي ... إلى أين؟ التجربة الخطأ والبديل المنشود. (Cairo: House of the Voice of Lebanese Arabism, 1987).

Noman, M. A. *The Stakeholders in Yemen* الأطراف المعنية في اليمن. (Beirut: Publications of Al Qiban Institute, 1965)

Al-Sharjabi, A., et al. *The Palace and the Diwan: The Political Role of the Tribe in Yemen* القصر والديوان: الدور السياسي للقبيلة في اليمن. (Sana'a: Yemeni Observatory for Human Rights, 2009).

Al-Hadad, M. Y. *The General History of Yemen: History of Yemen Before Islam* التاريخ العام لليمني: تاريخ اليمن قبل الإسلام (Part One). (Beirut: Al Madina Publications, 1986).

al-Hadi, Imam. *The Collection of Edicts by Imam al-Hadi* مجموع رسائل الإمام الهادي، يحيى بن الحسين بن القاسم بن إبراهيم. (Saada & Amman: Imam Zayd bin Ali Cultural Institute, 2001).

Omar, J. *The Memoir of Jarallah Omar (leader of the Northern National Liberation Front and a member of the Politburo of the Yemeni Socialist Party)* من مذكرات جار الله عمر. (Sana'a: Yemeni Cultural Development Foundation, 2007).

Qadara, F. R. 'The Ottoman Empire in the Traces of Sheikh Al-Taher Al-Zawi' الدولة العثمانية في آثار الشيخ الطاهر الزاوي. *Al-Majalla Al-Jami'a*, 4(16): November 2014).

BIBLIOGRAPHY

Al-Sharjabi, Q. N. *The Traditional Social Strata in Yemeni Society* الشرائح الاجتماعية التقليدية في المجتمع اليمني. (Sana'a: Dar Al Hadatha and Yemeni Centre for Studies and Research, 1986).

Ibn Khaldun, A. R. *The Introduction of Ibn Khaldun* مقدمة إبن خلدون (H. A. Altaher, Ed.). (Cairo: Dar Al Fagr lil Turath, 2004).

Al-Saidy, A. K. T*he Yemeni Opposition Movement During the Era of Imam Yehia ibn Mohammed Hamid al-Dien* حركة المعارضة اليمنية في عهد الإمام يحي بن محمد حميد الدين. (Sana'a, 1983).

Salim, S. M. *The Structure of Contemporary Yemen: Yemen and Imam Yihia* تكوين اليمن الحديث. (Cairo: Madbouli Library, 1984).

Sameh, A. *The Ottoman Turks in North Africa* الأتراك العثمانيون في إفريقيا الشمالية. (Beirut: Dar Lebanon, 1969).

Al Sarraf, A. *South Yemen: Political Life From Colonialism to Unity* اليمن الجنوبي: الحياة السياسية من الاستعمار إلى الوحدة. (UK: Riad El Rayyes Books, 1992).

Al-Sayaghi, H. B. A. (Ed.) *Unknown pages from the history of Yemen and the Sana'a law* صفحات مجهولة من تاريخ اليمن وقانون صنعاء (3rd ed.). (Sana'a: Yemeni Center for Studies and Research, 2008).

Al-Shahrastani, M. *Kitāb al–Milal wa al–Nihal* كتاب الملل والنحل (A. A. Muhanna & A. H. Faoud, Eds.). (Beirut: Dar El-Marefah, 1993).

Shubat, F. *The Organisation of Personal Status for Non-Muslims: Legislation and Judiciary in Syria and Lebanon* تنظيم الأحوال الشخصية لغير المسلمين: التشريعات والقضاء في سوريا ولبنان. (Damascus: The Higher Institute for Arab Studies, 1966).

Wannas, A. M. *The Libyan Character: The Trinity of the Tribe, the Booty, and the Victory* الشخصية الليبية: ثلاثية القبيلة والغنيمة والغلبة. (Tunis Mediterranean Publisher, 2014).

Al-Wasa'i, A. W. i. Y. *History of Yemen: The So-Called Venue of Concerns and Sadness in Accidents and History of Yemen* تاريخ اليمن: المسمى فرجة الهموم والحزن في حوادث وتاريخ اليمن. (Cairo: Salafi, 1944).

Zawi, T. A. *Explanation of the Book "Al Tithkar: The History of Western Tripoli" by Ibn Ghalboun* شرح لكتاب «التذكار: تاريخ طرابلس الغرب لإبن غلبون». (Cairo: Salafi Library, 1930).

Zayd, A. M. *Mu'tazila currents in Yemen in the sixth century Hijri* تيارات معتزلة اليمن في القرن السادس الهجري. (Sana'a: The French Center for Yemeni Studies, 1997).

Al Zubairi, M. M. *Waq al Waq* واق الواق. (Republished ed.). (Qatar: The Ministry of Culture, Arts and Heritage, 2015).

Books in Multiple Languages: English, German, and French

Abdelnasser, Gamal. 'Egypt: Succession Politics' In Volker Perthes (ed.), Arab Elites: *Negotiating the Politics of Change*. (Colorado: Lynne Rienner).

Ayubi, Nazih N. *Over-Stating the Arab State: Politics and Society in the Middle East*. 3rd edn. (London: I.B.Tauris, 2006).

Bassiouni, Cherif (ed.). *Libya: From Repression to Revolution*. (Leiden, The Netherlands: Brill, 2013). https://doi.org/10.1163/9789004257351

Batatu, Hanna. *Syria's Peasantry, the Descendants of Its Lesser Rural Notables, and Their Politics.* (Princeton: Princeton University Press, 1990).

Bonnefoy, Laurent. *Salafism in Yemen: Transnationalism and Religious Identity.* (New York: Columbia University Press, 2011).

Bonnefoy, Laurent. 'Salafism in Yemen: A 'Saudisation'?' In Madawi Al-Rasheed (ed.), *Kingdom without Borders: Saudi Political, Religious and Media Frontiers.* (London: Hurst, 2008).

Brandt, Marieke. *Tribes and Politics in Yemen: A History of the Houthi Conflict.* (Oxford: Oxford University Press, 2017). https://doi.org/10.1093/oso/9780190673598.001.0001

Brandt, Marieke. 'Inhabiting Tribal Structures: Leadership Hierarchies in Tribal Upper Yemen' In Andre Gingrich and Siegfried Hass (eds), *Southwest Arabia Across History: Essay to the Memory of Walter Dostal.* (Wien: Verlag der Österreichis Akademie der Wissenschaften, 2014).

Brehony, John Albert Noel. 'Explaining the Triumph of the National Liberation Front' In Clive Jones (ed.), *Britain and State Formation in Arabia 1962–1971.* (London: Routledge, 2019). https://doi.org/10.4324/9781315150338-3

Burchill, Scott et al. (eds). *Theories of International Relations.* 5th edn. (London: Palgrave, 2013).

Calvert, Peter. *The Foreign Policy of New States.* (London: Palgrave Macmillan, 1986).

Charrad, Mounira M. *States and Women's Rights: The Making of Postcolonial Tunisia, Algeria, and Morocco.* (Berkeley: University of California Press, 2001). https://doi.org/10.1525/9780520935471

Chubin, Shahram and Charles Tripp. *Iran and Iraq at War.* (London: Publisher not provided, 1988). https://doi.org/10.5040/9780755612567

Cederman, Lars-Erik, Kristian Skrede Gleditsch, and Halvard Buhaug. *Inequality, Grievances, and Civil War.* (Cambridge: Cambridge University Press, 2013). https://doi.org/10.1017/CBO9781139084161

Day., Stephen W. *Regionalism and Rebellion in Yemen: A Troubled National Union,* (Cambridge: Cambridge University Press, 2012). https://doi.org/10.1017/CBO9781139135443

Dresch, Paul. *A History of Modern Yemen.* (Cambridge: Cambridge University Press, 2000).

Dresch, Paul K. 'The Tribal Factor in the Yemeni Crisis'. In Jamal S. al-Suwaidi (ed.), *The Yemen War of 1994: Causes and Consequences.* (Abu Dhabi, 1995).

Dresch, Paul. *Tribes, Government and History in Yemen.* (Oxford: Clarendon Press, Oxford University Press, 1993). https://doi.org/10.1093/oso/9780198277903.001.0001

Kohlberg, Etan and Amin Ehteshami (eds). *In Praise of the Few: Studies in Shi'i Thought and History.* (Leiden: Brill, 2020). https://doi.org/10.1163/9789004406971

Farah, Caesar E. *The Sultan's Yemen: Nineteenth-Century Challenges to Ottoman Rule.* (London: I.B.Tauris, 2002).

Haider, Najam. *Shi'i Islam: An Introduction.* (Cambridge: Cambridge University Press, 2014).

Halliday, Fred. *Revolution and Foreign Policy: The Case of South Yemen 1967–1987.* (Cambridge: Cambridge University Press, 1990). https://doi.org/10.1017/CBO9780511622366

Harik, Illiya. 'The Origins of the Arab State System' In Ghassan Salamé (ed.), *The Foundation of the Arab State.* (London: Croom Helm, 1987).

BIBLIOGRAPHY

Haykel, Bernard. 'The Huthi Movement's Religious and Political Ideology and Its Relationship to Zaydism in Yemen' In Abdullah Hamidaddin (ed.), *The Huthi Movement in Yemen: Ideology, Ambition and Security in the Arab Gulf*. (London: I.B.Tauris, 2022). https://doi.org/10.5040/9780755644292.ch-001

Haykel, Bernard. *Revival and Reform in Islam: The Legacy of Muhammad al-Shawkani*. (Cambridge: Cambridge University Press, 2003).

Hinchcliffe, Peter, John T. Ducker, and Maria Holt. *Without Glory in Arabia: The British Retreat from Aden*. 1st edn. (London: I.B.Tauris, 2006). https://doi.org/10.5040/9780755607907

Hinnebusch, Raymond. *The International Politics of the Middle East*. 2nd edn. (Manchester: Manchester University Press, 2018).

Hinnebusch, Raymond. 'Foreign Policy in the Middle East' In Raymond Hinnebusch and Anoushiravan Ehteshami (eds), *The Foreign Policies of Middle East States*. 2nd edn. (London: Boulder, 2014. https://doi.org/10.1515/9781685850715

Hoyland, Robert G. *Arabia and the Arabs: From the Bronze Age to the Coming of Islam*. (London and New York: Routledge, 2001). https://doi.org/10.4324/9780203455685

Hudson, Michael C. 'Bipolarity, Rational Calculation and War in Yemen' In Jamal S. al-Suwaidi (ed.), *The Yemen War of 1994: Causes and Consequences*. (Abu Dhabi, 1995).

Ingrams, W.H. *Hadhramaut: A Report on the Social, Economic and Political Condition of the Hadhramaut*. (London: The Colonial Office, 1936).

Kaplan, Robert D. *The Revenge of Geography*. (New York: Random House, 2012).

Kaufman, Stuart J. 'Ethnicity as a Generator of Conflict' In Karl Cordell and Stefan Wolff (eds), *The Routledge Handbook of Ethnic Conflict*. (London: Routledge, 2016).

Khadduri, Majid. *Modern Libya: A Study in Political Development*. (Baltimore: The Johns Hopkins Press, 1963).

Khomeini, Ayatollah. *Islamic Government*. 2nd edn. (Rome: European Islamic Cultural Centre, 1982).

Korany, Bahgat. 'Alien and Besieged Yet Here to Stay: The Contradictions of the Arab Territorial State' In Ghassan Salamé (ed.), *The Foundation of the Arab State*. (London: Croom Helm, 1987).

Kostiner, Joseph. *Yemen: The Tortuous Quest for Unity, 1990–94*. (London: The Royal Institute of International Affairs, 1996).

Kour, Z.H. *The History of Aden 1839–1872*. (London: Frank Kass, 1981).

Kuehn, Thomas. *Empire, Islam, and Politics of Difference: Ottoman Rule in Yemen, 1849–1919*. (Leiden: Brill, 2011). https://doi.org/10.1163/ej.9789004211315.i-292

Leca, Jean. 'Democratisation in the Arab World: Uncertainty, Vulnerability and Legitimacy: A Tentative Conceptualisation and Some Hypotheses' In Ghassan Salamé (ed.), *Democracy without Democrats*. (London: I.B. Tauris, 1994).

Lynch, Marc. 'Thinking Big, Thinking New: Is the Muslim Brotherhood a Terrorist Organization or a Firewall Against Violent Extremism?' In N.N. *Evolving Methodologies in the Study of Islamism. Project on Middle East Political Science*, (George Washington University and Carnegie Corporation of New York, March 2016).

Lynch, Marc. *The Arab Uprising: The Unfinished Revolutions of the New Middle East.* (New York: Public Affairs, 2012).

MacQueen, Benjamin. *An Introduction to Middle East Politics.* Second edition. (UK: Sage Publications Ltd, [Year not provided]).

Madelung, Wilferd. *Der Imam al-Qāsim ibn Ibrahim und die Glaubenslehre der Zaiditen.* (Berlin: Walter De Gruyter & Co, 1965). https://doi.org/10.1515/9783110826548

Maxwell, Joseph A. *A Realist Approach for Qualitative Research.* (Los Angeles: Sage, 2011).

Manea, Elham. The Perils of Nonviolent Islamism. New York: Telos Press Publishing, 2021.

Manea, Elham. 'Jemen: Die Geschichte eines fragilen Staates' In Helmut Krieger and Magda Seewald (Hrsg.), *Krise, Revolte und Krieg in der arabischen Welt.* (Wiener Institut für Entwicklungsfragen (VIDC): Vienna, 2017).

Manea, Elham. 'The Significance of Gender in Arab-Spring Transitional Justice' In Kirsten Fisher and Robert Stewart (eds), *Transitional Justice and the Arab Spring.* (London: Routledge Studies on Middle Eastern Politics, 2014). https://doi.org/10.4324/9780203431146-9

Manea, Elham. 'Yemen's Arab Spring: Outsmarting the Cunning State?' In Larbi Sadiki (ed.), *Routledge Handbook of the Arab Spring.* (London: Routledge Studies on Middle Eastern Politics, 2014).

Manea, Elham. *The Arab State and Women's Rights: The Trap of Authoritarian Governance (Yemen, Syria, and Kuwait).* (London: Routledge Studies in Middle Eastern Politics, 2011). https://doi.org/10.4324/9780203807583

Manea, Elham. *Regional Politics of the Gulf.* (London: Saqi Books, 2005).

Manea, Elham. 'La tribu et l'Etat au Yémen' In Mondher Kilani (ed.), *Islam et changement social.* (Lausanne: Editions Payot, 1998).

de Maigret, Alessandro. *Arabia Felix: An Exploration of the Archaeological History of Yemen.* (London: Stacey International, 1996).

Migdal, Joel. *Strong Societies and Weak States: State–Society Relations and State Capabilities in the Third World.* (Princeton, NJ: Princeton University Press, 1989). https://doi.org/10.1515/9780691212852

Obeid, Amal S.M. 'Political Elites in Libya Since 1969' In Dirk Vandewalle (ed.), *Libya Since 1969: Qadhafi's Revolution Revisited.* 1st edn. (New York: Palgrave Macmillan, 2008). https://doi.org/10.1007/978-0-230-61386-7_5

el-Omari, Racha. 'The Muʿtazilite Movement (I): The Origins of the Muʿtazila' In Sabine Schmidtke (ed.), *The Oxford Handbook of Islamic Theology.* (Oxford: Oxford University Press, 2016). https://doi.org/10.1093/oxfordhb/9780199696703.013.31

Perthes, Volker. 'Politics and Elite Change in the Arab World' In Volker Perthes (ed.), *Arab Elites: Negotiating the Politics of Change.* (Colorado: Lynne Rienner, 2004). https://doi.org/10.1515/9781588269843

Petersen, Roger D. and Sarah Zuckerman. 'Anger, Violence, and Political Science' In Michael Potegal et al. (eds), *International Handbook of Anger.* (New York: Springer, 2010). https://doi.org/10.1007/978-0-387-89676-2_32

BIBLIOGRAPHY

Petersen, Roger D. *Understanding Ethnic Violence: Fear, Hatred, and Resentment in Twentieth-Century Eastern Europe*. (Cambridge: Cambridge University Press, 2002). https://doi.org/10.1017/CBO9780511840661

Philips, Sarah. *Yemen and the Politics of Permanent Crisis*. (London: The International Institute for Strategic Studies, 2011).

Philips, Sarah. Yemen's Democracy Experiment in Regional Perspective: Patronage and Pluralized Authoritarianism. (New York: Palgrave, 2008).

Quataert, Donald. *The Ottoman Empire, 1700–1922*. 2nd edn. (Cambridge: Cambridge University Press, 2005). https://doi.org/10.1017/CBO9780511818868

Raymond, André. 'The Ottoman Legacy in Arab Political Boundaries' In L. Carl Brown (ed.), *Imperial Legacy: The Ottoman Imprint on the Balkans and the Middle East*. (New York: Columbia University Press, 1996).

Acemoğlu, Daron and James A. Robinson. *Why Nations Fail*. (New York: Crown Business, 2012).

Rubin, Barry (ed.). *Political Islam*. (London: Routledge, 2007).

Saksena, Kashi Prasad. *Muslim Law as Administered in India and Pakistan*. 4th edn. (Lucknow: Eastern Book Company, 1963).

Salamé, Ghassan (ed.). *The Foundation of the Arab State*. (London: Croom Helm, [Year not provided]).

Salmoni, Barak A. et al. 'APPENDIX B: Zaydism: Overview and Comparison to Other Versions of Shi'ism' In N.N. *Regime and Periphery in Northern Yemen: The Huthi Phenomenon*. (RAND Corporation, 2010).

Smitson, Scott. 'The Road to Good Intentions: British Nation-building in Aden' In K. Guttieri, V. Franke and M. Civic (eds), *Understanding Complex Military Operations: A Case Study Approach*. (London: Routledge, 2014).

Articles

Alley, April Longley. 'Yemen's Houthi Takeover.' Middle East Institute, 22 December 2014. www.mei.edu/publications/yemens-houthi-takeover.

Anderson, Lisa. 'Absolutism and the Resilience of Monarchy in the Middle East.' *Political Science Quarterly* (Spring 1991): 106(1), 1–15.

Anderson, Lisa. 'The State in the Middle East and North Africa.' *Comparative Politics* (October 1987): 20(1), 1–18.

Amburn, Brad. 'The Failed States Index 2005.' *Foreign Policy*, 2005–07: 149, 56–65. http://foreignpolicy.com/2009/10/22/the-failed-states-index-2005.

Antunes, Sandrina, and Isabel Casisao. 'Introducing Realism in International Relations Theory.' *International Relations*, 27 February 2018. www.e-ir.info/2018/02/27/introducing-realism-in-international-relations-theory.

Behravesh, Maysam. 'Constructivism: An Introduction.' *International Relations*, February 2011. www.e-ir.info/2011/02/03/constructivism-an-introduction.

Bell, Christine. 'Power-Sharing, Conflict Resolution, and Women: A Global Reappraisal.' *Nationalism and Ethnic Politics* (2018): 24(1), 13–32.

Brandt, Marieke. 'The War in Yemen, Bottom-up: Tribal Politics in Depth and in Motion.' *British Yemeni Society Journal* (2019): 27, 11–18.

Burrowes, Robert D. 'The Famous Forty and Their Companions: North Yemen's First-Generation Modernists and Educational Emigrants.' *Middle East Journal* (Winter 2005): 59(1), 81–97. www.jstor.org/stable/4330098.

Burrowes, Robert D. 'Prelude to Unification: The Yemen Arab Republic, 1962–1990.' *International Journal of Middle East Studies* (1991): 23, 483–506.

Blumi, Isa. 'Speaking Above Yemenis: A Reading Beyond the Tyranny of Experts.' *Global Intellectual History* (2021): 6(6), 990–1014.

Bonnefoy, Laurent. 'Revolution, War and Transformations in Yemeni Studies.' *Middle East Report* (2021): 51(301), 1.

Carapico, Sheila. 'How Yemen's Ruling Party Secured an Electoral Landslide.' MERIP Middle East Research and Information Project, 16 May 2003. Available from: www.merip.org/mero/mero051603.

Carment, David, Joe Landry, Yiagadeesen Samy, and Scott Shaw. 'Towards a Theory of Fragile State Transitions: Evidence from Yemen, Bangladesh and Laos.' *Third World Quarterly* (2015): 36(7), 1316–1332.

Cederman, Lars-Erik, Andreas Wimmer, and Brian Min. 'Why Do Ethnic Groups Rebel? New Data and Analysis.' *World Politics* (January 2010): 62(1), 87–119.

Clausen, Maria-Louise. 'Understanding the Crisis in Yemen: Evaluating Competing Narratives.' *The International Spectator* (2015): 50(3), 16–29. DOI: 10.1080/03932729.2015.105370.

Deeb, Marius. 'Radical Political Ideologies and Concepts of Property in Libya and South Yemen.' *The Middle East Journal* (Summer 1986): 40(3), 445–461.

Faksh, Mahmud A. 'The Alawi Community of Syria: A New Dominant Political Force.' *Middle Eastern Studies* (April 1984): 20(2), 133–153.

Gause III, F. Gregory. 'Yemeni Unity: Past and Future.' *Middle East Journal* (1988): 41(1), 33–47.

Grigoriadis, Theocharis N., and Walied Kassem. 'The Regional Origins of the Libyan Conflict.' *Middle East Policy* (2021): 28(2), 119–129.

Halliday, Fred. 'Catastrophe in South Yemen: A Preliminary Assessment.' MERIP *Middle East Report* (1986), 139, 37–39.

Hinnebusch, Raymond 'Change and Continuity after the Arab Uprising: The Consequences of State Formation in Arab North African States.' *British Journal of Middle Eastern Studies* (2015): 42(1), 12–30.

Hudson, Michael C. 'Geopolitical Shifts.' *Contemporary Arab Affairs* (July 2013): 6(3), 458–66. www.jstor.org/stable/10.2307/48600160.

BIBLIOGRAPHY

Joya, A. 'The Egyptian Revolution: Crisis of Neoliberalism and the Potential for Democratic Politics.' *Review of African Political Economy* (2011): 38(129), 367–386. www.jstor.org/stable/23055361.

Johnston, Ron. 'The Revenge of Geography: What the Map Tells Us About Coming Conflicts and the Battle against Fate', *The AAG Review of Books* (2013), 1(1), 1–3. DOI: 10.1080/2325548X.2013.785741.

Katz, Mark N. 'Yemen Unity and Saudi Security.' *Middle East Policy* (1992): 1(1).

Keating, Joshua. 'Who First Used the Term Arab Spring.' Foreign Policy, November 2011. https://foreignpolicy.com/2011/11/04/who-first-used-the-term-arab-spring.

Kendall, Elisabeth. 'The Failing Islamic State Within the Failed State of Yemen.' *Perspectives on Terrorism* (2019): 13, 77–86.

Liebesny, Herbert J. 'Administration and Legal Development in Arabia: Aden Colony and Protectorate.' *Middle East Journal* (Autumn 1955): 9(4), 385–396.

Lynch, Marc. 'Obama's Arab Spring?' Foreign Policy, 6 January 2011. https://foreignpolicy.com/2011/01/06/obamas-arab-spring.

McNamara, Robert. 'The Nasser Factor: Anglo-Egyptian Relations and Yemen/Aden Crisis 1962–65.' *Middle Eastern Studies* (2017): 53(1), 51–68.

Manea, Elham. 'Absence of Violence or Sustainable Peace? Yemen's Road to Peace', Part One. pm perspektive mediation: Beiträge zur Konfliktkultur, 1 (February 2021), pp. 59–65.

Manea, Elham. 'Absence of Violence or Sustainable Peace? Yemen's Pathway Forward.' MAP Middle East and Asia Project on Transitional Justice, Middle East Institute, 6 July 2021. www.mei.edu/publications/absence-violence-or-sustainable-peace-yemens-pathway-forward.

Manea, Elham. 'Yemen's Contentious Transitional Justice and Fragile Peace. MAP Middle East and Asia Project on Transitional Justice, Middle East Institute, January 2014. www.mei.edu/publications/yemens-contentious-transitional-justice-and-fragile-peace.

Mavani, Hamid. 'Ayatullah Khomeini's Concept of Governance (wilayat al-faqih) and the Classical Shi'i Doctrine of Imamate.' *Middle Eastern Studies*, 47(5), 2011, 807–824.

N.N. 'Accounts and Extracts of the Manuscripts in the Library of the King of France.' Published in Paris under the inspection of a Committee of the Royal Academy of Sciences at Paris, 1789. Translated from the French.

Olssen, M. 'Radical Constructivism and Its Failings: Anti-Realism and Individualism.' *British Journal of Educational Studies*, 44(3), 1996: 275–95. https://doi.org/10.2307/3122456.

Palmer, Monte. 'The United Arab Republic: An Assessment of Its Failure.' Middle East Journal 20(1), 1966: 50–67. www.jstor.org/stable/4323954.

Perkins, Brian M. 'Yemen: Between Revolution and Regression.' *Studies in Conflict & Terrorism*, 40(4), 2017: 300–17. DOI: 10.1080/1057610X.2016.1205368.

Randeria, Shalini. 'Between Cunning States and Unaccountable International Institutions: Legal Plurality, Social Movements and Rights of Local Communities to Common

Property Resources.' *European Journal of Sociology* 44(1), 2003, 27–60. https://doi.org/10.1017/S0003975603001188

Robbins, R.R. 'The Legal Status of Aden Colony and the Aden Protectorate.' *The American Journal of International Law*, 33(4), 1939, 700–715.

Salisbury, Peter. 'Yemen and the Saudi–Iranian Cold War.' Chatham House: The Royal Institute of International Affairs, 18 February 2015. www.chathamhouse.org/publication/yemen-and-saudi-iranian-cold-war.

Snyder, Jack. 'One World, Rival Theories.' *Foreign Policy* 145, October 2009: 52–62. https://edisciplinas.usp.br/pluginfile.php/4245015/mod_resource/content/1/Snyder_2004.pdf.

Steele, Abbey, and Livia Schubiger. 'Democracy and Civil War: The Case of Colombia.' *Conflict Management and Peace Science*, 35(6), 2018, 587–600.

International Crisis Group. 'Iran's Priorities in a Turbulent Middle East.' *Middle East Report* 184, 13 April 2018. https://link.springer.com/chapter/10.1057/978-1-137-50675-7_3.

Ulrichsen, Kristian Coates. 'Bahrain's Uprising: Regional Dimensions and International Consequences.' Stability: International Journal of Security & Development 2(1): 14, 2013. DOI: http://dx.doi.org/10.5334/sta.be

Vatanka, Alex. 'Iran's Yemen Play: What Tehran Wants—And What It Doesn't.' *Foreign Affairs*, 4 March 2015.

Vu, Tuong. 'Studying the State through State Formation.' *World Politics* 62(1), 2010: 148–75. www.jstor.org/stable/40646194.

Warburton, David. 'The Conventional War in Yemen.' *The Arab Studies Journal* 3(1), 1995, 20–44.

Waterbury, Myra A. 'Ethnicity in International Relations.' *Oxford Bibliographies*, 9 July 2020. DOI: 10.1093/OBO/9780199743292-013.

Wiktorowicz, Quintan. 'Anatomy of the Salafi Movement. *Studies in Conflict & Terrorism*, 29(3), 2006: 207–39. https://doi.org/10.1080/10576100500497004

Wimmer, Andreas, Lars-Erik Cederman, and Brian Min. 'Ethnic Politics and Armed Conflict: A Configurational Analysis of a New Global Data Set.' *American Sociological Review* 74(2), 2009, 316–337.

Yaccob, Abdol Rauh. 'Yemeni Opposition to Ottoman Rule: An Overview.' *Proceedings of the Seminar for Arabian Studies* 42, 2012, 411–419. www.jstor.org/stable/41623653.

Yadav, Stacey Philbrick, and Marc Lynch (eds). 'Politics, Governance, and Reconstruction in Yemen.' Project on Middle East Political Science (POMEPS) 29, 2017. https://scholarspace.library.gwu.edu/work/fb494883w.

Yoder, Dale. "Current Definitions of Revolution" (1926), *American Journal of Sociology*, 32(3), 433–41, www.jstor.org/stable/2765544.

Index

Page numbers in *italics* refer to illustrations.

Abatha, Farouq 113
Abdallah, Hasan 163
Acemoğlu, Daron 137
Aden, 16 February 2011 40–1
Aden, Britain fortifying 112
Aden Colony 114
Aden Trade Union Congress (ATUC) 129
al-Abidine, Zine 16
al-Ahmar, Abdullah 165
al-Ahmar, Ali Mohsen 43, 152, 165–7, 187, 205
al-Ahmar, Hamid 45, 48
al-Ahmar, Sheikh Abdullah 43–4
Alahssab, Ahmed 84, 85
al-Alimi, Rashad 152
Al Amiri (Dhala) 115
Alamrani, Abdulwahab 89
Alamrani, Mohammed bin Ismail 89
Al Aqial Movement 77
al-Assad, Bashar 14, 146
al-Assad, Hafez 14
al-Azzi, Hussein 86
al-Beidh, Ali Salem 192
al-Bukiri, Nabil 87, 89
al-Deen, Maysaa Shuja 194
al-Dhari, Zayd 188–9
al-Din, Imam Yehia Hamid 69, 70, 89, 179
al-Eryani, Abdul Rahman Yahya 8, 158, 171
Algeria 106–8
al-Hadi, Imam 61–2, 69

Al-Haqq Islamic party 192
al-Hariri, Rafik 13
Al-Hasan, Muhammad ibn 59
Al Hibshi, Shikhan 128
al-Hirak movement 40
al-Houthi, Badreddin 183, 186, 190
al-Houthi, Hussein 186, 190–6
    radicalization of 190
Al-Huraizi, Ali Salem 83
Ali, al-Husayn ibn 58
Ali, Ben 39
Ali, Mohammad 112
Ali Pasha, Mohammad 99
Ali, Zayd bin 58
Ali, Zine al-Abidine Ben 18
Al-Jawf, Wadi 54, 157
Al Jifri, Mohammed Ali 129
Allah, Radya Ihas 82
al-Magariha tribes 24
Almane'ay, Sheikh Ahmed bin Saleh 47
Al-Maqaleh, Abdulaziz 60
al-Maqatirah tribe 157
al-Mutawakel, Radhya 135
al Muayydi, Majid al-Din 183–4
al Orf law 96
al-Qasim, Al Mutawakkil 69, 72
al-Qasim, Imam al-Mansur 69
al-Rashoud, Talal 180
Al Safwany, Sadiq Mohammed 180
al-Sarraf, Ali 163

al Sayaghi, Hussein 73
al-Sharjabi, Qaid 147
al-Tamimi, Yassin 87
al-Wadi'i, Muqbil bin Hadi 174
Alwaite 24, 199
al-Warfalla 24
Al-Wasa'i, Abd al-Was' ibn Yehia 100
al-Zawi, Al Ṭahir Aḥmad 93
Al Zindani, Abdel Majid 48
Amazigh (Berber) dynasty 94
Amran 187
ancient Yemen 53, 54
    Abbasid dynasty in Baghdad (750–1258 CE) 57
    Abyssinian Ethiopians 56
    Hadramawt Kingdom 54
    Himyar Empire 56
    Minaean kingdom (Maʿīn) 54
    Qataban Kingdom 54
    Saba kingdom 53
    Sassanid Persians 56
    Umayyad dynasty in Damascus (661–750 CE) 57
Anderson, Lisa 106–7
Antar, Ali 162–3
Aqial system 55
Arabia and Arabs (Hoyland) 55
Arab Nationalist Movement (ANM) 129
Arab Spring 13–32
    analysis 19–32
    Bahrain 31
    complex realism in 29
    constructivism in 30
    Contextual Realist approach to 20
    drivers of 16–17
    economic marginalization driving 16–17
    generational divide in 19
    historical sociology in 30
    internal level of analysis 31
    Marxist approach to 15
    mobilization in 17–19
    outcomes of 13–32
    political stagnation driving 17
    regional actors' behaviour towards 28

    regional actors' range/complexity, realist approach to 28–30
    regional level of analysis 32
    Saudi Arabia 31
    state formation, 20–1
    Sunni–Shia sectarian divide 31
    survival and complex realism, regional context 27–32
    term usage 13–16
Arab State and Women's Rights: The Trap of Authoritarian Governance, The (Manea) 21
Arab Uprising: The Unfinished Revolutions of the New Middle East, The (Lynch) 15
Asir 49, 69, 70, 99, 101
Asnag, Abdullah 129
Audhali 115
Ayubi, Nazih 25, 106
Azzan, Mohammed 185, 188, 193

Bafaqih (Yemeni historian) 56
Bahrain 20, 31
Bakr, Wafa Alsayed Abu 82
Bassiouni, Cherif 92
Batriyyaa 61
Bazamah, Muhammad Mustafa 92
Beaumont, Richard, Sir 118–19, 124
Beihan 115
Benomar, Jamal 34, 205
Birth of the Federation "Idea" 119–26
Bouazizi, Mohamed 16–18
Bourguiba, Habib 16
Bouzid, Sidi 16
Brandt, Marieke 9, 67, 181
British colonialism 106–9
Buhaug, Halvard 138–40
Burrowes, Robert D. 69

Calvert, Peter 28
Carment, David 138
Cederman, Lars-Erik 49, 138–40
Charrad, Mounira M. 107
1994 Civil War, politics of survival and 164–70
    Arab–Israeli Six-Day War of 1967 171

INDEX

factions that supported Saleh in 166–8, *167*
colonization legacies 105–34
   Britain in the southern Yemeni city of Aden 106
   of European powers 106–9
   French Algeria 106
   Gulf countries borders charted by 107
   Italian Libya 106
   see also state formation in the MENA region; state formation in Yemen
complex realism to Arab Spring 29
countries of new states and old societies 20–7
   Colonial rule 26–7
   Egypt 23
   ideology 27
   MENA region 25
   Ottoman rule 26
   political elites 27
   social structures and legacies of geography 26
   traditional power base in 21–2
cunning state and the politics of survival 135–54
   ethnically structured state 145–54
      countries of new states and old societies 145
      countries of old states and old societies 145
      historical facts 136
      north Yemen 146–8
      patterns 144–5
      post-2015 political elites 151–4
      regional/tribal representation in 149, *150*
      in traditional power base of Socialist Party/army 149, *150*
   south Yemen 148–50
   theoretical deliberations 137–40
   United Yemen 150–1
   Yemeni instability 140–4
      1994 civil war 143
      north Yemen 141
      south Yemen 141–2
      united Yemen 142–4

cunning state, role of 155–96
   1994 Civil War, politics of survival and 164–70
   Hashemite strata, ethnic targeting of 156–60
   regional geographical level 155–6
   sectarian (doctrinal)level 155–6
   Southern group grievances 161–4
   Tribal (clan) level 155–6
   see also Saada Group Grievances; Sunni Islamism, state success in promoting
Cyrenaica 26–7, 92

Da'an treaty 103, 179
Damascus Spring 14
Dasuqi, Asim 15
Dathina 115
Davis, Kevin Alexander 81
"divide and rule" principle 10, 71, 110, 147, 152, 157
"domino effect" theory 13–14
Dresch, Paul 64, 73, 84
Ducker, John 122

Eastern Aden Protectorate (EAP) 117, 123
economic marginalization and uprisings 16–17
Egypt 3–4, 10, 15, 20, 23, 94, 106
   Mamluk dynasty 94
ElBaradei, Mohammed 13
Erdoğan, Recep Tayyip 86
ethnicity 9–11

Famous Forty 7
Faulkner, William 74
Fezzan 26, 92
Forward Policy 119–26
Fragile State Index 137
French colonialism 106–9
Friday of Dignity 47
Front for the Liberation of South Yemen (FLOSY) 129–31, 149

265

General People's Congress (GPC) 166
geographical versus political Yemen 51–6
Gleditsch, Kristian Skrede 138–40
Gul, Abdullah 86
Gulf Cooperation Council (GCC) 34
Gulf Rivalry and the Yemeni Civil War (Manea) 4, 6, 20, 41
Gurr, Ted Robert 207

Habash, George 130
Hadawiya 61
Hadi, Abdrabbuh Mansur 2, 35, 152, 163, 169, 203
Hadramawt Kingdom 54–6, 85, 116
Hadrami 52
Hajjah 65, 187
Halmain 116
Hamdan tribes 68
Hashemite Adnanis 68
Hashemite strata, ethnic targeting of 156–60
Haushabi 115
Haykel, Bernard 72, 193
Herzog, Issac 86
hijrah 63, 64, 147
Hinnebusch, Raymond 6, 19, 30, 37
Hinterland control by British 112–13
Hirak 41
History of Modern Yemen, A (Dresch) 84
Hodeida 101, 187
Honvault, Juliette 180
house of war (*dar al Harb*) 73
Houthi Islamist ideology 191
Houthi militia 153, 182–96
Houthi rebellion 190
Hoyland, Robert G. 54–5
Hussein, Saddam 28

ihtisab 183
Illah Tribes 116
Imam, appointment of 59
imamah 183
Imamate Theory in Zaydism (Azzan) 184
Imam Yehia 7, 69, 90, 100–1, 103–4, 141, 156–8, 181
Imamyyah 59

Immunity Law 205
Implementation Mechanism 205
Ingrams, Harold 117
internal level of analysis to Arab Spring 31
Iraq 20, 28, 91, 106
Islamic Iranian Revolution in 1979 28
IslamistIslah Party 41
Ismail, Abdel Fatah 162
Italy, colonization legacy of 106
Ithna Ashari 59

Jarudiyya 61
jihad, jihadists 69, 169, 178
Jihadi Sunni Islamism 192
Joint Meeting Parties (JMP) 41, 44–6

Kaplan, Robert D. 51–2
Karman, Tawakkol 48
Kathiri sultanate 117
Kaufman, Stuart 11
Khadduri, Majid 92–3
Khaldun, Abd ar-Raḥman ibn 58–9
Khouri, Rami 14
khuruj doctrine 60, 62–3, 69–70, 178, 188
Kifaya (*Enough*) movement 18
King Idris 27
Korany, Bahgat 106
Kuehn, Thomas 102

land tax (*kharaj*) 73
Lebanon 20, 106
legitimate grievances 138
Libya 3, 15, 20, 24, 52, 106, 108
Logloughi 77
Lower Aulaqi 115
Luce, William, Sir 121
Lynch, Marc 13–15

MacNamara, Robert 120
MacQueen, Benjamin 25, 97
Madhhiki tribes 65
Mahra 116
Mahwit 187
Malazim (Fascicles) 191
Mamluk dynasty 94

INDEX

Marx, Karl 37
Massad, Joseph 15
Maxwell, Joseph A. 4–5, 198
MENA (Middle East and North Africa)
    region 3–6, 106–9
    colonization legacies in 105–34
    religious perspective 92
    state formation in 94–7, 106–9
        consequences of 108
Minaean kingdom (Ma'īn) 54
Minaeans 52
Min, Brian 49
Modern Libya: A Study in Political Development (Khadduri) 92
Mohammed, Ali Nasr 162
Mohsen, Ali 44, 46–7, 190
Morocco 106
Mubarak, Hosni 18, 23, 39, 145, 199
mukarrib (unifier) 55
Mutarrif bin Amr Al Shihabi 63
Mutarrifiyya 61, 63–4
Mutarrif, Zayd bin Ali 63
Mutawakkilite Kingdom 71, 146
Mutazili stream 60

Naga'il 73, 77
narrative dilemma 81–90
    British colonization 82
National Liberation Front for Occupied South Yemen (NLF) 129–30
Noman, Mohammed Ahmed 157–8
North Yemen
    instability 141
    survival politics of 146–8

O'Neill, Brian 78
Operation Decisive Storm 35
Orkaby, Asher 35–6
Othman, Arwa 48
Ottoman imperialism legacies 91–104
    Cyrenaica 92
    differentiated citizenship 97
    Fezzan 92
    MENA region 92–3
    military role 97

state–society relations 95–7
successor states, structure and behaviour of 94–5
Tanzimat reforms 94
see also MENA (Middle East and North Africa) region
Özbdun, Ergun 94

Palestine/Israel 106
People's Socialist Party (PSP) 127–9
perceived injustices 138
Perthes, Volker 20, 23
Petersen, Roger D. 5, 159, 161–2
Political Security Organization (PSO) 190
political stagnation and uprisings 17
politics of impoverishment, Yemen 69–74
    dynastic kingdom, creation 70
    indirect sources of income 72
        hospitality, Althaifa 72
        levy contractors 72
        punishments 72
        war financing 72
    Naga'il practice 73, 77
    political and economic ramifications 73
    Shafii populations in Lower Yemen as infidels 72–3
    Zayd, Ali Mohammed 71
Power Identity in Yemen: The Controversy of Politics and History (Alahssab) 84
Prophet Mohammed 57
Putin, Vladimir 1

Qadhadfa 24
Qadis 147
Qahtani tribes 67–8
Qarnaw (Karna) 54
Qasimi Zaydi imams 98
Qatabanians 52
Qataban Kingdom 54
Qu'aiti sultanate 117
Qurayshi ethnic background 59
Qutb, Sayyid 192

Radfan (in Dhala) 116
Randeria, Shalini 144

267

Rasulids (1229–1454) 66
Reading in the Thought of the Zaydis and the Mu'tazila: The Islamic Yemen (Al-Maqaleh) 60
realist approach to regional context of Arab Spring 28–30
regional geographical level identity in Yemen 85, 155–6
regional level of analysis to Arab Spring 32
regional rivalry 3
religious beliefs 49–80
Republican Yemen, The (Al-Baradouni) 70
Requiem for a Nun (Faulkner) 74
Revenge of Geography, The (Kaplan) 51
Rice, Condoleezza 15
Ridda War (War of Apostasy) 168
Robinson, James A. 137

Saada Group Grievances 170–96
    between 2004 and 2010 170
    dawa (Islamic proselytizing) 173
    jihad (used in the military sense) 173
    power struggles within the Republican side 191
    Salafi Islam promotion 174
    Yemen Arab Republic (YAR) political system 172
Sa'ada wars 35
Sabaeans 52
Saba kingdom 53
Sadah (Masters) 68, 147, 181, 183
Salamé, Ghassan 25
Saleh, Ali Abdullah 10, 37–8, 43, 203, 205
Saliḥiyya 61
Sana'a 39, 101–2
Saudi Arabia 31, 107, 120, 122
sectarian (doctrinal) level identity in Yemen 85, 155–6
    and state formation 100–4
    tribes towards Zaydi imam 101
sha'b (settled tribe) 55
Shabwa (Alwaliq) tribes 149
Shafite tribes 85, 101
Shakir, Wameedh 39
Shiites 34, 58, 60

Smith, Anthony D. 11
South Arabian identity construction 118–31
South Arabian political landscape 126
Southern group grievances 161–4
Southern Yemeni Socialist Party 166
South of Arabia 51
south Yemen
    instability 141–2
    survival politics of 148–50
Spain 106
Stakeholders in Yemen, The (Noman) 157
state formation in the MENA Region 3, 106–9
    colonization legacies in 105–34
    colonization consequences of 108
        Arab countries 108
        countries from the Ottoman Empire, carving out 109
        territorial states with borders, institutionalization/consolidation 109
    state formation in 106–9
state formation in Yemen 20–1, 97–104, 109–18
    background 98–100, 111–13
        Zaydi imams dominance 98–9
    Britain fortified Aden 112
    Britain interests in South of Arabia 112
    countries of new states and old societies 21
    countries of old states and old societies 20
    divergent state capacities and traditional leaders role 101
    divergent state and administrative capacities 113–18
        Aden Colony 114
    Hinterland control by British 112
    independence movements 126–7
        for Aden or for states within the protectorates 126–7
        for southern unification or Pan-Arab Unity 127
    sectarian difference and 103–4
    sectarian factor 100–1

INDEX

South Arabian identity construction 118–31
   Egyptian–Syrian unification 121
   Free Officers Movement 122
   Greenwood, Anthony 125
   South Arabian political landscape 126
   state and administrative capacities, regional divergence in 101–2
   traditional leaders role, reinforcing via indirect rule 102–3
   tribes towards Zaydi imam 101
   Turkish disdain of Zaydism 100
   western and eastern Aden protectorates 115–18
state–society relations in Ottoman imperialism legacy 95–7
Sudan 20
Sulaymaniyah 61
Sultan Hamid 97–8
Sultan Selim I 98
Sunni and Shia Islam, animosity between 58–9
Sunni Islamism, state success in promoting 175–82
   educational impoverishment 179–82
   group grievances and social structure 175–7
   regime's legitimacy, usefulness for 177–8
Sunni Islamist Islah party 203
Sunni–Shia sectarian divide and Arab Spring 31
Syria 3, 20, 24, 52, 106–8

Tahirids (1454–1539) 66
Taif Treaty 141
Ta'iz 39–40, 101
Talib, Ali ibn Abi 58
Taqiyya doctrine 59–60
Taymiyyah, Ibn 174
tevzi system 102
traditional leaders' role
   divergent state capacities and 101
   reinforcing via indirect rule 102–3
Transjordan 106
Trevaskis, Kennedy, Sir 123

Trevelyan, Sir Humphrey 110
tribal (clan) level identity in Yemen 85, 155–6
Tribal Order: Politics and Law in the Mountains of Yemen, A (Weir) 176
tribes 9–11, 49–80
Tribes and Politics in Yemen: A History of the Houthi Conflict (Brandt) 67
Tripolitania 26
Tunisia 3–4, 10, 15, 20, 106
   Amazigh (Berber) dynasty 94
Tunisian Jasmine Revolution 38
Tunisian uprisings 15, 18
   domino effect of 18

United Yemen, instability 142–4
Upper Aulaqi 115–16
Upper Yafa 116

Wahhabi movement 99
Wahidi 115
Walter, Barbara F. 206
Waterbury, Myra A. 11
Weir, Shelagh 176, 179
Western Aden Protectorate (WAP) 116, 123
Why Nations Fail (Acemoğlu and Robinson) 137
Wilaya (guardianship/rulership/governates) 57, 153
Wimmer, Andreas 49

Yemen 3, 15, 20, 24
   as a geographical space 49–50
   geographical versus political 51–6
   historical legacies 50
   modern Yemen, governorates and districts of 66
   political identity of power in 84–5
      Lower Yemen 86
      regional 84–5
      sectarian 4–5
      Taiz 89
      tribal (clan) 84–85
      Upper Yemen 85–86

religious beliefs and tribes 56–74
   Batriyyaa 61
   Jarudiyya 61
   sub-movements 60–4
transition towards chaos 197–212
   conflict resolution 211
   how things went wrong 202–9
   Yemeni conflict traps 209–12
see also ancient Yemen; state formation in Yemen
Yemeni history
   relevance today 74–80
      core ruling elites 76
      group grievances 76–7
      Mutazilite influence 75
      racial exclusion rise 77–80
      Yemen's decline on Islam 75
Yemeni Civil War 33–48
   constraining systematic structures 41–5
      core elites power struggle 43–5
      internal factors 41
      Yemeni regime characteristics 42
   economic pains and corruption 38
   Taiz, 11 February 2011 39–40
      Aden, 16 February 2011 40–1
      al-Hirak movement 40
      Hirak 41
      Islamist Islah Party 41
      Joint Meeting Parties (JMP) 41
   Youth Agency 39–41
      Sana'a, 15 January 2011 39
   and Youth Uprisings 33–48
      aspirations and structures trap 37–8
      Yemeni state formation 36
      youth think tanks 34

Yemeni Civil War: The Arab Spring, State Formation and Internal Instability, The 4
Yemeni dilemma 2
Yemeni instability 140–4
   1994 civil war 143
   north Yemen 141
   south Yemen 141–2
   united Yemen 142–4
Yemeni tribes 9, 67–8
Yemen Socialist Party (YSP) 203

Zabarah, Mohammed Ahmed 180
Zamil folk poetry 74
Zayd, Ali Mohammed 71
Zayd bin Ali 62
Zaydi ethnicity 76, 85
Zaydi Hadawi Imamate theory 63
Zaydi Hashemites 146
Zaydi imams 98
Zaydi Qahtani tribal stratum 146, 159
Zaydi religious revival and Houthi militia 182–96
   Iran–Iraq war (1980–1988) 186
Zaydism 50–2, 57–60
   geographical, tribal divisions of Zaydi followers 64
      Amran 65
      Dhamar 65
      Hajjah 65
      Saada 65
      Sana'a 65
   Mutarrifiyya Zaydis 63
Zaydi tribes 101, 156–7
Zuckerman, Sarah 161–2